The Process of Internationalization

THE ACADEMY OF INTERNATIONAL BUSINESS

Published in association with the UK Chapter of the Academy of International Business

Titles already published in the series:

International Business and Europe in Transition (Volume 1)
Edited by Fred Burton, Mo Yamin and Stephen Young

Internationalisation Strategies (Volume 2)
Edited by George Chryssochoidis, Carla Millar and Jeremy Clegg

The Strategy and Organization of International Business (Volume 3)
Edited by Peter Buckley, Fred Burton and Hafiz Mirza

Internationalization: Process, Context and Markets (Volume 4)
Edited by Graham Hooley, Ray Loveridge and David Wilson

International Business Organization (Volume 5)
Edited by Fred Burton, Malcolm Chapman and Adam Cross

International Business: Emerging Issues and Emerging Markets (Volume 6)
Edited by Carla C.J.M. Millar, Robert M. Grant and Chong Ju Choi

International Business: European Dimensions (Volume7)
Edited by Michael D. Hughes and James H. Taggart

Multinationals in a New Era: International Strategy and Management (Volume 8)
Edited by James H. Taggart, Maureen Berry and Michael McDermott

International Business (Volume 9)
Edited by Frank McDonald, Heinz Tüselmann and Colin Wheeler

Internatialization: Firm Strategies and Management (Volume 10)
Edited by Colin Wheeler, Frank McDonald and Irene Greaves

The Process of Internationalization

Strategic, Cultural and Policy Perspectives

Edited by

Frank McDonald

Michael Mayer

and

Trevor Buck

palgrave
macmillan

First published 2004 by
PALGRAVE MACMILLAN
Houndmills, Basingstoke, Hampshire RG21 6XS and
175 Fifth Avenue, New York, N.Y. 10010
Companies and representatives throughout the world

PALGRAVE MACMILLAN is the global academic imprint of the Palgrave Macmillan division of St. Martin's Press, LLC and of Palgrave Macmillan Ltd. Macmillan® is a registered trademark in the United States, United Kingdom and other countries. Palgrave is a registered trademark in the European Union and other countries.

ISBN 1–4039–3228–X

This book is printed on paper suitable for recycling and made from fully managed and sustained forest sources.

A catalogue record for this book is available from the British Library.

Library of Congress Cataloging-in-Publication Data
Academy of International Business. UK Chapter. Conference
(30th : 2003 : De Montfort University)
The process of internationalization : strategic, cultural, and policy perspectives / edited by Frank McDonald, Michael Mayer, and Trevor Buck.
p. cm.
Selection of papers from the 30th Annual Conference of the UK Chapter of the Academy of International Business, held April 11–12, 2003 at De Montfort University.
Includes bibliographical references and indexes.
ISBN 1–4039–3228–X (cloth)
1. International business enterprises—Congresses. 2. Strategic planning—Congresses. 3. Corporate culture—Congresses. 4. Investments, Foreign—Government policy—Congresses. 5. Globalization—Economic aspects. I. McDonald, Frank, 1951– II. Mayer, Michael, 1965– III. Buck, Trevor. IV. Title.
HD62.4.A223 2003
658′.049—dc22 2003065684

10 9 8 7 6 5 4 3 2 1
13 12 11 10 09 08 07 06 05 04

Printed and bound in Great Britain by
Antony Rowe Ltd, Chippenham and Eastbourne

Contents

Foreword

The 30th Annual Conference of the UK Chapter of the Academy of International Business (AIB UK) was held on 11 and 12 April 2003 at Leicester De Montfort University, hosted by Leicester Business School. This book contains a selection of papers from the conference.

To mark the 30th anniversary of the creation of AIB UK, a plenary session in honour of its founding chairman, Dr Michael Z. Brooke, was planned. Despite the significant health problems that he had suffered in recent years, Michael was very keen to attend this special occasion. It is a matter of great sadness that Michael was taken ill in March and died on 1 April 2003, aged 80 years. While his passing inevitably resulted in a solemn air at the conference, it was nevertheless a highly appropriate occasion to celebrate Michael's work.

The plenary session (papers from which will be published in a Special Issue of the *International Business Review*, guest edited by Peter Buckley) paid tribute to Michael's deep and wide-ranging contribution to international business research and teaching. After an earlier career as an Anglican priest, it was as a Lecturer in Sociology at the University of Manchester Institute of Science and Technology (UMIST) that Michael burst onto the IB scene in 1970, after completing his PhD. His doctorate was on the formulation of strategy in multinational companies, and formed the basis of his contribution to *The Strategy of Multinational Enterprise* (1970), with Lee Remmers. The book had a worldwide impact, particularly in North America.

Michael had a mission to create, as he put it, 'A body of knowledge'. He also had a strong desire to disseminate this knowledge, and he recognized that both he, and the UK, needed a professional network to support research and teaching in IB. He met these needs first by joining AIB himself in 1970, and then by forming the UK Chapter in spring 1973 with a conference at UMIST. Before 1973, AIB membership in the UK could be counted on the fingers of one hand. Michael commented that a tremendous amount of perseverance was needed to keep the Chapter going. But keep it going he did, until the mid-1980s when he stepped down as chair. Michael continued to regularly attend AIB UK annual conferences, and remained deeply involved. He gave great support and encouragement to young academics at the beginning of their careers, as well as to more established ones, both within and outside the formal conference sessions, right up to the point when his health prevented him from attending.

Michael's legacy also includes a large body of written work, and the grounding of his research in business practice meant that he generated academic studies of very considerable originality. His highly influential contribution to the academic understanding of licensing is a case in point. Another example was his work on management contracts, which was among the first in the field worldwide. The list is long, and it is impossible to do justice to it here. But any scholar of IB is well-advised to read Michael's work, to get a grasp of how international business really functions.

The 30th annual conference attracted a record number of participants – just over 140 delegates from 50 higher education institutions. The programme, which Michael had studied with much admiration, was a full one. It has produced a book (Volume 11 in the Palgrave Macmillan series) that testifies to the vitality of AIB UK. This is as fitting a tribute to Michael as it is possible to wish for.

JEREMY CLEGG
Chair, Academy of International Business
United Kingdom Chapter

Acknowledgements

Thanks to Trevor Buck and to Liz Myers and her team at Leicester Business School at Leicester De Montfort University for very efficient organization of the 30th annual conference of the Academy of International Business. The success of the conference was also due to the excellent work of referees who evaluated the submissions to the conference and provided comments to the contributors of the chapters in this volume.

Notes on the Contributors

Zuhair Al-Obaidi has a DSc degree from the Helsinki School of Economics and a BA from the University of Reading. His business experience includes 30 years of work and consultation for firms, governments, and international organizations. His current teaching and research interests include international technology transfer, globalization of SMEs, international marketing, and international business operation modes.

Ali Ataullah is a doctoral student at the University of Durham. His research interests include financial regulations in developing countries and their impacts on performance of financial institutions, financial innovations and direct foreign investment in developing countries.

Jim Bell is a Professor of International Business Entrepreneurship at the University of Ulster, Magee Campus, Northern Ireland. His research interests are in the area of small-firm internationalization and public policy in support of internationalization.

Cristina Boari is Professor of Business Policy and Management at the University of Bologna (Italy). Her research is focused on inter-firm rivalry and cooperation in industrial clusters and on interorganizational relationships and value creation in symbolic goods. Her work has been published in journals such as the *Journal of Management and Governance* and the *Scandinavian Journal of Management*.

Susan Bridgewater is a Lecturer in Marketing and Strategy at Warwick Business School. She has a BA (Hons) in French and German from Durham University and an MBA and PhD from Warwick University. Before joining Warwick in 1991, Susan worked in industry as Brand Manager and New Markets Manager for Nairn-Forbo and Unilever. Susan researches in the areas of internationalization, networks, emerging markets and branding. She was co-editor of *Innovation in Marketing* with Professor Peter Doyle and co-author of *International Marketing Relationships*. Until recently Susan was Academic Director of Warwick's Distance Learning MBA programme with students from over 100 countries. She teaches and directs programmes for a range of organizations, including Chrysalis, HSBC, KPMG, Nestlé, Philips, Prudential, the Football Association, the Professional Footballers' Association and the League Managers' Association.

Keith Brouthers is Associate Professor at Temple University's Fox School of Business. His work focuses on international strategic decision-making and the factors that drive these decisions. Keith's work has been published in leading academic journals including *Journal of International Business Studies, Strategic Management Journal, Management International Review, Journal of Management,* and *Journal of Management Studies*, among others.

Lance Brouthers is Professor of Western Hemispheric Studies and Director of the PhD programme in International Business in the College of Business Administration at University of Texas at El Paso. His research examines international strategy issues such as changes in the business environment, product strategies, emerging markets and entry mode choice, and has appeared in *Journal of International Business Studies, Strategic Management Journal, Long Range Planning and Management International Review*, among others.

Trevor Buck is Research Professor of Business Policy in the Department of Strategy and Management in the Leicester Business School, De Montfort University. His publications in the last five years include articles in *Academy of Management Journal, Journal of World Business, Journal of International Business Studies, Business History* and the *California Management Review.* His main research interests are executive remuneration in the USA, the UK and Germany, enterprise strategies among privatized firms of the former Soviet Union, and business history, particularly the development of international patterns of corporate governance. Trevor is a member of the Executive Committee of the UK Chapter of the Academy of International Business.

Giulio Cardilli is a PhD student in management of information systems at the LUISS Guido Carli University (Italy). After a degree in business administration at the University of L'Aquila (Italy), he obtained his Masters in management of food industry by the ISMEA (Italian Agency for Research in Food Industry). His research is focused on the potential of internet technologies to support the so-called virtual internationalization, especially with respect to regional products manufacturers.

Fabrizio Cocciola obtained a degree in economics and business at the University of L'Aquila (Italy). His main research field is the use of internet-based communication tools in companies adopting e-business strategy. Based on such research activity in 2000 he founded Brandner SRL, an operating company offering CRM services related to virtual communities.

Mark Cook is a Principal Lecturer in Economics at University College Northampton. His teaching and research interests centre on international business, the economics of Europe and small and medium sized businesses (SMEs). He has authored a number of texts, *International Business Economics, Managerial Economics* and *Supply-side Economics,* and has been involved with a range of externally funded projects, including, disabled workers in SMEs, local impact analysis studies, the Corby Regeneration Project and labour market developments, and a study of the motor sport industry in Northamptonshire. A selection of his publication can be found in *Local Economy,* the *Journal of European Business Education,* and the *International Small Business Journal.*

Pavlos Dimitratos is a Research Fellow at the University of Strathclyde. His research interests include international entrepreneurship, and international business strategy and management. He has published in the *European Management Journal, International Business Review* and *Journal of International Entrepreneurship,* among others. He has recently co-edited a text entitled *Emerging Paradigms in International Entrepreneurship* (2004).

Grahame Fallon is a Senior Lecturer in International Business at University College Northampton and Deputy Director of the International Research Group. His teaching and research interests centre upon foreign direct investment at the national and regional level in the EU, Eastern Europe and the former Soviet Union, together with economic transition issues and international political economy. He has also carried out research into international marketing strategies, small and medium sized businesses (SMEs) and into ethnic business. His previous work has been published in a range of journals, including the *Journal of Small Business and Enterprise Development,* the *European Business Review, Qualitative Research* and the *Journal of Contemporary European Studies.*

Luciano Fratocchi is an Assistant Researcher in business management at the University of L'Aquila (Italy). He obtained a PhD in business management from the University of Bologna (Italy) on headquarter–subsidiary relationships. His research is focused on internationalization processes of SMEs, and his work has been published in journals such as *International Journal of Business Performance Management* and *European Management Journal.*

Mika Gabrielson is Professor of International Business at the Helsinki School of Economics. His teaching covers areas such as exports and international and global marketing, and his research interests include multiple sales-channel strategies and rapid globalization. Before joining the academic world he held several senior positions in high-tech marketing and purchasing.

Luca Giustiniano is Assistant Professor of Business Organization at University of L'Aquila (Italy). He holds a PhD in management information systems from

Luiss Guido Carli University, Rome (Italy). He has published in the areas of management of information systems and ICT development.

Paul N. Gooderham is Professor of Strategy and Management at the Norwegian School of Economics and Business Administration. This is the third volume in this series in which Gooderham's work has featured. His most recent book is *International Management: Cross-Boundary Challenges* (co-authored with Odd Nordhaug). His recent publications include articles in *Administrative Science Quarterly, Employee Relations, Current Topics in Management, Management International Review, European Business Forum, The International Journal of the Economics of Business, Beta: Scandinavian Journal of Business Research, Scandinavian Journal of Management and International Small Business Journal.*

Ulrich Hoppe is the Director General of the German-British Chamber of Commerce and Industry in London. He previously worked as a lecturer at Manchester Metropolitan University and in New York in a variety of private sector organizations.

Robert Johnston is Professor of Operations Management at Warwick Business School. Before moving to academia Dr Johnston held several line management and senior management posts in a number of service organisations in both the public and private sectors. He continues to maintain close and active links with many large and small organizations through his research, management training and consultancy activities. His research interests include service excellence, service recovery and complaint management, and performance measurement. He is the co-author or editor of over 25 books and has contributed over 30 chapters to other texts. He has published around 50 articles in refereed journals and has written over 60 case studies and three computer-based simulations. He is the Head of the Operations Management Group and Academic Director of MBA Programmes and the Diploma in Service Leadership. He has served as Associate Dean of the Business School for four years and as a member of the School's management committee for twelve years. He has also been the academic director of two MBA programmes. He was the founding editor of the *International Journal of Service Industry Management* and he also serves on the editorial board of the *Journal of Operations Management*, the *International Journal of Internet and Enterprise Management* and the *International Journal of Tourism and Hospitality Research.* He is a founder member of the European Operations Management Association, a member of the steering committee of the International Academy of Services Research and Education, a member of the Services Management International Advisory Board, EGADE, Mexico, and a board member of the Performance Measurement Association.

Jorma Larimo is Professor of International Marketing at the University of Vaasa in Finland. His research is focused on foreign direct investment strategies and performance in internationalization in small and medium-sized enterprises. He is also the Director of the Finnish Graduate School of International Business. His work has been published in journals such as *Journal of International Business Studies*, *Journal of Business Research*, *Journal of Euromarketing*, *International Studies of Management and Organization* and *Management International Review*.

Hang Le is a Lecturer in Economics at Nottingham Trent University. Her chapter in this book is based on her PhD thesis completed at Durham University. Her current research interests are: foreign direct investment, its locations determinants and impacts on host economies; social responsibility of foreign affiliates in host countries; economic development and economic growth theories.

Lester Lloyd-Reason is Reader in International Enterprise Strategy and Director of the Global Enterprise Research Unit (GERU) at the Ashcroft International Business School in Cambridge, UK. He has considerable experience of managing international research projects in the field of small-business support structures, particularly in Central and Eastern Europe, and has published more than 80 papers in this area. He has developed two successful Action for Co-operation in Economics (ACE) projects for the European Union Phare Programme which have led to the development of strong international links with academics, NGOs and governmental agencies, and developed a number of enterprise support initiatives. He has acted as strategic adviser to a number of organizations within both the private and public sectors. He is a member of both the European and International Council for Small Business, the Board of Directors of the Institute of Small Business Affairs (ISBA) in the UK; and serves on the Editorial Board of a number of Journals, including the *International Small Business Journal* (ISBJ).

Sharon Loane is a Lecturer in Business Economics at the University of Ulster, Magee Campus, Northern Ireland. Her research interests are in the area of small-firm internationalization, specifically internet-enabled start-ups.

Brian Mathews is Professor of Marketing in the Department of Business and Marketing, Luton Business School. After completing his MBA and PhD at the University of Strathclyde, he has actively pursued research in a number of areas. To date he has published 47 articles in peer-reviewed journals, one book and over 70 papers. Articles have appeared in many journals, including *Industrial Marketing Management*, *Journal of Organizational and Occupational Psychology*, *International Journal of Research in Marketing* and *Managerial and Decision Economics*. He has won several prizes including the 'most outstanding paper' award by the Literati Club.

Jan Mattsson has been Professor in Business Administration at Roskilde University since May 1996. He has held several Professorships and visiting Professorships in New Zealand, Australia and Scandinavia. He graduated with a DBA from Gothenburg University in 1982 and was promoted there to Associate Professor in 1985. Professor Mattsson is currently active in service marketing and international marketing research. He has authored several books and journal articles. He serves on many editorial boards of international journals in marketing and services. He takes part in several international research projects and is a member of the Center for Service Studies at Roskilde University.

Michael Mayer is Reader in Strategic Management at the University of Edinburgh and was previously a Senior Lecturer at the University of Glasgow, UK. He is a graduate of the University of Augsburg, Germany and received his doctorate from the University of Warwick, UK. Michael is co-author of the book *The European Corporation* and has published in journals such as the *Strategic Management Journal, Organisation Studies* and *Industrial and Corporate Change,* as well as in the quality press such as the *Financial Times.* His current research interests include the relationship between strategy and organization. Michael is a member of the Executive Committee of the UK Chapter of the Academy of International Business.

Frank McDonald is Professor of International Business Strategy at the University of Plymouth. He has authored several books in the area of European and International Business, and contributed to journals such as *Environment and Planning C, European Journal of Industrial Relations, Journal of Small Business Management* and *Journal of International Entrepreneurship.* His current research interests are the impact on host locations of the strategic development of subsidiaries, and the contribution of clusters/industrial districts to international competitiveness. Frank is a member of the Executive Committee and Treasurer of the UK Chapter of the Academy of International Business.

Bruce Millett is Head of the Department of Human Resource Management and Employment Relations at the University of Southern Queensland, Toowoomba, Australia, and Sub-Dean for education at University of Southern Queensland. Bruce has written books on organizational behaviour and has published on the internationalization of services.

Anna Morgan-Thomas is a Lecturer in Business and Management at the University of Glasgow. Her research interests include international e-commerce, exporting and FDI in Central and Eastern Europe.

Trevor Morrow is a Lecturer in Strategic Human Resource Management at the University of Ulster's School of International Business. His research interests include strategic human-resource management, employee relations, international and comparative HRM, and HRM in SME's. His work has been published in journals such as the *Journal of Small Business and Enterprise Development*, the *Journal of European Industrial Training* and the *Irish Journal of Management*. He is the co-editor of the *Irish Journal of Management*.

Terry Mughan is Principal Lecturer in Intercultural Management at Anglia Polytechnic University in Cambridge, UK. His current research focuses on internationalization processes in small and medium-sized enterprises and the evolution of regional support strategies in the UK. He was the founding Chair of SIETAR UK (The Society for Intercultural Education, Training and Research). He has been at the forefront of intercultural development projects in the UK for several years. Terry has carried out government-funded research into international business development and has participated in LEONARDO projects, such as 'The International SME', and is currently an adviser to the East of England International Trade Forum.

George Nakos is Associate Professor at Clayton College and State University. George's work focuses on small and medium-sized organizations and entrepreneurial activities. His work has been published in leading journals including *Entrepreneurship Theory and Practice, Thunderbird International Business Review* and *Journal of Global Marketing*.

Odd Nordhaug is Professor of Administrative Science at the Department of Strategy and Management, Norwegian School of Economics. He has published numerous books in many countries, the latest being *International Management: Cross-Boundary Challenges* (Blackwell, 2003; co-authored with Paul N. Gooderham) and has contributed research articles to journals such as: *Administrative Science Quarterly, Human Relations, Journal of Portfolio Management, Management International Review, Scandinavian Journal of Management, Current Topics in Management, International Studies of Management & Organization, European Management Journal, International Journal of Human Resource Management, Human Resource Management Journal, International Small Business Journal*, and *Non Profit and Voluntary Sector Quarterly*. He is the editor of the scientific journal *Beta: Scandinavian Journal of Business Research*.

Manuela Presutti is a Post-Doctoral Fellow of Management at the University of Bologna (Italy). She obtained a PhD in business management at the University of Bologna (Italy) through her work on the role of social capital in interorganizational networks. Her research is focused on industrial clusters and on internationalization processes of SMEs.

Kristen Ringdal is Professor of Sociology (methodology) at the Department of Sociology and Political Science, Norwegian University of Science and Technology (NTNU). He has published several books, the most recent of which is a textbook on social science research methods. He has published articles in research journals in various fields including *Administrative Science Quarterly*, *Management International Review*, *European Sociological Review*, *Acta Sociological*, *British Journal of Cancer* and *Quality of Life Research*. He is the Norwegian national coordinator for the European Social Survey, and an elected member of the Royal Norwegian Society of Science and Letters.

Habte Selassie is Senior Lecturer in the Department of Business and Marketing, Luton Business School, University of Luton. He teaches international business, international marketing, and research methods; and his research interests include international business collaboration strategies, marketing orientation, and globalization. Dr Selassie has published a book, and several articles in journals including *Journal of International Food and Agribusiness Marketing* and *Journal of Consumer Behaviour: An International Research Review*. He has participated in several international projects such as TEMPUS and Phare Programmes for Eastern and Central European countries. He is a member of the Academy of International Business (AIB), the Market Research Society, and the Chartered Institute of Marketing (MCIM), and serves on the editorial boards of journals including the *Journal of African Business* and the *Journal of East–West Business*.

Bridgette Sullivan-Taylor is ESRC Research Fellow in the Marketing and Strategic Management Group at Warwick Business School. She has previously held management positions in both private and public sector organizations in New Zealand and the UK. She has also had academic appointments at Oxford, Cambridge and Durham Universities in the UK, Vlerick School of Management (Belgium) and Auckland University (New Zealand). Her current research interests include strategic change (intent and practice); the alignment of corporate strategy with organizational processes; the design and implementation of international business and global strategies in the service industry, and the management of international strategic alliances and partnerships.

James H. Taggart is Professor of International Business Strategy at the University of Glasgow. His research interests include international management of technology, strategy of multinational subsidiaries, and the impact of soft management issues on international business management.

Jennifer M. Taggart is a Research Fellow at the University of Glasgow. An economist by profession, she has also published in the fields of international business strategy and the impact of national culture on international management.

Denise Tsang is a Lecturer at the School of Business, University of Reading. She was previously a Lecturer in the Bristol Business School. Denise obtained a first-class degree in management and business administration from Reading University in 1994, and completed her PhD in economics at Reading in relation to foreign direct investment within the European microcomputer industry in 1998. Her research interests include strategic issues in high-technology sectors and comparative management; her current project is on entrepreneurial ventures within the Chinese and Irish software industry. Her first book was *Business Strategy and National Culture: US and Asia Pacific Microcomputer Multinationals in Europe*.

Heinz Tüselmann is Reader in International Business at Manchester Metropolitan University. His research is focused on HRM issues in international business and German direct foreign investment. Heinz has published in many journals including, *Journal of World Business, Transnational Corporations, Environment and Planning C, European Journal of Industrial Relations* and the *Industrial Relations Journal*.

David Williams is Senior Lecturer in Economics at Nottingham Trent University. His research is centred on sourcing by multinational corporations, and he has published in *International Business Review* and *Environment and Planning C*.

Introduction: Strategic, Cultural and Policy Perspectives of Internationalization

Michael Mayer and Frank McDonald

This volume of the Academy of International Business (AIB) series, based on selected papers presented at the 30th annual AIB conference, is organized around the theme of the strategic, cultural and policy perspectives of internationalization. Part I of the book, including the best paper by Anna Morgan-Thomas and Susan Bridgewater, is devoted to the strategic and organizational development of the internationalized firm. Part II investigates the role of culture and institutions in internationalization; Part III is concerned with internationalization by small and medium-sized enterprises; and Part IV deals with the impact and policy implications of foreign direct investment.

International business is a field characterized by a multiplicity of perspectives and approaches. It is a plurality that mirrors the complex and multifacetted nature of the practice and policy of internationalization. While covering the key perspectives of strategy and organization and the impact of foreign direct investment (FDI) and policy implications it pays particular attention to two contextual perspectives of particular current interest: the continued role and impact of national culture and institutions and the increasing importance of small and medium-sized enterprises in the international arena. The themes help to shed light on a variety of thematic foci, particularly ongoing processes of internationalization and entry-mode choice; the management and impact of subsidiaries; e-commerce; and HR and employment issues. The relationships between the themes expounded in the chapters are illustrated in Table 1.

The strategic and organizational development of the internationalized firm

In a world beset by continued political and technological uncertainties, clear paths to success in international business remain elusive. The first two papers in this volume set out to explore in some detail the relationship between two

Table 1 Structure of the book

Theme and focus	*FDI impact and policy*	*Strategy and organization*	*SME*	*Culture and institutions*
Internationalization and entry modes	Chapter 14	Chapters 1, 2, 3 and 5	Chapters 10, 12 and 17	Chapter 6
Subsidiaries and FDI	Chapter 15			Chapters 7 and 8
e-commerce		Chapter 1	Chapter 11	
HR and employment	Chapter 15	Chapter 4		
Other themes	Chapters 16 and 17 (regional focus)	Chapter 3 (supply-chain issues)	Chapter 13 (pricing issues)	Chapter 9 (corporate-governance issues)

of the most significant developments in international business, e-commerce and increased collaborative strategies, and performance.

Arguably, one of the most significant changes in the international business environment over recent years has been the arrival of international e-commerce. In Chapter 1, Anna Morgan-Thomas and Susan Bridgewater indicate in their AIB-UK best-paper award-winning contribution to this volume 'Winners and Losers in the Internet Game' the development of information and communication technologies that challenge the very foundations of the theory and practice of international business. Their chapter offers two contributions to this emerging field of study, both indicating that it is not technological sophistication on its own that offers the key to success. Firstly, they suggest that contrary to expectations sophisticated e-commerce models are not necessarily conducive to export success, but that simple but well-managed information-based web-sites are most conducive to success. Secondly, they highlight that even in an 'e-commerce' world conventional factors such as level of internationalization and export experience remain central to the determination of success.

While companies are puzzling as to how best to exploit the new opportunities afforded by new communication technologies, the ability to successfully manage the already well-established collaborative arrangement of international joint ventures (IJVs) remains similarly elusive. Jorma Larimo highlights these issues in Chapter 2, which investigates the performance of Finnish IJVs using two measures, survival and stability. The results indicate that many IJVs were identified as being in some sense failures. Key factors associated with performance were found in the study, including size, age, and difference in uncertainty avoidance.

In Chapter 3, Denise Tsang continues the focus on interorganizational linkages and relationships but places the emphasis on downstream activities by exploring the management of supply-chain relationships. By studying the supply-chain strategies of four major US microcomputer companies in the UK, Tsang identifies the evolutionary nature of industry-specific factors as most important in strategies adopted by these US firms. Supply-chain management tended to be adapted to the specific conditions that prevailed in the UK market, but the general industry trends were the dominant factor for the evolution of management systems. Tsang highlights the importance of what she calls 'human capital', and related factors. Chapter 4 by Loane *et al.* accordingly explores the role of international human-resource management strategies as a critical factor in supporting successful competition in international business (IB). The chapter considered the international human-resource practices of 14 Irish international companies. The findings suggest that the models of internationalization that have been developed from research in large MNEs do not adequately explain the approaches taken in smaller and medium-sized firms. In particular, these firms need to be more flexible, adaptable and opportunistic than their larger counterparts.

The final chapter in this section, by Pavlos Dimitratos, brings together the diverse strands of research into international business strategies to develop a systematization of the field, and sets the scene for Part II in which the role of national cultures and institutions in shaping international business strategy are explored. In the chapter a classification of international business strategies is provided that identifies IB strategies at two levels – the overall international marketplace context, and the specific foreign country context. The chapter also explores recommendations for future research in this area.

The role of culture and institutions in the internationalization process

In Chapter 6, Brouthers *et al.* pick up on one of the dimensions of international business strategy identified by Dimitratos, the mode of foreign involvement. They consider the joint effect of home and host-country culture as well as cultural distance in affecting managerial choices between alternative modes of market entry. Using transaction cost analysis the chapter explores the simultaneous impact of national cultural distance and two well-known measures of home and target country culture – power distance and uncertainty avoidance. The findings suggest that when all three (host, home and distance) measures of national culture are considered simultaneously, their collective impact plays a very important role in explaining entry-mode choice.

While Brouthers *et al.* find that national culture plays a notable role in shaping market entry, the effect of culture on the management of established subsidiaries is more varied. Taggart and Taggart explore, in Chapter 7, national cultural differences and find that they are of lesser significance to managers of foreign subsidiaries than is frequently assumed. Nevertheless, they do find linkages between cultural distance and performance but suggest, in light of their overall findings, that appropriate managerial policies emphasizing learning and communication can go a long way towards avoiding possible negative effects of cultural distance and disparity.

The focus on subsidiary management is continued in Chapter 8 by Gooderham *et al.*, who consider the role of national institutional structures in shaping the human-resource practices of subsidiaries of American multinationals in Europe. Just as in the earlier chapter by Brouther's *et al.* this chapter considers both home and host-country contexts in their investigation. The chapter compares the use of characteristically US human-resource management (HRM) practices in indigenous firms and subsidiaries of US multinational companies in the UK, Ireland, Germany and Denmark/Norway, and investigates differences in human-resource management practices between indigenous firms, as well as between indigenous firms and subsidiaries, by country. The findings indicate that US multinational enterprises tend to apply their own, nationally idiosyncratic, repertoire of HRM practices in their subsidiaries in Western European countries.

In Chapter 9 Trevor Buck continues the exploration of the importance of culture and institutions by considering whether international corporate governance will converge to US-style market capitalism. The analysis is conducted on two main fronts. Firstly, by considering imposed US-style reforms that can be observed in business history during large-scale institutional change in Germany, Japan and Russia. Secondly, a particular US-style corporate governance factor, the executive stock option, is considered in the context of developments in modern Germany. The chapter focuses on resistance by national governance institutions to 'alien' innovations because of different cultural and institutional environments. The analysis in the chapter is used to generate research hypotheses that indicate how rigorous tests may be applied to the convergence thesis.

Internationalization by small and medium-sized enterprises (SMEs)

While, traditionally, most research in international business has focused on the strategies pursued by large firms, changing institutional and technological conditions have facilitated the internationalization of small firms so much that Selassi *et al.* in Chapter 10 find that SME's in the East of England were more involved in exporting and importing than their larger counterparts. An important role in this context is played by internet/web-site-based modes of internationalization, which is particularly used by the smaller firms. The chapter provides an overview of the main characteristics, especially the size of firms, that impact on export behaviour of SMEs in East England. The major obstacles to exporting by SMEs are also identified and measured.

Given this importance of 'web'-facilitated internationalization, Cardilli *et al.* in Chapter 11 examine whether location matters any more, even for the small firm. Investigating the use of the internet for the internationalization of regionally-based products they find that e-commerce can indeed provide a significant impetus for foreign market expansion but that firms often do not make the necessary investments or develop the necessary integrated strategies. Both the ability to learn and the characteristics of the entrepreneur running the firm are important here, both factors which can be found in slightly different manifestations in Chapter 12 which focuses on patterns and processes of small-firm internationalization. In this chapter, Bridgewater *et al.* investigate both firms, in the services sector, that internationalize in an incremental fashion, and those that internationalize more rapidly. The primary aim of the chapter is to increase understanding of how small, service firms expand within and across international markets by examining the nature of the learning and knowledge-transfer processes that underpin this process. By exploring this process, useful insights are gained that make a contribution to the field of SME internationalization.

In Chapter 13, Gabrielson and Al-Obaidi focus on those small firms characterized by a rapid, almost instantaneous process of internationalization, the so called 'born-globals'. The focus of the chapter is on the pricing strategies of 'born-globals' using evidence from eight case studies. A schema is developed for pricing by 'born globals' that involves key factors such as products, brand names, types of supply channels and relationships with customers.

The impact and policy implications of foreign direct investment

Up to this point the book has focused primarily on the various strategic and organizational policies adopted by internationalizing and international firms. In Part IV the discussion considers both the effect that international investments have on their host economies and on the ways in which governmental policies may shape these effects and the investment decisions themselves. The chapters in this section consider the relationship between FDI and three key dimensions of economic development – exports, growth and employment – and suggest a complex set of relationships between foreign direct investment and the development of host economies.

In Chapter 14, Hang Le and Ataullah cast a positive light on export-orientated policies by arguing that the implementation of such an economic approach is crucial to the development of a virtuous circle linking growth in FDI and economic growth in ASEAN countries. The emphasis is on the bi-directional relationship between inward FDI and economic growth; that is, inward FDI affects economic growth and economic growth affects inward FDI. The study found that there was a positive relationship in this bi-directional process and that an export-orientated policy seems to reinforce these positive effects.

Chapter 15, by Frank McDonald *et al.*, investigates the relationship between the embeddedness in host locations by German-owned subsidiaries in the UK and the growth of employment and of skilled labour by these firms. The results indicate that few German subsidiaries are deeply embedded in their host location. Moreover, embeddedness factors have no significant effect on employment growth by German subsidiaries and only a marginal impact on the demand for skilled labour. Some policy implications for regional development are drawn from the results. The link between FDI and regional development is also examined by Grahame Fallon and Mark Cook in Chapter 16, where the focus is on the major factors that attract inward FDI. This is done by examining and comparing those factors far four regions of the UK, the results indicating that FDI is attracted to those regions because of different locally available resources. Policy implications for regional development are derived from the results.

The final chapter by Cristina Boari *et al.* investigates the importance of globalization versus localization forces in the context of an Italian industrial district based in Rome. The study found that where tacit knowledge and high levels of trust were important, proximity was regarded as crucial for good performance, whereas globalization forces were strongly evident in matters connected to reaping economies of scale in operations where tacit knowledge was less important. The chapter concludes that because the success of the industrial district was connected to the complementary use of global and local networks, policy should be geared towards helping firms within industrial districts to develop such an integrated approach.

Part I

The Strategic and Organizational Development of the Internationalized Firm

1

Winners and Losers of the Internet Game: A Study of British Exporters

Anna Morgan-Thomas and Susan Bridgewater

Introduction

The notion of overcoming distance, which lies at the heart of international business, has recently been threatened by developments in information and communication technologies (ITC). The advent of a global information network which is said to 'compress space' and 'put an end to geography' was forecast to revolutionize the word business (de la Torre and Moxon, 2001). With its ability to link suppliers, manufacturers and customers at near-zero cost, the internet was said to affect the very fundamentals of international business enquiry (Samiee, 1998a), and, not surprisingly, was welcomed with much excitement and expectations of new opportunities for international commerce (Hamill, 1997).

These forecasts give rise to an interesting question: are the opportunities presented by the internet open for all businesses or are some better suited to rake the benefits? The literature offers conflicting answers to this question. One popular opinion, especially prominent in the days of internet euphoria, suggests that the global nature of the net makes it automatically suited for international business in any setting. As reflected by Quelch and Klein (1996), 'any company that establishes a web-site becomes a global company'. A different view is expressed by more cautious commentators who point to factors that might moderate the effects. For example, the e-commerce literature suggests that e-models (Dutta *et al.*, 1998; Geiger and Martin, 1999; Voss, 2000), product characteristics (Deighton, 1997; Sakar *et al.*, 1998) or the nature of the environment matter (Yoris and Kaufmann, 2001). International business scholars suggest that export experience or intensity might influence e-commerce returns (Samiee, 1998b), and IT research draws attention to the ways in which the available technology is used and managed (Gerwal *et al.*, 2001).

To date, the evidence supporting the above claims is scarce, and much of the literature is purely conceptual and theoretical in nature (see Hamill and Gregory, 1997; Samiee, 1998a; Quelch and Klein, 1996). Although empirical work in the area has started with some important contributions from e-commerce research (Dutta and Segev, 1999; Geiger and Martin, 1999; Gerwal *et al.*, 2001), much of the theory is constructed without any allowance for the international dimensions of the phenomena. In fact, a search of major research journals did not generate a single study that specifically addressed the success factors in international e-commerce. As voiced by de la Torre and Moxon (2001), what seems absent in the study of international aspects of e-business is an understanding which would link the theoretical expectations with data about the actual effects. In an effort to provide this connection, we build on existing conceptualizations and empirical studies from three broad themes of literature, namely exporting (Cavusgil and Zou, 1994; Shoham, 1998; Madsen, 1987; Zou and Stan, 1998; Leonidou, 1998), e-commerce (Samiee, 1998a; Hamill, 1997; Quelch and Klein, 1996; Hamill and Gregory, 1997; Dutta and Segev, 1999; Peterson *et al.*, 1997), and information technology (IT) value-stream research (Willcocks *et al.*, 1998; Mahmood and Mann, 1993; Sethi and King, 1994; Palvia, 1997; Mahmood and Soon, 1991) to find an answer to the following question: which factors contribute to a higher effectiveness of international e-commerce?

To answer this question, we first set the conceptual boundaries of the study by placing it within the context of e-commerce, IT and exporting. Then, we develop a range of research hypotheses (H1–H8) which are tested on a sample of British exporters. This is followed by a discussion of results and research implications, closing with directions for further research and limitations.

Research background

E-commerce in general and international e-commerce in particular represent emerging fields of academic enquiry, and whilst widely acknowledged and discussed they remain largely undefined and lacking broadly accepted conceptualizations. A variety of terms are used to describe digital economic activity and these terms are often used interchangeably and with no common understanding of their scope and relationship. It is, therefore, imperative that before outlining research hypotheses we supply the basic definitions and place the study within a context.

The study lies within a narrowly defined area of e-activity which is set within technological, functional and operations boundaries. According to the technology research, e-activity appears in various types of networks, for example cellular phones, EDI, or extranets (Christianse and Venkatraman, 2002). The focus here is on one type of commuter mediated network – the internet – and only one type of application – the corporate web-site. Consequently, outside the scope lie issues related to e-mail, user groups and web communities, search engines and all other applications that are not web-site related. Moreover, the scope is further narrowed by the type of function affected by the e-activity. Potentially, various business processes might be transferred to a corporate web-site including purchasing, inventory management or recruitment (Bakos, 1997; El Sawy *et al.*, 1999). All these fall outside the boundaries of this project because the focus here is on marketing-based applications; that is, where the function performed by the web-site concerns supporting the transaction and relationship with a customer (Hoffman and Novak, 1996).

Finally, the geographical constraint concerns the operationalization of effectiveness. The latter is defined in terms of gains in export performance and only non-domestic effects of e-commerce are of interest. To capture those we focus on international businesses, more specifically on exporters, which were chosen for three reasons. First, exporting represents the most common mode of international involvement (Leonidou, 1995) and is inclusive of a wide range of internationally-oriented firms, at various stages of internationalization (Cavusgil, 1999; Samiee *et al.*, 1993; Shoham, 1998; Madsen, 1987). Second, it has been subject to widespread empirical research and an extensive theoretical base exists for further studies (Leonidou, 1996; Cavusgil and Zou, 1994; Aaby and Slater, 1989; Madsen, 1987). Finally, exporting is about trading and not investment and, as such, seems to be more in tune with the market-making or exchange-oriented capabilities of the internet (Peterson *et al.*, 1997).

Research hypotheses

Based on the literature, eight hypotheses are derived on the relationship between various aspects of e-commerce systems and performance.

E-model

The e-commerce literature offers a range of taxonomies describing various business models that can be adopted when e-channels are added to existing channel structures (Earl, 2000; El Sawy *et al.*, 1999), and one feature differentiating the models is the type of marketing function that is transferred to the electronic channel (Peterson *et al.*, 1997). Following a classification proposed by Berthon *et al.* (1999), these functions can be described as transaction, distribution, and communication-type functions. The literature is undecided as to which of these generates the highest returns. Some suggest that the final stage of internet capability is reached when an organization achieves on-line transaction capability (Quelch and Klein, 1996). Others claim that sustaining the customer relationship represents the ultimate goal (Geiger and Martin, 1999; Hoffman and Novak , 1996). In any case, it has been hypothesized that organizations progress from communication-based applications towards more complex relationship and transaction-based models, and that this move is associated with greater gains in terms of effectiveness of international marketing (Earl, 2000; El Sawy *et al.*, 1999).

H1 The more advanced the e-model, the greater the impact of the internet.

Network push and pull effects

The decision to adopt the internet as a marketing channel is not made in a vacuum; rather it is responsive to the social and relational context in which it takes place (Gerwal *et al.*, 2001). There are two important elements of that context: customers and competitors. Some organizations, for example, engage in internet activities simply because other firms do (Deephouse, 1996). This mimicking behaviour can occur because organizations dealing in technologically intensive environments are perceived as technologically savvy – and having such an image is an advantage. For others, the adoption represents an act of 'competitive necessity' (Clemons and Row, 1991). The more competitors and customers become internet-capable, the more inclined firms are to adopt it in order to maintain their competitive position (Iacovou *et al.*, 1995). With the growing size of the network of users, the competitive pressures to use the network increase (Yoris and Kaufmann, 2001), and as the number of adopters increases so does the value of the network and the benefits to the user (Katz and Shapiro, 1985). It is expected that operating in an environment where the network of other users is well-developed will stimulate higher returns for the network members.

H2 The odds of being successful are increased in environments where the network of users is well-developed.

Export experience and export intensity

Companies differ in terms of their commitment to exporting and the level of international activities, and the exporting literature generally links increased international competences with improved performance (Jonhanson and Vahlne, 1977; Tallman and Li, 1996). The level of internationalization has been suggested as a major factor in export-channel management (Erramilli and Rao, 1990; Leonidou, 1996), and it is therefore reasonable to expect that it plays a role in a decision concerning virtual-channel addition. We consider two facets of internationalization: export experience and export intensity.

Export intensity

Export intensity, as expressed by the value of export sales as a proportion of total sales (Burton and Schlegelmilch, 1987; Shoham, 1998), denotes a firm's increased reliance on foreign markets as a means of growth (Tallman and Li, 1996). It has been suggested that export intensity affects the extent of the benefits realized by adopters of international e-commerce (Samiee, 1998a), in particular that greater returns are expected to be gained by intensive exporters who can use e-commerce to further leverage their already highly developed international strategies. When significant marketing and sales expertise has been built into the existing channels, greater economies can be achieved by adding a virtual one (Geyskens *et al.*, 2002). In the case of irregular and less-intensive exporters, large knowledge barriers faced when integrating IT into existing channel systems may not be economically justifiable (Samiee, 1998b).

Export experience

The inverse relationship seems to be advocated with regard to the length of export experience (Quelch and Klein, 1996), and the argument is based on two premises. First, the relatively less-developed international competences of firms which have only briefly been engaged in exporting, might result in a lack of alternative marketing channels and efficient ways of conducting international business. This might force less-experienced exporters to rely on technology to a much greater extent and the greater reliance should, in turn, generate greater benefits. Secondly, such companies might also be less committed to existing procedures, routines and ways of doing business, and as a result they might be more proactive when faced with technological change (Geyskens *et al.*, 2002).

H3 The internet's impact is affected by the level of internationalization and (a) is positively related to export intensity; and (b) is negatively related to export experience.

Product characteristics

By introducing the concept of asset specificity, transaction-cost analysis (TCA) research has established a link between product characteristics and export-channel arrangements (Anderson and Gatignon, 1986; Klein, 1989). Asset specificity refers to the transaction-specific assets that must be borne for the transaction to take place. These assets are often operationalized by learning required to commercialize the product, or by product complexity (Anderson and Coughlan, 1987). TCA argues that if such assets are present, it is more efficient to carry out the transaction within the company rather than to deal with a partner (Klein *et al.*, 1990). A similar link has been proposed in the e-commerce literature (Daniel and Klimis, 1999). For example, Malone *et al.* (1987) suggest that the greater the complexity of a product, the more information is needed to specify the attributes to the customer, and therefore the greater the utility of electronic channels. Information-intensive products, that is products that can be strategically enhanced through information technology, are generally complicated to order and require accompanying information. This enhanced information component can be stored, processed and effectively communicated through computerized information systems (Porter, 2001).

H4 Product characteristics affect the odds of success in that (a) a specialist character increases the odds; and (b) product complexity increases the odds.

Level of investment

The underlying theme for most IT research concerns the effect of IT investment on returns, and the basic proposition is that the scale of gains is determined by the timely allocation of resources supporting adoption and implementation (Iacovou *et al.*, 1995). Even in the case of such a seemingly free-for-all application as a company web-site, financial resources are required for the initial development and installation (Samiee, 1998a). More resources, often in the form of an ongoing budget, are needed to cover the cost of running the system, maintenance, subsequent enhancements and upgrading (Premkumar and Ramamurthy, 1996). Aside from financial investment, other resources must be allocated, for example human resources might be important to support the infrastructure. Because web marketing represents investment oriented towards a long-term perspective, the adoption is typically preceded by a significant amount of planning and preparation, and management commitment is necessary to facilitate integration with existing marketing processes and ensure continuity over time (Premkumar and Ramamurthy, 1996).

H5 The greater the level of investment, the greater the odds of being successful.

Experience-based learning

Neo (1988), analysing 14 well-known IT cases, concluded that the most successful implementers were those who had already implemented similar systems, having built an infrastructure of experience and learning. Firms with adequate infrastructure and experiences are less threatened by the complexity of new technology. In general, highly computerized firms are better prepared to undertake IT projects and more likely to be successful. Conversely, a relatively low computerized level of operations makes the integration of sophisticated information systems difficult, necessitating costly expenditure an capital, people, and technology (Premkumar and Ramamurthy, 1996).

H6 Previous experience and the presence of complementary IT resources has a positive impact on the odds of being successful.

Age-based learning

Technology assimilation is best characterized as a process of organizational learning wherein individuals and the organization as a whole acquire knowledge and skills necessary to effectively apply technology (Attewell, 1992). Organization learning is a function of time; experience is a prime source of learning by capturing the trial-and-error process by which organizations acquire information (Garvin, 1993). Age-based learning helps capability development, and experiential learning has been shown to predict performance (Sinkula, 1994).

H7 The odds of success are increased with time.

Sophistication

Any IT application might be applied with varying degrees of success depending on the manner in which the technology is utilized and managed. This is particularly true of advanced IT applications and complex technologies, which can be used in more or less completed and sophisticated ways. Sophistication reflects the effectiveness of use – the extent to which a given application is managed effectively (Fichman, 2001). In the long run, the competitive and financial returns depend on how well the technological base is managed (Fichman and Kemerer, 1999).

H8 Sophistication increases the odds of being successful.

Methods

A mailed cross-sectional survey was used to collect the data. To qualify for the sampling frame a company had to have international sales and a web-site, and the *British Export Directory* published by the Institute of Export was used to find target firms and the database search generated a sample of 3,136 companies.

The survey instrument was developed using procedures recommended by Churchill (1979). Following the literature search, an initial sample of possible items was generated and edited to form a draft questionnaire. The questionnaire was evaluated by three academic experts from the University of Warwick, pretested with three export executives, and then piloted on a random sample of 98 exporting companies.

Data collection involved two mailshots and in both cases an envelope containing a covering letter, a copy of the questionnaire, a reply card and a return pre-paid envelope was sent to a named export executive. In 208 instances the letters contained wrong details either with regard to the address or the company or the person. These were deducted from the original sample thus reducing the actual sample to 2,828 companies. By the closing date, the final number of replies reached 727, yielding an overall response rate of 25.7 per cent. Upon closer examination, 22 questionnaires were identified as unusable, leaving an effective response rate of 24.9 per cent, which is quite satisfactory given that (1) the survey was unsolicited, (2) the instrument was extensive, and (3) that top executives are less likely to reply (Hunt and Chonko, 1987). Overall, the response rate compares favourably with other reported rates of 15 to 20 per cent (Menon *et al.*, 1999).

The non-response bias was assessed by examining the differences between early and late respondents with regard to the mean values of the key variables (Armstrong and Overton, 1977). No significant differences were found.

Although the letters were addressed specifically to a person in charge of exporting, the majority of replies came from non-exporting senior executives. Most replies were sent by managing directors (MDs) (38 per cent) and sales/marketing managers (35 per cent), with the remaining 15 per cent accounted for by export managers and 11 per cent by others. The resulting sample is representative of various company sizes ranging from 1 to 8,000 employees, with an average of 266 employees. In terms of the general company type, 75 per cent of companies represent the manufacturing category, and more specifically high-tech (20.1 per cent), machinery/components (27.7 per cent), chemicals/raw materials (14.3 per cent) and other manufacturing (12.9 per cent). The remaining service category is comprised of consultancy/research services (8.8 per cent), retail/distribution (10.9 per cent) and other services (5.2 per cent).

We used both single and multiple indicator measures and, in the latter case, a measure-development procedure suggested by Churchill (1979) and updated by Anderson and Gerbing (1988) was followed. In order to ensure the initial validity of constructs the literature was searched for previous conceptualizations and whenever possible existing measures were used. If these were not available, new measures were developed on the basis of the literature search, conceptual definitions and pre-study interviews. The multi-item measures were validated with principal component analysis (PCA) and confirmatory factor analysis (CFA). First, PCA was used to examine unidimensionality and discriminant validity of scales. We applied four commonly used decision rules to identify factors: (1) a minimum eigen value of 1; (2) a minimum factor loading of .30 for each indicator variable; (3) simplicity of factor structure; and (4) exclusion of single-item factors from the standpoint of parsimony (Hair *et al.*, 1998). The initial set of factors was then analysed using CFA and the results show a satisfactory model-fit with $\chi^2=458.25$, $df=288$; root-mean-square error of approximation RMSEA=.054; comparative fit index CFI=.97; normed fit index NFI=.95. All constructs display satisfactory levels of reliability with alpha values higher than the recommended threshold of .60–.70 (Nunnally, 1978); high internal stability with the amount of variance captured larger than .50 (Fornell and Larker, 1981); and good composite reliability with a CR index >0.7 (Hair, 1998). The details of the measurement model are presented in the Appendix, and Table 1.1 presents correlation matrix and descriptive statistics. All multi-item constructs in this study were measured using 7-point scales anchored by 1 = strongly disagree and 7 = strongly agree, unless otherwise indicated.

As it was intended to assess the positive effect of a web-site on export performance, we build on well-established export performance measures and capture this construct using four indicators: sales, profits, number of foreign markets served, and overall performance (Cavusgil and Zou, 1994; Shoham, 1998).

A web-investment measure taps on financial and non-financial resources allocated to e-marketing. Because there were no marketing measures, items taken from the IT literature were adopted (Mahmood and Mann, 1993; Mahmood and Soon, 1991). The initial pool consisted of five indicators, but two of them were dropped in the purification procedures. The remaining three show good reliability.

We found no suitable measure for network effects – the extent to which sources outside the company affect the adoption of virtual export channels. Two sources of imitation were identified: customers and competitors. Again the indicators are based on the IT and internet literature (Geiger and Martin, 1999; Sillince *et al.*, 1998). Reliability is below the recommended 0.7, but this could be expected with two item measure and in an in an exploratory context - above 0.5 (Nunnally 1978).

To capture product characteristics we build on two constructs derived from TCA research: the specialist nature of the product (learning), and product complexity. The former reflects the level of specialization of a product and is measured by how much one must learn about the product in order to effectively sell it. The scale was adopted from Anderson and Coughlan (1987). The latter, product complexity, was operationalized using four semantic differential items adapted from Anderson (1985).

We found no existing measures for the adopted e-model, which is to capture one of three possible web-site functions: information provision, transaction or relationship (Hoffman and Novak , 1996). Building on existing theoretical conceptualizations, in particular Berthon *et al.* (1999) and Geiger and Martin (1999), we developed a set of dichotomous scales (yes/no) covering a range of possible web-site facilities related to either information (7 items), transaction (3 items) or relationship function (6 items – see Table 1.1 for details). We assume that a web-site performs a given function if a single item from a given group is present, for example a business is defined as trading on-line if it enabled its customers to either order on-line or pay on-line or deliver on-line.

Channel sophistication aims to assess the extent to which technology is used and managed in the most advanced format (Fichman, 2001). We elaborated on

Table 1.1 Measurement Model

Mulit-items measures (CFA model)	*Standardized factor loading*
Network effects (own, based on Sillince *et al.*, 1998) (α=.68, *CR*=.66, *AVE*=.50)	
We are under pressure from our customers to adopt the internet	.67
Many of our competitors use the internet	.74
Product characteristics – specialist character (based on TCA literature e.g. Klein *et al.*, 1990; Klein, 1989) (α=.84, *CR*=.77, *AVE*=.54)	
Specialized know-how is required to market our products/services	.85
It takes a long time to learn about our products/services	.71
It is difficult for an outsider to learn our customers' requirements	.52
Product complexity (adapted from Anderson and Coughlan, 1987) (measured on 7-point semantic differential scale) (α=.68, *CR*=.84, *AVE*=.57)	
technological intensity	.77
engineering content	.71
complexity	.84
sophistication	.71
Experience-based learning (items adapted from Gerwal *et al.*, 2001; Mahmood and Mann, 1993; Premkumar and Ramamurthy, 1996) (α=.82, *CR*=.82, *AVE*=.54)	
My company operates complex and very sophisticated IT infrastructure	.78
Employs a high proportion of IT support and IT literate staff	.65
Invests heavily in IT systems and applications	.90
Prior to the internet, has been using IT system(s) that support sales and marketing (e.g. electronic databases, EDI)	.56
Web investment (own, based on Mahmood and Mann, 1993; Gerwal *et al.*, 2001) (α=.79, *CR*=.78, *AVE*=.54)	
*Level of initial investment in internet related hardware/software was high**	
Ongoing internet budget is very high	62
There is substantial planning for internet activities	.70
*Top management is commited and supportive of the internet**	
Overall investment in terms of time and resources is high	.87
Impact (scale based on export performance literature e.g. Cavusgil and Zou, 1994; Madsen, 1987) (α=.93, *CR*=.93, *AVE*=.62)	
The internet has significantly improved	
... export profits	.88
... number of foreign markets served	.87
... export sales	.94
... overall performance	.80
Competition intensity (adopted from Klein *et al.*, 1990) (α=.79, *CR*=.78, *AVE*=.64)	
The level of competition in my industry is very high	.66
There are many competitors in our market	.92

**Items dropped during the purification procedure.*

Table 1.1 (Continued)

E-model (based on Dutta and Segev, 1999; Geiger and Martin, 1999)

Information	Relationship	Transaction	Sophistication
Company information	On-line customer service	On-line ordering	Multiple pages
Product/service information	Visitor recognition software	Payment facilities	Regular content update
Product catalogues	Customer feedback forms	On-line delivery	Different language versions
Product/service prices	Personalized interface		Own domain name
Sales promotions/ offers	Customer profiling/ capturing customer data		Registered with major search engines
Links to other companies			
Foreign distributor contact information	Order tracking/ shipping		Other facilities

previous conceptualizations by Dutta *et al.* (1998) and Geiger and Martin (1999) to construct six dichotomous scales (see Table 1.1). For the regression model, the summated score was transformed into a nominal category with a score of three as the cut-off point: a score <3 indicates a less-sophisticated user, whilst a score >3 indicates a more sophisticated user.

We used two indicators of the level of internationalization: the number of years in exporting and export intensity. The items were measured as continuous variables and transformed by logarithmic function.

Time of adoption has traditionally been used to capture age-related learning. We use one indicator, which measures how long a company has been using their web-site as expressed by years and months.

Control variables

Company size and industry group have been suggested as important determinants of the internet usage. Accordingly, we included six dummy variables to represent the industry sectors of the sample and a firm-size measure based on the logarithm of the number of employees. Furthermore, we controlled for competition intensity using variables from TCA research (Klein *et al.*, 1990).

Model specification

To test the research hypotheses, we have used logistic regression, a technique that estimates the odds of the dependent variable occurring (Hair *et al.*, 1998). In our case the dependent variable reflects the level of success with international web-site marketing and concerns two types of web-site users: successful and unsuccessful. We used the individual average scores for the web-site impact on export performance, dividing the cases into three groups: those with a score equal to or lower than three (unsuccessful), those with a score equal to or higher than five (successful), and the mid-category with scores greater than three but smaller than five. The latter represents cases where the effect of the internet was somewhat neutral and, as neither successful nor unsuccessful, these cases were excluded from further analysis.

The final model includes the average scores for all multi-item construct, interval variables and dummy variables as specified in the measurement model. In addition to the main effects, we included moderator effects concerning e-model indicators (see Table 1.2). The two recommended tests for the overall model are both insignificant, providing support for the acceptance of the model: $\chi^2 = 8.845$ for the change in the -2LL value (log likelihood value); the Hosmer and Lemeshow measure of overall fit=.356. Several fit indicators provide further support for the model: (1) the log likelihood value (-2LL) value has reduced from 555.483 in the base model to 355.711 indicating fit improvement; (2) the Cox and Snell R^2 and Negelkerke R^2 are quite satisfactory at .392 and .523 respectively; and (3) finally the pseudo R^2 is also acceptable at .360.

Model interpretation

The individual coefficients are assessed with Wald statistics and eight indicators are significant at the level of .05 or higher. We find no support for H1: neither the ability to transact, the relationship capability nor the moderator effect transaction × relationship had any significant effect on the probability of being successful. The probability of being successful are, however, significantly increased when the network effects are present – H2 is strongly supported ($B = .451$, $p < .001$). The probabilities are also enhanced by export intensity and decreased by export experience as posited by H3a and H3b. Furthermore, there is a positive, although not very strong ($B = .295$, $p < .05$) relationship between the specialist nature of the product and the chances of success supporting H4a. We found, however, no evidence that the complexity of the product affects the probabilities.

The second highest regression coefficient concerns the relationship between the investment in web marketing and odds of being successful. H5 is strongly supported suggesting that the level of investment in e-marketing represent a highly important determinant of returns.

Contrary to the expectations and predictions from IT theories, we found no evidence that experience-based learning or time-based learning affect the odds. Neither H6 nor H7 is supported. Possibly the most important result concerns H8, which is strongly supported with $B = 1.382$, $p < .001$. The coefficient for

Table 1.2 Logistic regression on successful and unsuccessful web-site users

Independent variables	*B*	*Sig.*	*Probability (odds) ratio*	*Hypothesis*	*Supported?*
Transaction	0.512	0.389			
Relationship	0.427	0.169		H1	No
Relationship × transaction	–0.334	0.642			
Network effect	**0.451******	0.000	**1.57**	H2	Yes
Export intensity	**0.449*****	0.002	**1.57**	H3a	Yes
Export experience	–0.484**	0.012	**1.62**	H3b	Yes
Specialist	**0.295****	0.029	**1.34**	H4a	Yes
Product complexity	–0.178	0.165		H4b	No
Investment	**0.575******	0.000	**1.77**	H5	Yes
Experience-based learning	–0.040	0.718		H6	No
Time-based learning	0.014*	0.095		H7	No
Sophistication	**1.382** ****	0.000	**3.98**	H8	Yes
Size	–0.393****	0.000			
Competition	–0.350***	0.001			
High-tech	–0.080	0.913			
Machinery	–0.295	0.682			
Chemical	0.004	0.996			
Other manufacturing	0.458	0.548			
Consultancy	0.768	0.363			
Retail/distribution	0.009	0.991			
Intercept	–3.768	0.317			

Log likelihood (-2LL) = 355.711 | Chi-square = 8.845 | Hosmer and Lemeshow test = .356
Cox and Snell R^2 = .392 | Negelkerke R^2 = .523 | Pseudo – R^2 = .360
Correct classifications (%) = 78.1

**** significant at $p < 0.001$ | *** $p < 0.01$ | ** $p < 0.05$ | * $p < 0.10$

B=Logistic coefficient
Sig=Significance

sophistication is also the highest of all coefficients, more than twice as high as the next in size, which suggests that sophistication represents the single most important variable in the equation. The interpretation of individual regression coefficients in logistic regression is difficult because the dependent variable concerns odds and the coefficients represents log values which have to be transformed by e to enable meaningful interpretation. By transforming the sophistication coefficient we find that the odds are increased by four for sophisticated users.

In general, we found that the strongest factor in increasing the odds of being successful is the sophistication of web-site use. This is followed by web-investment, export intensity and network effects. The odds decrease with export experience, level of competition and size.

Conclusions and future research

Although marketers have long recognized the potential significance of the internet for international marketing, the empirical research of international e-commerce is still in its infancy. This study provides some preliminary insights into factors which determine the impact of virtual-channel additions, substantially adding to the emerging stream of literature on the internet in the international context.

The empirical results are important for several reasons. First, there are some very interesting implications concerning e-commerce. The results show that against common wisdom, success with the internet is not dictated by the ability to transact on-line. In particular, problems with on-line ordering, payment and security have often been linked with a lower propensity to e-commerce and lower returns, but in our study we have found no evidence supporting this theory. On the contrary, the results suggest that even basic information models can be very successful provided the internet is managed correctly. In other words, the irrelevance of having transaction facilities is offset by the paramount importance of sophistication when managing the web-site.

In general, the results indicate that there is no link between the business model and the odds of success. We found no evidence of increased returns in the case of transaction or relationship-based models. Surprisingly, no such evidence was found even when the model adopted involved both transaction and relationship-building capabilities. Also important are the implications for IT research. It is quite significant that neither of the well-established learning constructs represents a significant determinant of success. It remains debatable whether such a result is related to the specific nature of the internet and its applications, or whether it is symptomatic of the increasingly 'outsourced' nature of organizational information systems. This feature of IT systems has possibly been rather overlooked in IT research.

The study represents an important step forward towards the measurement of e-business phenomena in the context of marketing and strategic management. Complex IT applications are notoriously difficult to capture, particularly when the research setting concerns diverse companies. The measures utilized in this study represent an important step towards operationalization of e-commerce phenomena. Although the findings are a significant step towards understanding the role and impact of e-commerce in international business, they are based on cross-sectional data which do not fully capture the dynamics of e-business and the complex system of interactions between e-marketing and international marketing. The approach to data presented here is, by default, broad but shallow, and as a result many of the analysed relationships are only touched upon. Further research should concentrate on longer-term studies and a more detailed exploration of constructs, possibly within more contextualised settings.

The study is also somewhat superficial in the treatment of various e-models. This is particularly important, considering that our results show no relationships between business models and the effectiveness of international e-marketing. It is plausible that more detailed investigation and broader conceptualization of e-model constructs would lead to different results, but it is also likely that the results are indicative of differences between domestic and international e-commerce.

References

Aaby, N.-E. and Slater, S.F. (1989) 'Management influences on export performance: a review of the empirical literature 1978–88', *International Marketing Review* 6(1), 7–26.

Anderson, E. (1985) 'The salesperson as an outside agent or employee: a transaction cost analysis', *Marketing Science* 4(3), 234–54.

Anderson, E. and Coughlan, A.T. (1987) 'International market entry and expansion via independent or integrated channels of distribution', *Journal of Marketing* 51(1), 71–82.

Anderson, E. and Gatignon, H. (1986) 'Modes of entry: a transaction cost analysis and propositions', *Journal of International Business Studies* 17(1), 1–26.

Anderson, J. and Gerbing, D. (1988) 'An updated paradigm for scale development incorporating unidimensionality and its assessment', *Journal of Marketing Research* 25(3), 186–92.

Armstrong, J.S. and Overton, T.S. (1977) 'Estimating non-response bias in mail surveys', *Journal of Marketing Research* 16(4), 396–400.

Attewell, P. (1992) 'Technology diffusion and organisational learning: the case of business computing', *Organisation Science* 3(1), 1–19.

Bakos, J.Y. (1997) 'Reducing buyer search costs: implications for electronic marketplaces', *Management Science* 43(4), 1677–92.

Berthon, P., Pitt, L. and Katsikeas, C.S. (1999) 'Virtual services go international: international services in the marketspaces', *Journal of International Marketing* 7(3), 84–105.

Burton, F.N. and Schlegelmilch, B.B. (1987) 'Profile analysis of non-exporters versus exporters grouped by export involvement', *International Marketing Review* 27(1), 38–49.

Cavusgil, T.S. (1999) 'Differences among exporting firms based on their degree of internationalisation', in Buckley, P.J. and Ghauri, P.N. (eds), *The Internationalisation of the Firm: A Reader*, pp. 208–18. London: International Thomson Business Press.

Cavusgil, T.S. and Zou, S. (1994) 'Marketing strategy–performance relationship: an investigation of the empirical link in export market ventures', *Journal of Marketing* 58(1), 1–24.

Christianse, E. and Venkatraman, N. (2002) 'Expertise exploitation in electronic channels', *MIS Quarterly* 26(1), 15–39.

Churchill, G.A.Jr. (1979) 'A paradigm for developing better measures of marketing construct', *Journal of Marketing Research* 16(1), 64–73.

Clemons, E.K. and Row, M.C. (1991) 'Sustaining IT advantage: the role of structural differences', *MIS Quarterly* 15(4), 275–94.

Daniel, E. and Klimis, G. (1999) 'The impact of electronic commerce on market structure: an evaluation of the electronic market hypothesis', *European Management Journal* 17(3), 318–25.

de la Torre, J. and Moxon, R.W. (2001) 'E-commerce and global business: the impact of the information and communication technology revolution on the conduct of international business', *Journal of International Business Studies* 32(3), 617–39.

Deephouse, D.L. (1996) 'Does isomorphism legitimate?' *Academy of Management Journal* 39(4), 1024–39.

Deighton, J. (1997) 'Commentary on "Exploring the implications of the Internet for consumer marketing"', *Journal of the Academy of Marketing Science* 25(3), 347–51.

Dutta, S., Kwan, S. and Segev, A. (1998) 'Business transformation in electronic commerce: a study of sectoral and regional trends', *European Management Journal* 16(4), 540–51.

Dutta, S. and Segev, A. (1999) 'Business transformation on the Internet', *European Management Journal* 17(4), 466–76.

Earl, M.J. (2000) 'Evolving the e-Business', *Business Strategy Review* 11(1), 33–8.

El Sawy, O.A., Malhotra, A., Gosain, S. and Young, K.M. (1999) 'IT-intensive value innovation in the electronic economy: insights from Marshall Industries', *MIS Quarterly* 23(3), 305–35.

Erramilli, M.K. and Rao, C.P. (1990) 'Entry mode by service firms: role of market knowledge', *Management International Review* 30(1), 50–62.

Fichman, R.G. (2001) 'The role of aggregation in the measurement of IT-related organisational innovation', *MIS Quarterly* 25(4), 427–55.

Fichman, R.G. and Kemerer, C.F. (1999) 'The illusory diffusion of innovation: an examination of assimilation gap', *Information Systems Research* 10(3), 255–75.

Fornell, C. and Larker, D. (1981) 'Evaluating structural equation models with unobservable variables and measurement error', *Journal of Marketing* 28(1), 39–50.

Garvin, D.A. (1993) 'Building a learning organization', *Harvard Business Review* 71(1), 78–91.

Geiger, S. and Martin, S. (1999) 'The Internet as a relationship marketing tool – some evidence from Irish companies', *Irish Marketing Review* 12(1), 24–36.

Gerwal, R., Comer, J.M. and Mehta, R. (2001) 'An investigation into the antecedents of organizational participation in business-to-business electronic markets', *Journal of Marketing* 65(1), 17–33.

Hair, J.F., Anderson, R.E., Tatham, R.L. and Black, W.C. (1998) *Multivariate Data Analysis*, 5th edn. Upper Saddle River: Prentice-Hall.

Hamill, J. (1997) 'The Internet and international marketing', *International Marketing Review* 14(3), 300–23.

Hamill, J. and Gregory, K. (1997) 'Internet marketing in the internationalisation of UK SMEs', *Journal of Marketing Management* 13(1), 9–28.

Hoffman D.L. and Novak T.P (1996) 'Marketing in hypermedia computer-mediated environments: conceptual foundations', *Journal of Marketing* 60(1), 24–37.

Hunt, S.D. and Chonko, L.B. (1987) 'Ethical problems of advertising agency executives', *Journal of Advertising* 16(1), 16–24.

Iacovou, C.L., Benbasat, I. and Dexter, A.S. (1995) 'Electronic data interchange and small organisations: adoption and impact of technology', *MIS Quarterly* 19(3), 465–85.

Johanson, J. and Vahlne, J.-E. (1977) 'The internationalisation process of the firm – a model of knowledge development and increasing foreign market commitments', *Journal of International Business Studies* 8(1), 23–32.

Katz, M.L. and Shapiro, C. (1985) 'Network externalities, competition and compatibility', *The American Economic Review* 75(4), 424–40.

King, D., Lee, J., Warkentin, M. and Chung, H.M. (2002) *Electronic Commerce: A Managerial Perspective*, 1st edn. New Jersey: Prentice-Hall.

Klein, S. (1989) 'A transaction cost explanation of vertical control in international markets', *Journal of the Academy of Marketing Science* 17(3), 253–60.

Klein, S., Frazier, G. and Roth, V.J. (1990) 'A transaction cost analysis model of channel integration in international markets', *Journal of Marketing Research* 27(3), 196–208.

Leonidou, L.C. (1995) 'Export simulation research: a review, evaluation and integration', *International Business Review* 4(2), 133–56.

Leonidou, L.C. (1996) 'The export development process: an integrative review of empirical models', *Journal of International Business Studies* 27(3), 517–51.

Leonidou, L.C. (1998) 'Organisational determinants of exporting: conceptual, methodological, and empirical insights', *Management International Review* 38(1), 7–53.

Madsen, T.K. (1987) 'Empirical export performance studies: a review of conceptualisations and findings', *Advances in International Marketing* 2(3), 177–98.

Mahmood, M.A. and Mann, G.J. (1993) 'Measuring the organisational impact of information technology investment: an exploratory study', *Journal of Management Information Systems* 10(1), 97–122.

Mahmood, M.A. and Soon, S.K. (1991) 'A comprehensive model for measuring the potential impact of information technology on organisational strategic variables', *Decision Science* 22(4), 869–97.

Malone, T., Yates J. and Benjamin R. (1987) 'Electronic markets and hierarchies', *Communications of the Academy of Chapter Marketers ACM* 6(4), 485–97.

Menon, A., Bharadwaj, S.G., Adidam, P.T. and Edison, S.W. (1999) 'Antecedents and consequences of marketing strategy making: a model and test', *Journal of Marketing* 63(1), 18–40.

Neo, B.S. (1988) 'Factors influencing the use of information technology for competitive advantage: an exploratory study', *Information and Management* 15(2), 191–201.

Nunnally, J.C. (1978) *Psychometric Theory*. New York: McGraw-Hill.

Palvia, P.C. (1997) 'Developing a model of the global and strategic impact of information technology', *Information and Management* 32(3), 229–44.

Peterson, R.A., Balasubramanian, S. and Bronnenberg, B.J. (1997) 'Exploring the implication of the Internet for consumer', *Journal of the Academy of Marketing Science* 25(3), 329–46.

Porter, M.E. (2001) 'Strategy and the Internet', *Harvard Business Review* 80(1), 62–78.

Premkumar, G. and Ramamurthy, K. (1996) 'The role of interorganizational and organizational factors on the decision mode for adoption of interorganizational systems', *Decision Sciences* 26(3), 303–36.

Quelch, J.A. and Klein, L.R. (1996) 'The Internet and international marketing', *Sloan Management Review* 37(1), 60–76.

Sakar, M., Butler, B. and Steinfield, C. (1998) 'Cybermediaries in electronic marketspace: toward theory building', *Journal of Business Research* 41(2), 215–21.
Samiee, S. (1998a) 'Exporting and the Internet: a conceptual perspective', *International Marketing Review* 15(3), 413–26.
Samiee, S. (1998b) 'The internet and international marketing: is there a fit?', *Journal of Interactive Marketing* 12(1), 7–21.
Samiee, S., Walters, P.G.P. and DuBois, F.L. (1993) 'Exporting as an innovative behaviour: an empirical investigation', *International Marketing Review* 10(1), 5–25.
Sethi, V. and King, W. (1994) 'Development of measures to assess the extent to which an information technology application provides competitive advantage', *Management Science* 40(5), 1601–27.
Shoham, A. (1998) 'Export performance: a conceptualisation and empirical assessment', *Journal of International Marketing* 6(1), 39–81.
Sillince, J.A.A., Macdonald, S., Lefang, B. and Frost, B. (1998) 'E-mail adoption, diffusion, use and impact within small firms: a survey of UK companies', *International Journal of Information Management* 18(3), 231–42.
Sinkula, J.M. (1994) 'Market information processing and organizational learning', *Journal of Marketing* 58(1), 35–45.
Tallman, S. and Li, J. (1996) 'Effects of international diversity and product diversity on the performance of multinational firms', *Academy of Management Journal* 39(2), 179–96.
Voss, C. (2000) 'Developing an eService Strategy', *Business Strategy Review* 11(1), 21–33.
Willcocks, L., Graeser, V. and Lester, S. (1998) 'Cybernomics and IT productivity: not business as usual', *European Management Journal* 16(2), 272–83.
Yang, Y.S., Leone, R.P. and Alden, D.L. (1992) 'A market expansion ability approach to identify potential exporters', *Journal of Marketing* 56(2), 84–96.
Yoris, A.A. and Kaufmann, R.J. (2001) 'Should we wait? Network externalities, compatibility, and electronic billing adoption', *Journal of Management Information Systems* 18(1), 47–63.
Zou, S. and Stan, S. (1998) 'The determinants of export performance: a review of the empirical literature between 1987 and 1997', *International Marketing Review* 15(3), 333–56.

2

International Joint Venture Performance: Empirical Evidence from Finnish International Joint Ventures

*Jorma Larimo**

Introduction

The past three decades have been characterized by a multiplicity of studies focusing on the subject of international joint ventures (IJVs) and alliances. Behind this great interest towards IJVs and other forms of cooperation arrangements by academics and managers are (1) the increasing use of collaborative arrangements by companies and various public organizations, and (2) the relatively high failure rate of various types of collaborative arrangements.

As regards the reasons for the increasing use of various types of cooperation arrangements including IJVs, Contractor and Lorange (1988) present seven more or less overlapping objectives for the formation of IJVs:

1 risk reduction;
2 economies of scale and/or rationalization;
3 technology exchanges;
4 co-opting or blocking competition;
5 overcoming government mandated trade or investment barriers;
6 facilitating initial international expansion of inexperienced firms; and
7 vertical quasi-integration advantages of linking the complementary contributions of the partners in a 'value chain'.

It is evident that the reasons for forming IJVs are manifold and reach into all areas of business strategy. Although there may be very diverse motivations, the motivations can probably be distilled into three broad categories:

*The author wishes to offer his thanks to Sami Rumpunen and Jukka Harju for their help in data collection and statistical analysis, and to thank an anonymous reviewer for useful comments. Finally, financial support for the research project from the Wihuri Foundation is gratefully acknowledged.

(a) resource-driven IJVs;
(b) market driven IJVs; and
(c) risk-driven IJVs (see for example Parkhe, 1996).

These three categories are often interrelated, and several of the IJVs established in the late 1980s and in the 1990s are distinguishable from earlier counterparts in their straddling of multiple objectives.

Failure rates of collaborative arrangements in several studies have been high, depending on the measure used, with rates as high as two-thirds being reported in some empirical studies (Geringer and Hebert, 1991; Chowdbury, 1992). Furthermore, results about the influence of various variables on IJV performance have been rather mixed.

This chapter aims to provide additional evidence on the relationships between selected partner firms, target countries, and IJV-related variables and IJV performance. An additional goal is to analyse whether there is variation in the results depending on the measure of performance – in this case survival and stability. The empirical part of the paper will be based on a sample of 657 IJVs established by 130 Finnish companies in over 60 foreign countries during 1970–99. The study is the first large-scale study focusing on IJV performance of firms originating from any of the Nordic countries. By 'IJV' is meant a unit of at least two partners with one having its headquarters outside the target country of the unit. The unit may have been established as a greenfield investment, or the IJV may be a partial acquisition of a local unit. The share of the foreign partner in the IJV must be in the range 10–94 per cent. Finally, our focus is on IJVs having manufacturing operations; thus, IJVs in the service sector and IJVs between firms in the manufacturing sector which concentrate only on sales or R&D operations are excluded. Our focus is also from the viewpoint of the foreign partner in the IJV.

The structure of the chapter is as follows. In the next section an overview of performance measures is made. This is followed by a discussion of the relationships between various variables and IJV performance, and hypotheses (H1–H11) are developed for the empirical part that follows. The sample selection, operationalization of variables used and key methodological issues in the study are discussed, and the results presented and analysed. The final section includes a summary and conclusions.

Measurement of IJV performance

A major difficulty in evaluating the success of IJVs is due to the definitions and measures of performance used. Academics have used numerous measures of performance, many of which are conceptually ill-founded and have *prima facie* caused inconsistency in empirical findings (Geringer and Hebert, 1991; Olk, 1997; Robson and Katsikeas, 1998). In several studies only one criterion for

IJV performance has been used, but in others there has been great variation in how performance has been evaluated and which criteria have been used. Also, evaluation can be directed towards either the performance of the operation itself (JVPERF), or towards the performance of the partners (PARTPERF) (that is, how the IJV characteristics influence the partner(s)' performance). Furthermore, the evaluation can be realized using subjective or objective measures or a combination of both (see Blanchot and Mayerhofer, 1997).

Reviews of empirical IJV studies (see Larimo, 2001, and Robson, Leonidou and Katsikeas, 2002) indicate that an overwhelming majority of proxies identified in the literature correspond to JVPERF. Only a few studies assess PARTPERF. Objective measures of JVPERF have included longevity, survival, stability, combinations of longevity/survival and stability, and various types of business indicators (for example profitability, market share and so on). Subjective measures have also been used, such as items assessed by partner firm(s), various items assessed by the IJV general manager, or a combination. Furthermore, different combinations of objective and subjective measures have been used. All measures have their own strengths and weaknesses, but in this study the evaluation will be directed towards the JVPERF and we will focus on the two measures – survival and stability.

Survival has usually been accepted as a good indicator of performance; a divestment is usually regarded as an indicator that the unit has not reached the goals set for it, or that the unit has clearly been a failure. The latter may not necessarily be the case (see for example Yan and Zeng, 1999), but results in several studies (for example Beamish, 1985; and Harrigan, 1988) reveal that most ventures that have ceased operations did so because they failed. Also, in a rather recent study by Glaister and Buckley (1998) a high correlation was found between survival and subjective measures of IJV performance (see also Geringer and Hebert, 1991).

Stability is another commonly used measure for IJV performance; stability increases internal harmony and trust between partners. Only if it is clearly evident that the inputs of partners do not equal the desired levels, and they agree about this, is a rapid change in ownership distribution justified. Another exception includes cases where such a change was already planned at the time of establishing the IJV (for a good review related to the concept and use of instability as the measure of IJV performance see Yan and Zeng, 1999). In this study instability includes both divestments and greater changes in ownership distribution.

Relationships between variables and IJV performance

In two reviews covering over 90 empirical studies focusing on IJV performance, over 100 variables were found to have been used (Larimo, 2001; Robson *et al.*, 2002).

A great majority of the variables were used only in a very few studies, and even for those used in several studies the results were usually rather mixed. Thus additional analysis is needed of the relationships between all variables and IJV performance. For this study 13 variables were selected based on data collected for a large FDI databank by Finnish and other Nordic companies. The variables are: parent size, international and target-country-specific experience, unit relatedness, cultural distance and four individual dimensions of culture (uncertainty avoidance, masculinity–feminity, power distance, individualism), form of establishment, number of partners, dominant foreign ownership, and age of the IJV. Factors such as cultural distance and age of the IJV have been included in several earlier studies, but as stated above the earlier results have been rather mixed. Other variables such as the relationships between the four separate dimensions of culture with IJV performance have been analysed only limitedly so far, and additional evidence is clearly needed.

Size of the partner firm

One might expect that because larger firms usually have more financial and management resources, and their international experience is greater than that of smaller companies, their need for a local partner is likely to be smaller. Also, if they do need a partner, then their ability to negotiate and their bargaining power is likely to be greater than that of smaller firms. It could also, then, be expected that they would enjoy better performance with their IJVs. The empirical results are, however, very mixed. From the eight studies where the relationship between the size of the foreign partner and IJV performance has been analysed, three indicate support for a positive relationship (Tomlinson, 1970; Makino and Delios, 1996; Soonkyo, 2000) and three for a negative relationship (Koh and Venkatraman, 1991; Hennart *et al.*, 1998; Garcia-Canal *et al.*, 1999). In two studies no statistically significant relationship could be found (Chen, Hu and Shieh, 1991; Merchant, 1997). One possible explanation for the negative relationship is that larger firms have made more relatively unrelated types of FDIs and in this kind of FDI/IJV the performance has often been poorer than in more related types of FDI/IJV. Another explanation is that larger firms may have greater pressure to integrate various foreign units more tightly into their global networks than SMEs, and therefore may more often buy the share(s) of the other partner(s) causing greater instability than in IJVs by SMEs. Based on the above, it seems that there does not exist any direct relationship between size of the foreign partner and IJV performance.

H 1 There is no direct relationship between the size of the foreign partner and IJV performance.

International experience and target-country-specific experience

Experience can improve performance/longevity of a FDI in several ways. First, experienced firms are probably better market and partner 'scanners' than novices in the international arena. More accurate evaluations of potential sites and IJV partners for a FDI should increase the probability of better performance and reduce the risk of subsequent divestment. Second, as experience is accumulated it becomes easier to avoid many of the problems involved in running foreign subsidiaries, and to find workable solutions if problems should arise after all. Finally, international operations take place in environments that are often subject to seemingly dramatic changes, for example sudden changes in exchange rates and prices, competition and so forth. The interpretation of such events and how to respond to them can vary greatly, depending on how experienced the decision-makers are. An event that from the viewpoint of an unexperienced firm is regarded as quite extraordinary, may be interpreted by an experienced firm as simply a normal fluctuation. What could lead to withdrawal from an operation in the first case may well barely raise any concern in the latter. In sum, higher levels of experience should lead to lower dissolution rates and therefore to better performance. However, based on the greater international experience and usually greater need for integrating the operation of various units to the international network of the foreign partner than in cases of less experienced foreign parents, the stability of the units could be expected to be lower in the former than in the latter cases. Empirical support for a positive relationship between international experience and IJV performance is given by Barkema and Vermeulen (1997), whereas Chen *et al.* (1991) and Sim and Ali (2000) did not found any relationship, and Hu *et al.* (1992) found a negative relationship. Related to the performance in FDIs in general, results by Mariotti and Piscitello (1997) and Larimo (1998, 2000) indicated that international experience decreased the probability of divestment, that is increased the probability of survival.

For the case of target-country-specific experience, we might expect reduced uncertainty related to the operation environment, thus increasing the possibilities for better performance. However, target-country-specific experience may also reduce the need for a local partner after the starting period of the operation. Thus, as in the case of international experience, it could be expected that based on survival the relationship would be positive but based on stability it would be negative. The relationship has been reviewed in five studies of which three indicate support for a positive relationship (Artisien and Buckley 1985, Makino 1995, Barkema and Vermeulen 1997), one for a negative relationship (Makino and Delios 1996), and one no statistically significant relationship (Chen *et al.* 1991).

Lasserre (1999) reviewed the influence of earlier IJV experience in other Asian countries on IJV performance, but no statistically significant relationship was found. Although the empirical results related to international and target-country-specific experience are somewhat mixed, we expect that:

H 2a International experience has a positive impact on IJV performance if the performance is measured by survival.

H 2b International experience has a negative impact on IJV performance if the performance is measured by stability.

H 3a Target-country-specific experience has a positive impact on IJV performance if the performance is measured by survival.

H 3b Target-country-specific experience has a negative impact on IJV performance if the performance is measured by stability.

Unit relatedness

An issue of greater interest related to partner selection has been the presence of an overlap between business operations of the foreign partner and the IJV, and those of the foreign partner and of the local partner. Business-field-related experience reduces the amount of uncertainty and should therefore improve the possibilities for better performance. Unrelatedness of the operation to the foreign partner increases uncertainty, and especially if the foreign partner does not have any target-country-specific experience the risks related to the IJV are very high. Relatedness between the IJV's business and the parents' business should facilitate the transfer of tacit knowledge due to similarities in organizational processes (Saxton, 1997). Transfer of tacit knowledge is likely to be a key source of synergies in several inter-firm relationships (Hedlund, 1994; Teece, 1977). Furthermore, due to similarity with the parent, related IJVs are more likely to be tightly integrated with their parents which should increase possibilities for better performance; for example in low-cost supply units (either for one or both of the parents). Finally, in some Asian countries such as China, the host governments view related types of units more favourably than unrelated units and grant them preferential treatment.

In the IJV context, the influence of overlapping industries between the foreign partner and IJV performance have been analysed in 11 studies and in the partners' fields of businesses in nine studies. For the overlap of business fields of the foreign partner and the IJV seven of the studies indicated support for a positive relationship and three for a negative one, and in one study no relationship was found. For the influence of the overlap between partners' industries the results are more surprising. In five of the nine studies a negative relationship was found, in two a positive relationship, and in two no relationship was found. One explanation for the negative findings in several studies is that performance was often measured using stability as the criterion. If both partners are operating in the same field this means that they are more competitors, and in order to increase market power and better integr foreign units to their global networks they might easily tend to increase their ownership in the IJV or buy the other partner totally out of the venture, therefore increasing instability. If the operations of the local partner are partly or totally different from those of the foreign partner, the foreign partner might need the contribution of the local partner more which may increase the stability of the IJV. However, in general the results in several studies confirm that the performance has been better and the probability of divestment lower in related than in unrelated types of FDIs (see for example Li, 1995; Yamawaki, 1995; Hennart *et al.*, 1998). Thus, in summary, the results concerning the relatedness of operations are somewhat mixed, although because of better possibilities to reach synergy effects, lower uncertainty and partly also based on greater empirical support we expect that:

H 4 There is a positive relationship between relatedness of the IJV and performance of the unit.

Cultural distance

Cultural distance between partners and its impact on IJV performance has so far been the most commonly reviewed variable. The distance has usually been expressed multi-dimensionally, based on Hofstede's (1980) five cultural dimensions and the index developed by Kogut and Singh (1988). Cultural similarity decreases problems caused by cultural issues – for example different norms of behaviour and productivity, measurement and goals related to performance – and should facilitate trust and cooperation between partners. Therefore a negative relationship between cultural distance and IJV performance could be expected. Twelve of 27 studies including cultural distance give support to the expectation of a negative relationship between this distance and IJV performance. In six studies no relationship was found, while in as many as 10 studies support for a positive relationship was found. Regarding a positive relationship, it has been suggested that partners from culturally distant countries might have more to learn from each other, and that the potential opportunities to realize synergies may be increased through the different kind of strengths between Western and Asian companies (see for example, Pangarkar and Lee, 2001).

Barkema and Vermeulen (1997) tried to analyse in more detail the impact of culture on IJV performance. Using Hofstede's (1980) five different cultural dimensions – power distance, uncertainty avoidance, individualism, masculinity, and long-term orientation – they expected differences in the impact of various dimensions. Differences in uncertainty avoidance are difficult to cope with because they imply differences in how people perceive opportunities and threats in their environment and how they act upon them (Schneider and De Meyer, 1991). In high uncertainty-avoidance countries, organizations tend to respond to uncertainty by building up a system of high formalization and hierarchy. In low uncertainty-avoidance countries people are more attracted to flexible, *ad hoc* structures that leave more room for improvization and negotiation. Differences in uncertainty avoidance lead to differences in how partners perceive and respond to events in the environment of the IJV, which will likely breed disagreement and disputes between the partners, and have a detrimental impact on the IJV's performance. Power distance and individualism directly bear on issues of internal integration and influence relationships with personnel, such as the organization's choice of control forms, reward systems, and so on (see for example Hofstede, 1980, 1993, 2001). Management of personnel is usually one of the first activities to be left to the local partner, and there is also evidence that MNCs do not transfer cultural values related to power distance and individualism to their foreign subsidiaries (Soeters and Schreuder, 1988). Thus tensions between partners with differences along those dimensions may be avoided. Hofstede (1993, 2001) and Shenkar and Zeira (1992) suggest that having partners from both 'feminine' and 'masculine' cultures may even benefit the IJV. The aggressive attitude of one partner and the relationship orientation of the other may complement each other rather than collide.

The above suggests that differences in uncertainty avoidance would be more important than the other dimensions. Barkema and Vermeulen's (1997) empirical results supported the expectations that uncertainty avoidance and long-term orientation had greater differential negative impact on IJV survival than masculinity, while the two other dimensions (individualism and power distance) had no impact. For the empirical part of our study we expect that:

H 5 There is a negative relationship between cultural distance of the home country of the foreign partner and the target country of the unit and IJV performance.

H 6 There is a negative relationship between uncertainty avoidance and masculinity dimensions and IJV performance.

H 7 There is a non-significant relationship between power distance and individualism dimensions and IJV perfomance.

Form of establishment

A FDI including IJVs can be made either in the form of an acquisition or a greenfield investment. The main differences are:

1 an acquisition (in IJVs a partial acquisition) means buying a going concern, a bundle of assets (management, production etc.), whereas in greenfield investments everything is built from scratch;
2 building a unit from scratch takes much more time than buying part or all of a going concern; and
3 a greenfield investment increases total supply while a partial acquisition does not expand total supply.

Analysis of the impact of the form of establishment is excluded from most IJV studies mainly because they include only IJVs established by greenfield investments. The definition of an IJV in this study includes, however, also partial acquisitions. Soonkyo (2000) did not find any relationship between forms of establishment and IJV survival in his study of Japanese IJVs in the USA. However, as concerns the impact of the form of investment in general on FDIs, there is strong opposite evidence. Several authors (see for example Larimo, 2000) have found that an acquisition form of investment significantly increased the probability of divestment, that is it had a negative impact on performance. The key reasons for higher divestment rates have been the unrealistic levels of synergy goals and problems in the integration of the foreign unit. Furthermore, there is evidence that staged acquisitions seem to be rather common (see for example Larimo, 1993). Therefore we expect that:

H 8 There exists a negative relationship between acquisition forms of IJV entry and IJV performance.

Number of partners

The number of partners could also be expected to have an influence on IJV performance, in affecting coordination costs and the managerial complexity of the unit. Thus, one would expect that the greater the number of partners in an IJV, the greater the chance for poorer performance/instability of the unit. Interestingly, the results of studies referred to above (p. 25) indicate a negative relationship in one study whereas in three studies no relationship was found. It may be that in cases of three or more IJV partners the benefits of extra partners in the form of financial support or good relationships with important governmental institutions or distribution outlets have been overriding the drawbacks of additional partners in the IJV. Thus we expect that:

H 9 The number of partners does not significantly influence the IJV performance.

Distribution of ownership

One of the most commonly reviewed variables so far has been the influence of the distribution of ownership in the IJV. According to Killing (1983), the dominance of one partner will increase stability, because effective control will enable the parent to manage the IJV as a wholly-owned subsidiary, avoiding the managerial costs inherent in an IJV. Thus dominance may reduce transaction costs and stabilize the IJV. However, Beamish (1985) and Blodgett (1992) argue that roughly equal equity shares will result in greater stability because the partners are equally committed to the JV and possess roughly equal bargaining power. Dominant partner ownership has been included in 16 studies of which nine report a non-significant relationship with IJV performance. However, in five studies a positive relationship has been found. The results can be combined with the findings in three additional studies where it was found that there had not existed any statistically significant relationship between 50–50-ownership and IJV performance (Erden, 1997; Kachra and Hebert, 1999; Soonkyo, 2000). Thus, other issues than ownership distribution seem to have been more influential and/or the influence of ownership shares on IJV performance depends on other decisions made. Thus we expect that:

H 10 The ownership distribution of the IJV does not significantly influence the IJV performance.

Age of unit

The age of the unit may also influence the IJV performance. Young units may have problems because of 'liability of newness'; according to population ecologists organization mortality rates tend to decrease with age (Hannah and Freeman, 1984) as the external and internal legitimacy of the unit increases and it succeeds in developing needed networks for its operations. On the other hand, 'old' units are more likely than newly established units to produce and market products that are in the mature and declining stages of their product life-cycles. This provides a rationale for divesting 'old' units that may override even significant age-dependent barriers to exit (Harrigan, 1985). Also, over the years, the probability of changes in the strategies of the partner companies increases, increasing the probability of changes in the ownership structure of the IJV.

The age relationship has been reviewed in 17 studies so far; nine found a positive relationship and the rest found no relationship between age and IJV performance. The findings in some studies suggest that the impact of age, or timing of the IJV, on performance is a little more complicated than a straight linear relationship. Kogut (1988), for example, observed a dip in performance in years five and six. Results in any of the earlier studies do not give support to a negative relationship between age and IJV performance (e.g. Chen *et al.*, 1991). Because the measures of performance in this study are survival and stability, we expect that companies have survived the 'liability of newness' stage. Instability of ownership, however, is assumed to increase over the years because of various internal and external changes related to the partner companies and the environment of the IJV. Thus:

H 11a There is a positive relationship between the age of the IJV and performance of the unit when the performance is measured by survival.

H 11b There is a negative relationship between the age of the IJV and performance of the unit when the performance is measured by stability.

Methodology, sample and operationalization of variables

Because of the nature of the dependent variable, a logit model is used in the analysis. In the model, the probability that a certain type of situation – performance – is found is explained by the reviewed variables. The points of interest in this study are, in the first model, the probability that the unit has survived, and in the second model whether the ownership distribution has been stable or not. The regression coefficients estimate the impact of independent variables on the probability that the IJV has survived or the ownership distribution has been stable. A positive sign means that the variable has increased the probability of survival (stability), and negative that the variable has decreased the probability of survival.

Based on various data sources (business journals, company reports, earlier surveys made by the author), 728 IJVs established by Finnish companies around the world during 1970–99 were identified. This represents about 40 per cent of all manufacturing FDIs made by Finnish companies in the same period. Of the identified units, 71 could not be included to the sample because of missing information, so that the final sample is based on 657 IJVs. Of these, 130 were located in 63 countries, but about two-thirds were located in OECD countries.

The operationalization of the variables used in the analysis is presented in Table 2.1, following the approaches of earlier studies. The performance of the unit was evaluated in this data-set in two different ways: (1) survival – the IJV was still in Finnish ownership vs the unit was divested, and (2) stability – the IJV was still in Finnish ownership with no significant increase in the ownership share vs where the increase was small. In the second alternative significant increase in ownership refers to changes of at least 20% or changes where the minority changed to 50–50 ownership or to majority ownership.

The Appendix includes descriptive statistics of the sample. The majority of the IJVs were established by companies which already had extensive international

Table 2.1 Operationalization of variables

Partner size (PARSIZE): Total sales of the company in the year preceding the FDI is changed to Finnish Mark values in 2001. A logarithmic version is taken because it may be expected that the influence is not linear.

International experience (INTEXP): The number of foreign manufacturing investments made by the Finnish firm before making the reviewed IJV.

Target country experience (TCEXP): The length of earlier manufacturing experience in the target country.

Relatedness of the unit (URELATEDNESS): Dummy variable equal to one if the foreign company had experience from the same SIC field of industry of the IJV, otherwise zero.

Cultural distance (CULTDIST): Cultural distance between Finland and the target country of the IJV based on Hofstede's (1980, 1993, 2001) four dimensions, and the formula developed by Kogut and Singh (1988) using all countries for which Hofstede informs the values of the four cultural dimensions.

Power distance (PDI), **Individualism** (IDV), **Masculinity** (MAS), **Uncertainty avoidance** (UAI): Distance between Finland and the target country of the IJV along the four dimensions of Hofstede (1980, 1993, 2001).

Acquisition form of establishment (ACQFORM): Dummy variable equal to one if the IJV was a partial acquisition and zero if it was a greenfield investment.

Number of partners (NUMPART): Number of partners in the IJV.

Dominant Finnish partner ownership (DFPO): Whether the share of the Finnish firm was 51–94 (= 1) or less (= 0).

Age of the IJV (AGE): Number of years from the establishment of the units to 2001, or to the divestment of the unit.

experience, and in several cases already one manufacturing unit in the target country. The field of business of the IJV was in a clear majority closely related to the field of the Finnish partner. A majority of the IJVs were partial acquisitions. As noted above, about two-thirds of the units were located in various OECD countries, and the mean cultural distance between Finland and the target countries was 1.67 using Hofstede's four dimensions and the formula developed by Kogut and Singh (1988). Along various dimensions of culture the difference related to PDI and MAS variables was about 18 in both cases, whereas related to IDV and UAI variables the mean difference was approximately minus four. The Finnish partner had majority (dominant) ownership in about 40 per cent of cases. On average there was 2.2 partners in the IJVs. As may be expected, the highest correlations were between cultural distance and the various dimensions of cultural distance. Otherwise the correlations were rather low indicating severe problems with multicollinearity (see Appendix).

Results

As discussed above, the first sample was based on 657 IJVs established in 1970–99 by Finnish companies in various foreign countries. The first analysis was made based on the survival of the unit. Of the 657 IJVs, 275 (41.9%) were later divested and thus 382 IJVs (58.1%) were still in existence in 2002. Thus, the results indicate a very high divestment rate.

The results of the first regression model are presented in Table 2.2 (the Nagelkerke R^2 of the model is satisfactory at 22.5%). The estimated coefficients represent the utility whether the IJV was existing or not: a positive coefficient means that the unit was existing and a negative coefficient that the unit was divested. The results of the first regression model indicate that five of the reviewed 13 variables had significantly influenced the IJV performance. As expected, UNITRELATEDNESS had positively affected performance. Thus an overlap between the operation of the IJV and the Finnish partner increased the possibility of reaching synergy and lowered uncertainty related to the operation. CULTDIS also has the expected negative sign. The results give support to the hypothesis that greater cultural distance between Finland and the target country of the IJV caused more problems with management and/or integration of the

Table 2.2 Results of the binomial regression analysis for survival and stability

	Expected sign	*1. Survival*		*2. Stability*	
		coefficient	*significance*	*coefficient*	*significance*
CONSTANT		4.309	0.000	2.873	0.000
PSIZE	0	–0.599	0.001****	–0.516	0.007***
INTEXP: Survival	+	0.114	0.651	–	–
INTEXP: Stability	–	–	–	0.011	0.967
TCEXP: Survival	+	0.014	0.362	–	–
TCEXP: Stability	–	–	–	0.014	0.329
UNIT RELATEDNESS	+	1.107	0.003***	0.907	0.057*
CULTDIST	–	–0.260	0.091*	–0.051	0.736
UAI	–	0.010	0.059*	0.009	0.076*
MAS	–	0.000	0.980	0.002	0.781
PDI	0	0.006	0.364	0.004	0.593
IDV	0	–0.008	0.226	–0.008	0.237
ACQFORM	–	0.088	0.662	–0.482	0.018**
NUMPART	0	0.054	0.740	0.220	0.164
DFPO	0	0.064	0.731	0.120	0.536
AGE: Survival	+	–0.157	0.000****	–	–
AGE: Stability	–	–	–	–0.179	0.000****
Number of observations		657		657	
% of correct observations		68.2		70.9	

Level of significance denoted by * (0.1), ** (0.05), *** (0.01), **** (0.001).

unit than possible synergies based on the differences in culture. In three other cases the results did not support our expectations. For PSIZE no sign was expected because it was supposed that the relationship between PSIZE and IJV performance is more complicated than a linear relationship. The results, however, clearly indicated that larger firms had more often divested their IJVs than smaller companies. Perhaps the integration problems had been greater and/or barriers to exit lower in larger than in smaller companies. Furthermore, there were greater restructuring operations in several large Finnish companies leading to the divestment of whole business sectors, which were not their core business areas; this may partly explain the finding. For the uncertainty avoidance index (UAI) a negative sign was expected, but the results indicated the opposite. This is in contrast with the findings of Barkema and Vermeulen (1997) who found that difference in the uncertainty-avoidance dimension had the most detrimental influence on IJV performance. The very small mean difference along the UAI dimension in this study may at least partly explain the difference in the results. The negative sign for AGE indicates that overtime there seems to be increasing amounts of detrimental factors inside and outside the IJV, and in partner companies, increasing the probability of divestment and therefore overriding the problems of 'liability of newness' during the first years of operation.

For NUMPART, FPDO, PDI and IDV, non-significance was expected and also found. Thus, the number of partners and foreign-partner dominance in the IJV do not closely influence performance, but other issues related to the IJV are more important. Also, the power-distance and individualism dimensions of culture seem not to be so important, in line with Barkema and Vermeulen's (1997) findings. In addition, four other variables – INTEXP, TCEXP, MAS and ACQFORM – were against expectations non-significant. The two first results indicate that, surprisingly, that the experience factor is not so important for IJV performance. The non-significance of MAS is opposite to the results of Barkema and Vermeulen (1997), and the non-significance of ACQFORM is against the findings of several studies focusing on the probability of divestments in FDIs in general, but in line with the finding of Soonkyo (2000).

Of the 657 IJVs, 238 (36.2%) were stable (no significant increase in ownership), but significant increases occurred in 419 cases. Thus the instability rate was very high (63.8%). Because 275 of the unstable cases were divestments, a change in ownership had occurred in an additional 144 cases (also in about 100 of those cases which were divested). The instability rate is much higher than, for example, in a more recent study by Sim and Ali (2001), which found an instability rate of 34%. The results in the second regression model are also presented in Table 2.2. The estimated coefficients represent the value whether the IJV was stable (unit not divested and no greater changes in ownership distribution) versus instable (unit divested or greater change in ownership distribution). The second model is somewhat better than the first (Nagelkerke R^2 26.2%).

Five of the reviewed 13 variables were statistically significant in the second model, and for four of those five – PSIZE, UNITRELATEDNESS, UAI and AGE – the results were very similar. All of them had the same signs as in the first model, and only in the case of UNITRELATEDNESS had level of significance decreased more compared to the results in the first model. Thus those four variables seem to be significant determinants of IJV performance whether performance was measured based on survival or stability. It is also noteworthy that in the second model the expected sign for AGE was negative. Thus using stability as the measure of performance, the results supported expectations. CULTDIST was statistically significant in the first model, but not in the second model. Instead, the variable ACQFORM was now statistically significant. The negative influence of acquisition-forms of IJV establishment on IJV stability was as expected. Thus the results now support the findings of most earlier studies. Partial acquisitions often include staged increases in ownership of the foreign partner, and failures in acquisitions seem to be more common than in greenfield investements, therefore causing more instability in the former than in the latter cases.

As in the first model, for NUMPART, FPDO, PDI and IDV non-significance was expected and also found in the second model. Thus, these four variables at least seem not to have any direct relationship with IJV performance. In addition, three additional variables were insignificant in the second model – INTEXP, TCEXP and MAS – so that in total seven of the variables were non-significant as measures of performance. The results of the second model also give support to the surprising view that experience variables seem not to have been so important in the IJV operations by Finnish firms.

Summary and conclusions

The role of IJVs in international business operations has been significant and there are no signs that this role will be any the less significant in future. The situation may in fact be the opposite. Although the use and importance of IJVs is very common, the failure rate of such ventures is high, which raises the question of how to evaluate performance and how to secure success in IJV operations? Furthermore, there is variation in the results depending on the measure of performance. The goal of this chapter has been to analyse the relationships between 13 variables and IJV performance, with an additional goal of analysing variation between different measures of performance. Survival and stability were selected as measures of performance, with the empirical work based on 657 manufacturing IJVs established by 130 Finnish companies in over 60 countries during 1970–99.

Table 2.3 Summary of the hypothesis and results

		Expected sign	*Based on survival*	*Based on stability*
H1	PSIZE	0	Not supported	Not supported
H2A	INTEXP: Survival	+	Not supported	–
H2B	INTEXP: Stability	–	–	Not supported
H3A	TCEXP: Survival	+	Not supported	–
H3B	TCPEXP: Stability	–	–	Not supported
H4	UNIT RELATEDNESS	+	Supported	Supported
H5	CULTDIST	–	Supported	Not supported
H6	UAI and MAS	–	Not supported	Not supported
H7	PDI and IDV	0	Supported	Supported
H8	FORM: ACQ	–	Not supported	Supported
H9	NUMPART	0	Supported	Supported
H10	DFPO	0	Supported	Supported
H11A	AGE: Survival	+	Not supported	–
H11B	AGE: Stability	–	–	Supported

A summary of the hypotheses developed and the results is presented in Table 2.3. In both models five of the reviewed 13 variables were significant and four of them were the same in both models. Those four variables which significantly influenced performance independent of the measure used were PSIZE, UNITRELATEDNESS, UAI and AGE. A large size of the Finnish partner or a longer age of the unit both negatively influenced performance, whereas an overlap between the operations of the IJV and Finnish partner and a difference in uncertainty avoidance positively influenced performance. In the case of UNITRELATEDNESS the results supported expectations, which was also the case with AGE when performance was measured based on stability. Other results, however, were against expectations. The significance of some variables depended on the measure of performance; thus based on survival CULTDIST negatively influenced performance, whereas based on stability ACQFORM had a negative impact on performance.

Furthermore, for four variables – NUMPART, DFPO, PDI and IDV – a non-significant relationship with IJV performance was expected and also found independent of the measure of performance. In addition, three of the reviewed variables were, against expectations, non-significant in both models: INTEXP, TCEXP and MAS. Thus experience in FDIs and IJVs, the number of partners, dominance of the foreign partner, and dimensions of culture other than uncertainty avoidance seem not to have had any significant influence on IJV performance in IJVs established by Finnish companies. Some of these variables have been analysed in limited ways in earlier studies with mixed findings. In summary, it is noteworthy in the results that based on both measures of performance significant and non-significant variables included foreign-partner-specific, target-country-specific, and local-partner-specific variables.

Appendix 1: descriptive statistics and the correlation matrix of the independent variables

	Mean	*Std.*	*1*	*2*	*3*	*4*	*5*	*6*	*7*	*8*	*9*	*10*	*11*	*12*	*13*
PSIZE (LOG) (1)	3.575	0.781	1.000												
UNITRELATEDNESS (2)	0.932	0.250	–0.060	1.000											
INTEXP (LOG) (3)	1.117	0.591	0.777	–0.090	1.000										
TCEXP (4)	3.470	6.540	0.273	0.027	0.310	1.000									
CULTDIST (5)	1.670	1.074	0.059	–0.075	0.108	–0.089	1.000								
PDI (6)	18.420	22.520	0.037	–0.115	0.075	–0.140	0.684	1.000							
IDV (7)	–4.190	22.510	0.003	0.130	–0.057	0.239	–0.574	–0.702	1.000						
MAS (8)	17.120	22.320	0.110	–0.016	0.163	0.007	0.548	0.262	–0.083	1.000					
UAI (9)	–3.750	21.460	0.070	–0.078	0.111	–0.032	0.189	0.362	–0.234	0.414	1.000				
ACQFORM (10)	0.620	0.490	0.016	0.089	–0.032	0.148	–0.297	–0.362	0.364	–0.146	–0.079	1.000			
NUMPART (11)	2.184	0.555	–0.024	–0.068	–0.015	–0.055	–0.007	0.074	–0.096	0.026	0.008	–0.032	1.000		
DFPO (12)	0.390	0.490	–0.060	0.090	–0.095	–0.103	–0.128	–0.115	0.057	–0.064	–0.040	0.173	–0.110	1.000	
AGE (13)	11.138	5.026	–0.267	0.100	–0.336	–0.152	–0.044	–0.080	0.165	–0.130	–0.107	0.086	0.050	–0.040	1.000

There were several limitations in this study and therefore many avenues for future research. First, the study focused on only two objective measures of performance. Although results in several studies have indicated high correlations between objective and subjective measures of performance this is not always the case, and of future interest would be comparisons of both objective and subjective measures. The second limitation of this study was the great focus on *ex ante* variables. Although there are some additional *ex ante* variables such as previous IJV experience (see for example Padmanabhan and Cho, 1999, who noted that ownership-structure-specific experience had a great influence on FDI behaviour) and size symmetry between partners which would be of interest in future work, there is a greater need in future to integrate *ex post* variables such as commitment to the IJV, trust, and other ties between the partners. Of the single variables a more detailed analysis of the influence of culture and cultural difference would be of interest. In this study the analysis was based on Hofstede's (1980, 1993) four dimension of culture, whilst in future studies the addition of Hofstede's fifth dimension – long-term orientation – as well as other views and categorizations of culture and cultural distance would be of interest (see for example Barkema and Vermeulen 1997, and Brouthers and Brouthers, 2001). Furthermore, in this study the ownership structure of the IJV (majority-owned, co-owned, or minority-owned) or other target-country-related variables than cultural distance were not included. Thus in future more analysis is needed about their influence on IJV performance. Finally, this study focused only on IJVs established by Finnish companies, and an interesting alternative would be to compare the behaviour and influencing factors among samples from other countries. Comparisons of the performance of IJVs established by other Nordic firms would be of particular interest.

References

Artisien, P and Buckley, P.J. (1985) 'Joint ventures in Yugoslavia: opportunities and constraints' *Journal of International Business Studies*, 18(1), 111–34.

Barkema, H. and Vermeulen, F. (1997) 'What differences in the cultural backgrounds of partners are detrimental for international joint ventures?' *Journal of International Business Studies* 28(4), 845–64.

Beamish, P.W. (1985) 'The characteristics of joint ventures in developed and developing countries', *Columbia Journal of World Business* 20(3), 13–19.

Beamish, P.W. (1988) *Multinational Joint Ventures in Developing Countries*. New York: Routledge.

Blanchot, F. and Mayrhofer, U. (1997) 'Empirical literature on joint venture success: a review of performance measures and of factors affecting longetivity', in Macharzina K., Oesterle, M.-J. and Wolff, J. (eds), *Global Business in the Information Age*, 23rd Annual EIBA Conference, Stuttgart.

Blodgett, L.L. (1992) 'Factors in the instability of international joint ventures: an event history analysis', *Strategic Mangement Journal* 13(4), 475–81.

Brouthers, K.D. and Brouthers, L.E. (2001) 'Explaining the national culture paradox', *Journal of International Business Studies* 32(1), 177–89.

Chen, H., Hu, M.Y. and Shieh, J.C.P. (1991) 'The wealth effect of international joint ventures: the case of U.S. investment in China', *Financial Management* 20(4), 31–41.

Chowdhury, J., (1992) 'Performance of international joint ventures and wholly owned foreign subsidiaries. A comparative perspective', *Management International Review* 32(2), 115–33.

Contractor, F. and Lorange, P. (1988) 'Why should firms cooperate? The strategy and economic basis for cooperative ventures', in Contractor, F. and Lorange, P. (eds), *Cooperative Strategies in International Business*, Lexington, MA: Lexington Books.

Erden, D. (1997) 'Stability and satisfaction in cooperative FDI', in Beamish, P.W. and Killing, J.P. (eds), *Cooperative Strategies: European Perspectives*, San Francisco: New Lexington Press.

Garcia-Canal, E., Valdes, A. and Arino, A. (1999) 'More than two are a crowd. Different paths to effectiveness in dyadic and multi-party joint ventures', Research Paper no. 385, IESE, University of Navarra, Spain.

Geringer, J.M. and Hebert, L. (1991) 'Measuring performance of international joint ventures', *Journal of International Business Studies* 22(2), 249–63.

Glaister, K. and Buckley, P. (1998) 'Measures of performance in UK international alliances', *Organization Studies* 19(1), 89–118.

Hannah, M.T. and Freeman, J. (1984) 'Structural inertia and organizational change', *American Sociological Review* 49(2), 149–64.

Harrigan, K.R. (1985) *Strategies for Joint Ventures*. Lexington, MA: Lexington Books.

Harrigan, K.R. (1988) 'Joint ventures and competitive strategy', *Strategic Management Journal* 9(2), 141–58.

Hedlund, G.H. (1994) 'A model of knowledge management and the N-form corporation', *Strategic Management Journal* 15(1), 73–90.

Hennart, J.-F., Kim, D.-J. and Zeng, M. (1998) 'The impact of joint venture status on the longevity of Japanese stakes in U.S. manufacturing affiliates', *Organization Science* 9(3), 1–14.

Hofstede, G. (1980) *Culture's Consequences: International Differences in Work-related Values*. Beverly Hills, CA: Sage.

Hofstede, G. (1993) 'Cultural constraints in management theories', *Academy of Management Executive* 7(1), 81–94.

Hofstede, G. (2001) *Cultural Consequences. Comparing Values, Behaviors, Institutions, and Organizations Across Nations*. Thousand Oaks, CA: Sage.

Hu, M.Y., Chen, H. and Shieh, J.C. (1992) 'Impact of U.S.-China joint ventures on stockholders' wealth by degree of international involvement', *Management International Review* 32(2),135–48.

Kachra, A. and Hebert, L. (1999) 'Managerial behavior, IJV structure and venture performance', Working Paper no. 199–22, Richard Ivey School of Business, University of Western Ontario, London, Ontario, Canada.

Killing, J.P. (1983) *Strategies for Joint Venture Success*. New York: Routledge.

Kogut, B. (1988) 'A study of the life cycle of joint ventures', in Contractor, F. and Lorange, P. (eds), *Cooperative Strategies in International Business*, Lexington, Mass.: Lexington Press.

Kogut, B. and Singh, H. (1988) 'The effect of national culture on the choice of entry mode', *Journal of International Business Studies* 19(3), 411–32.

Koh, J. and Venkatraman, N. (1991) 'Joint venture formations and stock market reactions: an assessment in the information technology sector', *Academy of Management Journal* 34(4), 869–92.

Larimo, J. (1998) *Determinants of Divestments in Foreign Production Operations made by Finnish Firms in OECD Countries*. Proceedings of the University of Vaasa. Discussion Paper no. 233.

Larimo, J. (2000) *Divestment of Foreign Production Operations: Similarities and Differences Determinants?* AIB Annual Conference, Phoenix, Arizona.

Larimo, J. (2001) *International Joint Venture Performance: An Integrative Review of Empirical Literature in 1970–2001*. 26th European International Business Academy Annual Conference in Paris.

Lasserre, P. (1999) 'Joint venture satisfaction in Asia Pacific', *Asia Pacific Journal of Management* 16(1), 1–28.

Li, J. (1995) 'Foreign entry and survival: effects of strategic choices on performance in international markets', *Strategic Management Journal* 16(4), 333–51.

Makino, S. (1995) *Joint venture ownership structure and performance: Japanese joint ventures in Asia,* PhD dissertation, University of Western Ontario, Ontario, Canada.

Makino, S. and Delios, A. (1996) 'Local knowledge transfer and performance: implications for alliance formation in Asia', *Journal of International Business Studies* (special issue), 905–27.

Mariotti, S. and Piscitello, L. (1997) 'Divestment as failure or part of a restructuring strategy', in *Global Business in the Information Age*, 23rd Annual European International Business Academy Annual Conference, Stuttgart.

Merchant, H. (1997) 'International joint venture performance of firms in the non-manufacturing sector', in Beamish, P.W. and Killing, J.P. (eds), *Cooperative Strategies: North American Perspectives*. San Francisco: New Lexington Press.

Olk, P. (1997) 'The effect of partner differences on the performance of R&D consortia', in Beamish, P.W. and Killing, J.P. (eds), *Cooperative Strategies: North American Perspectives*. San Francisco: New Lexington Press.

Padmanabhan, P. and Cho, K. (1999) 'Decision specific experience in foreign ownership and establishment strategies: evidence from Japanese firms', *Journal of International Business Studies* 30(1), 25–44.

Pangarkar, N. and Lee, H. (2001) 'Joint venture strategies and success: an empirical study of Singaporean firms', *Journal of Asian Business* 17(3), 1–13.

Parkhe, A. (1996) 'International joint ventures', in Punnett, B.J. and Shenkar, O. (eds), *Handbook of International Management Research*. Cambridge, MA: Blackwell Business.

Robson, M., Leonidou, L. and Katsikeas, C. (2002) 'Factors influencing international joint venture performance', *Management International Review* 42(4), 385–418.

Saxton, T. (1997) 'The effects of partner and relationship characteristics on alliance outcomes', *Academy of Management Journal* 40(2), 443–61.

Schneider, S. and de Meyer, A. (1991) 'Interpreting and responding to strategic issues: the impact of national culture', *Strategic Management Journal* 12(4), 307–20.

Shenkar, O. and Zeira, Y. (1992) 'Role conflict and role ambiquity of chief executive offices in international joint ventures', *Journal of International Business Studies* 23(1), 55–75.

Sim, A. and Ali, M. (2000) 'Determinants of stability in international joint ventures: evidence from a developing country context', *Asia Pacific Journal of Management* 17(3), 373–97.

Soeters, J. and Schreuder, H. (1988) 'The interaction between national and organizational cultures in accounting firms', *Accounting, Organizations and Society* 13(1), 75–85.

Soonkyo, C. (2000) *Partner Nationality, Network Relations, and Venture Survival: The Case of Japanese Cooperative Ventures in North-America*. AIB Annual Conference in Phoenix, Arizona.

Teece, D. (1997) 'Technological transfer by multinational firms: the resource cost of international technology transfer', *Economic Journal* 87(3), 242–61.

Tomlinson, J.W.C. (1970) *The Joint Venture Process in International Business: India and Pakistan*. Cambridge, MA: MIT Press.

Yamawaki, H. (1995) 'Exit of Japanese multinationals in U.S. and European manufacturing industries', unpublished working paper (Department of Economics, Catholic University of Louvain, Belgium).

Yan, A. and Zeng, M. (1999) 'International joint venture instability: a critique of previous research, a reconceptualization, and directions for future research', *Journal of International Business Studies* 30(2), 397–414.

Zeira, Y., Newburry, W. and Yeheskel, O. (1997) 'Factors affecting the effectiveness of equity international joint ventures in Hungary', *Management International Review* 37(3), 259–79.

3

US Foreign Direct Investment within the UK Microcomputer Industry: The Interaction between Supply-Chain Strategy and Industry Environment

Denise Tsang

Introduction

The microcomputer industry, which incorporates personal computers, workstations and servers, is a leading manufacturing industry with worldwide sales in 2000 of approximately 140 million units (AFX Asia, 2002a, 2002b and 2002c). It is associated with the rise and the decline of some fascinating firms in the contemporary industrial landscape, which highlights the rapid pace of change in the industry environment and the subsequent challenges encountered by global firms. This chapter discusses the ability of successful US microcomputer firms to determine their strategic orientations in the supply chain within the context of UK investment, and therefore provides insight into the relationship between supply-chain strategy and the dynamic industry environment. The supply chain is tremendously significant within the microcomputer industry as it impinges directly upon firms' profitability (Rappaport and Halevi, 1991; Curry and Kenney, 1999; Ozsomer and Cavusgil, 2000). The concept of supply-chain strategy in the context of the microcomputer industry relates to the product strategy (that is the physical design and the psychological positioning of the microcomputer), the sourcing strategy (that is the organization of components for the assembly process), as well as the channel strategy (that is the structural arrangement in relation to the distribution of fully assembled products).

There has been a persisting debate over the abilities of firms to determine their strategy orientations (Astlely and Van de Ven, 1983; Hrebiniak and Joyce, 1985; Varadarajan, Clark and Pride, 1992; Li, 2001; Aragon-Correa and Sharma, 2003; St John, Pouder and Cannon, 2003). Furthermore, researchers such as Craig and Douglas (2000), Prahalad and Doz (1987) as well as Porter (1986) have emphasized the tension between implementing strategies that have been pursued in the headquarters, and devising strategies that suit the host-country market characteristics when firms' undertake foreign investment. Tsang (2002) pointed out the dominance of American microcomputer firms in Europe during the past two decades; in particular, how they imposed the traditional American model and the new American model of sourcing strategies, which served as industry recipes in the supply chain. This chapter utilizes the perspectives of industry-creation and industry-evolution to examine the environment-strategy relationship within the product and channel elements among successful US microcomputer firms' supply chains (De Wit and Meyer, 1998). The product and channel elements are sensitive to different environments and therefore are appropriate to investigate the issue concerning the ability of firms (as actors within the UK microcomputer industry) to determine their strategies.

The industry-evolution perspective suggests, at a holistic level, that successful firms pursued supply-chain strategies that complied with the evolutionary demands of the industry. It embodies the work of systems theorists (Thompson, 1967; Silverman 1970), contingency theorists (Burns and Stalker, 1961; Lawrence and Lorsch, 1967), industrial economists (Bain, 1957; Scherer, 1980) and the population-ecology theorists such as Hannan and Freeman (1977). It advocates a deterministic influence of the environment and proposes an interdependent relationship between supply-chain strategy and the microcomputer industry environments; accordingly, firms will attain success only if their supply-chain strategies conform to the prevailing industry dynamics and adapt to the opportunities and threats. For example, Scherer (1980) stated that firms' performance were associated with their pricing, R&D, innovation strategies and so on, and that these variables were in turn influenced by external environments such as barriers to entry, levels of concentration and degrees of product differentiation.

The industry-evolution perspective has been applied in the areas of strategy during the past few decades, and can be seen in product life-cycle analysis, product portfolio planning, the profit impact of market strategies, the five-forces model as well as the institutional environment analysis of the market channel (Levitt, 1965; Kotler, 1973; Porter, 1979; Buzzell and Gale, 1987; Suchman, 1995; Grewal and Dharwadkar, 2002). Within this perspective, one can therefore argue that the microcomputer industry proceeds in a life-cycle that can be divided into the stages of introduction, growth, maturity and decline, and it follows that there are corresponding product and channel strategies that are critical for achievement within each stage. Namely, an innovative product strategy is the base to capture the demand of affluent buyers during the introductory stage, whereas a strategy to gain economies of scale in distribution will be the most important factor when the industry approaches the growth stage. During the mature stage, the critical factor for success within a mass market is to reduce overheads by rationalizing functional activities. Finally, the strategy for competing in the decline stage will be the further minimization of overheads and the fostering of a reputable brand.

The industry-creation perspective, as a contrast, argues that supply-chain strategies are derived from microcomputer firms' ingenious creativity to tackle favourable and unfavourable environments; it stems from the belief that firms as autonomous economic agents are capable of exerting their influence on the formation of business strategies. This perspective can be traced from writers such as Child (1972), Tellis and Crawford (1981), Pfeffer and Salancik (1978), Zeithaml and Zeithaml (1984), Baden-Fuller and Stopford (1992), Hamel and Prahalad (1994) as well as Lynn and Akgun (2001). For example, Pfeffer and Salancik (1978) wrote that rather than designing the firm to fit the environment, it was more likely that the firm would attempt to design its environment to fit its present structural arrangements. Hence, a successful supply-chain strategy is dependent upon the resource endowment of the firm; in most cases, the insight and intuition associated with the human capital of an exceptional firm enables it to formulate an innovative approach that defies convention, which results in its gaining market share.

The industry-creation perspective therefore argues that successful microcomputer firms are those that build upon their internal resources and manipulate the industry environment to enhance their strategic, technological or market competitiveness in any stage of the industry development. For example, Tellis and Crawford (1981) argued that there were no sequences of marketing events between the introduction and decline stages within the life-cycles of products; they concluded that growth was limited only by management's ability to harness market dynamics and the efforts of meditative agencies. In addition, Buaron (1981), Chakravarthy (1984), Hamel and Prahalad (1994) as well as Steffens (1994) stated that successful firms were able to increase their chances of gaining market share by redefining or rewriting the rules of competition, rather than competing according to the prevailing rules. Buaron (1981) believed that such innovative strategies would allow firms to establish a new set of key success factors in the market. Indeed, Lynn and Akgun (2001) found that managerial visions were critical towards successful product developments within Apple, IBM and Hewlett-Packard.

The UK microcomputer industry was and is still intensely competitive. Between 1977–99 successful US firms encountered a rapidly changing environment coupled with challenges from indigenous entrepreneurial firms. The setting therefore provides an excellent ground to explore the intriguing relationship between industry environment and the supply-chain strategy among firms. For purposes of this chapter, a successful firm is manifested in attaining a market-share position that leads to superior financial performance. The following section describes the supply-chain strategies of the US firms Apple, IBM, Compaq, Sun, and Dell, which has resulted in periods of extraordinary market leadership.

It then discusses the nature of their supply chain within the UK microcomputer industry. An indirect method of data collection was adopted in relation to the study of the five firms; it consists of content analysis of primary and secondary firm and industry materials for the late 1970s, the 1980s and the 1990s. The central issue addressed in this chapter is: did the supply chain strategies that led to their creation of specific market segments derive from unique firm innovations in the areas of product and market channel, or, conversely, did they denote the compliance to the demand of the evolving UK microcomputer market?

American investment and the UK supply chain

The first wave of American microcomputer investment in the UK in 1977 was led by Apple, Tandy and Commodore, while subsequent investments were pursued by IBM, Hewlett-Packard, Texas Instruments, Digital, Compaq, Sun, Dell and others during the 1980s. US firms have not only created the UK microcomputer industry, but also dominated the industry since its inception. In this section I will discuss the product and channel strategies within the supply chains of eminent US firms Apple, IBM, Compaq, Sun, and Dell between 1977 and 1999, to evaluate the relative importance of the industry-creation and industry-evolution perspectives. The five firms were selected as they have led in sub-segments of the UK microcomputer industry at the introduction, growth or mature stages of the market; in addition, they have fitted into different categories of the life-cycle and their experiences illustrate the philosophical basis of supply-chain strategies in this fast-paced industry.

I will, however, elaborate the life-cycle stages undertaken in the UK prior to the discussion of the intriguing relationship between supply-chain strategy and the industry environment. The *introduction stage* of microcomputers corresponds to the period prior to 1984. During this stage, product configurations for microcomputers were specified, and the total market demand exhibited a continuous growth pattern. There was the shaping of the technology standard, in the form of Apple versus IBM/IBM-compatibles as well as personal computers versus workstations. The *growth stage* for microcomputers extended from 1985 to 1989, and was a period where the total market demand rapidly increased; microcomputer sales at the firm level and within the UK reached 40 per cent. The *mature stage* of microcomputers between 1990–99 featured a price–performance paradox. There continues to be a downward movement of the selling price for microcomputers, the average selling price has decreased throughout this stage, but parallel with this price reduction has been the increase in the processing capacities of microcomputers. As a result, a Pentium-based IBM-compatible system in the mid-1990s was cheaper than a similar model with the inferior 286-based microprocessor in the mid-1980s. Indeed, the watershed period

1990–91 witnessed a 2.3 per cent increase in the number of units sold, which was accompanied by an 8.4 per cent decrease in the value of sales within the UK (Cane, 1992).

Though the decline stage is not covered here, it refers to the period beginning from 2000 where the year-over-year increase in the total volume of microcomputer sales has been slow. Indeed, the industry analyst Dataquest commented that for this product-cycle stage in the UK and overall European market, 'the days of double-digit growth are behind us forever. We are looking at a market in Western Europe that is primarily a replacement market' (*Birmingham Post*, 2003). However, demand varied across different segments of microcomputers; for instance, unit sales for personal computers declined by 5 per cent between 2000–01, while those for servers fell by 2 per cent (IDC, 2002).

Production innovations in Apple

The emergence of Apple Computer in the late 1970s as well as its further expansion in the late 1980s is attributed to two major product innovations – the launch of Apple II and the introduction of the Macintosh. Apple's first personal computer product, Apple II, was launched by its UK dealer EuraApple. Built on externally procured components, it could generate colour graphics as well as being equipped with a keyboard and memory. Above all, it was presented in an attractive beige plastic case endorsed by Apple's corporate logo, which was designed by the reputable public-relations consulting firm Regis McKenna.

As shown in Table 3.1, the Apple II was targeted as a premium-priced consumer product. Indeed, its rainbow striped, half-eaten apple logo symbolized the dawn of an era where the computer has become a consumer product, in addition to its previous industrial product status. Apple II was an instant success; its

Table 3.1 Top ten UK home microcomputers in 1983

Firm	*Model*	*Retail price*
Commodore	Commodore 64	£220
Sinclair	Spectrum	£99
Acorn	BBC	£399
Commodore	VIC 20	£140
Oric	Oric 1	£99
Dragon Data	Dragon 32	£170
Texas Instruments	TI 994a	£90
Sinclair	ZX81	£40
Atari	Atari 800	£300
Apple	Apple IIe	£750

Note: Home microcomputers refers to personal computers under £1,000.
Source: Based on data from *Financial Times* (12 December 1983).

sales rose rapidly and had taken approximately 50 per cent of the UK personal-computer market prior to IBM's entry. Apple II's physical design generated mass appeal within the consumer segment. Apple's product strategy was therefore similar to successful indigenous firms such as Sinclair Research and Acorn. Sinclair's early products, the ZX80 and ZX81, allowed users to program the system in BASIC computer language and perform functions which varied from plotting a graph to setting up a database. However, the design of Sinclair's computers economized on the display and tape-drive functions and they were priced at unprecedentedly low levels, £40 for the ZX81 in 1983.

Accompanying the gain of market share in its first five years was the growth of Apple's dealer networks, which had risen to 500 in the UK in 1982. Apple II's channel strategy was innovative as it departed from those of existing computer firms such as IBM and ICL in their dependence on person-to-person sales teams. However, Apple did not expand to the retailer channel during the introductory stage as in the USA, since its products were more expensive than other consumer computers, only eventually doing so when the market moved towards maturity. Another point of note is that the successful entrepreneurial British firms Sinclair and Acorn utilized the mail-order channel when entering the market in 1979; buyers would ring the firms to order their respective ZX80 or System 1, which were then dispatched to their addresses by mail. Apple did not explore the mail-order channel until the late 1990s.

The Macintosh denoted another era of successful product innovation in Apple after the intermittent failures of Apple III and Lisa. The first Macintosh model, the Macintosh 128K, was launched in 1984. Its graphical user interface which allowed users to interact with the system by moving and pointing to positions on the screen via a mouse, was at the frontier of microcomputer technology. This distinctive user-friendly feature was widely acknowledged:

> If you wanted a friendly machine and could afford a premium price, you bought an Apple Macintosh. It came with Apple's software, which transformed the screen into an electronic desktop with nifty icons to help you keep track of data programs, and pull-down menus to help you select and issue commands. (Kirkpatrick, 1993, p. 57)

Despite a slow start, the sales for Macintosh gradually picked up with the increasing number of software applications such as HyperCard, AppleShare and AppleTalk.

To demonstrate the pioneering technology of Macintosh, Apple incorporated the concept of company retail outlets which had previously been adopted by Tandy. Its appointed dealers opened a number of Apple stores throughout the UK during the mid-1980s; Personal Computers plc, for instance, obtained the contractual rights to operate 'The Macintosh Centre' in London and Leeds.

Its activities were depicted in its marketing material as: 'there's a place where you can buy a Macintosh, choose Macintosh software, consult with Macintosh experts, see the latest Macintosh add-ons, join Macintosh training courses, rent a Macintosh system and arrange a Macintosh maintenance contract' (Apple Computer Inc., 1986). The simplicity of the Macintosh fuelled the growth of the UK microcomputer industry and enabled Apple to reach the peak of its UK market share with an average of over 10 per cent prior to the early 1990s. Apple, in particular, had a strong clientele encompassing artists, writers and specialists from other domains of the creative industry.

Market redefinition by IBM

By 1980, IBM finally acknowledged that the computer market had progressed and that the sub-segment of microcomputers (though dominated by youthful US firms such as Apple, Tandy and Commodore) could not be ignored. IBM launched its first personal computer, the IBM PC, in 1981 after 18 months' concerted effort from members of an autonomous team in Boca Raton, Florida. (This may be compared to the standard product development cycle of 42 months at the time.) IBM assigned its Greenock plant in Scotland as the manufacturing site for the IBM PC in Europe; a choice made after vigorous competition from IBM's other 16 sites in Europe (including France, Germany, Sweden, Italy and Spain). The IBM PC, priced at £2,080 in its basic form, could not be regarded as a technological breakthrough; nevertheless, it was received by UK dealers with considerable enthusiasm (Meredith and Cane, 1983).

It should also be noted that IBM had an unprecedentedly heavy dependence on external components; indeed the only part of its personal computer that was supplied exclusively by IBM subsidiaries in its initial year of production was the keyboard (De Jonquières, 1983a). IBM, nevertheless, reversed this policy and internalized the production of a variety of components from the mid-1980s before it gradually took another U-turn in the 1990s. IBM exploited its technological and marketing heritage, and positioned its personal computer (which bears the same colour as the mainframes) as a high-quality product that was perfectly compatible with businesses operating in the mainframe and minicomputer environment. Thus, among mainframe and minicomputer users, the IBM PC was a logical choice for their corporate computing needs. Indeed, De Jonquières (1983b) stated the IBM's sales force was highly skilled at exploiting its competitors' weaknesses and capitalizing on 'fear, uncertainty and doubt' among users faced with purchasing decisions. The IBM PC's key selling point was actually the least-risk option in the industry, and was supported by the saying that 'no data processing manager was ever fired for buying from IBM'.

It was not surprising that the IBM PC captured a majority of the corporate accounts during its first four years. Cane (1985) commented on IBM's performance as:

> IBM has probably achieved in the UK its highest share of direct sales and has converted to the personal computer a vast number of large corporations including the banks. This strength added to the large sales volume which some of their bigger dealers achieved, confirmed their strong hold over this market.

Table 3.2 shows that IBM achieved a commanding market share of 25 per cent in business personal computers in the UK in 1987. However, as IBM personal computers were more expensive than those offered by competitors such as Amstrad, it generated sales revenues accounting for 31.8 per cent while Amstrad only gained 7.5 per cent of the market by sales value.

Other than its reputation for technological compatibility, IBM's achievement can also be attributed to its channel strategy that facilitated the distribution of its personal computers. It should be remembered that various established firms such as Digital Equipment and Hewlett-Packard attempted to impose their own standards in the early 1980s. Indeed, Digital used similar selling points to IBM in the UK and advertised: 'The gap, believe us, is wide... Digital was the first company to mass-produce minicomputers, and the PDP-11 is, in fact, the world's most popular minicomputer today... And the Digital difference becomes even wider when you consider Digital's unique service back up' (Digital Equipment Corporation, 1983, p. 31). However, Digital failed in its personal computer venture and withdrew its technically sophisticated Rainbow personal computer.

IBM departed from sole reliance on the traditional market channel of personal selling by replicating its US channel practice to appoint dealers, distributors and retailers in the UK (which gradually emerged as the norm during the market growth stage). IBM appointed two distributors to manage the UK dealers in the

Table 3.2 Market shares within the UK business microcomputer segment, 1987

Firm	*Headquarters*	*Market share (% by volume)*
Amstrad	UK	26.0
IBM	USA	24.7
Olivetti	Italy	7.7
Compaq	USA	4.3
Apple	USA	4.3
Apricot	UK	4.1
Tandon	USA	5.9
Others	Various	23.0

Note: Business microcomputers refers to systems over £1,000.
Source: Based on data from *Financial Times* (11 April 1988, p. 5).

early 1980s, and then increased the total number of distributors to eight in 1987. However, it tried to eliminate the layer of distributors by altering the discount structure that worked in favour of the dealers in 1989 (Houlder, 1989). Though indigenous UK firms such as Acorn and Sinclair and the youthful US firm Commodore had been utilizing retailers such as W.H. Smith, Boots and Dixons to market their products, IBM did not engage actively in the retail channel when distributing the IBM PC. Nevertheless, it increasingly turned to retailers as the market approached maturity. Six Dixons stores, for instance, retailed the PS2 model-30 range computer together with software, printer and aftersales service for about £2,000 in 1987 (Urry, 1987).

Channel development by Compaq

Compaq was founded in 1982 (a few months after the IBM PC was introduced) by three ex-engineers of Texas Instruments. Its target product was IBM-compatible machines; hence the firm's name Compaq, which stands for compatibility and quality. Buxton (1987, p. 13) commented that Compaq 'had always intended to be big from the start, it installed an in-house computer designed to cope with the demands of a one billion dollars corporation'. Compaq set up a marketing subsidiary in the UK in 1984, and opened an impeccably built plant in Scotland in 1987, which was extended in 1994. It quickly established a reputation for innovative technology, high quality and premium price; for instance, IBM's first portable personal computer in 1984 was heavier and had fewer features than the original 28 pounds Compaq portables. It was also reported in 1987 that Compaq 'builds machines to the industry standard set by IBM but which are frequently acknowledged to have superior performance to IBM equipment and are sold at prices comparable to those of IBM products' (Buxton, 1987).

Compaq adopted a policy of cooperating with UK dealers by granting them very generous discounts as well as not competing with them via a direct sales force. The dealers handled all Compaq's clients, including corporate accounts. It should be noted that in the 1980s, microcomputer firms' sales personnel tended to cut out resellers when handling potential big orders. Compaq's channel strategy thus paved the way for its rapid market penetration first in portable computers and then in desktop systems. One UK survey in 1985 showed that among 800 speciality stores, 66 per cent of them carried Compaq products compared to 80 per cent for IBM and 65 per cent for Apple (*Management Today*, 1985). Table 3.2, above, shows that Compaq had gained a 4.3 per cent share of the business market in the UK by 1987. Compaq also operated a dealer-buying price to regulate its retail pricing. This meant that leading retailers such as Dixons would have to sell within the range of the dealer-buying price and could not undercut small dealers. Nevertheless, Compaq incorporated direct sales such as person-to-person sales and telephone sales as the market matured during the 1990s. The former handled government and corporate businesses, while the latter was responsible for small businesses of 20–200 employees. However, it had no representation for businesses with less than 20 employees, and therefore avoided channel conflict with retailers.

Compaq has grown continuously in the UK during the 1980s; however, it suffered a setback in 1990 when other IBM-compatibles producers began price competition. Compaq's new CEO acknowledged the problem and changed the product culture to one of sparing no expense to launch the very best personal computers on the market. As a consequence, Compaq's position continuously improved during the 1990s; and it secured the largest market share in the UK by the end of the decade. Compaq undertook a series of merger and acquisition activities that has affected its UK manufacturing and marketing operations over recent years. It acquired US firms Tandem in 1997 and Digital in 1998; in addition, it merged with Hewlett-Packard in 2002. This last merger, in particular, has meant that the new firm has obtained a dominant position in the worldwide microcomputer market.

Technology commercialization at Sun

Back in the late 1980s, Sun visualized the emerging technological trajectory in the computer industry, and announced the importance of a computer network. The idea, since then, has been widely practised by personal computer-based internet users, such as those who log in to a web-site and use the software at the site to send electronic mail messages. The original S.U.N. workstation was a generic workstation to run on the Stanford University Network project. Apollo Computer first launched workstations in 1980; they were similar to personal computers but had more computing power, and their data storage catered for complex graphics and calculations. Most importantly, they were designed for network integration. Apollo's technical customer bases during the 1980s were therefore users who demanded considerable processing power on their desktop systems, but which was unavailable from the widespread low-capacity personal computers. Apollo developed a workstation market of technical applications in areas of electrical computer-aided design and computer-aided software engineering; nevertheless, it adhered to the mainframe and minicomputer industry strategy and built its workstations with proprietary network and operating systems.

Sun was aware of an emerging need among engineers and scientists for workstations with higher performance relative to the personal computer, and lower price when compared to the minicomputer network. It proposed the concept of affordable and powerful workstations based on an open system; that is, the adoption of standard hardware and software components such as Motorola's microprocessor and the Unix operating system. The rationale behind non-proprietary components was that no single company could be at the forefront of every important breakthrough, since technological change in the computer industry was continually accelerating. Sun's CEO Scott McNealy commented that: 'in the past, computer companies have been able to charge a premium for proprietary technology. In the future, they will have to offer a discount' (Gannes, 1987, p. 60). Sun set up its person-to-person sales operation in the UK in 1984, and then expanded into manufacturing in 1988. The state-of-the-art manufacturing plant at Linlithgow, Scotland, provided Sun greater flexibility to serve the markets in Europe and the Middle East.

Suns' ability to differentiate its workstations in terms of price and performance allowed it to become, within a few years, an important player in the UK, well-ahead of competitors such as IBM, Hewlett-Packard and Digital in terms of the Unix-based workstation market. Sun consolidated its leadership by the late 1980s in the engineering/scientific workstation market, and continuously designed more powerful models each year to keep ahead of imitators. As the market matured and profit margins deteriorated during the 1990s, Sun recruited UK dealers to complement its sales teams and successfully stimulated greater demand from the workstation market to sustain its growth.

Unsatisfied with the performance of the available microprocessors incorporated into workstations, Sun designed and released its proprietary reduced-instruction-set computer microprocessor, the SPARC, in 1989; since then, it gradually phased out Intel and Motorola's complex-instruction-set computer microprocessor-based workstation models, and has specialized in SPARC workstations. Sun also licensed the SPARC architecture to firms such as Fujitsu and ICL. Sun rightly identified that financial analysts would be able to understand complex financial data more quickly if the data were conveyed in graphical form, and opened the City of London office in 1989 to exploit the needs of financial institutions. During the 1990s, it set up a pilot programme with prospective firms to demonstrate the advantages of using workstations. Overall, Sun's efforts resulted in the establishment of new market segments such as banks, insurance, financial institutions, airlines, healthcare, education, government and the internet. Sun also successfully developed new customer bases, and was selling a third of its workstations to commercial, non-technical users in the UK by the mid-1990s.

Channel compression by Dell

Dell was created by Michael Dell in 1984 with US$1,000 start-up capital; the key marketing point of the firm was to sell custom-built computers directly to end-users. According to Dell (2000), it chose the UK as the first country for expansion in 1984 owing to his identification of market opportunity as well as the common language factor. Dell (2000, p. 28) stated:

> I'd been to London for a family vacation during the spring break of my freshman year in college...I had taken the opportunity to roam into a couple

> of computer stores, and I observed the same high mark-up/lousy service phenomenon in the United Kingdom as I had in the United States.

Dell compressed the market channel vertically and eliminated the intermediary function of dealers and retailers; this defied the conventional wisdom in the industry and resulted in the creation of a successful operation in the UK. Dell confirmed its position as the leading player in the UK by 2000, with a 17.5 per cent market share (IDC, 2002).

Dell revitalized the mail-order market channel adopted by early UK firms such as Sinclair and Acorn, who had, nevertheless, broadened their market channels with retailers and dealers during the period of significant market growth. Against the prevailing practices in the UK microcomputer industry, Dell not only eliminated the entrenched dealer channel and sold personal computers to customers directly, it built the computers *after* it received customer orders. An industry analyst commented on Dell's market channel when it entered the market in 1987: 'As in the US, you can't walk into a dealer in the UK and buy a Dell machine – you have to order it over the phone and it will be delivered by courier to your door' (*Personal Computer World*, 1987). Though none of Dell's US counterparts replicated Dell's telephone marketing during the 1980s, its cost-effective channel strategy was adopted by UK entrants such as Elonex and Opus Technology. By the mid-1990s, Dell and its US counterpart Gateway, together with Elonex, Opus and Viglen, became the leading firms within the UK mail-order channel.

Dell not only operated on a build-to-order rather than the traditional build-to-forecast model, it reinforced this model with complete reliance on external component suppliers in its manufacturing plant in Ireland, which was opened at the Irish Development Agency's Raheen Industrial Estate in Limerick in 1991. It further expanded its operation by acquiring the AST plant in Limerick in 1998. Commenting on his insight into the sourcing strategy within the supply chain, Dell's CEO stated: 'As a small start-up, Dell couldn't afford to create every piece of the value chain. But more to the point, why should we want to? We concluded that we'd be better off leveraging the investments others have made and focusing on delivering solutions and systems to customers' (Magretta, 1998, p. 74). Indeed, Dell's UK advertisement reflected this philosophy 'Performance and value. Perfectly balanced without the middleman' (Dell Computer Corporation, 1999). Dell's sourcing of components enabled the firm to offer the most up-to-date system at least cost. As one of its managers commented in 2001: 'Low inventory is critical to our cost advantage. Component costs have been reducing at a rate of about 1 per cent a week, and that is still continuing' (Daniel, 2001).

Dell has rationalized its market segments into large customers and small customers as the market has matured. The former encompasses large firms (businesses with more than 500 employees in the UK) as well as the public sector (for example healthcare, education, local and central government), and Dell has tackled these customer accounts with face-to-face selling teams where account executives visit prospective clients to explore their information system needs. Small customers include individuals and small firms, and Dell has approached this market segment with its innovative toll-free telephone marketing and internet sales; individuals contact Dell for product enquiries or to place orders. Dell's prospective customers in the UK can contact its European telephone marketing team 12 hours a day during the week, during nine hours on Saturdays and six hours on Sundays. Customers can also utilize the internet and order from the firm 24 hours a day. Following its tremendous success at home, Dell began internet sales in the UK in 1998, and was the first microcomputer firm to embark an internet sales at that time. Its web-site was regarded as a top web-site with channel functions such as 'customers can review, configure and price systems within Dell's entire product line, order systems online or by telephone, and track orders from manufacturing through shipping' (*Financial Times*, Survey, 1998, p. 22). Another useful feature of Dell's web-site is its service and support pages, which include account information, software support, technical information and technical advice.

Discussion

The above sections have shown that the superior performance of Apple, IBM, Compaq, Sun, and Dell within the UK are the result of implementing innovative product and channel strategies; however, their overall strategic orientations followed the development of the UK microcomputer industry and targeted the critical success factors towards different stages of the industry life-cycle. The ideas of Apple II, the Macintosh, the IBM PC, Compaq's IBM-compatible systems and the Sun workstation derived from existing product technologies, while Dell's notion of build-to-order captured benefits in relation to the abundant supply of third-party components. The central theme of their product strategies therefore continued with the trajectory of growth that had been previously tested in the industry. In addition, they adapted channel strategies to the requirements of the UK microcomputer market. The use of dealers during the introductory product stage allowed Apple and IBM to diffuse their product knowledge, while Compaq enlisted the support of dealers by not setting up company sales teams to compete with them in the expanding UK market. IBM, Apple and Compaq's active pursuit of retailing coincided with the maturity of the market, which demanded economies of scale in the distribution channel. Finally, the shift from personal sales to dealer networks in Sun as well as the vertical-channel compression in Dell enabled them to reduce costs in the mature stage of the product cycle. However, it may not be ignored that the success of these five firms has defied the traditions of the computer industry in terms of abandoning proprietary component technology and pioneering new marketing channels. Therefore, their supply-chain strategies challenged the existing rules if one considers the overall picture where the microcomputer is a segment of the computer industry.

Apple entered the UK market in 1977 through indirect export and then established its direct marketing and manufacturing presence in Ireland in 1980. Apple's rise in the UK was associated with the unique product concept during the transitional period when microcomputers replaced microcomputer kits. Apple II was an attractively designed personal computer with real graphics, sound and colour. It was also widely known during its time as a general-purpose computer whose usage was limited only by the user's imagination; for example, it could be programmed as an oscilloscope. Apple's next innovation, the Macintosh, was far more user-friendly than the prevailing IBM PC standard; users could view and switch between several applications at the same time by pointing with a mouse to the relevant icons. Thus, the Macintosh allowed the non-technical user to interact with the machine via easily comprehensible graphics rather than mechanical function keys as used in the IBM-style PC. The distribution of these innovative products to small businesses and individual users was facilitated by Apple's channel strategy, which consisted of a network of corporate and value-added dealers. The interaction of product and strategy therefore enabled Apple to rise to a prominent position and increase market share when the UK market grew considerably during the 1980s. Though Apple's market share declined throughout the 1990s as a result of internal inefficiencies and the diffusion of the Windows operating system, it demonstrated signs of revival in 1999 with another innovative product, the iMac, which is a stylish design in colours such as tangerine, strawberry, lime, blueberry and grape.

The product strategy in relation to the IBM PC captured the essence of marketing in projecting differentiation from other competitors in a rapidly expanding market, and supports the industry-evolution perspective. To service the European market, IBM designated its Scottish plant, built in 1954, as its manufacturing site for personal computers. The IBM PC standard competed with those offered by Apple, Hewlett-Packard, Digital Equipment, Wang, Honeywell, Zenith, Tandy, Texas Instruments, NEC and others, within an industry still dominated by mainframes and minicomputers. The emergence of the IBM PC standard during the 1980s can be attributed mainly to IBM's person-to-person sales force's ability to convey the message that IBM PCs were universally compatible with IBM mainframes and minicomputers, together with pre-sales and after-sales services unrivalled within the computer industry. Most importantly, IBM supported its direct-channel strategy with the help of dealers and retailers, which were widely used by industry participants during the early 1980s. For example, there were hundreds of dealers in the UK serving firms such as Apple; in addition, retailers such as W.H. Smith, Boots, Dixons and Currys were outlets for Commodore and Sinclair's products. Though IBM had set the technical trajectory in the personal computer market, its market share gradually declined as it was not able to compete in price with IBM-compatible personal-computer manufacturers during the 1990s.

Compaq's entry into the personal-computer market with high performance IBM-compatibles represented an innovative product positioning. Compaq also refined the dealer channel and provided dealers with above-industry discounts and committed not to compete with them via its own sales teams. These strategies allowed the firm to create a new market segment, subsequently passing IBM to become the market leader during the 1990s. Table 3.3 shows that Compaq led the UK personal computer market with a 17 per cent market share in 1998. Compaq responded to the mature market in the mid-1990s by altering its founders' visions to compete in price, and widened its channel strategy by incorporating direct sales and retail sales. As a result it operated from within a retail network, through direct sales teams, telephone marketing and internet sales, as well as its traditional dealer network.

Sun's early success in engineering and scientific workstations provided a genuine alternative for technical users who were not able to take advantage of personal computers because of their limited processing power, therefore suffering delays on timeshared minicomputers. Sun's affordable and powerful workstation products successfully targeted this special niche of technical users that existing firms such as Apollo or Digital had neglected. Sun's continuous success in the 1990s with the commercialization of workstations and the appointment of corporate dealers again demonstrated its response towards changing market

Table 3.3 Leading firms in the UK personal computer market, 1998

Firm	*Units sold*	*Market share (% units sold)*
Compaq	174,784	16.6
Dell	148,315	14.1
Toshiba	66,552	6.3
Hewlett-Packard	41,928	4.0
IBM	41,364	3.9
Packard Bell/NEC	41,309	3.9
Gateway	35,215	3.3
Elonex	32,414	3.1
Apple	29,410	2.8
Fujitsu	25,255	2.4
Others	417,486	39.6

Source: Based on data from *PC Dealer* (16 September 1998).

dynamics during the stage of maturity. It should also be noted that to meet the market demand for more powerful workstations in the late 1980s (caused by the lack of suitable microprocessors), Sun even launched its own SPARC design. Therefore, Sun's supply-chain strategy that led to its continuous success was driven by the evolution of the microcomputer industry.

Despite being a late entrant in the UK microcomputer market, Dell has become a market leader towards the end of the 1990s. Dell's first British model was an Intel 80286-based IBM AT-style system, priced at £2,199. A reviewer wrote that this system 'is a few hundred pounds cheaper than any comparable system I know of', and 'if Dell can overcome the British prejudices and confusing legislation about mail order purchases, the company seems set to make a killing' (*Personal Computer World*, 1987, p. 113). Most importantly, Dell was able to maintain its cost advantage when component prices continuously fell dramatically throughout the 1980s. Dell built personal computers according to customers' orders; in other words, it did not carry inventory on finished stock and adopted a just-in-time component delivery schedule that was based on the actual volume of orders. This therefore argues in favour of the deterministic view that the industry's environment governs the strategic orientation of high-performing firms. Dell combined build-to-order with its telephone and internet-driven individual marketing system to consolidate its low-cost position during the mature stage of the industry life-cycle. In addition, the first-hand information about customers gathered by Dell's direct marketing teams provided the firm with up-to-date market intelligence that further enhanced its competitiveness. Dell maintained at least 50 per cent of its sales from repeat purchases, which confirms that Dell has considerable proprietary knowledge about its customers in terms of microcomputer ownership and the problems they might have experienced, providing an invaluable market asset.

This chapter has demonstrated that the supply-chain strategies among successful US microcomputer firms were based on a thorough understanding of the evolving industry and the subsequent alignment of their strategies with the requirement of the particular life-cycle stage, hence substantiating the environmental determinism perspective of supply-chain strategy. Arthur (1996) has further refined this perspective in terms of technological determinism; he considered that the competition of knowledge-based industries such as computer hardware was about the search for a winning product in each new wave of technology development. Successful firms in this perspective are those that transform considerable amounts of knowledge and relatively small amounts of traditional resources into products that are subject to increasing (rather than diminishing) returns to scale. Accordingly, successful microcomputer supply-chain strategies have been about positioning firms' products or processes to capture increasing returns to scale in each new wave of the industry. Apple, Compaq and Sun's product designs as well as IBM and Dell's product positioning shaped the development of the industry and generated success for those firms within the technological domain of the time.

This chapter has also touched on another interesting issue – the differing responses of firms in pursuing supply-chain strategies compatible to the evolutionary stages of microcomputers. For example, why did indigenous UK firms such as Elonex and Opus duplicate Dell's mail-order channel as early as the mid-1980s, while firms such as IBM only implemented mail-order practices in the 1990s? The differences in firms' apparent differentials in replicating an optimal supply-chain strategy during the course of the industry's evolution can be explained by the legacy problem. The legacy problem focuses on the internal constraints of firms that have their origins in the elaboration of structural arrangements during external expansion. It arises from the historic context of the firm, and provides insight into the variations of firms. For instance, to adopt Dell's channel strategy to tackle the cost structure when the industry approached maturity would alienate existing dealer networks, which would regard direct marketing practices as competition from the firm. Indeed, the investment within the channel network is not only a structural contractual arrangement that can be written off with a single decision, it also encapsulates human-capital investment such as cultivating relationships with dealers. This means that the internal constraint is not simply about consolidating the business operation in relation to the environmental demand, it also involves the delicate handling of a large number of dealers that generate a substantial proportion of a firm's sales. In other words, firms can react strategically within the microcomputer industry's life-cycle only if they are not weighed down by their historic legacies.

The concept of the legacy problem is therefore synonymous with Ghoshal and Bartlett's (1998, p. 40) administrative heritage:

> a company's ability to respond to the strategic task demands of today's international operating environment is constrained by its internal capabilities, which are shaped by the company's administrative heritage.

They considered the determinants of administrative heritage, including national culture, company history and the impact of founders/key executives. The presence of the legacy problem therefore improvizes the philosophical basis of supply-chain strategies among successful US microcomputer firms, and suggests that strategies are co-determined by the evolution of the industry and the firm. In other words, the microcomputer industry environment first determines the type of supply-chain strategy for competitive success, and then the presence or absence of the legacy problem within the firm determines the possibility of pursuing the strategy that corresponds to the evolutionary stage of the industry.

Conclusion

Earlier sections have demonstrated that the successes of Apple, IBM, Compaq, Sun and Dell have been due to the implementation of supply-chain strategies aligned with different life-cycle stages of the UK microcomputer industry. The strategy that led to Apple's and IBM's histories of extraordinary achievements in the early stages of the UK microcomputer industry, as well as the continuous success of Compaq, Sun and Dell during the industry-growth and maturity stages, illustrates the skilful deployment of innovative products and the development of market channels. Apple and IBM demonstrated superb skills in defining the market with product and channel approaches. Apple in particular undertook an active marketing programme towards educational institutions and creative industries whereas IBM established a strong position in the corporate sector. Sun combined elements of the innovative-product technology strategy with a strong focus on niche markets. Sun's performance, to a great extent, was due to its ability to achieve economies of scale by widening the customer base of workstations and realigning its channel strategy with the changing environment. Compaq utilized an IBM-compatible product strategy and a unique channel approach to enter the fast expanding UK market; it built on a reputation of superior product performance and became the leading personal computer firm in the 1990s. Furthermore, Dell's success originated from its ability to improvize existing practices and to adopt processes that minimized costs in its supply chain. It can therefore be seen that the five US firms' supply-chain strategies were evolutionary rather than revolutionary in nature; they did not challenge the status quo of the industry or exhibit signs of discontinuity with the general direction of industry evolution. Indeed, industry evolution takes on significant importance in their strategic orientations within the UK.

The picture which has emerged is that superior performance among US microcomputer multinational firms' operations abroad depends on leveraging the strategies in the product and channel components of the supply chains they developed at home (Buckley and Casson, 1976; Dunning, 1988; Porter, 1990; Kogut and Zander, 1993; Teece, Pisano and Shuen, 1997). These five successful US firms have pursued to a considerable degree a global approach in their product launches within the UK, with appropriate timing; furthermore, they implemented their US-driven market-channel practices discriminatively during 1977–99. Their alignment of a standard US approach to suit the UK market channel could be considered as a response to the structural differences and the slower pace of channel development. Hence, their successes represented adapting global strategies to the specific circumstances in the UK, and are parallel to the notion of balancing global efficiency with local responsiveness (Prahalad and Doz, 1987; Ghoshal and Bartlett, 1998).

The findings here add to previous research in relation to the transfer of US microcomputer firms' sourcing models in Europe, and reiterate the importance of capability-based supply-chain competitive advantages when firms invest abroad. As US microcomputer firms' successes in the UK are closely intertwined with the leverage of headquarter capabilities in the supply chain, as well as deploying them strategically during the process of direct investment, future theory development on industry evolution could therefore focus on the sources of multinational firms' home-grown capabilities within the supply chain. The microcomputer industry has matured within two decades; the speed of evolution means that only firms with a long view and an understanding of the success factors critical at different life-cycle stages within the local context will be able to respond appropriately to the industry dynamics during international expansion.

References

AFX Asia (2002a) 'World PC shipments down in 2001, first fall since 1985', *Global News Wire*, 18 January 2002.

AFX Asia (2002b) 'Global 2001 workstation shipments down 11.2 per cent', *Global News Wire*, 30 January 2002.

AFX Asia (2002c) 'Global 2001 server shipments up 1.8 per cent', *Global News Wire*, 30 January 2002.

Apple Computer Inc. (1986) Advertisement in *Personal Computer World*, November 1986, back cover.

Aragon-Correa, A. and Sharma, S. (2003) 'A contingency resource-based view of proactive corporate environmental strategy', *Academy of Management Review* 46(1), 71–88.

Arthur, W.B. (1996) 'Increasing returns and the new world of business', *Harvard Business Review* 74(4), 100–9.

Astley, G. and Van de Ven, A.H. (1983) 'Central perspectives and debates in organization theory', *Administrative Science Quarterly* 28(2), 245–73.

Bain, J.S. (1957) *Industrial Organisations*. New York: John Wiley.

Baden-Fuller, C.W.F. and Stopford, J.M. (1992) *Rejuvenating the Mature Business*. London: Routledge.

Buaron, R. (1981) 'New-game strategies', *The McKinsely Quarterly*, Spring issue, 24–40.

Buckley, P. and Casson, M. (1976) *The Future of the Multinational Enterprise*. London: Macmillan – Palgrave.

Burns, T. and Stalker, G.M. (1961) *The Management of Innovation*. London: Tavistock.

Buxton, J. (1987) 'Why Compaq will not be frozen out', *Financial Times*, 24 July 1987, S1 p. 13.

Buzzell, R.D. and Gale, B.T. (1987) *The PIMS Principle*. New York: The Free Press.

Cane, A. (1985) 'Europeans take a wary view', *Financial Times*, 24 June 1985, p. 6.

Cane, A. (1992) 'Growth in personal computer sales slows', *Financial Times*, 18 February 1992, p. 10.

Chakravarthy, B.S. (1984) 'Strategic self-renewal: a planning framework for today', *Academy of Management Review* 9(3), 536–47.

Child, J. (1972) 'Organisational structure, environment and performance: the role of strategic choice', *Sociology* 6(1), 1–22.

Craig, C.S. and Douglas, S.P. (2000) 'Configurational advantage in global markets', *Journal of International Marketing* 8(1), 6–26.

Curry, J. and Kenney, M. (1999) 'Beating the clock: corporate responses to rapid change in the PC industry', *California Management Review* 42(1), 8–36.

Daniel, C. (2002) 'Dell Europe moves up a gear as PC industry declines', *Financial Times*, 9 November 2001, p. 26.

Digital Equipment Corporation (1983) Advertisement in *Management Today*, July 1983, pp. 30–1.

Dell, M. (2000) *Direct from Dell*. London: HarperCollins Business.

Dell Computer Corporation (1999) Advertisement in *PC Direct*, January 1999, pp. 2–5.

De Jonquières, G. (1983a) 'Going for broke to stay number one', *Financial Times*, 15 August 1983, p. 12.

De Jonquières, G. (1983b) 'IBM's rivals strike back: Europe's computer industry', *Financial Times*, 21 November 1983, p. 18.

De Wit, B. and Meyer, R. (1998) *Strategy: Process, Content, Context*. London: International Thompson Business Press.

Dunning, J. (1988) 'The eclectic paradigm of international production: a restatement', *Journal of International Business Studies* 19(1), 1–32.

Gannes, S. (1987) 'Sun's sizzling race to the top', *Fortune* 122(8), 58–61.

Ghoshal, S. and Bartlett, C.A. (1998) *Managing Across Borders*. London: Random House.

Grewal, R. and Dharwadkar, R. (2002) 'The role of the institutional environment in marketing channels', *Journal of Marketing* 65(3), 82–97.

Hamel, G. and Prahalad, C.K. (1994) *Competing for the Future*. Boston: Harvard Business School Press.

Hannan, M. and Freeman, J. (1977) 'The population ecology of organizations', *American Journal of Sociology* 82(4), 929–64.

Hrebiniak, L.G. and Joyce, W.F. (1985) 'Organizational adaptation: strategic choice and environmental determinism', *Administrative Science Quarterly* 30(3), 336–49.

Houlder, V. (1989) 'A turbulent market that defies gravity', *Financial Times*, 27 February 1989, p. 22.

International Data Corporation (IDC) (2002) 'UK PC sales better than expected despite continued lack of corporate demand', *IDC Press Release*, 18 February 2002.

Kirkpatrick, D. (1993) 'Mac vs Window', *Fortune* 128(8), 57–60.

Kogut, B. and Zander, U. (1993) 'Knowledge of the firm and the evolutionary theory of the multinational corporation', *Journal of International Business Studies* 24(4), 637–45.

Kotler, P. (1973) 'The major tasks of marketing management', *Journal of Marketing* 37(4), 42–9.

Lawrence, P.R. and Lorsch, J.W. (1967) *Organization and Environment: Managing Differentiation and Integration*. Cambridge, MA: Harvard University Press.

Levitt, T. (1965) 'Exploit the product life cycle', *Harvard Business Review* 43(6), 81–94.

Li, H. (2001) 'How does new venture strategy matter in the environment–performance relationship?', *Journal of High Technology Management Research* 12(2), 183–202.

Lynn, G.S. and Akgun, A.E. (2001) 'Project visionary: its components and impact on new product success', *Journal of Product Innovation Management* 18(6), 374–87.

Magretta, J. (1998) 'The power of virtual integration: an interview with Dell Computers', *Harvard Business Review* 76(2), 74–84.

Management Today (1985) 'Compaq's compact fortunes', May 1985, pp. 92–6.

Meredith M. and Cane, A. (1983) 'IBM launches new computer in Europe', *Financial Times*, 19 January 1983, p. 1.

Miller, D. (1987) 'The structural and environmental correlates of business strategy', *Strategic Management Journal* 8(1), 55–76.

Ozsomer, A. and Cavusgil, S.T. (2000) 'The effects of technology standards on the structure of the global PC industry', *European Journal of Marketing* 34(9/10), 1199–1220.

Personal Computer World (1987) 'Bench Test', July 1987, pp. 113–18.

Pfeffer, J. and Salancik, G.R. (1978) *The External Control of Organizations: A Resource Dependence Perspective*. New York: Harper & Row.

Porter, M.E. (1979) 'How competitive forces shape strategy', *Harvard Business Review* 57(2), 137–45.

Porter, M.E. (1980) *Competitive Strategy*. New York: The Free Press.

Porter, M.E. (1986) 'Changing patterns of international competition', *California Management Review* 27(2), 9–40.

Porter, M.E. (1990) *The Competitive Advantage of Nations*. New York: The Free Press.

Prahalad, C.K. and Doz, Y.L. (1987) *The Multinational Mission: Balancing Local Demands and Global Vision*. New York: The Free Press.

Rappaport, A.S. and Halevi, S. (1991) 'The computerless computer company', *Harvard Business Review* 69(4), 69–80.

Scherer, F.M. (1980) *Industrial Market Structure and Economic Performance*. Boston: Houghton Mifflin.

Silverman, D. (1970) *The Theory of Organizations*. Exeter, NH: Heinemann.

St John, C.H., Pouder, R.W. and Cannon, A.R. (2003) 'Environmental uncertainty and product process life cycles: a multi-level interpretation of change over time', *Journal of Management Studies* 40(2), 513–41.

Steffens, J. (1994) *NewGames: Strategic Competition in the PC Revolution*. Oxford: Pergamon Press.

Suchman, M.C. (1995) 'Managing legitimacy: strategic and institutional approaches', *Academy of Management Review* 20(5), 571–610.

Teece, D., Pisano, G. and Shuen, A. (1997) 'Dynamic capabilities and strategic management', *Strategic Management Journal* 18(7), 509–33.

Tellis, G.J. and Crawford, C.M. (1981) 'An evolutionary approach to product growth theory', *Journal of Marketing* 45(4), 125–32.

The Birmingham Post (2003) 'E-business: PC deliveries rise 6 per cent', 28 January 2003.

The Financial Times Survey (1998) 'Information Technology', *Financial Times*, 2 December 1998, p. 22.

Thompson, J.D. (1967) *Organizations in Action*. New York: McGraw-Hill.

Tsang, D. (2002) *Business Strategy and National Culture*. Cheltenham: Edward Elgar.

Urry, M. (1987) 'Dixons to stock IBM personal computers', *Financial Times*, 5 December 1987, p. 3.

Varadarajan, R.P., Clark, T. and Pride, W.M. (1992) 'Controlling the uncontrollable: managing your market environment', *Sloan Management Review* 39(2), 39–47.

Zeithaml, C.P. and Zeithaml, V.A. (1984) 'Environmental management: revising the marketing perspective', *Journal of Marketing* 48(1), 46–53.

4

The Role of Human Resource Policy in the Internationalization of Irish Organizations

Sharon Loane, Trevor Morrow and Jim Bell

Introduction

Dowling (2002) believes that the globalization of business is forcing managers to grapple with complex issues as they seek to gain or sustain a competitive advantage. Dowling (2002) cites Morgan (1986) in analysing international human-resource management (IHRM) based on three dimensions:

1. The three broad human activities of procurement, allocation and utilization.
2. The three national or country categories involved in IHRM activities: the host country where a subsidiary may be located, the home country where the firm is headquartered, and 'other' countries that may be the source of labour or finance.
3. The three types of employees of an international firm: *host country nationals* (HCNs), *parent country nationals* (PCNs) and *third country nationals* (TCNs).

Schuler, Budhwar and Florkowski (2002) believe international human resource management is about the worldwide management of human resources (see Brewster, 2002; Adler and Ghandar, 1990; Tung, 1984; Punnett and Ricks, 1992; Cascio and Bailey, 1995; Poole, 1999; Harris and Brewster, 1999). The purpose of IHRM is to enable the firm, the multinational or internationalizing enterprise to be successful globally. This entails being (a) competitive throughout the world; (b) efficient; (c) locally responsive; (d) flexible and adaptable within the shortest time periods; and (e) capable of transferring knowledge and learning across globally dispersed units.

This chapter has two aims. The first is to examine the key IHRM issues facing Irish international firms as they undergo the internationalization process. Irish international firms are usually large by national standards, but medium-sized when compared with European and North American multinational corporations. The second is to examine to what extent Irish international firms face the same

IHRM problems and issues as large international firms and, if so, whether there are variations in how these are tackled. The chapter begins with a discussion and analysis of the nature of IHRM before describing research in 14 Irish international firms.

Defining international human resource management

There is no consensus about what the term international human resource management (IHRM) covers, although most studies in the area have traditionally focused on the area of expatriation (Brewster and Harris, 1999).

IHRM may be defined as 'the human resource management issues and problems arising from the internationalization of business, and the human resource management strategies, policies and practices which firms pursue in response to the internationalization process' (Scullion, 1995: 352). Scullion argues that the advantage of such a definition is that it covers a far broader spectrum than the management of expatriates and involves the worldwide management of people (see Dowling *et al.*, 1999). Reviews of the literature have suggested that international HRM is more complex than domestic HRM, and that the complexities of operating in different countries and employing different national categories of workers are the main factors that differentiate domestic and international HRM, rather than any major differences between the HRM functions performed (Dowling *et al.*, 1994).

Brewster and Scullion (1997) identify a number of reasons why an understanding of IHRM is of growing importance at the present time. Firstly, recent years have seen rapid increases in global activity and global competition, which has resulted in an increase in the number and influence of multinational companies (MNCs) (Young and Hamill, 1992). Secondly, the effective management of human resources internationally is being increasingly recognized as a key source of competitive advantage in international business (Edwards, Ferner and Sisson, 1996). Thirdly, it is increasingly recognized that the effective implementation of international business strategies will depend on the ability of companies to develop appropriate human-resource strategies for the recruitment and development of their 'international managers' (Bartlett and Ghoshal, 1992). Fourthly, there is growing evidence that the human and financial costs of failure are more severe than in domestic business and that many companies underestimate the complex nature of the HRM problems involved in international operations (Tung, 1984). Fifthly, the advent of the Single European Market and the rapid growth of Irish direct investment abroad mean that IHRM issues are increasingly important concerns for a far wider range of companies than the traditional giant MNCs: particularly amongst the growing number of smaller and medium-sized enterprises (SMEs) who have significantly internationalized their operations in recent years.

International HRM in an Irish context is particularly pertinent for several reasons. First, recent research suggests the emergence of a group of indigenous MNCs within Ireland (Donnelly, 1996). Given the current economic climate of steady growth, low inflation and interest rates, Irish companies are reported to be increasingly internationalizing, primarily through overseas acquisitional activities (Chapman Flood, 1993). Second, Irish MNCs, while large in national terms, are small to medium-sized when compared with other European and North American MNCs. Evidence suggests that small and medium-sized enterprises (SMEs) are becoming increasingly 'internationalized' and face HRM constraints such as a lack of managerial capability and limited foreign experience (UN, 1993). Third, many Irish MNCs are relatively new to the international scene; with the exception of a few companies such as CRH and Smurfit who pioneered the route to internationalization in the 1970s, the majority of Irish MNCs have only begun to diversify into overseas markets since the early 1980s.

Within Irish-based research there is virtually no previous research on the IHRM policies and practices of indigenous companies. Indeed, the majority of Irish-based research hitherto has either centred on the role of HRM in foreign-owned MNCs (Gunnigle, 1992; Monks, 1996), or, alternatively, on issues of convergence between the HRM practices of foreign and domestic companies (Enderwick, 1986; Kelly and Brannick, 1985; Roche and Geary, 1997). Moreover, Dineen and Garavan (1994) argue that the growth in HRM research is indeed largely the result of a growth in the number of foreign-owned MNCs within the Irish economy.

The development of Irish international firms

As the internationalization of Irish business gains momentum, IHRM has become firmly on the agendas of a growing number of Irish companies. While specific data regarding outward investment flows are not readily available, evidence does suggest that the number of Irish-owned enterprises investing overseas, particularly since the mid-1980s, have been increasing (OECD, 1994). Research conducted by the United Nations in the early 1990s identified 17 indigenous small to medium-sized transnationals within Ireland (UN, 1993), and more recent research into the approach of Irish companies to industrial relations identified a conservative estimate of 20 indigenous MNCs (Donnelly, 1996).

These Irish MNCs were found to be predominately located within what Lynch and Roche (1995) define to be 'traditional' and 'resource-based' sectors of Irish industry. The sectoral location of Irish MNCs would, at first sight, seem to support O'Malley's (1985) 'late industrialization' thesis, the basic premise of which is that as a result of Ireland's late industrialization, 'barriers to entry for latecomers' have constrained and shaped the internationalization of indigenous industry. O'Malley (1992) argues that barriers to entry have resulted in the 'clustering' of Irish international companies into sectors with a 'significant degree of natural protection' or 'virtually non-traded sectors'. Large in domestic terms but small in international terms, Irish international firms are either 'survivors of intensifying competition or young companies established in a competitive environment' (O'Malley, 1992).

Internationalization strategies of Irish companies

While the number of Irish companies internationalizing is reported to be increasing, evidence suggests that the pace of overseas business expansion amongst Irish companies is also accelerating.

Acquisitional growth strategies are the most prevalent means of internationalization amongst Irish companies, and after organic growth strategies, mergers and joint ventures are the least popular (Chapman Flood, 1993; Donnelly, 1996). As O'Malley (1992: 38) notes, Irish companies have predominately 'engaged successfully in international markets in the form of taking over foreign firms and becoming multinational companies'. Irish companies, in the main, tend to pursue small to medium-sized overseas acquisitions, many of them 'bolt-ons' to existing operations. The internationalization of Irish companies is expected to continue given the limitations of domestic markets, the further opening of the economy, the shift in state policy toward the development of indigenous companies in international markets, the growing need to locate facilities close to the main overseas markets, and the need to achieve critical mass to compete in the deregulated markets of the twenty-first century.

Strategy and international HRM

One area of international business research has concentrated on identifying the methods by which firms seek to penetrate foreign markets, and the rationale for adopting their chosen foreign market entry strategy (for example, see McKiernan, 1992). Scandinavian research has attempted to explain the process of internationalization in terms of well-defined stages, with firms moving sequentially from exporting to licensing and then to foreign direct investment, each step involving greater commitment to the internationalization process (Johanson and Vahlne, 1977; Johanson and Mattson, 1988). Such approaches to internationalization have problems accommodating recent developments in international business. First, these models have been complicated by the rapid growth, in the last decade, of collaborative arrangements such as international joint ventures and strategic alliances (Hendry, 1994). Second, with the upsurge in international joint ventures and acquisitions in the last decade (Hamill, 1992), many firms were able to effectively 'leapfrog' the internationalization process. This is particularly significant in the Irish context given the primary role of acquisitions in the foreign market entry strategies of Irish firms.

One of the central issues concerning companies with overseas operations is the balance between globalizing forces and local market responsiveness (Bartlett and Ghoshal, 1989). Problems of control are exacerbated in international companies when operations are dispersed over considerable geographic and cultural distances and when the environment is complex and heterogeneous (Baliga and Jaeger, 1984). Edstrom and Galbraith (1977) suggest three modes of control – personal or direct control, bureaucratic control that relies on recording and reporting, and, lastly, control by socialization where the functional behaviours and rules are learned and internalized by individuals. It has been argued, however, that control modes may change as the firm's strategy evolves over time. During the early ethnocentric or home-country-focused stage of a firm's international involvement, parent-country expatriates exercise tight control. As strategy becomes host-country-focused or polycentric, there is a marked decline in the number of expatriates abroad and their function shifts to the communication and coordination of strategic objectives. Finally, with globalization and evolution of a globally-focused or geocentric strategy, there is a need for a broad range of executives with international experience (Adler and Bartholomew, 1991).

There is growing evidence to suggest that the international human-resource management (IHRM) policies of firms organized on a multidomestic basis differ from globally integrated firms (Kobrin, 1992; Schuler *et al.*, 1993). Other researchers have suggested linkages between the product life-cycle stage and international strategy, and HRM policy and practice (Milliman *et al.*, 1991). With the recent emergence of the concept of strategic international human-resource management (SIHRM) defined as – 'human resource management issues, functions and policies and practices that result from the strategic activities of multinational enterprises and that impact the international concerns and goals of those enterprises' (Schuler *et al.*, 1993: 56) – came a growing recognition that the success of global business depends more importantly on the quality of the MNC's human resources and how effectively the enterprise's human resources are managed and developed (Bartlett and Ghoshal, 1992).

In the following sections we consider the available research into the IHRM practices of Irish international firms. The analysis is based on a study of 14 international firms, using semi-structured interviews with the HR director as the main source of information, supplemented by questionnaires to expatriates. Table 4.1 presents a profile of the organizations and shows that the companies were drawn from a wide range of sectors. All have reported rapid growth of their international business operations in recent years.

There are four areas normally encompassed within international human-resource management, and each is considered in turn. The first is international staffing, an area which to date has enjoyed the bulk of research on IHRM. The

Table 4.1 Profile of organizations

Company	*Total staff*	*Industry*	*Established*	*Commenced international operations*
A	5,450	Retail	1970	1975
B	1,655	Travel	1956	1991
C	9,600	Financial services	1969	1987
D	6,200	Property	1975	1986
E	16,500	Insurance	1984	1989
F	24,000	Banking	1922	1972
G	460	Advertising	1969	1973
H	1,750	Hospitality & tourism	1905	1936
I	12,900	Construction	1952	1982
J	18,400	Pulp & paper	1943	1973
K	6,000	Textiles	1968	
L	4,480	Textiles	1977	1985
M	2,370	Agri-business	1971	1983
N	800	Food	1910	1990

second is expatriate performance and assessment. The third focuses on IHRM policies such as recruitment, selection training and repatriation. The fourth examines international management development.

International staffing policies and practice

As highlighted in the introduction to this chapter, international companies face three alternatives with respect to the staffing of management positions abroad; the employment of parent-company nationals (PCNs), host-country nationals (HCNs), or third-country nationals (TCNs). The choice between the various alternatives is influenced by several factors, both internal and external to the international firm, which are discussed below. As Scullion (1995) outlines, there are a number of options open to MNCs with respect to their staffing policies: ethnocentric, polycentric, geocentric, mixed and *ad hoc*. Companies with ethnocentric predispositions will tend to favour the employment of PCNs, while companies with a polycentric value system will tend to employ HCNs (Heenan and Perlmutter, 1979). In regio or geocentric international firms, overseas management positions may be staffed by TCNs. In practice, geocentric staffing policies are unusual even in the giant MNCs. Evidence suggests that, in general, Irish MNCs tend not to adopt a geocentric approach to the management of their overseas operations (Donnelly, 1996).

The international business strategy of the firm also influences staffing policies at the subsidiary level. Multinational integration strategies require a greater use of PCNs in order to control and coordinate integrated activities (Porter, 1986), and multidomestic or nationally responsive strategies would require the use of HCNs to ensure sensitivity to local market and cultural considerations (Scullion, 1993). The availability of local management talent in host countries and government restrictions on the employment of local nationals are other factors influencing the choice of staffing policy, as are the relative costs of the alternatives. The characteristics of the subsidiary will also have an impact. The employment of PCNs will be greater in new subsidiaries, particularly in the start-up phase. Similarly, the employment of PCNs will be greater in greenfield sites as compared with acquisitions and in subsidiaries, which are strategically important to the international company (Hamill, 1989).

There was considerable variation in the international staffing practices of the Irish companies involved in the research, not surprising given the range of factors influencing the choice of staffing policy as discussed above. In the very early stages of internationalization, the staffing policies of the majority of Irish companies were largely ethnocentric in character, an approach which is relatively common at this stage in the internationalization process where a company is setting up a new business process or product in another country and knowledge of the company's culture and reporting systems are considered essential (Zeira, 1976). The studies also identified a number of other reasons for employing expatriates in Irish MNCs, which were consistent with recent European research (Banai, 1992; Brewster and Scullion, 1997). Firstly, the lack of management skills available in some countries; secondly, the need for specific product and business knowledge provided an incentive to use expatriates; thirdly, the need for training and development of local staff was identified as a motivation; and finally, international assignments were increasingly seen as a central part of management development.

Although there were variations in practice, the general philosophy of all these firms was towards employing PCNs for very specific purposes and, as a consequence, this sometimes entailed for very limited time spans. It was relatively unusual for Irish expatriates to continue in senior management positions abroad beyond the early years of internationalization, and the commitment to develop host-country managers for senior positions was reflected in the importance the Irish firms attached to recruiting and retaining high-calibre local managers. The international human-resource strategy was to localize management in the subsidiary companies by developing HCNs to take over the running of foreign businesses and withdrawing expatriates. The implementation of the localization strategy was a major challenge for Irish firms given that many international firms have tended to neglect the training and development needs of their host-country managers and focus their development efforts on the PCNs (Shaeffer, 1989; Scullion,1994). However, the ways in which this common philosophy may work very differently in practice is illustrated by the cases of companies B and C.

Companies B and C made major international acquisitions in the 1990s and company B developed a senior management team of combined PCNs and HCNs. The main rationale for using Irish expatriates in this case was for development purposes – to develop future senior managers with the international management perspective and capability to run an increasingly international business. A very different approach was followed by company C; post-acquisition, the staffing practice was to continue with HCN managers running the business. The company was very concerned with ensuring a friendly bid, and felt, for political reasons, it was appropriate to continue with local managers rather than bringing in expatriates. In addition, the company was very satisfied with the quality and performance of the HCN senior management in the acquired company.

Companies B and C also had a number of branches abroad, in addition to their recently acquired businesses, particularly in the USA and the UK. In contrast to the staffing approach in the acquired businesses, the senior management of the foreign branches were usually Irish expatriates. This is linked to the strategic marketing approach of the companies to focus on the niche ethnic markets in the UK and the USA, and the strong preference expressed by some major customers that top managers in host countries should be parent-country nationals. In this context, public relations and marketing were usually the key roles. Previous research had largely ignored this factor because it has concentrated largely on the very largest multinationals and has tended to neglect the service sector (Brewster, 1991).

In other firms in the sample, as they moved beyond the early phase of internationalization and adopted a highly decentralized approach to international business, the shift was towards a polycentric staffing policy. The limited promotion and development opportunities for local managers was a major disadvantage of the ethnocentric approach, and in addition the adaptation of PCNs to some host counties frequently took longer than anticipated. A number of advantages of the polycentric approach were identified which were consistent with findings in the literature (Dowling *et al.*, 1994). Firstly, this approach enhanced the ability of firms to recruit, retain and motivate high-calibre local staff. Secondly, local managers were more sensitive to local culture and local market trends. Thirdly, it helped to maintain the local identity of the business. Fourthly, HCN managers generally cost less than PCN managers. Finally, this approach was a better fit with the decentralized business approach and the international growth strategy based on international acquisitions pursued by the majority of the Irish firms. The present research highlights examples of firms which pass through various stages of internationalization between evolution from a domestic to a mature international business. The research highlights that an international staffing strategy must be linked to the strategic evolution of the firm, and that for Irish multinationals the recruitment and development of HCN managers are key HRM challenges associated with the internationalization of Irish business.

The performance of expatriate managers

The companies varied in their overall approach to expatriate management. In four firms (companies A, L, N and D) the approach was centralized: head office managed the expatriates. Company H and company I adopted a decentralized approach, with little or no contact between head office and the expatriate. In the remainder there was a mixture of strategies. In company M, for example, the expatriate was ultimately accountable to head office, but day-to-day management lay with the overseas unit. The extent of the control structure also depended on the assignment and whether or not the expatriate had any previous overseas experience.

An important issue in the IHRM literature is that of expatriate failure, which is usually defined as the premature return of an expatriate manager (Dowling and Welch, 1988). The literature suggests that expatriate failure remains a significant problem, particularly for US multinationals, ranging between 25 and 40 per cent (Mendenhall and Oddou, 1985). Recent research suggests that these figures are somewhat exaggerated (Harzing and Van Ruysseveldt, 1995) and that expatriate underperformance is a far more frequent problem than failure of the type that requires repatriation (Scullion, 1995). A major conclusion which emerges from the Irish study, is that the expatriate failure rate in Irish companies is similar to other European countries and is considerably lower than in comparison with US companies. None of the 14 companies reported expatriate failure rates in excess of 5 per cent and the majority (9 out of 14) had rates of around 1 per cent. Four reasons were given for the low Irish expatriate failure rate. First, Irish managers were considered to be more international in their orientation and more internationally mobile than some of their foreign counterparts. Second, international assignments were generally seen to be a key part of the overall management development process and, as a result, as one personnel manager suggested, even those that did not like the assignment were inclined to 'stick it out'. Third, the relatively small numbers of expatriates involved in smaller MNCs and the personal knowledge of managers may have resulted in more reliable selection. Finally, failure to return to the company at the end of an assignment was not viewed as expatriate failure. In company I and company E, the HR managers indicated that some expatriates 'stay on the circuit' as they get used to working in an international environment and prefer the lifestyle abroad. However, this was viewed in a positive way and an indication of the expected mobility of international employees.

Family-related problems were identified as the major reason for poor performance in an international assignment in Irish MNCs, a finding that is consistent with recent European research (Brewster and Scullion, 1997). At the same time, Irish companies paid little attention to the family factor in relation to their selection decisions. Finally, the research illustrates the complexity of the issues surrounding the question of performance measurement in MNCs (Schuler *et al.*, 1991). Despite the growing tendency to see expatriates as key human assets, the criteria used for the performance appraisal of international managers had, in practice, received relatively little attention and indeed none of the companies had introduced separate appraisal systems for expatriate managers.

Repatriation

A significant finding of the research was the identification of the repatriation of managers as a significant problem for Irish international companies. Whereas none of the companies reported serious concerns with the performance of expatriates, many said they faced or anticipated significant problems regarding the re-entry of expatriate managers. The research highlighted that concerns over re-entry may lead to low morale and a higher turnover of expatriates (Harvey, 1989; Scullion, 1994). A key problem for the Irish international firms was finding suitable posts for repatriates, of similar status and responsibility to those positions they held abroad. It was anticipated that the repatriation problem would become more acute in future years because some companies expected continued expansion overseas at the same time as undertaking rationalization of domestic operations, thereby limiting opportunities at home. The research also highlighted other problems associated with re-entry such as loss of status, loss of autonomy, loss of career direction and a feeling that international experience is undervalued by the company (Johnston, 1991).

Most of the companies did not consider the issue of repatriation, although that issue is widely debated in the literature (Guzzo *et al.*, 1992; Adler, 1991; Brewster, 1991). In the Irish companies the expatriate was simply expected to fit back into the position which had been vacated some years previously. In part, this lack of emphasis on repatriation stemmed from a lack of expatriate failure as none of the companies recognized this as a problem. As a consequence of these experiences, only two companies (companies B and L) were exploring the possibility of repatriation policies. However, some measures had been introduced to minimize the repatriation problem. Firstly, to reduce the duration of the international assignment as it was generally felt that repatriation problems were more acute in longer assignments. Secondly, companies were paying greater attention to the career-planning of expatriates, and in particular were planning the return of expatriates earlier. Thirdly, one of the financial-service companies had begun to offer sabbaticals to some senior expatriates on completion of their international assignment.

However, some of the firms also faced an increasing reluctance among domestic employees to take international assignments. There were several reasons given for this phenomenon: the feeling that expatriates were 'out of sight and out of mind', the single-status nature of some contracts, the growth of the dual-career family and the consequent reluctance of one of the partners to move abroad, the fact that international experience was not appreciated by the domestic company and, related to this last factor, the perception that expatriate assignments were damaging to careers.

International HRM policies

The firms varied in the extent to which they had well-developed policies covering the recruitment, selection, predeparture briefing, repatriation and compensation of expatriates. The firms which had internationalized after 1980 were more likely to have put in place policies to deal with specific IHRM issues. These firms were taking a more proactive approach to internationalization than their more established counterparts, and their experience supports the prescriptive argument of Svard and Luostarinen (1982) that appropriate international human-resource policies should precede rather than follow international operations. These results are particularly interesting because they do not fit well with previous research findings, which suggest there is little or no formal HR involvement in the early stages of international involvement. The more usual pattern is that as international activities expand, with an accompanying increase in the number of expatriates, more formal HR policies begin to emerge (Welch and Welch, 1997). A number of factors may help to explain the relatively more proactive HRM approach of the Irish firms. To some extent it reflected competitive pressures quickly to establish a position in the international market and an attempt to make up the time they had lost in this arena. It also reflected the absence of a fund of knowledge and experience accumulated over time by the firms with more international experience. Moreover, the firms which entered international markets after the 1980s may also have benefited from the attention paid in the general management literature to the value of human-resource assets to the firm, and their more comprehensive policies were a means of gaining competitive advantage through this route. Finally, the majority of Irish firms leapfrogged the normal incremental approach to international business development by the use of acquisitions as the dominant mode of foreign market entry. As a result there were not the opportunities to accumulate knowledge and learning about international markets in a slower stage-by-stage approach.

Recruitment and selection

The high costs of expatriate failure highlight the importance of effective recruitment and selection procedures to the international firm. A key recruitment issue is whether firms recruit internally or externally, and an important selection issue is whether the criteria used for selecting expatriates should be different from those used for domestic appointments (Scullion, 1994). The majority of firms had a clear preference to recruit internally for international assignments, although four firms (companies L,M, I and F) employed external staff in exceptional circumstances. Two main advantages of internal as opposed to external recruitment were cited by the companies. Firstly, knowledge of the individual and the family, which was particularly important for those companies establishing new international operations in the early phase of the internationalization process. Secondly, the growing tendency to use international assignments for career development purposes. Two firms, (companies B and F) had separate international streams, although even here expatriates were recruited from within the domestic operation where possible. In these two firms, the majority of expatriates were contract staff.

In terms of the selection criteria used for international assignments, a candidate's domestic track record and general management and technical skills were the main factors considered (Tung, 1982). However, some of the companies also took into account a wider range of factors including cultural empathy, family situation, and previous international experience. Foreign-language ability was important for younger graduates and the development potential of the graduate was increasingly important. For more senior expatriate appointments the ability to operate independently and to develop cross-cultural leadership skills were seen as key factors (Scullion, 1992). However, while all companies felt that the effective selection of managers was vital to successful performance abroad, only four of the companies had introduced psychometric testing for expatriates. It was felt that the candidates for international postings would be well-known within the company and this finding is consistent with research which has noted that often the applicant for an international posting is selected prior to the interview on track record alone, and the interview is used merely for negotiating the expatriate package (Barham and Oates, 1991).

International briefing and training

An effective briefing on the nature of the international assignment prior to departure was also regarded as important to the success of an international assignment (Ronen, 1989). All of the companies conducted briefings, which usually involved interviews with senior managers to clarify the key objectives of the assignment. In addition, there was sometimes the opportunity to hold discussions with former and current expatriates who had knowledge of the country in question. This latter form of briefing was particularly valued by the managers because they could ask questions and learn from the experiences of their predecessors. The companies which had the largest number of expatriates also tended to have the most comprehensive training packages. In three of the companies (companies B, G and L), the training comprised visits to the overseas location and the involvement of the spouse of the expatriate as well as an extensive induction programme. The focus on training was undoubtedly fuelled by the problems of expatriate adaptation and possible failure, a topic extensively documented in the literature (Barham and Oates, 1991; Rothwell, 1992; Tung, 1981).

The level of communication between head office and expatriate may be a deciding factor in the success, or otherwise, of the international assignment (Newman, 1992; Brewster, 1991; Tung, 1981), as the feeling of abandonment and isolation is a major difficulty for expatriates. The level of communication varied considerably in these companies: some corresponded on a daily basis with their expatriates, whilst for others communications were much more erratic. The type of communication ranged from the normal business channels of telephone, fax or telex to more personal measures designed to provide expatriates with an ongoing link with home. For example, in company B a collage of newspaper articles was put together each day and faxed to expatriates.

None of the companies had established their own cultural-awareness training programmes. This was partly because the two most important foreign markets, the USA and the UK, were not felt to be so culturally dissimilar to the domestic culture. The relatively small size of the Irish companies was also a factor here; there were limited resources available at the corporate headquarters for training and development (Scullion and Donnelly, 1998). Some of the companies used external training organizations to help prepare their managers for international assignments, and one of the financial-service companies sent senior international managers to courses run by US business schools.

International management development

The effective implementation of global strategies depends, to a large degree, on the existence of an adequate supply of internationally experienced managers (Adler and Bartholomew, 1992), and Scullion (1992) identified shortages of international managers as an increasingly important problem for British multinationals. There were growing concerns in some of the Irish MNCs that shortages of international managers and restrictions on managerial mobility were recently emerging as significant constraints on their internationalization strategies. Shortages of qualified host-country (HCN) managers were a particularly acute concern for the manufacturing MNCs due to the very rapid internationalization of their businesses in recent years.

There was also growing recognition of the importance of developing effective international management-development programmes (Scullion, 1997), but the ways in which this development was carried out varied considerably. Two companies operated international management-development programmes. In the case of one of the service firms, this programme extended over two years and was made up of 17 managers drawn from throughout the company: expatriates, host-country managers and managers from the domestic operation. The dairy firms included exchanges between Irish and overseas operations in their management-development programme and operated these programmes with the explicit aim of developing an internal resource to meet their future international needs. In one of the dairy companies the personnel manager pointed out that 'there's a shortage of people that would have worked in different worlds, that actually would have worked on the international scene'. Certainly many of the companies reported that they were spending more on international management education, particularly for top and senior management. The companies used a combination of internal and external international development programmes, one interesting feature of which in the case of the banks was the use of leading European and US business schools. Yet, in most of the firms the emphasis was on developing general rather than international management competencies. The personnel manager in company N suggested that 'there are qualities of managers that are unique and if you don't have them, no matter how much you've travelled, you won't get them'. International management development was also utilized as a component of culture change and the transference of managers between locations was certainly viewed in this way in three of the food companies.

The key international HR issue facing these companies was the need to develop the next generation of top managers with the capacities to run an international business. International management development, succession planning and international career planning were seen as vital areas for the corporate human-resource function in the international firm. One of the ways in which this was achieved was through the use of graduate training programmes and there was a view in some of the firms that mistakes in the international arena could be made with fewer repercussions by graduate trainees than by fully-fledged managers. In addition, should senior managers with international experience leave the firm, there were potential replacements available through the graduate training scheme.

Discussion

The description of HRM practices in the Irish international firms reveals both similarities and differences, with the types of approaches discussed in the general IHRM literature. In addition, there are many differences between the firms themselves; from this research it is certainly not possible to say that there is

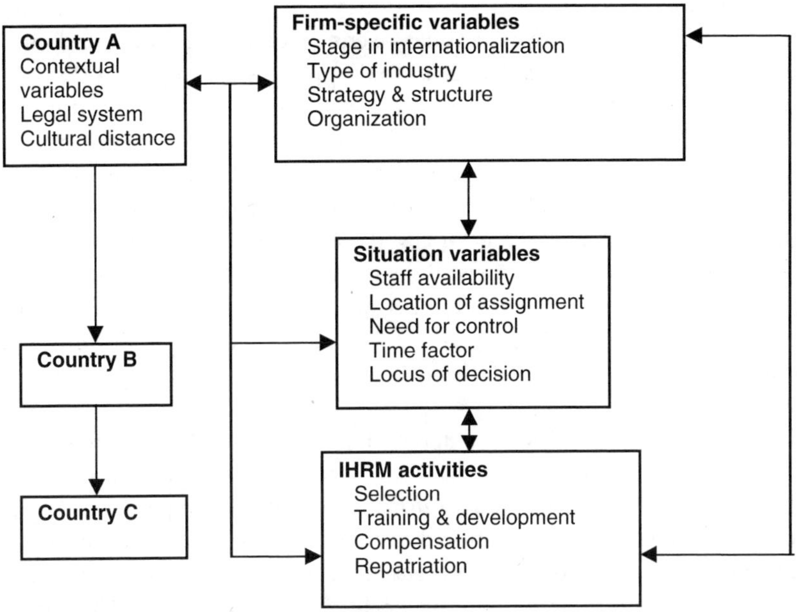

Figure 4.1 Determinants of IHRM approaches and activities
Source: Based on Welch and Welch, 1994.

a small firm or an 'Irish' approach to internationalization. However, certain trends do emerge in how international issues are managed. Thus, firms have a set of choices available on the approaches they wish to adopt in managing HR issues and they have to make decisions on those choices. For example, they have to consider whether to design new HR policies to deal with the impact of internationalization; whether to adopt a centralized or decentralized approach in dealing with matters; whether to have uniform or individual arrangements in their subsidiaries and with their expatriates. In trying to understand the differences between firms in the approaches they took, the framework provided by Welch and Welch (1994) and outlined in Figure 4.1 is a useful starting point. Welch and Welch, from research in four Australian firms, put forward the proposition that 'international HRM approaches and activities are a function of firm specific and situational activities' (p. 150). The Irish research did not explore all the dimensions suggested in the Welch framework, but does give insights into three of the firm-specific elements: the stage of internationalization, the type of industry, and strategy and structure.

Stage in the internationalization process

The Welchs research indicated that the stage of internationalization is 'a major determinant of staffing policy' (p. 151) and that, as a firm evolves through the various stages of the internationalization process, its staffing requirements change to suit specific organizational needs at each stage. The stage in the internationalization process is a useful tool in understanding the HRM policies adopted by the Irish firms. The Irish firms could be broadly grouped into two categories: firms which had entered the international market before 1980, and those which had entered after that date. In firms which had entered 'early' (for example, companies G, H, I and J), the process of internationalization was to a certain extent passive: circumstances dictated that they go international because the nature of the business demanded this approach, because external events or crises triggered the need, or because plans for expansion led naturally to international markets. These firms tended to adopt a more *laissez faire* attitude to IHRM issues and dealt with HR issues on an *ad hoc*, reactive and individual basis.

In contrast, the 'late' firms entered the international arena much more aggressively and, because they were late entrants, had to devise ways in which to get up to speed with their competitors. For example, companies B, L and M, who did not enter the international market until the 1980s, were trying to internationalize as quickly as possible and were much more proactive in their HR strategies than their more long-established counterparts. This need to internationalize rapidly also meant that these companies had to design and implement specific IHRM policies and systems; whilst their more established counterparts relied extensively on the experience they had gained over time in dealing with HR issues. This finding therefore supports the Welch suggestion that the assumption that there is a 'sequential evolutionary development' to the internationalization process is flawed in that the number of stages involved 'varies from firm to firm' (p. 151).

Some of the Irish companies, primarily through the use of international acquisitions as the main foreign market entry strategy, were trying to bypass some of the stages of internationalization in their attempts to catch up with or overtake their more established international competitors. They could not rely on experience in managing HR matters and were therefore more likely to develop HR policies and practices which to some extent sought to anticipate the HR problems arising from internationalization rather than just reacting to events in the international arena.

Strategy and structure

Welch and Welch contend that 'strategy and structure can dominate at a given point in time and thus influence the IHRM activity' (p. 154). There was evidence of the impact of both strategy and structure in the Irish research. For example, the dairy companies were fairly small and had entered the international market very aggressively. They needed to expand rapidly in order to survive and had developed their HR policies to cope with this expansion. The larger firms such as companies E and J operated a more decentralized approach towards internationalization. The Irish research also suggests that the first target country for the newly international firm and the number of locations are important factors in the strategy adopted towards internationalization and the way in which HR practices emerge. Whereas some research suggests that familiar markets, in both geographic and 'psychic' terms, are the most likely targets for international firms (see for example Johansson and Mattson, 1988), many of the Irish companies did not follow this route.

Type of industry

The type of industry also appears to have an impact on the IHRM practices adopted. The Welch study suggests that 'the service company may be more vulnerable than the manufacturing firm as it has not experienced that preparatory stages of exporting which allow exposure to some of the inherent difficulties involved in offshore business ventures' (pp. 152–3). However, evidence from the Irish study indicated that a service company might be able to leverage certain advantages. Thus, company B, as a service organization, was able to enforce a reasonably uniform set of HR practices and to interchange employees between locations. In contrast, company I, a manufacturing firm, had a very diverse set of practices throughout the company and this militated against movement between even the various domestic sites; adding the international dimension to its activities complicated matters further. Here the personnel manager remarked enviously on 'the IBMs of this world who are able to move their people about internationally as on a chess board'.

Firm-specific interactions

Although the Welch study does not explore this issue, it was apparent in the Irish study that the firm-specific factors do not operate in isolation; there is a process of interaction between the variables, which results in a variety of outcomes. In addition, it may be useful to differentiate between internal and external firm-specific variables and to identify the range of choices in the HR practices that firms pursue. Some of these choices are identified in Figure 4.2. The research suggests that firms have several choices in their approach to HR issues: centralization or decentralization; flexibility or uniformity; a set of HR policies which offer general guidelines for action, or one which indicates specific action; a strategy which is proactive or one which is reactive. The Irish study gives some indications that a combination of certain variables may lead to the adoption of particular approaches. Thus there was evidence that where companies go through a process of rapid internationalization and choose more distant markets, they will adopt a centralized HR policy. Conversely, where they have undertaken a slow approach to internationalization and choose closer markets they will adopt a decentralized HR policy.

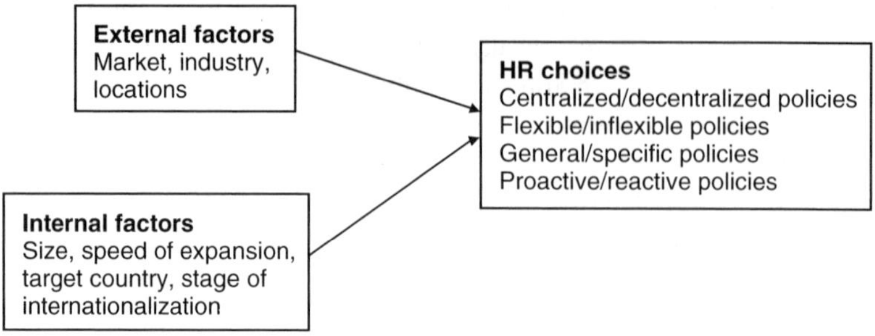

Figure 4.2 External and internal factors and HR choices

Conclusions

This chapter has considered the IHRM practices of 14 Irish international companies. The findings of the research suggest that the models of internationalization which have been developed from research in large MNEs do not adequately explain the approaches taken in smaller and medium-sized firms: these firms may need to be more flexible, adaptable and opportunistic than their larger counterparts, and likewise their HR practices may need to be tailored to specific demands. The research has indicated the usefulness of the framework proposed by Welch and Welch (1994) in identifying linkages between IHRM activities and organizational factors such as the stage in internationalization, the type of industry, strategy and structure. Welch proposed the framework as one conducive to theory-building rather than theory-testing, based on a study of expatriate management rather than human-resource practices in general. However, the Irish research suggests that the framework is a robust mechanism for identifying the range of variables which impact on human-resource choices in international activities. The research supports some of the findings from Welch's research and also suggests that attention needs to be paid to identifying the ways in which variables interact with one another in their impact on HR practices

The argument presented in this chapter suggests that international HRM is becoming increasingly important not only in the traditional giant MNCs but also amongst a growing number of medium-sized firms who have internationalized their operations in recent years. The preliminary evidence presented here suggests that a number of Irish MNCs, who in this case are amongst the largest Irish firms, are beginning to have problems in the management of expatriates: the ability to continue to make expatriation an attractive proposition together with repatriation appear to be growing problems for Irish MNCs. The recruitment and retention of the high-quality host-country (HCN) managers needed to effectively manage the acquired international businesses was a vital component of IHRM strategy in those companies committed to a policy of using local managers. More generally, the integration of the acquired foreign businesses was a key challenge facing Irish MNCs.

Finally, while previous research would suggest that as international activities expand with an accompanying increase in the number of expatriates, more formal HR policies emerge (Welch and Welch, 1997), the present research highlights interesting contrasts between the *ad hoc* and experience-based ways in which the more established firms managed their HR issues and the more proactive and policy-conscious methods of the newer entrants to the international arena. Further research should reveal which approach is proving more effective. Indeed, there is a need for a new research agenda in international HRM to establish better information about the role and management of HRM activities across frontiers in small and medium-sized firms, as well as in giant MNCs, to clarify and measure current developments and to place such developments in the context of more adequate theories of international HRM.

While the study of 14 Irish firms was a good sample size given the relative rarity of indigenous, independent medium-sized enterprises, it has identified the need for more extensive in-depth case study research that would facilitate cross-case comparisons. This type of research is needed in order to develop more sophisticated theoretical frameworks for identifying the range of variables which impact upon human-resource choices in the international arena.

References

Adler, N.J. and Bartholomew, S. (1992) 'Managing globally competent people', *Academy of Management Executive* 6(1), 52–64.

Adler, N.J. and Ghadar, E. (1990) *Strategic Human Resource Management: A Global Perspective. Human Resource Management in International Comparison*. Berlin: De Gruyter.

Baliga, B.R. and Jaeger, A.M. (1984) 'Multinational corporations: control systems and delegation issues', *Journal of International Business Studies* 2(1), 25–40.

Banai, M. (1992) 'The ethnocentric staffing policy in multinational corporations: a self-fulfilling prophecy', *International Journal of Human Resource Management* 3(3), 451–72.

Barham, D. and Oates, D. (1991) *The International Manger*. London: The Economist Books.

Bartlett, C. and Ghoshal, S. (1989) *Managing Across Borders: The Transnational Solution*. Boston: Harvard Business School Press.

Bartlett, C. and Ghoshal, S. (1992) 'What is a global manager?', *Harvard Business Review*, September/October, 124–32.

Brewster, C. (1991) *The Management of Expatriates*. London: Kogan Page.

Brewster, C. (2002) 'Human resource practices in multinational companies', in Gannon, M. and Newman, K. (eds), *Handbook of Cross-Cultural Management*. London: Blackwell.

Brewster, C. and Harris, H. (eds) (1999) *International HRM: Contemporary Issues in Europe*. London: Routledge.

Brewster, C. and Scullion, H. (1997) 'Expatriate HRM: a review and an agenda', *Human Resource Management Journal* 7(3), 32–41.

Casico, W. and Bailey, E. (1995) 'International human resource management: the state of research and practice', in Shenkar, O. (ed.), *Global Perspectives on Human Resource Management*. London: Prentice-Hall International

Creaner, J. and Monks, K. (1996) 'Entering the international market: opportunities and choices in human resource practices', *Research Papers Series*, Dublin City University Business School.

Dineen, D. and Garavan, T. (1994) 'Ireland: the Emerald Isle – management research in a changing European context', *International Studies of Management and Organisation* 24(1–2), 137–64.

Donnelly, N. (1996) 'The management of industrial relations in Irish-owned multinational companies: some exploratory findings', paper presented at the Management Research in Ireland Conference, University College Cork.

Dowling, P.J. (2002) 'International human resource management', in McDonald, F., Tuselmann, H. and Wheeler, C. (eds), *International Business: Adjusting to New Challenges and Opportunities*. London: Palgrave.

Dowling, P.J. and Welch, D. (1988) 'International human resource management: an Australian perspective', *Asia-Pacific Journal of Management* 6(1), 39–65.

Dowling, P.J., Schuler, R.S. and Welch, D. (1994) *International Dimensions of Human Resource Management* (2nd edn). California: Wadsworth.

Edstrom, A. and Galbraith, J. (1977) 'Transfer of managers as a coordination and control strategy in multinational organizations', *Administrative Science Quarterly* 22(3), 248–63.

Edwards, P.K., Ferner, A. and Sisson, K. (1996) 'The conditions for international human resource management: two case studies', *International Journal of Human Resource Management* 7(1), 20–40.

Enderwick, P. (1986) 'Multinationals and labour relations: the case of Ireland', *Journal of Irish Business and Administrative Research* 8(1), 1–11.

Forster, N. and Johnsen, M. (1996) 'Expatriate management policies in UK companies new to the international scene', *International Journal of Human Resource Management* 7(1), 179–205.

Government Publications (1994) *National Development Plan 1994–1999*. Dublin: The Stationery Office.

Gunnigle, P. (1992) 'Management approaches to employee relations in greenfield sites', *Journal of Irish Business and Administrative Research* 3(1), 20–36.

Hamill, J. (1989) 'Expatriate policies in British multinationals', *Journal of General Management* 14(4), 18–33.

Hamill, J. (1992) 'Cross-border mergers, acquisitions and alliances in Europe', in Young, S. and Hamill, J. (eds), *Europe and the Multinationals*. London: Edward Elgar.

Harris, H. and Brewster, C. (1999) 'An integrative framework for pre-departure preparation', in Brewster, C. and Harris, H. (eds), *International HRM: Contemporary Issues in Europe*. London: Routledge.

Harvey, M.G. (1989) 'Repatriation of corporate executives: an empirical study', *Journal of International Business Studies* 34(2), 131–44.

Harzing, A.W.J. and Van Ruysseveldt, J. (1995) *International Human Resource Management*. London: Sage.

Heenan, D.A. and Perlmutter, H.V. (1979) *Multinational Organisation Development*. Reading, MA: Addison-Wesley.

Hendry, C. (1994) *Human Resource Strategies for International Growth*. London: Routledge.

Johansson, J. and Mattson, L.G. (1988) 'Internationalization in industrial systems – a network approach', in Hood, N. and Vahlne, J.E. (eds), *Strategies in Global Competition*. London: Croom Helm.

Johanson, J. and Vahlne, J.E. (1977) 'The internationalization process of the firm – a model of knowledge development and increasing foreign commitment', *Journal of International Business Studies* 8(1), 23–32.

Johnston, J. (1991) 'An empirical study of repatriation of managers in UK multinationals', *Human Resource Management Journal* 1(4), 102–8.

Kelly, A. and Brannick, T. (1985) 'Industrial relations practices in multinational companies in Ireland', *Journal of Irish Business and Administrative Research* 7(3), 98–111.

Kobrin, S.J. (1992) 'Multinational strategy and international human resource management policy', unpublished paper, The Wharton School, University of Pennsylvania.

Lynch, J. and Roche, F. (1995) *Business Management in Ireland: Competitive Strategies for the 21st. Century*. Dublin: Oak Tree Press.

McKiernan, P. (1992) *Strategies of Growth*. London: Routledge.

Mendenhall, M. and Oddou, G. (1985) 'The dimensions of expatriate acculturation: a review', *Academy of Management Review* 10(1), 39–47.

Mendenhall, M.E. and Oddou, G. (1987) 'Expatriate selection, training and career pathing: a review and critique', *Human Resource Management* 23(3), 331–48.

Milliman, J., Von Glinow, M. and Nathan, B. (1991) 'Organizational life cycles and strategic international human resource management in multinational companies: implications for congruence theory', *Academy of Management Review* 16(3), 318–39.

Monks, K. (1996) 'Global or local? HRM in the multinational company: the Irish experience', *Journal of Human Resource Management* 7(3), 721–35.

Morgan, P. (1986) 'International human resource management: fact or fiction?', *Personnel Administrator* 31(9), 43–7.

O'Malley, E. (1985) 'The performance of Irish indigenous industry: some lessons for the 1980s', in Fitzpatrick, J. and Kelly, J. (eds), *Perspectives on Irish Industry*. Dublin: Irish Management Institute.

O'Malley, E. (1992) 'Problems of industrialisation in Ireland', in Goldthorpe, J. H. and Whelan, C.T. (eds), *The Development of Industrial Society in Ireland*. Oxford University Press for the British Academy.

Organisation for Economic Co-operation and Development (1994) *Reviews of Foreign Direct Investment: Ireland*. Paris: OECD.

Poole, M. (ed.) (1999) *Human Resource Management: Critical Perspectives on Business and Management*, Vols I, II, III. London: Routledge.

Porter, M. (1986) *Competition in Global Industries*. Boston: Harvard Business School Press.

Punnett, B.J. and Ricks, D.A. (1992) *International Business*. Boston: PWS Kent.

Roche, W.K. and Geary, J.F. (1997) 'Multinationals and industrial relations practices', in Murphy, T.V. and Roche, W.K. (eds), *Industrial Relations in Practice* (Revised and Expanded). Dublin: Oak Tree Press.

Ronen, S. (1989) 'Training the international assignee', in Goldstein, I. (ed.), *Training and Career Development*. San Francisco: Jossey-Bass.

Schaeffer, R. (1989) 'Managing international business growth and international management development', *Human Resource Planning* 34(1), 29–36.

Schuler, R.S., Fulkerson, J.R. and Dowling, P.J. (1991) 'Strategic performance measurement and management in multinational corporations', *Human Resource Management* 30(3), 365–92.

Schuler, R., Dowling, P.J. and De Cieri, H. (1993) 'An integrative framework of strategic international human resource management', *International Journal of Human Resource Management* 4 (4), 717–64.

Schuler, R., Budhwar, P. and Florkowski, G. (2002) 'International human resource management: review and critique', *International Journal of Management Reviews* 4(1), 41–70.

Scullion, H. (1992) 'Strategic recruitment and development of the international manager: some European considerations', *Human Resource Management Journal* 3(1), 57–69.

Scullion, H. (1993) 'Creating international managers: recruitment and development issues', in Kirkbride, P. (ed.), *Human Resource Management in Europe*. London: Routledge.

Scullion, H. (1994) 'Staffing policies and strategic control in British multinationals', *International Studies of Management and Organisation* 3(4), 86–104.

Scullion, H. (1995) 'International human resource management', in Storey, J. (ed.), *Human Resource Management: A Critical Text*. London: Routledge.

Scullion, H. (1997) 'The key challenges for international HRM in the 21st century', in *Association of European Personnel Managers Handbook*. London: Institute of Personnel Managers.

Scullion, H. and Donnelly, N. (1999) 'International HRM in medium sized MNCs: evidence from Ireland', in Brewster, C. and Harris, H. (eds), *Contemporary Issues in European Human Resource Management*. London: Routledge.

Svard, M. and Loustarinen, R. (1982) 'Personnel needs in the internationalising firm', FIBO Publication no. 19. Helsinki: Helsinki School of Economics.

Tung, R.L. (1982) 'Selection and training procedures of U.S. European and Japanese multinationals', *California Management Review* 25(1), 57–71.

Tung, R.L. (1984) 'Strategic management of human resources in the multinational enterprise', *Human Resource Management* 23(2), 129–43.

United Nations (1993) *Small and Medium-sized Transnational Corporations: Role, Impact and Policy Implications*. New York: UN Publications.

Welch, D. and Welch, L. (1994) 'Linking operation mode diversity and IHRM', *International Journal of Human Resource Management* 5(4), 139–64.

Welch, D. and Welch, L. (1997) 'Pre-expatriation: the role of HR factors in the early stages of internationalization', *International Journal of Human Resource Management* 8(4), 402–13.

Young, S. and Hamill, J. (1992) *Europe and the Multinationals*. London: Edward Elgar.

Zeira, Y. (1976) 'Management development in ethnocentric multinational corporations', *California Management Review* 18(4), 34–42.

5

A Typology of International Business Strategies

Pavlos Dimitratos

Introduction

The goal of strategy is the continuous pursuit for and sustainability of economic rents (Amit and Schoemaker, 1993; Bowman, 1974; Mahoney, 1995; Penrose, 1959). Hence, it is posited that international business strategy (IBS) aims at achieving such rents in international markets, and so IBS encompasses all strategic tools targeted on attaining and exploiting a competitive advantage abroad.[1] If viewed in this broad context, one can understand why this term has been defined differently in the related literature. Indeed, researchers have used it in a variety of instances, with no unanimity on what this concept involves. For instance, researchers include the mode of foreign involvement as a related IBS that a firm can implement abroad, but they also include global, multifocal and multidomestic functions as other IBSs without having reached agreement on their definition and classification (Birkinshaw *et al.*, 1995; Fleenor; 1993; Ghoshal, 1987; Harzing, 2000).

This situation generates tension in the international business literature because further advancement of the IBS study appears problematic without attempting to identify and classify the various strategic choices available to the firm abroad. In this conceptual chapter we seek to clarify the IBS construct through a typology[2] of its various manifestations. By doing so, we expect that further development and testing of empirical classifications of IBSs will be facilitated. IBSs examined in this chapter are largely business- rather than corporate-level strategies, since they apparently do not refer to the scope of the firm but rather to how the firm can compete within a particular product-market abroad. Additionally, the content of strategy (that is, what is decided and what must be done) as opposed to the process of strategy-making (how strategy is formed) is explored.

In this chapter, we initially provide an overview of the overall typology referring to IBSs. We then discuss the five dimensions and relevant strategic choices existing for the firm at the overall international marketplace level. Afterwards we elaborate on the strategies at a specific foreign-country level by referring to four related dimensions. We conclude by suggesting future directions for international business researchers stemming from this typology.

International business strategy: context and dimensions

Kutschker and Bäurle (1997) suggest that a firm should decide upon the following four dimensions as far as its IBS is concerned: choice of foreign countries and modes of penetration; extent of localization and globalization in international markets; degree of coordination among scattered worldwide operations; and timing of internationalization plans. Thus, in line with this categorization that provides a good starting point as regards classification of IBSs, we posit that these may be viewed in two broad contexts (Figure 5.1). The first refers to strategic choices in *the overall international marketplace*, that is the total number of countries in which the firm has business activities. These are strategic tools that seek to enhance organizational performance on the 'worldwide map' of the firm. The second dimension refers to strategic choices in *a specific foreign country*. If we assume that the firm has international activities in 10 foreign countries, it has to decide on specific strategic tools in each of them, notwithstanding their likely similarity from one country to another.

We suggest that the dimensions of IBS at the overall international marketplace context include: (a) worldwide integration of operations; (b) responsiveness to individual markets; (c) geographic range of operations; (d) geographic focus of operations; and (e) rate of resource allocation worldwide. The dimensions of IBS within a specific foreign-country context include: (a) level of resources committed; (b) closeness of collaboration; (c) pursuit of competitive advantage; and (d) order/timing of entry. In order to derive this typology we performed an extensive search of the international-business literature focusing on strategies and strategic tools. Related studies were obtained through computer-aided (ABI/Inform, Emerald, Ingenta) and manual searches.

International business strategies within the overall international marketplace

Three dimension – worldwide integration of operations, responsiveness to individual markets, and geographic range of operations – are examined together because they deal with closely related IBSs. The distinction between a global and a multidomestic industry is the starting point in this discussion. Morrison (1990) posits that a global industry is identified by many competing multinationals that market a standardized product worldwide and exhibit a presence in all key international markets. Hout *et al.* (1982) define a global industry as one in which a company's competitive position in one country is critically influenced by its competitive positions in other countries. The opposite of a global industry is the multidomestic industry wherein customer demands and firms' strategies differ across individual countries. A *global strategy* is presumed to be an effective organizational strategic tool in global industries, and similarly a *multidomestic strategy* in multidomestic industries.

Yip (1989) elaborates on the concept of global strategy by arguing that it is characterized by (a) carrying out competitive moves in the whole international market as part of a 'global' competitive plan; (b) locating value-added activities (R&D, production, marketing and sales) in separate places to maximize global efficiency; (c) selecting target countries based on expected gains from a worldwide presence and globalization rather than individual nation benefits; (d) offering a standardized product or service to all markets; and (e) presenting very similar marketing mixes to all countries. Generally, with a global strategy a firm competes worldwide with a uniform plan and a standardized marketing mix. In contrast, with a multidomestic strategy a firm carries out distinct 'national' sub-strategies, adapts its product mix across countries, and, in fact, each of its establishments abroad constitutes a separate profit centre (Hout *et al.*, 1982; Leontiades, 1985; Quelch and Hoff, 1986).

Thus, a multidomestic strategy involves a relatively much higher degree of responsiveness to local needs and requirements, and, furthermore, does not incorporate considerable integration demands of organizational activities at an international level. This is because value-added activities and competitive considerations occur at individual country levels, and hence worldwide integration of operations seems to be minimal. This is the reason why the two strategies take their respective positions in Figure 5.2, which shows all relevant strategies along the dimensions of worldwide integration of operations and responsiveness to individual markets.

In terms of geographic range of operations worldwide, the two strategies might not vary significantly. The likely difference being that to achieve maximum gains, the global strategy with its 'global' plan may call for presence in as many countries as possible in order to result in economies of scale and scope worldwide. Therefore, the global strategy could lie at a higher position compared with its multidomestic counterpart in Figure 5.3, which presents the relevant strategies along the dimensions of geographic range of operations and responsiveness to individual markets. It can be added that numerous researchers (Hamel and Prahalad, 1985; Hout *et al.*, 1982; Johansson and Yip, 1994; Morrison and Roth, 1992) argue that global strategies are associated with superior performance. Nonetheless, others (Baden-Fuller and Stopford, 1991; Morrison *et al.*, 1991; Rugman, 2000) find that firms implementing global strategies are losing out to competitors with regional strategies.

A *regional strategy* (Baden-Fuller and Stopford, 1991; Morrison *et al.*, 1991; Roth, 1992; Schlie and Yip, 2000) appears to be an alternative to its global

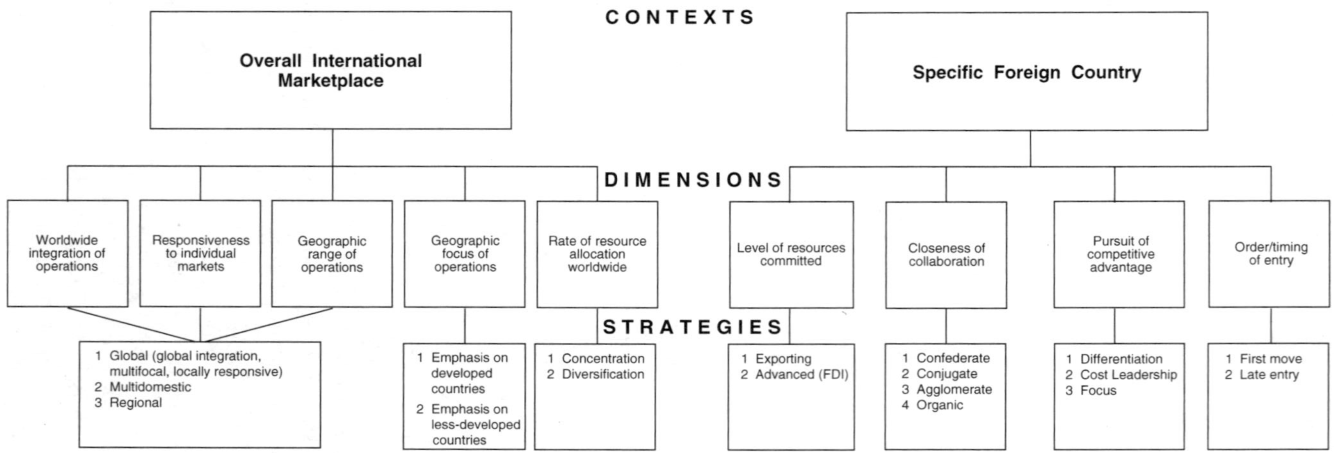

Figure 5.1 A typology of international business strategies

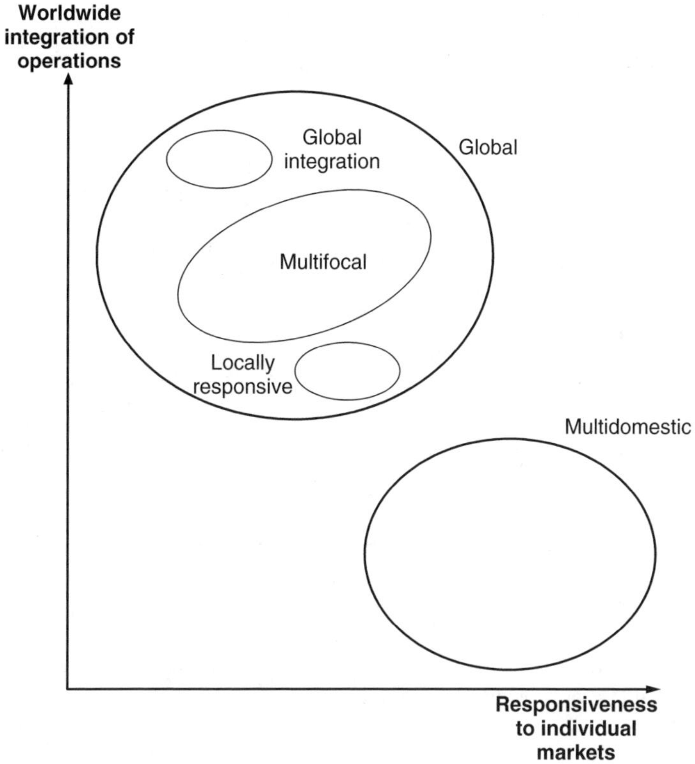

Figure 5.2 A typology of international business strategies along 'worldwide integration of operations' and 'responsiveness to individual markets'

counterpart in global industries. The regional strategy calls for pursuit of competitiveness within regionally trading groups of countries, such as the EU, East Europe, North America, Latin America and so on. Similar country-group characteristics in global industries may call for a regional emphasis due to similar demands by customers, rivals or governments within nation blocs. The scope for a regional strategy occurs since a global industry, wherein the regional strategy is implemented, is different from a multidomestic industry that is characterized by many divergent individual country idiosyncrasies. Consequently, the regional strategy is considered to be similar to the global one, meaning that both regard target countries as one uniform large market. The likely difference between them is that the regional strategy has a more limited geographic range and a higher emphasis on regional demands. This is why these categories of IBS are represented in the way shown in Figure 5.3.

Moreover, in Figure 5.2, three IBSs appear as separate divisions of global strategy. These mainly originate from researchers who introduce the integration–responsiveness framework (Ghoshal, 1987; Prahalad and Doz, 1987; Roth

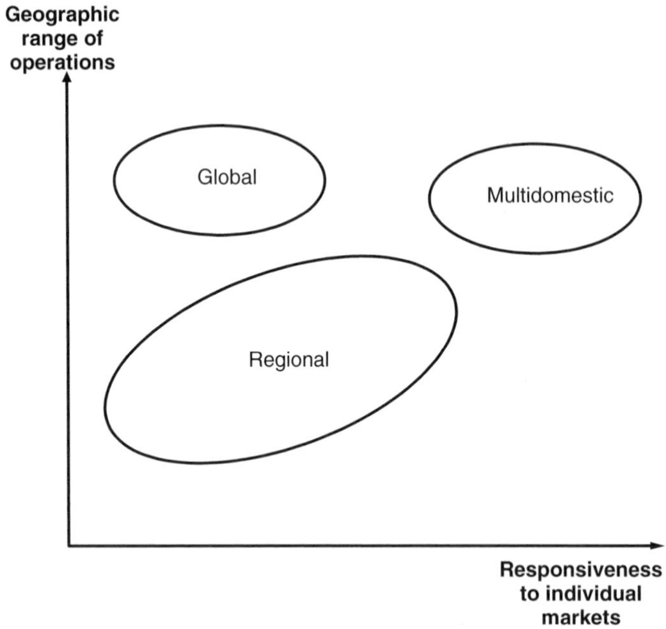

Figure 5.3 A typology of international business strategies along 'geographic range of operations' and 'responsiveness to individual markets'

and Morrison, 1990), which can be applied to global industries and presents these three types of strategies, namely locally responsive, global integration and multifocal.

A firm pursues a *locally responsive strategy* if demands for country-level adaptation are intense. One should note that this strategy would not be considered identical to the multidomestic one, since the former mainly refers to global industries, as the study of Roth and Morrison (1990) shows.[3] A *global integration strategy* is appropriate if intense pressures for worldwide coordination of operations are met in the global industry. Many firms nowadays can implement this strategy, as they are likely to be multinationals with a strong home-base but with operations in foreign countries necessitating effective integration of value-added activities (cf. Hu, 1992). Also, if requirements for both individual-country adaptation and worldwide coordination are present to an intermediate degree, a *multifocal strategy* can be implemented (Martinez and Jarillo, 1991; Prahalad and Doz, 1987).[4]

In short, it is argued that global strategy can embrace locally-responsive, global-integration and multifocal types of strategies.[5] Along with multidomestic and regional strategies, global strategy is posited to be the third major type of

IBS encompassing the dimensions of worldwide integration of operations, responsiveness to individual markets and geographic range of operations.

Geographic focus of operations

Organizational characteristics and strategies can be influenced by conditions of the foreign market (Aulakh *et al.*, 2000; Buckley, 1990; Dunning, 1980, 1988; Erramilli *et al.*, 1997; Itaki, 1991; Kuemmerle, 1999), and a growing stream of literature in international business maintains that developed and less-developed countries are two distinct categories that possess dissimilar characteristics (Aulakh *et al.*, 2000; Dimitratos and Lioukas, 2003; Erramilli *et al.*, 1997; Kuemmerle, 1999). This fourth dimension of IBS deals with whether firms *focus their operations on developed or less developed countries* of the world.[6]

The literature has examined to some degree the relative prevalence of strategic tools and associated performance achieved in the two country groups. Studies in favour of concentrating international business activities on developed countries exist (Christensen *et al.*, 1987; Das, 1994; Denis and Depelteau, 1985; Dominguez and Sequeira, 1993; Douglas, 1996), but in spite of this, evidence in favour of expansion into less-developed countries is present also (Da Rocha *et al.*, 1990). Further complicating this issue, Collins (1990) finds that performances of firms with international operations in both developed and developing countries do not significantly differ.

More studies will have to investigate this interesting theme in the future. Additionally, a related issue refers to whether there are performance 'synergies' between the two country categories or not. It may be likely that because the market characteristics of the two country groups are so fundamentally different, firms fail to achieve such synergies when they simultaneously operate in countries with dissimilar stages of economic development, as Dimitratos and Lioukas (2003) find.

Rate of resource allocation worldwide

In studies that deal with this dimension of IBS in the overall international market, two associated strategic choices are encountered (Ayal and Zif, 1979). A *concentration strategy* is distinguished by the concentration of efforts in only one or a few key countries and the subsequent gradual expansion into new ones over time. Conversely, a *diversification strategy* is characterized by the rapid entry into many foreign countries and the simultaneous allocation of resources across those markets. Although research on these two strategies has largely dealt with activities of exporting firms, the two strategies can be studied in the context of other advanced modes of foreign involvement also.

As regards the question of which of the two strategies leads to superior performance, empirical results are mixed. Most researchers favour a diversification strategy (Cooper and Kleinschmidt, 1985; Lee and Yang, 1990; Piercy, 1981a), but others argue that a concentration strategy yields superior performance (Katsikeas and Morgan, 1994). Still other studies find that the choice between the two strategies does not differentiate between high and low performers abroad (Bourantas and Halikias, 1991; Piercy, 1981b). It is likely that, increasingly, more firms will employ diversification strategies given the increased use of the internet and modern information and technological systems. These systems allow firms to reach international partners and customers easily with fewer available resources than those needed to tap foreign markets in the recent past.

International business strategies in a specific foreign country

Four factors contribute to the IBS in a specific country:

1 Level of resource committed;
2 Closeness of collaboration;
3 Pursuit of competitive advantage;
4 Order/timing of entry.

Level of resources committed

The firm services foreign markets through *exporting* (indirect exporting, direct exporting) or *advanced* (licensing/franchising, joint ventures, strategic alliances, subsidiaries) *modes*. The level of resources committed is high in advanced (or foreign direct investment, FDI) modes, while relatively low in exporting modes. The level of resources is commensurate to the degree of expected return in the foreign market. However, the proposition that FDI modes yield comparatively superior performance (Hill *et al.*, 1990; Leontiades, 1985; Root, 1987; Young *et al.*, 1989) appears to have received little empirical support.

There are two main theoretical streams that attempt to explain the mode of involvement in foreign countries (cf. Andersen, 1997). These are the incremental frameworks (Bilkey and Tesar, 1977; Johanson and Vahlne, 1977, 1990; Johanson and Wiedersheim-Paul, 1975), which are behaviourally oriented, and the transaction-cost theories (Buckley and Casson, 1976; Dunning, 1980, 1988; Hennart, 1982; Rugman, 1981), which are based on economics (for a discussion of these theoretical streams see Andersen, 1997; Coviello and McAuley, 1999; Madhok, 1997).

It should be emphasized that the international-business literature has seemingly treated the mode of foreign involvement as the principal, and often sole, strategic choice that the firm can undertake abroad (Andersen, 1997; Anderson and Gatignon, 1986; Bradley, 1995; Hill *et al.*, 1990; Kogut and Singh, 1988). Nevertheless, this is a narrow view, since modes of involvement available to firms in foreign markets should be regarded as strategic choices in a broader set encompassing other interrelated strategies within a specific foreign country (Fiegenbaum and Lavie, 2000), such as those discussed in this chapter.

Closeness of collaboration

When the organization employs collaborative strategies it reduces environmental uncertainty by preventing unpredictable behaviour by other firms and stabilizing the organization's exchanges with the environment (Astley and Fombrun, 1983; Dollinger and Golden, 1992). Collaborative activities have dramatically increased in international business in recent years, while the degree of interest given by researchers to them has also grown more recently. Dunning (1995) reports that while interorganizational cooperation is not a new phenomenon, the growing significance of such ventures as an organizational form appears to be quite recent.

A classification of collaborative strategies is provided by Astley and Fombrun (1983), Dollinger (1990) and Dollinger and Golden (1992). This classification refers to whether such partnerships are direct or indirect as well as whether they take place with competitors or non-competitors. There are four associated distinctions: First, if activities are direct with competitors, they are of a *confederate type* (for example, engaging in a joint venture with a foreign competitor). Second, if activities are direct with non-competitors, they are of a *conjugate type* (for example, participation in R&D activities with foreign suppliers). Third, if activities are indirect with competitors, they are of an *agglomerate type* (for example, being a member of a trade association in the foreign country). Fourth, if activities are indirect with non-competitors, they are of an *organic type* (for example, having strong liaisons with universities in the foreign country). Direct types assume a higher degree of closeness of collaboration compared with indirect types.

Figure 5.4 presents the different modes of foreign involvement that the firm can implement at a specific foreign country level along the dimensions of level of resources committed and closeness of collaboration. While the level of resources committed is comparatively lower in exporting modes, if the firm uses a sales subsidiary to export its products in the foreign market, the level of resources committed can be very high. But even if the firm does not have a sales subsidiary, and rather exports through agents or distributors located in the foreign market (direct exporting), the level of resources committed in the foreign country may be significant: exporting firms have to devote a sufficient amount of resources in order to locate, develop and maintain effective relationships with foreign intermediaries and partners. Therefore, exporting and FDI modes can involve numerous combination levels of resources committed and closeness of collaboration. The two mode categories should not be viewed narrowly as possessing diagonally different positions in Figure 5.4, and in this chapter we seek to highlight this point.

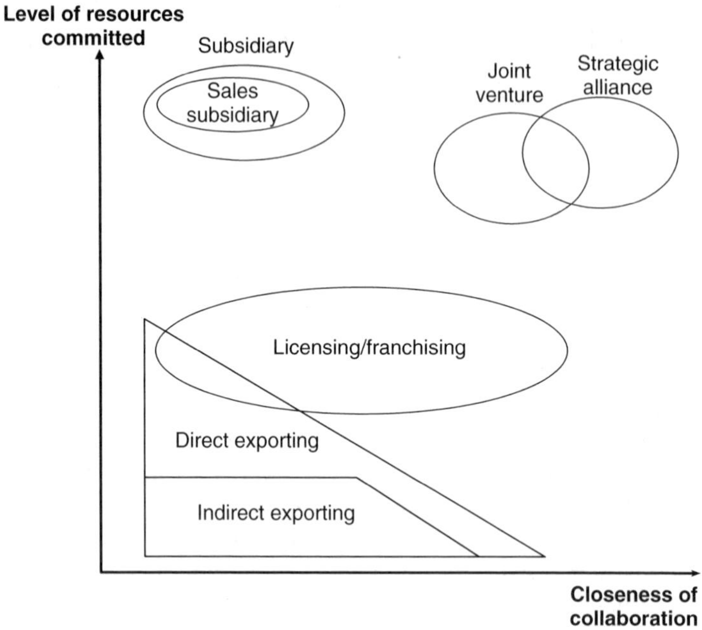

Figure 5.4 A typology of international business strategies along 'level of resources committed' and 'closeness of collaboration'

In addition, the level of closeness of collaboration that a firm can have in its exporting modes may be considerable, inasmuch as the firm can cooperate intimately with distributors, agents, or even competitors in the foreign market. This may be the case for indirect exporting also, in which the firm can export through a larger company located in its domestic market. This last mode presupposes a very close relationship between the two organizations.

Hence, it is valid to posit that a significant part of the international-business literature has treated exporting as a rather basic and premature mode of foreign entry, disregarding that it may necessitate a large extent of organizational resources and networking activities. Furthermore, because exporting is frequently the first step in the firm's international activities, it may involve a high level of 'start-up' internationalization costs, which are likely to be proportionately lower in subsequent FDI modes.

Pursuit of competitive advantage

The traditional view in the strategic-management literature was that the firm through implementation of a competitive strategy aims at outperforming its rivals. Porter (1980, 1985) provides the perhaps most widely used categorization of competitive strategies, which has also been followed in studies investigating international business activities (Katsikeas, 1994; Moon and Lee, 1990; Simon, 1996). A *differentiation strategy*, the first competitive strategy suggested by Porter, seeks to create value perceived as unique by the firm's customers. By implementing a differentiation strategy a firm aims at achieving brand loyalty by customers who are not particularly price-sensitive for the extra value. A differentiation strategy does not disregard costs and prices, but certainly does not make them a first priority either. *Cost leadership*, the second competitive strategy proposed by Porter, is frequently attained by elimination of innovation or advertising costs, removal of 'no-frills' product offerings, thereby emphasing that all products are price competitive and implementation of tight cost controls and scale economies (Porter, 1980).[7] Additionally, when a firm implements a *focus strategy*, the third competitive strategy suggested by Porter, it seeks to satisfy the needs of a market niche and directs its efforts to the demands of this small segment of customers. The focus strategy can be further classified into cost-focus and differentiation-focus substrategies (Porter, 1985). Other classifications of competitive strategies can be found in Hambrick (1983), Miles and Snow (1978), Miller (1986) and Mintzberg (1988) (cf. Campbell-Hunt, 2000).

The modern view in strategic management and international business is that cooperative and competitive activities should not be viewed as mutually exclusive operations in the host market, and many scholars (Bresser, 1988; Dollinger and Golden, 1992; Lado *et al.*, 1997; Ohmae, 1989; Young *et al.*, 1996) adopt a positive stance on the issue of a possible coexistence of collaborative and competitive operations. Nonetheless, repeatedly, strategy researchers have tended to regard competition and cooperation as opposite ends of a bipolar scheme (Lado *et al.*, 1997). A similar approach appears to have erroneously been adopted in international-business research, wherein one of the key questions in studies that investigate entry-mode decisions has been whether a firm should implement a collaborative or a non-collaborative mode of involvement. Studies in international business should examine to a larger extent strategies seeking to achieve a competitive advantage in conjunction with collaborative and other strategies within the specific foreign country context (as is the case in the study of Chetty and Wilson, 2003).

Order/timing of entry

This fourth strategic dimension at the specific foreign country level, which refers to the order of entry into the international market, has not received notable attention in international-business research. In spite of this, the few available studies (Mascarenhas, 1992a, 1992b, 1997; Mitchell *et al.*, 1994; Pan *et al.*, 1999) show that *first movers* in foreign markets maintain higher market shares than *late entrants*. These results verify the research findings on first-mover advantages in a market (Lambkin, 1988; Robinson, 1988; Robinson and Fornell, 1985; Urban *et al.*, 1986). They also explain why many Western companies have been eager to be among the first to enter East European countries, despite the significant political and economic risks existing in them. It would be interesting to investigate what is the level of resources that first movers or late entrants commit upon entry because there is scant research on this topic.[8]

The theme of order/timing of entry into a foreign country can be associated with that of the competitive interplay between competitors in the market, which has received some attention in the international-business literature. The decision, behaviour and timing concerning entry into foreign markets may be affected by actions of competitors in the domestic marketplace (Hennart and Park, 1994; Ito and Pucik, 1993; Kim and Lee, 2001; Mascarenhas, 1986) or in the international marketplace (Dimitratos *et al.*, 2003; Graham, 1974, 1978; Kim and Hwang, 1992; Morrison and Roth, 1992). Collectively these studies suggest that imitation, 'follow the leaders' or 'avoid the leaders' patterns of behaviour can be developed by internationalized firms, possibly influencing their order and timing of entry abroad.

Future research directions

In this chapter we have offered a typology of the various IBSs along with a discussion of what each of these strategies involves. The examination has differentiated between IBSs at the overall international marketplace level and at the level of a specific foreign country. It is expected that through this typology researchers can refer to an integrated conceptual framework involving related strategic tools that a firm employs in order to achieve superior performance abroad. Additionally, international-business scholars may empirically test this suggested framework deriving relevant taxonomies of IBSs.

While the emphasis in this chapter was *solely* on the strategic choices that a firm can decide on and implement abroad, one should also consider that a firm's selection of strategic choices abroad is context-specific. This suggests that the selection of strategic choices can be explained by heterogeneous resource patterns, market opportunities and environmental characteristics (Hennart and Park, 1993, 1994; Melin, 1992; Young *et al.*, 1989; Zou and Cavusgil, 1996). Therefore, effective implementation of an appropriate IBS is contingent on organizational and environmental variables existing in each particular case. For instance, it would be interesting to examine the impact of industry type ('traditional' vs 'knowledge-intensive') and characteristics on the choice of strategies at the overall international marketplace level. Holistic examinations incorporating contextual variables have to take place in order to investigate under what conditions IBSs can produce best results.

Additionally, with the exception of some modes of foreign involvement, it is especially surprising how underinvestigated is the IBS–performance association in the international-business literature (Devinney *et al.*, 2000). It would be particularly interesting to test the association between performance and the global–multidomestic–regional strategy scheme suggested in this chapter. Similarly, the literature has dealt extensively with whether a collaborative entry mode will be selected or not, and has to a significant degree disregarded the performance associations of the various modes of foreign involvement. Undoubtedly, more studies have to investigate empirically performance relationships of IBSs.

Moreover, as regards the dimensions within a specific foreign country context, researchers have to examine relevant strategic choices as a set of interrelated decisions, in which the level of resources committed is only one of four available dimensions. The four-pillar scheme put forward in this chapter can serve as a guideline encompassing all related strategies, because emphasis merely on the mode of foreign involvement tends to offer a restricted and one-sided view of internationalization. Furthermore, another research avenue worth considering would be to examine to what extent strategies at a specific foreign country level are replicated from one country to another for a given firm.

Researchers also have to delve into associations between IBSs of the two contexts. For instance, it would be interesting to find out what is the level of resources that firms with global, multidomestic or regional strategies commit in each of their foreign countries (Hill *et al.*, 1990). Relationships between the dimensions of the two contexts are largely unexplored, with one of the few exceptions being the study by Proff (2002). International business researchers can examine this interesting theme in future studies to analyse possible interdependencies between dimensions of the two contexts.

Notes

1 Although the outcomes of IBSs primarily relate to international markets, the IBS of a firm may use its broader international scope and leverage to develop a competitive advantage also at home. A classic example here is the 'exchange-of-threats behaviour', wherein an effective response for the firm which sees a foreign company invading its home market is to retaliate by entering the foreign firm's own market (Graham, 1974, 1978).

2 Classifications can be expressed either in a typology or a taxonomy scheme. The former is derived conceptually, the latter empirically (McKelvey, 1982; Venkatraman, 1989). As this classification is based on literature sources, it would be a typology rather than taxonomy.

3 Nevertheless, there is no accord on these differences between strategies. For example, in their attempt to differentiate between global and multidomestic strategies, Roth *et al.* (1991) perform an empirical study focusing on business units which all operate in *global* industries.

4 Worldwide integration of operations may be a composite construct. Analytically, Roth (1992) argues that two dimensions are involved in global strategies: configuration and coordination. The former dimension refers to where on the globe the

company will perform each of the activities of the value chain. The latter dimension refers to how such activities in different countries will be associated with one another. Both configuration and coordination can be incorporated in the worldwide integration of operations construct, reinforcing Porter's (1986) related suggestion. Porter's suggestion is that in order for global strategy to succeed, the firm should rely on concentrating its activities on a few countries, on coordinating effectively dispersed activities, or both. The first of these alternatives refers to a geographically concentrated configuration, as the global integration strategy is likely to be; the second to a high degree of coordination, as the locally responsive strategy is likely to be; and the third to a mixture of configuration and coordination, as possibly the multifocal strategy might be.

5 A few researchers (e.g. Devinney *et al.*, 2000) also discuss the 'transnational' strategy that firms can implement in the international marketplace. This term stems mainly from Bartlett and Ghoshal (1989), who refer to four types of corporations that exist in modern industries worldwide, namely global, multinational, international and transnational. Nonetheless, their classification primarily refers to types of *firms* rather than strategies. Also, it is difficult to distinguish transnational and international firms both from each other and from their global and multidomestic counterparts (Harzing, 2000; Leong and Tan, 1993; Prahalad and Doz, 1987; Roth and Morrison, 1990). Hence, we do not include in our typology transnational *strategies* as a separate type of strategy that a firm can pursue abroad.

6 For some firms, emphasis on developed or less-developed countries does not represent a free choice issue, because the type of product, industry or competition can direct a particular course of action. An example here is the firm that produces and markets technologically advanced products. It is almost inevitable that this firm markets its products in developed countries due to their sophisticated demand compared with that of less-developed countries. Additionally, it should be stressed that this dimension concerning geographic focus of operations refers to a great extent to 'market-seekers' (cf. Dunning, 1993). After all, it may be the case that firms which market their products in developed countries source from less-developed ones.

7 The dumping strategy can be considered a separate category of cost-leadership in international business activities. It involves selling a product abroad below the price of the domestic country or below the cost of producing it (e.g. Cateora, 1996). Therefore, a dumping strategy assumes a view of maximizing short-term sales through low prices (Leontiades, 1985).

8 Mascarenhas (1997) finds that the level of committed resources upon entry does not play a decisive role on the subsequent market share in the foreign country.

References

Amit, R. and Schoemaker, P.J.H. (1993) 'Strategic assets and organizational rent', *Strategic Management Journal* 14, 33–46.

Andersen, O. (1997) 'Internationalisation and market entry mode: a review of theories and conceptual frameworks', *Management International Review* 37(2) (special issue), 27–42.

Anderson, E. and Gatignon, H. (1986) 'Modes of foreign entry: a transaction cost analysis and propositions', *Journal of International Business Studies* 17, 1–26.

Astley, W.G. and Fombrun, C.J. (1983) 'Collective strategy: social ecology of organizational environments', *Academy of Management Review* 8, 576–87.

Aulakh, P.S., Kotabe, M. and Teegen, H. (2000) 'Export strategies and performance of firms from emerging economies: evidence from Brazil, Chile, and Mexico', *Academy of Management Journal* 43, 342–61.

Ayal, I. and Zif, J. (1979) 'Market expansion strategies in multinational marketing', *Journal of Marketing* 43(2), 84–94.

Baden-Fuller, C. and Stopford, J.M. (1991) 'Globalization frustrated: the case of white goods', *Strategic Management Journal* 12, 493–507.

Bartlett, C.A. and Ghoshal, S. (1989) *Managing Across Borders: The Transnational Solution.* Boston: Harvard Business School Press.

Bilkey, W.J. and Tesar, G. (1977) 'The export behavior of smaller-sized Wisconsin manufacturing firms', *Journal of International Business Studies* 8(1), 93–8.

Birkinshaw, J., Morrison, A. and Hulland, J. (1995) 'Structural and competitive determinants of a global integration strategy', *Strategic Management Journal* 16, 637–55.

Bourantas, D. and Halikias, J. (1991) 'Discriminating variables between systematic and non-systematic exporting manufacturing firms in Greece', *Journal of Global Marketing* 4(2), 21–38.

Bowman, E.H. (1974) 'Epistemology, corporate strategy, and academe', *Sloan Management Review* 15(2), 35–50.

Bradley, F. (1995) *International Marketing Strategy*. Englewood Cliffs, NJ: Prentice-Hall.

Bresser, R.K.F. (1988) 'Matching collective and competitive strategies', *Strategic Management Journal* 9, 375–85.

Buckley, P.J. (1990) 'Problems and developments in the core theory of international business', *Journal of International Business Studies* 21, 657–66.

Buckley, P.J. and Casson, M.C. (1976) *The Future of Multinational Enterprises*. London: Holmes & Meier.

Campbell-Hunt, C. (2000) 'What have we learned about generic competitive strategy? A meta-analysis', *Strategic Management Journal* 21, 127–54.

Cateora, P.R. (1996) *International Marketing*, 9th edn. Chicago: Irwin.

Chetty, S.K. and Wilson, H.I.M. (2003) 'Collaborating with competitors to acquire resources', *International Business Review* 12, 61–81.

Christensen, C.H., Da Rocha, A. and Gertner, R.K. (1987) 'An empirical investigation of the factors influencing exporting success of Brazilian firms', *Journal of International Business Studies* 18, 61–77.

Collins, J.M. (1990) 'A market performance comparison of U.S. firms active in domestic, developed and developing countries', *Journal of International Business Studies* 21, 271–87.

Cooper, R.G. and Kleinschmidt, E.J. (1985) 'The impact of export strategy on export sales performance', *Journal of International Business Studies* 16(1), 37–55.

Coviello, N.E. and McAuley, A. (1999) 'Internationalisation and the smaller firm: a review of contemporary empirical research', *Management International Review* 39(3), 223–40.

Da Rocha, A., Christensen, C.H. and Da Cunha, C.E. (1990) 'Aggressive and passive exporters: a study in the Brazilian furniture industry', *International Marketing Review* 7(5), 6–15.

Das, M. (1994) 'Successful and unsuccessful exporters from developing countries: some preliminary findings', *European Journal of Marketing* 28(12), 19–33.

Denis, J.E. and Depelteau, D. (1985) 'Market knowledge, diversification and export expansion', *Journal of International Business Studies* 16(3), 77–89.

Devinney, T.M., Midgley, D.F. and Venaik, S. (2000) 'The optimal performance of the global firm: formalizing and extending the integration-responsiveness framework', *Organization Science* 11, 674–95.

Dimitratos, P. and Lioukas, S. (2003) 'Greek perspectives of international entrepreneurship'. In L.-P. Dana, editor, *Research on International Entrepreneurship*. Aldershot, UK: Edward Elgar.

Dimitratos, P., McDonald, F., Tüselmann, H. and Ennis, S. (2003) *The Changing Patterns of Internationalisation: Firms, Markets and Regions*. Göttingen, Germany: Curvillier Verlag.

Dollinger, M.J. (1990) 'The evolution of collective strategies in fragmented industries', *Academy of Management Review* 15, 266–85.

Dollinger, M.J. and Golden, P.A. (1992) 'Interorganizational and collective strategies in small firms', *Journal of Management* 18, 695–715.

Dominguez, L.V. and Sequeira, C.G. (1993) 'Determinants of LDC exporters' performance: a cross-national study', *Journal of International Business Studies* 24, 19–40.

Douglas, M. (1996) 'The strategies and characteristics of exporting SMEs: a study of Peruvian firms', *Journal of Global Marketing* 9(4), 35–56.

Dunning, J.H. (1980) 'Towards an eclectic theory of international production', *Journal of International Business Studies* 11, 9–31.

Dunning, J.H. (1988) 'The eclectic paradigm of international production: a restatement and possible extensions', *Journal of International Business Studies* 19(1), 1–31.

Dunning, J.H. (1993) *Multinational Enterprises and the Global Economy*. London: Addison-Wesley.

Dunning, J.H. (1995) 'Reappraising the eclectic paradigm in an age of alliance capitalism', *Journal of International Business Studies* 26, 461–91.

Erramilli, M.K., Agarwal, S. and Kim, S.-S. (1997) Are firm-specific advantages location-specific too? *Journal of International Business Studies* 28, 479–502.

Fiegenbaum, A. and Lavie, D. (2000) 'Strategic management of MNCs' entry into foreign markets: experience of Israel in the 1990s', *European Management Journal* 18, 93–105.

Fleenor, D. (1993) 'The coming and going of the global corporation', *Columbia Journal of World Business* 28(4), 6–16.

Ghoshal, S. (1987) 'Global strategy: an organizing framework', *Strategic Management Journal* 8, 425–40.

Graham, E.M. (1974) *Oligopolistic Imitation and European Direct Investment in the United States*. Boston: Harvard Business School.

Graham, E.M. (1978) 'Transatlantic investment by multinational firms: a rivalistic phenomenon', *Journal of Post- Keynesian Economics* 1(1), 82–99.

Hambrick, D.C. (1983) 'High profit strategies in mature capital goods industries: a contingency approach', *Academy of Management Journal* 26, 687–707.

Hamel, G. and Prahalad, C.K. (1985) 'Do you really have a global strategy?' *Harvard Business Review* 63(4), 139–48.

Harzing, A.-W. (2000) 'An empirical analysis and extension of the Bartlett and Ghoshal typology of multinational companies', *Journal of International Business Studies* 31, 101–20.

Hennart, J.-F. (1982) *A Theory of Multinational Enterprise*. Ann Arbor, MI: University of Michigan Press.

Hennart, J.-F. and Park, Y.-R. (1993) 'Greenfield vs. acquisition: the strategy of Japanese investors in the United States', *Management Science* 39, 1054–70.

Hennart, J.-F. and Park, Y.-R. (1994) 'Location, governance, and strategic determinants of Japanese manufacturing investment in the United States', *Strategic Management Journal* 15, 419–36.

Hill, C.W.L., Hwang, P. and Kim, W.C. (1990) 'An eclectic theory of the choice of international entry mode', *Strategic Management Journal* 11, 117–28.

Hout, T., Porter, M.E. and Rudden, E. (1982) 'How global companies win out', *Harvard Business Review* 60(5), 98–108.

Hu, Y.-S. (1992) 'Global corporations are national firms with international operations', *California Management Review* 34(2), 107–26.
Itaki, M. (1991) 'A critical assessment of the eclectic theory of the multinational enterprise', *Journal of International Business Studies* 22, 445–60.
Ito, K. and Pucik, V. (1993) 'RandD spending, domestic competition, and export performance of Japanese manufacturing firms', *Strategic Management Journal* 14, 61–75.
Johanson, J. and Vahlne, J.-E. (1977) 'The internationalization process of the firm: a model of knowledge development and increasing foreign market commitments', *Journal of International Business Studies* 8(1), 23–32.
Johanson, J. and Vahlne, J.-E. (1990) 'The mechanism of internationalisation', *International Marketing Review* 7(4), 11–24.
Johanson, J. and Wiedersheim-Paul, F. (1975) 'The internationalization of the firm: four Swedish cases', *Journal of Management Studies* 12, 305–22.
Johansson, J.K. and Yip, G.S. (1994) 'Exploiting globalization potential: U.S. and Japanese strategies', *Strategic Management Journal* 15, 570–601.
Katsikeas, C.S. (1994) 'Perceived export problems and export involvement: the case of Greek exporting manufacturers', *Journal of Global Marketing* 7(4), 29–57.
Katsikeas, C.S. and Morgan, R.E. (1994) 'Differences in perceptions of exporting problems based on firm size and export market experience', *European Journal of Marketing* 28(5), 17–35.
Kim, W.C. and Hwang, P. (1992) 'Global strategy and multinationals' entry mode choice', *Journal of International Business Studies* 23(1), 29–53.
Kim, B. and Lee, Y. (2001) 'Global capacity expansion strategies: lessons learned from two Korean carmakers', *Long Range Planning* 34, 309–33.
Kogut, B. and Singh, H. (1988) 'The effect of national culture on the choice of entry mode', *Journal of International Business Studies* 19, 411–32.
Kuemmerle, W. (1999) 'The drivers of foreign direct investment into research and development: an empirical investigation', *Journal of International Business Studies* 30, 1–24.
Kutschker, M. and Bäurle, I. (1997) 'Three + one: multidimensional strategy of internationalisation', *Management International Review* 37(2), 103–25.
Lado, A.A., Boyd, N.G. and Hanlon, S.C. (1997) 'Competition, cooperation, and the search for economic rents: a syncretic model', *Academy of Management Review* 22, 110–41.
Lambkin, M. (1988) 'Order of entry and performance in new markets', *Strategic Management Journal* 9, 127–40.
Lee, C.S. and Yang, Y.S. (1990) 'Impact of export market expansion strategy on export performance', *International Marketing Review* 7(4), 41–51.
Leong, S.M. and Tan, C.T. (1993) 'Managing across borders: an empirical test of the Bartlett and Ghoshal [1989] organizational typology', *Journal of International Business Studies* 24, 449–64.
Leontiades, J.C. (1985) *Multinational Corporate Strategy – Planning for World Markets*. Lexington, MA: Lexington Books.
Madhok, A. (1997) 'Cost, value and foreign market entry mode: the transaction and the firm', *Strategic Management Journal* 18, 39–61.
Mahoney, J.T. (1995) 'The management of resources and the resource of management', *Journal of Business Research* 33(2), 91–101.
Martinez, J.I. and Jarillo, J.C. (1991) 'Coordination demands of internationalization strategies', *Journal of International Business Studies* 22(3), 429–44.
Mascarenhas, B. (1986) 'International strategies of non-dominant firms', *Journal of International Business Studies* 17(1), 1–25.

Mascarenhas, B. (1992a) 'First-mover effects in multiple dynamic markets', *Strategic Management Journal* 13, 237–43.

Mascarenhas, B. (1992b) 'Order of entry and performance in international markets', *Strategic Management Journal* 13, 499–510.

Mascarenhas, B. (1997) 'The order and size of entry into international markets', *Journal of Business Venturing* 12, 287–99.

McKelvey, B. (1982) *Organizational Systematics – Taxonomy, Evolution, Classification*. Berkeley, CA: University of California Press.

Melin, L. (1992) 'Internationalization as a strategy process', *Strategic Management Journal* 13 (Special Issue), 99–118.

Miles, R.E. and Snow, C.C. (1978) *Organizational Strategy, Structure and Process*. New York: McGraw-Hill.

Miller, D. (1986) 'Configurations of strategy and structure: towards a synthesis', *Strategic Management Journal* 7, 233–49.

Mintzberg, H. (1988) 'Generic strategies: toward a comprehensive framework', in Lamb, R. and Shrivastava, P. eds, *Advances in Strategic Management*, 5. Greenwich, CT: JAI Press.

Mitchell, W, Shaver, J.M. and Yeung, B. (1994) 'Foreign entrant survival and foreign market share: Canadian companies' experience in United States medical sector markets', *Strategic Management Journal* 15, 555–67.

Moon J. and Lee, H. (1990) 'On the internal correlates of export stage development: an empirical investigation in the Korean electronics industry', *International Marketing Review* 7(5), 16–26.

Morrison, A.J. (1990) *Strategies in Global Industries: How U.S. Businesses Compete*. Westpoint, CT: Qorum Books.

Morrison, A.J., Ricks, D.A. and Roth, K. (1991) 'Globalization versus regionalization: which way for the multinational?', *Organizational Dynamics* 19(3), 17–29.

Morrison, A.J. and Roth, K. (1992) 'A taxonomy of business-level strategies in global industries', *Strategic Management Journal* 13, 399–418.

Ohmae, K. (1989) 'The global logic of strategic alliances', *Harvard Business Review* 67(2), 143–54.

Pan, Y., S.L. and Tse, D.K. (1999) 'The impact of order and mode of market entry on profitability and market share', *Journal of International Business Studies* 30, 81–104.

Penrose, E.T. (1959) *The Theory of the Growth of the Firm*. London: Blackwell.

Piercy, N. (1981a) 'British export market selection and pricing', *Industrial Marketing Management* 10, 287–97.

Piercy, N. (1981b) 'Company internationalisation: active and reactive exporting', *European Journal of Marketing* 15(3), 26–40.

Porter, M.E. (1980) *Competitive Strategy – Techniques for Analyzing Industries and Competitors*. New York: The Free Press.

Porter, M.E. (1985) *Competitive Advantage – Creating and Sustaining Superior Performance*. New York: The Free Press.

Porter, M.E. (1986) 'Competition in global industries: a conceptual framework', In Porter, M.E., editor, *Competition in Global Industries*. Boston: Harvard Business School Press.

Prahalad, C.K. and Doz, Y.L. (1987) *The Multinational Mission: Balancing Local Demands and Global Vision*. New York: The Free Press.

Proff, H. (2002) 'Business unit strategies between regionalisation and globalisation', *International Business Review* 11, 231–50.

Quelch, J.A. and Hoff, E.J. (1986) 'Customizing global marketing', *Harvard Business Review* 66(3), 59–68.

Robinson, W.T. (1988) 'Sources of market pioneer advantages: the case of industrial goods industries', *Journal of Marketing Research* 25, 86–94.

Robinson, W.T. and Fornell, C. (1985) 'Sources of market pioneer advantages in consumer goods industries', *Journal of Marketing Research* 22, 305–17.

Root, F.R. (1987) *Entry Strategies for International Markets*. Lexington, MA: Lexington Books.

Roth, K. (1992) 'International configuration and coordination archetypes for medium-sized firms in global industries', *Journal of International Business Studies* 23, 533–49.

Roth, K. and Morrison, A.J. (1990) 'An empirical analysis of the integration-responsiveness framework in global industries', *Journal of International Business Studies* 21, 541–64.

Roth, K., Schweiger, D.M. and Morrison, A.J. (1991) 'Global strategy implementation at the business unit level: operational capabilities and administrative mechanisms', *Journal of International Business Studies* 22, 369–402.

Rugman, A.M. (1981) *Inside the Multinationals*. New York: Columbia University Press.

Rugman, A.M. (2000) *The End of Globalisation*. London: Random House.

Schlie, E. and Yip, G. (2000) 'Regional follows global: strategy mixes in the world automotive industry', *European Management Journal* 18, 343–54.

Simon, H. (1996) *Hidden Champions*. Boston: Harvard Business School Press.

Urban, G.L., Carter, T., Gaskin, S. and Muchia, Z. (1986) 'Market share rewards to pioneering brands: an empirical analysis and strategic implications', *Management Science* 32, 645–59.

Venkatraman, N. (1989) 'Strategic orientation of business enterprises: the construct, dimensionality, and measurement', *Management Science* 35, 942–62.

Yip, G.S. (1989) 'Global strategy in a world of nations', *Sloan Management Review* 31(1), 29–41.

Young, S., Hamill, J., Wheeler, C. and Davies, J.R. (1989) *International Market Entry and Development*. Englewood Cliffs, NJ: Prentice-Hall.

Young, S., Huang, C.-H. and McDermott, M. (1996) 'Internationalization and competitive catch-up processes: case study evidence on Chinese multinational enterprises', *Management International Review* 36(4), 295–314.

Zou, S. and Cavusgil, S.T. (1996) 'Global strategy: a review and an integrated conceptual framework', *European Journal of Marketing* 30(1), 52–69.

Part II

The Role of Culture and Institutions in the Internationalization Process

6

How National Culture Influences International Entry-Mode Choice

Lance Brouthers, Keith Brouthers and George Nakos

Introduction

Do systematic and measurable differences in national cultural values result in predictable cross-national differences in firms' choices between joint ventures and wholly-owned international entry modes? Relationships between national cultural attributes and strategic choice have been found (Geletkanycz, 1997; Schneider, 1989), but still it is unclear which specific national cultural attributes influence entry-mode decisions. For example, Shane (1994), Erramilli (1996) and Kogut and Singh (1988) each found that *national cultural distance* significantly influenced entry-mode selection, and Kogut and Singh (1988) and Erramilli (1996) found two *home-country national cultural attributes* (uncertainty avoidance and power distance) influenced mode selection. Furthermore, Shane (1994) found that *target-country power distance* levels affected mode choice. Shane (1994) provides one possible explanation for these equivocal findings. He suggests that scholars appear to be unsure as to whether home-country culture, target-country culture, or the differences in culture influence firm's mode choice.

No previous study has examined the simultaneous impact of home *and* host-country culture. Yet when firms make international entry-mode decisions they need to deal with both home and host-country cultural influences (Shane, 1994). Thus, past research, by ignoring part of the impact of national culture on mode choice, leaves us at best with an incomplete explanation of the entry-mode choice decision and, at worst, a misleading one. The purpose of this chapter is to provide a more complete understanding of how national culture influences firms' entry-mode decisions. Responding to Shane's (1994) recommendation, this chapter becomes the first to incorporate cultural distance, home-country and host-country culture into a single analysis. We use transaction-cost (TC) theory to investigate *simultaneous* influences of home-country culture, target-country culture and cultural distance on international entry-mode choice. More specifically, we explore the concurrent impact of national cultural distance and two familiar measures of home and target-country culture (power distance and uncertainty avoidance) on international entry-mode choice.

Cultural attributes and mode choices

Transaction-cost theory suggests that firms select the governance structure that offers the most efficient mode of operation. Mode efficiency is concerned with (1) the ability to write complete contracts (which influences the costs of opportunism and shirking), (2) the costs of controlling the actions of host-country personnel, and (3) the costs of monitoring host-country personnel performance (Shane, 1994; Erramilli and Rao, 1993; Gatignon and Anderson, 1988). As detailed below, scholars have suggested that national cultural attributes may affect these costs and, hence, may influence the mode choice decision.

Cultural distance

Kogut and Singh's (1988) initial work suggests that cultural differences influence equity entry-mode choice. Large differences between national cultures typically result in managers having perceptions of higher costs and risks associated with international investment, and hence they prefer joint-venture modes of entry.

In contrast, more recent scholarship using transaction-cost (TC) theory posits that firms entering culturally distant markets prefer to use wholly-owned modes of entry rather than joint ventures (JV) for several reasons. First, differences in cultures may make it impossible for firms to anticipate all contingencies and include them in JV agreements. Second, cultural distance may make enforcement of JV agreements difficult. And third, cultural differences may make it difficult to assess the performance of partner firms (Shane, 1994; Klein, Frazier and Roth, 1990). Each of these conditions increases transaction costs which in turn leads firms to choose wholly-owned modes of entry. Hence, TC theory suggests the following hypothesis:

> H1 As the cultural distance between home and target country increases, managers tend to prefer wholly-owned modes.

Home-country culture

Home-country culture may influence TC perceptions and entry-mode choice because (1) it influences decision-makers' perceptions of target-market risks and costs (Geletkanycz, 1997; Schneider, 1989), and (2) because of differences in trust which may mitigate transaction costs (Doney, Canon and Mullen, 1998; Erramilli, 1996). Two important home-country cultural attributes have been identified in past research: uncertainty avoidance and power distance.

Previous research indicates that managers from home cultures that are characterized by high uncertainty avoidance 'tend to feel uncomfortable dealing with uncertainty' (Geletkanycz, 1997: 620; Nakata and Sivakumar, 1996). Managers from high uncertainty-avoiding cultures perceive JVs as risky because organizational decisions and processes are shared. This increased risk means TC perceptions are also high; managers may suffer from a fear of opportunism and try to establish contractual arrangements that increase monitoring and control costs (Geletkanycz, 1997). To reduce these perceptions of high risk and transaction costs, managers may use highly structured organizations, such as wholly-owned subsidiaries, which minimize the uncertainty of dealing with other cultures' managers and/or management systems (Erramilli, 1996; Hennart and Larimo, 1998).

Conversely, managers from low uncertainty-avoiding cultures are 'more tolerant of different ideas, approaches and concepts' (Geletkanycz, 1997: 620; Nakata and Sivakumar, 1996), and do not perceive cross-cultural work environments as being inherently 'risky'. Managers from low uncertainty-avoiding cultures tend to be 'more willing to delegate, be flexible and assume risks' (Erramilli, 1996: 232), perceive lower TCs, and thus are more likely to use JV modes of entry (Hennart and Larimo, 1998). Thus:

H2a Managers from high uncertainty-avoiding cultures tend to prefer wholly-owned modes of entry.

A number of scholars have suggested that Hofstede's (1980) power-distance attribute may represent individual levels of trust (Erramilli, 1996; Doney *et al.*, 1998; Shane, 1994; Tse, Pan and Au, 1997), and research suggests that managers from high power-distance cultures typically have low levels of trust in others, preferring to retain power and authority (Doney *et al.*, 1998; Tse *et al.*, 1997). Such managers typically desire greater monitoring and control of foreign subsidiaries, which increases TCs (Doney *et al.*, 1998). As a consequence, Tse, Pan and Au (1997) maintain that firms from high power-distance countries prefer wholly-owned modes of entry.

In contrast, managers from low power-distance cultures exhibit higher levels of trust, which reduce TC perceptions (Doney *et al.*, 1998; Erramilli, 1996). Because of these increased trust levels, managers from low power-distance cultures are typically 'more open-minded' and are 'more open to teaming up with other foreign firms' (Tse *et al.*, 1997: 786). They tend to rely on trust, instead of formal monitoring and control systems, and prefer more decentralized modes of entry such as JVs (Doney *et al.*, 1998; Erramilli, 1996). Hence, TC theory suggests:

H2b Managers from high power-distance cultures tend to prefer wholly-owned modes of entry.

Target-country culture

Other scholarship suggests that transaction-cost perceptions and mode choice may be influenced by two target-country cultural attributes: power distance and uncertainty avoidance. Target-country power distance may affect TCs through its influence on opportunism (Shane, 1994), and target-country uncertainty avoidance levels may affect TCs in managing changes in an organization (Harzing and Hofstede, 1996).

Host-country power distance may influence entry-mode choice by affecting the degree of trust in the target market (Shane, 1994, 1993). For instance, Shane (1994, 1993) suggests that in high power-distance cultures trust is low. As a consequence, target-firm personnel may be more willing to engage in opportunistic behaviour, increasing transaction costs. Opportunistic behaviour may be engaged in because target-market workers may not believe they are being treated fairly by the parent firm (Shane, 1993, 1994), and to minimize trust-related problems of opportunism, Shane (1994) suggests using wholly-owned subsidiaries (to safeguard assets).

In low power-distance cultures people are open to change (Geletkanycz, 1997) and have a higher level of trust (Shane, 1994). Cooperation with home-country managers is less of a problem (Harzing and Hofstede, 1996), and opportunistic behaviour is much lower because target-market workers feel a sense of trust in the parent firm. As a consequence, TC perceptions will be low (Harzing and Hofstede, 1996). In such situations joint ventures are preferred (Shane, 1993, 1994). Hence, TC theory suggests:

> H 3a Managers selecting modes of entry into high power-distance cultures tend to prefer wholly-owned configurations.

Research has provided two explanations as to how target-market uncertainty avoidance may influence transaction costs and mode choice. The first explains how uncertainty avoidance levels may influence monitoring and control costs. The second explains how uncertainty avoidance levels may influence opportunistic behaviour and the safeguarding of assets. Both explanations lead to the same hypothesis.

First, personnel in target markets characterized by high uncertainty avoidance typically feel threatened by changes to the status quo (Geletkanycz, 1997; Harzing and Hofstede, 1996). For this reason target-market workers may perceive JVs as less uncertain than wholly-owned modes; in JVs target-market personnel still have some control over the venture. In wholly-owned modes of entry target-market personnel may feel a lack of control (Harzing and Hofstede, 1996; Shane, 1993); High levels of uncertainty avoidance lead to resistance to change, increasing the costs of monitoring and controlling the actions of target-market workers (Harzing and Hofstede, 1996). Joint ventures can reduce these higher costs by relying on the target-market partner firm to monitor and control workers.

In contrast, for target markets low in uncertainty avoidance the introduction of new (even foreign) management is typically not perceived as a threat, making adaptation much easier (Harzing and Hofstede, 1996). Hence, in lower uncertainty-avoidance markets there is less resistance to change (Harzing and Hofstede, 1996). Wholly-owned subsidiaries are preferred because the costs associated with monitoring and control of host-market workers are relatively low.

Doney, Canon and Mullen (1998) provide a second explanation. They suggest that uncertainty-avoidance levels affect the perceived costs and rewards of opportunistic behaviour. Workers in high uncertainty-avoidance cultures strongly resist change and, therefore, do not act opportunistically because they attach a high cost to doing so (getting caught will lead to change). This low affinity for opportunistic behaviour (1) results in lower TC perceptions, and (2) increases the preference for joint-venture modes of entry in high uncertainty-avoidance countries.

Conversely, individuals in low uncertainty cultures are more likely to engage in opportunistic behaviour because they do not perceive the costs of getting caught as being high (they are not afraid of change). This potential for opportunistic behaviour increases TC perceptions; firms respond by using wholly-owned modes of entry to protect firm assets (Doney *et al.*, 1998). Hence, target-market uncertainty-avoidance levels tend to influence both monitoring and control costs as well as opportunism costs such that:

H3b Managers selecting entry modes into low uncertainty-avoiding cultures tend to prefer wholly-owned modes of entry.

Methodology

To test our hypotheses, data were collected from key informants at firms in four home countries (the Netherlands, Germany, Greece and the USA) doing business in five Central and Eastern European target countries (Hungary, Poland, the Czech Republic, Russia and Romania). Dutch data were collected from a sample of 419 Dutch firms selected because they either had indications of investments in Central and Eastern Europe (CEE) or had attended a seminar on doing business in CEE. The German sample was taken from the top 400 firms (based on sales) as recorded in the AMADEUS cd-rom system. The Greek sample of 450 firms came from a variety of sources (Greek newspaper articles, magazine articles, exporter associations as well as various government sources) that identified Greek firms doing business in CEE. US data came from a random sample of 500 firms taken from the Dun and Bradstreet listing of the top 5,000 US firms. A total of 180 usable questionnaires (77 Dutch, 73 German, 16 Greek, 14 US) was obtained for this chapter.[1]

These particular home and host countries were selected for several reasons. First, we needed to gather data on current entry-mode decisions – otherwise our decision-making variables (control variables) would suffer from recall bias. Second, we needed to be able to translate documents (questionnaires, letters and responses) into the appropriate language – otherwise return rates would be unacceptably low (Harzing, 1997). Third, we needed to be present in the home country for data collection (have a local sponsor and return address) – this based on past international surveys (Harzing, 1997) that tend to show extremely low return rates for out-of-country participants. Fourth, we needed a sufficient number of participants to assure an acceptable level of usable responses. These criteria limited potential host countries to Central and Eastern Europe and/or China. Examining the cultural attributes of CEE countries revealed a wide range of attributes (power distance ranged from 95 to 19, while uncertainty avoidance ranged from 95 to 55), and adding China as a host country would add little to that variance (Chinese power distance 80 and uncertainty avoidance 40).

Previous literature about CEE indicates that German, US, Dutch and Greek firms are among the largest investors. Thus, once host countries were selected we examined the home countries that had made the largest number of investments in these host countries.[2]

Dependent variable

The dependent variable was obtained by having firm managers identify the mode of entry for their most recent CEE market investment. As in most previous research efforts that have examined the impact of culture on mode choice (Gatignon and Anderson, 1988; Hennart and Larimo, 1998; Kogut and Singh, 1988; Shane, 1993) we chose to restrict our examination to wholly-owned (95 per cent equity or more) and joint-venture modes of entry.

National cultural variables

National cultural attributes were taken from previous studies (see Table 6.1). Measures of home-country culture were taken from Hofstede and Bond (1988); measures of target-country culture were taken from Brouthers and Brouthers (2001). Similar to Barkema, Shenkar, Vermeulen and Bell (1997), cultural distance was calculated by taking the sum of the absolute value of the difference between home-country and target-country values for all four cultural attributes.[3] Hofstede's measures have been criticized for methodological weaknesses and cultural biases (see Harzing and Hofstede, 1996: 307–9), but, these measures, (1) are 'regarded as the most extensive examination of cross-national values in a managerial context' (Nakata and Sivakumar, 1996: 62); (2) they have been validated in previous

Table 6.1 Cultural attributes by country

Country	*Power distance*	*Uncertainty avoidance*
Netherlands	38	53[1]
Germany	35	65[1]
Greece	60	112[1]
USA	40	46[1]
Poland	50	55[2]
Czech Republic	35	60[2]
Hungary	19	83[2]
Russia	95	75[2]
Romania	90	95[2]

Sources: [1] Based on data from Hofstede and Bond (1988); [2] based on data from Brouthers and Brouthers (2001).

studies (see Harzing and Hofstede, 1996); and (3) were the measures used in most past studies that examined national culture's influence on entry-mode choice. For these reasons, we used Hofstede's measures in our effort to gain a better understanding of the relationship between national cultural attributes and entry-mode choice.

Control variables

We controlled for ownership, location and internalization variables. Previous research has found these types of variables can be used to predict entry-mode choice (Brouthers, Brouthers and Werner, 1999; Dunning, 1993; Agarwal and Ramaswami, 1992).

Ownership variables included firm size, international experience and product differentiation. We followed Gatignon and Anderson's (1988) approach and measured *firm size* as the total number of employees worldwide. *International experience* was based on the number of years of experience outside the home country (Agarwal and Ramaswami, 1992). *Product differentiation* was determined using three Likert-type questions (Cronbach alpha = .67) which examined the level of training of personnel, the ability to produce new products or services, and the level of resource availability within the firm (Agarwal and Ramaswami, 1992; Brouthers *et al.*, 1999).

Location variables included market potential and investment risk. *Market potential* was identified using a set of five Likert-type questions (alpha = .69) which examined the market and growth potential in the target market, the acceptability of the firm's products or services and the host government attitude towards the industry and foreign firms in general (Agarwal and Ramaswami, 1992; Brouthers *et al.*, 1999). We used a set of three Likert-type questions to measure *investment risk* (alpha = .77); these questions examined the stability of the political, social and economic conditions in the target market, the risk of repatriating/converting income, and the risk of expropriations in the target market (Agarwal and Ramaswami, 1992; Brouthers *et al.*, 1999).

Finally, internalization variables (*contractual risks*) were measured with a set of three Likert-type questions (alpha = .65) which measured the costs of making and enforcing agreements, the costs of maintaining quality standards, and the risk of dissipation of proprietary know-how (Agarwal and Ramaswami, 1992; Brouthers *et al.*, 1999).

In addition, scholars have noted that industry type and legal restrictions may also influence mode choice. Consistent with Kogut and Singh (1988), we included a variable, *industry type*, which was given the value of 0 if the firm was a manufacturer and a value of 1 if the firm was a service provider. To control for potential legal restrictions (Gatignon and Anderson, 1988) we included a variable, *legal restrictions*, which was measured with a single Likert-type question that read, 'At the time you entered this country, were there restrictions on the mode of servicing the market, i.e. were you restricted to licensing or joint venture modes?', covering the range 1 (many restrictions) to 7 (few restrictions).[4]

Findings

The data were analysed using logistic regression analysis (Hair, Anderson, Tatham and Black, 1995). Prior to running the logistic regression tests, a correlation analysis was prepared (Table 6.2), and numerous significant correlations were found between the variables. To test for multicollinearity we examined variance inflation factors (VIF) for the variables in our regression equations, and VIF scores ranged from 1.1 to 6.6. None of the VIF scores was greater than 10.0, the value suggested by Hair *et al.* (1995) as indicating multicollinearity.

Table 6.3 shows the results of the logistic regression analyses used to test the influence of home, target and cultural distance attributes on entry-mode choice. Model 1 shows the impact of the control variables on mode choice; this model was significant ($p = .00$) with a moderate chi-square (40.20) and explained 70.35 per cent of the mode-choice decisions, higher than the 55 per cent explained by chance. Model 2 shows the results of adding the cultural variables to the analysis, and this model was significant ($p = .00$) and the increase in chi-square value (13.90) was also significant ($p < .01$). Model 2 explained 77.91 per cent of the mode choices, substantially higher than the chance rate.

All five cultural measures were significantly related to mode choice. Support was found for (a) hypothesis 1, *firms entering culturally-distant markets preferred wholly-owned modes of entry* ($p < .05$), (b) hypothesis 2a, *firms from high uncertainty-avoiding home cultures preferred wholly-owned modes* ($p < .05$), and (c) hypothesis 3b, *firms entering low uncertainty-avoiding markets preferred wholly-owned modes* ($p < .01$). We found the opposite of what was hypothesized for our two measures of power distance (hypotheses 2b and 3a): firms from high

Table 6.2 Correlation matrix

Variables		*Mean*	*s.d.*	*1*	*2*	*3*	*4*	*5*	*6*	*7*	*8*	*9*	*10*	*11*	*12*	*13*
1	Size	17.5 k	45.3 k	–												
2	Int exp	41.4	30.5	.31*	–											
3	PD-H	43.9	10.6	–.12	–.29*	–										
4	UA-H	73.0	26.0	–.13	–.22*	.77*	–									
5	PD-T	59.4	28.3	.14	–.13	.27*	.20*	–								
6	UA-T	69.4	13.6	–.04	–.10	.35*	.39*	.33*	–							
7	C.D.	22.7	10.0	.14	.01	.10	–.18	.60*	.57*	–						
8	C.Risk	4.0	1.3	–.09	–.12	.39*	.24*	.41*	.25*	.22*	–					
9	I.Risk	4.6	1.3	–.04	.18	–.46*	–.40*	–.52*	–.39*	–.26*	–.58*	–				
10	P.Dif.	5.1	1.1	.24*	.17	.00	–.11	–.01	.02	.08	.03	–.07	–			
11	M.Pot.	5.2	0.9	.10	.02	–.27*	–.17.	–.01	–.03	.06	–.25*	.19	.01	–		
12	Type	0.3	0.5	–.16	–.16	.00	–.07	–.03	–.19	.01	.01	.06	.06	–.12	–	
13	Legal	4.8	1.9	–.32*	–.10	–.03	.03	–.22*	–.16	–.26*	–.12	.25*	–.12	.06	–.13	–
14	Mode	0.6	0.5	.20*	.29*	–.18	–.15	–.15	–.33*	–.14	–.10	.22*	.20	–.02	.13	.09

Note: * $p < .01$, $n = 172$, H = home country, T = target country.

Table 6.3 Logistic regression results

	Model 1	*Model 2*
Power distance – Home		−1.19*
		(.67)
Uncertainty avoidance – Home		1.87*
		(.82)
Power distance – Target		−.46+
		(.32)
Uncertainty avoidance – Target		−1.27**
		(.40)
Cultural distance		.94*
		(.47)
Firm size	.38**	.35*
	(.16)	(.17)
Experience	.57**	.52**
	(.20)	(.22)
Prod. differentiation	.35+	.45*
	(.22)	(.24)
Market potential	−.13	−.16
	(.20)	(.23)
Investment risk	.40*	.28
	(.23)	(.26)
Contractual risk	.15	.34+
	(.22)	(.25)
Industry type	.56**	.42*
	(.21)	(.22)
Legal restrictions	.44**	.42*
	(.19)	(.20)
Constant	.30	.65*
	(.19)	(.34)
n	172	172
chi-square	40.20	54.10
change in chi-square		13.90**
correctly classified	70.35	77.91
Significance	.0000	.0000

Note: $+p<.10$, $*p<.05$, $**p<.01$ (one-tailed tests), joint venture = 0.

power-distance cultures ($p<.05$) and firms entering high power-distance markets ($p<.10$) preferred joint-venture modes.

Discussion, limitations and implications

We began this chapter by noting that previous international entry-mode research, which examined both cultural distance and individual attributes of national culture, had begun to ask which components of national culture relate to mode decisions (Erramilli, 1996; Hennart and Larimo, 1998; Tse *et al.*, 1997; Shane, 1994). In this chapter we have attempted to advance this new line of inquiry by using TC theory to explain the simultaneous influence of two home-country, two host-country, and cultural-distance measures on the international entry-mode choices of Western firms entering CEE. Hence, we have extended previous research by investigating a more complete set of national cultural attributes, examining entry-mode selection from home-country and host-country (as well as cultural differences) perspectives.

Our results show that a firm's TC perceptions and, as a consequence, mode choice appears to be influenced by facets of home-country culture, target-country culture and cultural distance. We found that (1) home-country power distance, (2) home-country uncertainty avoidance, (3) target-country uncertainty avoidance, (4) target-country power distance, and (5) national cultural distance all significantly influenced mode choice. When all five cultural factors were considered simultaneously, the impact of the measures was not always in the predicted direction.

As hypothesized, it appears that wholly-owned modes were preferred when target-country uncertainty avoidance was low, when home-country uncertainty avoidance was high, and when cultural distance was high. Contrary to our TC-based predictions, joint ventures were preferred when home-country power distance and target-country power distance were high.

Strong and Weber (1998) provide one possible TC explanation for why our power-distance results were the opposite of what was hypothesized; power distance may not be a reliable proxy for trust, and instead may represent attitudes towards authority. In high power-distance cultures individuals are more inclined to respect and honour authority, hence reducing the TCs related to monitoring and controlling activities and encouraging the use of joint ventures. Conversely, in low power-distance cultures individuals typically prefer to operate without strict hierarchical controls. These more self-interested people create potential opportunism problems, which, in turn, leads to higher TC perceptions resulting in firms' preferring wholly-owned modes of entry. Future research efforts may wish to explore this issue.

We found support for the influence of several control variables on mode choice. Similar to Agarwal and Ramaswami (1992) and consistent with Dunning's (1993) OLI framework, we found that large firms and firms with greater experience preferred wholly-owned modes. Again, consistent with Dunning's (1993) framework, we found that firms with greater product differentiation, firms perceiving higher contractual risk, and firms entering markets with few legal restrictions preferred wholly-owned modes. We found no support for the influence of the location variables (market potential or investment risk) on mode choice. It may be that target-country cultural variables are more important than other location variables in determining mode choice, and future research efforts along these lines may help to clarify this issue. Finally, as suggested by Erramilli and Rao (1993), we found that service firms had a greater preference for wholly-owned modes than did manufacturing firms.[5]

Limitations

Our work has limitations. First, only estimated measures of Hofstede's (1980) cultural attributes were available for the target countries; actual cultural attributes may differ widely which may create a different set of findings and behavioural relationships. Second, we only utilized Hofstede's four original dimensions of culture, whilst Hofstede has since added a fifth dimension; however, no estimates of this attribute were available for the CEE locations. In addition, as pointed out earlier in the chapter, there is some debate about the reliability of Hofstede's measures; future studies using other measures of culture may help resolve this issue.

Management implications

In this chapter we used TC theory to examine the simultaneous influence of two home-country, two host-country, and cultural distance measures on entry-mode choice and found that international entry-mode choices appear to be influenced by all three cultural components. This has several implications for managers wishing to make international entry-mode decisions. First, it appears that managers consider not only the traditional issue of cultural distance, but also take into account their own national cultural biases as well as the potential benefits/problems associated with host-country cultural behaviour when choosing entry modes. Therefore, eliminating any of the three cultural components may significantly alter the international entry-mode choice.

Second, when choosing an international entry mode managers may need to consider the host-country culturally-based attitudes of potential employees/ managers. For instance, entering host countries with trusting cultures may provide firms with greater entry-mode choice flexibility than entering countries where the culture is untrusting. Host-country-specific attributes combined with home-country attitudes may significantly alter which entry mode a firm chooses.

Finally, firms wishing to expand internationally through alliances (both equity-based joint ventures and non-equity-based licensing agreements) may also wish to consider home-country, host-country and cultural-distance implications. Alliances require trust and are normally associated with greater risk (less control). Firms need to consider both their home-country cultural attitudes towards trust and risk as well as the attitudes of potential partner organizations. Assessing both these criteria may help a firm select better partner organizations and lead to more successful alliances.

Notes

1 We had responses from 47 per cent of firms contacted. Of those, the majority indicated that they did not have operations in the target markets used in this chapter. A total of 386 entries was provided in 21 different CEE markets.
2 Adding specific third-world home countries (like Guatemala, Malaysia, Panama or the Philippines) would have increased the home-country power-distance cultural attribute variation. Unfortunately, firms from these countries have made few investments in CEE markets, making data collection unfeasible.
3 The Kogut and Singh (1988) formula for calculating cultural differences was not used because the estimated target-market values did not have variance values to complete the formula.
4 Responding firms tended to be very large (average worldwide employment was 32,346 and ranged from 6 to 315,000), and also very experienced internationally. On average, respondents had over 41 years, international experience (ranging from 1 to 98). Our respondents made 39 investments in the Czech Republic, 50 in Poland, 28 in Hungary, 44 in Russia and 12 in Romania. Seventy-two of the investments were joint ventures, while 100 were wholly-owned subsidiaries. Finally, because we were dealing primarily with the largest firms in each country, there were many more manufacturing firms than there were service firms. Approximately 70 per cent of our respondents were manufacturing firms while about 30 per cent were service firms.
5 Typically, a service firm is able to establish a wholly-owned subsidiary at a lower cost than a manufacturing firm (Erramilli and Rao, 1993). In addition, service-firm competitive advantage is typically derived through intangible knowledge, which can more easily be transferred within an organization than between organizations; this encourages the use of wholly-owned subsidiaries (Erramilli and Rao, 1993).

References

Agarwal, S. (1994) 'Socio-cultural distance and the choice of joint ventures: a contingency perspective', *Journal of International Marketing* 2(2), 63–80.

Agarwal, S. and Ramaswami, S.N. (1992) 'Choice of foreign market entry mode: impact of ownership, location, and internalization factors', *Journal of International Business Studies* 23(1), 1–27.

Barkema, H.G., Shenkar, O., Vermeulen, F. and Bell, J.H.J. (1997) 'Working abroad, working with others: how firms learn to operate international joint ventures', *Academy of Management Journal* 40(2), 426–42.

Brouthers, K.D. and Brouthers, L.E. (2001) 'Explaining the national cultural paradox'. *Journal of International Business Studies* 32(1), 177–89.

Brouthers, L.E., Brouthers, K.D. and Werner, S. (1999) 'Is Dunning's eclectic framework descriptive or normative?', *Journal of International Business Studies* 30(4), 831–44.

Doney, P.M., Canon, J.P. and Mullen, M.R. (1998) 'Understanding the influence of national culture in the development of trust', *Academy of Management Review* 23(3), 601–20.

Dunning, J.H. (1993) *Multinational Enterprises and the Global Economy*. Harlow: Addison-Wesley.

Erramilli, M.K. (1996) 'Nationality and subsidiary ownership patterns in multinational corporations', *Journal of International Business Studies* 27(2), 225–48.

Erramilli, M.K. and Rao, C.P. (1993) 'Service firms' international entry-mode choice: a modified transaction-cost analysis approach', *Journal of Marketing* 57(July), 19–38.

Gatignon, H. and Anderson, E. (1988) 'The multinational corporation's degree of control over foreign subsidiaries: an empirical test of a transaction cost explanation', *Journal of Law, Economics and Organization* 4(Fall), 305–36.
Geletkanycz, M.A. (1997) 'The salience of "Culture's Consequences": the effects of cultural values on top executive commitment to the status quo', *Strategic Management Journal* 18(8), 615–34.
Hair, J.F. Jr., Anderson, R.E., Tatham, R.L. and Black, W.C. (1995) *Multivariate Data Analysis: With Readings*, 4th edn. New Jersey: Prentice-Hall.
Harzing, A.W. (1997) 'Response rates in international mail surveys: results of a 22 country study', *International Business Review* 6(6), 641–65.
Harzing, A.W. and Hofstede, G. (1996) 'Planned change in organizations: the influence of national culture', in Bamberger, P.A., Erez, M. and Bacharach, S.B. (eds), *Research in the Sociology of Organizations*. London: JAI Press, 14(1), 297–340.
Hennart, J.F. and Larimo, J. (1998) 'The impact of culture on the strategy of multinational enterprises: does national origin affect ownership decisions?' *Journal of International Business Studies* 29(3), 515–38.
Hofstede, G. (1980) *Culture's Consequences*. New York: Sage.
Hofstede, G. and Bond, M.H. (1988) 'The Confucius connection: from cultural roots to economic growth', *Organizational Dynamics* 16(4), 4–21.
Klein, S., Frazier, G.L. and Roth, V.J. (1990) 'A transaction cost analysis model of channel integration in international markets', *Journal of Marketing Research* 27(May), 196–208.
Kogut, B. and Singh, H. (1988) 'The effect of national culture on the choice of entry mode', *Journal of International Business Studies*, 19(Fall), 411–32.
Nakata, C. and Sivakumar, K. (1996) 'National culture and new product development: an integrative review', *Journal of Marketing* 60(1), 61–72.
Schneider, S.C. (1989) 'Strategy formulation: the impact of national culture', *Organization Studies* 10(2), 49–168.
Shane, S.A. (1993) 'The effect of cultural differences in perceptions of transaction costs on national differences in the preference for international joint ventures', *Asia Pacific Journal of Management* 10(1), 57–69.
Shane, S.A. (1994) 'The effect of national culture on the choice between licensing and direct foreign investment', *Strategic Management Journal* 15(4), 627–42.
Strong, K. and Weber, J. (1998) 'The myth of the trusting culture', *Business/Society* 37(2), 157–83.
Tse, D.K., Pan, Y. and Au, K.Y. (1997) 'How MNC's choose entry modes and form alliances: the China experience', *Journal of International Business Studies* 28(4), 779–805.

7

Impact of National Culture Differences on MNC Subsidiary Management

James H. Taggart and Jennifer M. Taggart

Introduction

The impact of differences in national culture has been among the most frequently and deeply researched international business topics in the last 20 years. Much of this stems from the natural inquisitiveness of the academic researcher; some of it has been driven by an obligation to ease the complex cross-border task of managers in multinational companies (MNCs); and yet other research seems to be motivated by a rejection of the basic notion that the culture of a nation may be encapsulated in a few quantitative dimensions, perhaps tending to caricature the individual as an unwanted consequence.

However, the importance of the topic may not be doubted, and Hofstede (1991) sees it as a natural outcome of the globalization of markets. National culture differences can have an enduring impact on the conduct and result of international business negotiations, affecting the use and training of expatriate managers, with extensive implications for a MNC's choice of entry mode into a new foreign market, especially when this includes some form of extended cooperation with host-country nationals and institutions. Cross-border cultural difficulties also play a major role in the nature and extent of international coordination, though researchers like Porter (1986), Martinez and Jarillo (1991) and Moon (1994) largely ignore this.

Koopman (1991) emphasizes the need for compatibility between a firm's strategy and the nature of the cultural differences it faces. This approach also encompasses the management of change on an international basis, focusing on the need to sensitize managers to the issues involved, especially those managers who are active across the headquarters–subsidiary interface. In effect, the levels of shared values, and understanding of those (mainly cultural) ideals that are not shared, limit the rate and extent of change and strategic transf[illegible]ion.

Viewing management from a strictly national basis is becoming an i[illegible] problematic standpoint. Jackson (1995) points out that even h[illegible] managers have to deal more widely with overseas customers, suppliers and regulators. This inevitably brings them into contact with different national cultures and, accordingly, different ways of approaching and dealing with the same situation. In this context, Puffer (1996) makes the evident point that managers with international experience are invaluable in the MNC. Even where such an executive is not familiar with the cultural norms in a particular host country, s/he will at least understand that different norms and attitudes are at work.

Cross-cultural management is not only about problems. As Schneider and Barsoux (1997) have indicated, every cultural interaction is an opportunity for the international manager to learn 'new possibilities, new ways of thinking, new ways of learning'. The purpose of this chapter is to look at such learning opportunities by assessing the impact of national culture differences between home and host countries on the way MNC subsidiaries in Britain may be managed. The results of a postal survey are discussed, focusing on the influence of cultural differences on subsidiary performance and various organizational attributes. Implications of the findings for academics, managers and policy-makers are reviewed and some conclusions drawn.

Conceptual background

Schneider and Barsoux (1997) define national culture as follows:

> Culture is founded on basic assumptions (where things are taken for granted, neither challenged or questioned). They give rise to different beliefs and values, and manifest themselves in different behaviours and artefacts.

Hofstede (1991) gives a somewhat different perspective, though it is clearly complementary to that above:

> Culture in the broader sense is a collective phenomenon. It is the collective programming of the mind which distinguishes one group or category of people from another.

Nations and cultures have generally been equated in the management literature and, indeed, most studies compare managers from different countries. Though this approach has occasionally been questioned (see for example Smith, 1992), it is adopted here as an appropriate methodology. Hofstede's (1980, 1991) seminal work draws principally on management theory, cross-cultural psychology and organizational psychology to explore the concept of national cultures and their differences. From a very large empirical study of IBM's subsidiaries in many countries he derived four primary determinants of national culture that have been used in many subsequent studies by researchers from many countries. These four dimensions of culture are both mutually exclusive and insightful:

- *Power distance*: the extent to which less-powerful members of a group accept and expect that power be unequally distributed.
- *Individualism versus collectivism*: in individualist societies ties between individuals and groups are loose, individuals and families are expected to be self-sufficient. In collectivist societies, from birth onwards, people are associated with strong cohesive in-groups, extended families that offer protection in return for undivided loyalty.
- *Masculinity versus femininity*: Hofstede argues that masculine values contain a dimension of assertiveness and competitiveness not present in feminine values. Masculinity pertains to societies in which social roles are distinct. In feminine societies, gender roles overlap.
- *Uncertainty avoidance*: describes a society's tolerance for uncertainty and ambiguity. Uncertainty-avoiding cultures try to minimize the possibility of unstructured situations by strict laws and rules, safety and security measures and a belief in the absolute truth of religion. People from these cultures tend to be more emotional and motivated by inner nervous energy. Those from uncertainty-accepting cultures are more tolerant, less bigoted and tend to have fewer rules.

Performance has been closely linked with corporate strategy for at least 25 years (see Hofer and Schendel, 1978). According to Schein (1985), there is a link between culture and the way a firm develops, implements and assesses its broad strategy objectives. He recognizes five strategy and performance questions that may be linked to a thriving organizational culture, and it may be supposed that these could have similar linkages with aspects of national culture:

- *Mission and strategy*: obtaining a shared understanding of core mission, primary task, manifest and latent functions.
- *Goals*: developing consensus on goals, as derived from the core mission.
- *Means*: developing consensus on the means to be used to attain goals, such as organization structure, division of labour, reward system and authority system.
- *Measurement*: developing consensus on the criteria to be used in measuring how well the firm is fulfilling its goals.
- *Correction*: developing consensus on the appropriate remedial or repair strategies to be used if goals are not being met.

Weick (1985) went a step further, arguing that strategy and culture are one and the same, but Fiol (1991) is more likely to be right in suggesting that cultural belief systems provide the 'glue' that binds the customs of the company to its strategic requirements. Prahalad and Bettis (1986) have also argued that the way in which managers perceive and utilize tangible assets is as big a contributor to competitive advantage and firm performance as is the actual quantity and nature of those assets. Competitive performance, say Murray and Richardson (2000), must be defined by effectiveness, efficiency and speed, but they suggest a need for cultural sensitivity within the firm by underlining the importance of a shared sense of vision and strategic intent.

The notion of corporate culture was popularized by Peters and Waterman (1982) and Deal and Kennedy (1982), but Mowday *et al.* (1982) articulated the concept more formally. They depicted corporate culture as encompassing a strong belief in and acceptance of the organization's goals and values, a willingness to exert considerable effort on its behalf, and a strong desire to maintain membership of the firm. Hofstede (1991) underlined the close connection, in the situation of the international firm, between national and corporate cultures. Lau and Ngo (1996) have established four types of corporate culture that embrace these ideas, and their results were confirmed by a further detailed study by Dosoglu-Guner (2000). The four types are:

- *Group culture* that has a primary focus on human relations within the internal organizational structure.
- *Developmental culture* that emphasizes flexibility and change, particularly in the external environment.
- *Hierarchical culture* focuses on internal stability, uniformity coordination and efficiency.
- *Rational culture* that centres on productivity, performance-goal fulfilment and achievement.

Procedural justice is about how people judge the fairness of social decision-making (Lind and Earley, 1992), and is a powerful determinant of conformity with group rules and laws. In the industrial context, it also influences whether managers' decisions are perceived to be ethical and unbiased. Kim and Mauborgne (1993) adapted the concept to international business management, linking it to the effective implementation of MNC global strategy. Thus, the link with firm performance is fairly explicit. Pillai *et al.* (1999) have developed good evidence of cross-cultural differences with respect to procedural justice, and this may be especially important at the headquarters–subsidiary interface.

According to O'Donnell (2000), decision-making autonomy at the level of the MNC subsidiary refers to the extent to which it has influence over its business activities, while subsidiaries with high autonomy allow their top managers to exercise greater discretion in dealing with local demands. As many of these local requirements are at least partly driven by local customs and needs, this suggests a link with national culture. This is supported by O'Donnell's (2000) view that one important way to manage foreign subsidiaries entails such culture-sensitive elements as contact among subsidiary managers, joint decision-making with the HQ, and inter-subsidiary committees.

Research questions

This chapter poses a general research problem. Do cultural differences between headquarters and foreign subsidiary have a systematic impact on the affiliate's organizational attributes like performance, corporate culture, procedural justice and autonomy? Hofstede's (1991) underlying message is that MNCs will benefit economically by reducing cultural conflict within its routines, operations and management activities. More specifically, both individualism and high power distance appear to have a negative impact on economic growth (Franke *et al.*, 1991); there is, in addition, a suggestion that masculinity is positively correlated with economic performance. Jain and Tucker (1995) argue that uncertainty avoidance may be positively linked with long-term performance objectives. In the case of all four Hofstede indices, it seems reasonable to suggest that smaller differences between the home country and the foreign subsidiary will yield less friction, more cooperation, and better potential for improved performance. Thus, we have the proposition:

> H1 Higher levels of subsidiary performance will be associated with lower differences of power distance, individualism, masculinity and uncertainty avoidance, as well as lower levels of overall cultural distance.

Both Hofstede (1991) and Smith (1992) maintain that a strong link exists between national culture and corporate culture, as Lau and Ngo's (1996) empirical study confirmed. It may be argued that such links apply to cultural distance as well as to home-country culture, hence the first research question:

> RQ1 Does the predominant corporate culture at the MNC subsidiary vary systematically with differences in power distance, individualism, masculinity and uncertainty avoidance, as well as differences in overall cultural distance?

Kim and Mauborgne (1993) have indicated clearly that high levels of procedural justice positively affect subsidiary managers' feelings of commitment, trust and satisfaction with the outcomes of HQ decisions. This, in turn, leads subsidiary managers to a higher level of compliance with HQ strategy aims and directives. They found that this applies more powerfully in global than in multidomestic industries which suggests, following the general argument of Jain and Tucker (1995), that there is a national cultural dimension at work here. The direction of its impact has not, however, been explored by previous research. By a similar process of reasoning, Vachani's (1999) identification of a link between MNC subsidiary autonomy and the nature of the parent company's global diversification may indicate some, as yet unidentified, link with national culture differences. Note, though, O'Donnell's (2000) warning that interdependence among sister subsidiaries may be at least as important as the hierarchical view of the HQ–subsidiary relationship. Accordingly, we may pose the following research questions:

RQ2 Does the level of procedural justice at the MNC subsidiary vary systematically with differences in power distance, individualism, masculinity and uncertainty avoidance, as well as differences in overall cultural distance?

RQ3 Does the level of autonomy at the MNC subsidiary vary systematically with differences in power distance, individualism, masculinity and uncertainty avoidance, as well as differences in overall cultural distance?

Young *et al.*'s (1988) observation that the age of a subsidiary and its level of exports both appeared to vary with subsidiary ownership lead to two further corresponding research questions:

RQ4 Does the age the MNC subsidiary vary systematically with differences in power distance, individualism, masculinity and uncertainty avoidance, as well as differences in overall cultural distance?

RQ5 Does the MNC subsidiary's export propensity vary systematically with differences in power distance, individualism, masculinity and uncertainty avoidance, as well as differences in overall cultural distance?

Boyacigiller (1990) proposed that the use of expatriates in overseas subsidiaries was closely linked to, among other things, cultural distance. It could be argued that this also applies to those host-country nationals who have had a spell of working at HQ before returning to the local subsidiary. Therefore, tentatively, we put forward a final research question:

RQ6 Does HQ work experience on the part of the subsidiary CEO vary systematically with differences in power distance, individualism, masculinity and uncertainty avoidance, as well as differences in overall cultural distance?

Research method

Sample and data collection

The research instrument was tested with 19 firms drawn from the Irish Development Agency's list of foreign subsidiaries operating in Ireland and from Scottish Enterprise's equivalent list for Scotland. A postal survey was the chosen data capture method for reasons of cost and results generalization. The amended instrument was posted to 600 Irish and 400 Scottish firms drawn from the above lists. The authors requested that only the plant chief executive or senior director should complete the research instrument. A month after the original mailing a reminder was sent out.

In all, 478 questionnaires were returned, of which 385 were completed. Of these, 255 were fully completed by an appropriate executive. Chief executives completed 214 (84%) of the accepted questionnaires, and 31 (16%) were filled in by other senior executives. The response sample was broadly representative of the overall sample in terms of size and industry structure. Ten per cent of all non-responders were telephoned to check for non-response bias, but no systematic variation was detected.

Measures

While other measures of national culture characteristics are available (see Trompenaars and Hampden-Turner, 1997). Hofstede's (1980) have been most often used and confirmed. Accordingly, his four dimensions of national culture (power distance, individualism–collectivism, masculinity–femininity and uncertainty avoidance) are used here. Four measures for each case were derived by subtracting the Hofstede indices for the host country from those of the home county, giving an algebraic difference. Where the subsidiary's CEO was not a host-country national, his/her national culture indices were used instead. A fifth measure, which may be regarded as expressing overall culture difference, was derived as the sum of the absolute values of the Hofstede indices.

Financial performance measures are useful though not always reliable, and often not available at subsidiary level (Roth and Morrison, 1990). Morrison (1990) argues that comparative performance data represent an acceptable alternative, and suggests useful comparators as headquarters' anticipation of subsidiary performance, the subsidiary's own anticipation, and industry norms. In our case the specific variables chosen were overall performance expectations, return on capital, profit, new product development and export market share. All measures were assessed on a five-point Likert scale.

Lau and Ngo (1996) and Dosoglu-Guner (2001) used a set of 16 variables to assess four types of corporate culture (group, developmental, hierarchical, rational). In this study the four variables for each culture type were summed to give overall measures. Procedural justice was evaluated using Kim and

Mauborgne's (1993) five variables. Autonomy was assessed through the use of 10 variables previously tested and used by Gates and Egelhoff (1986), Young *et al.* (1988) and Taggart (1998). These included responses on marketing, R&D, production, finance and HR decisions. All measures were assessed on a five-point Likert scale.

Three additional variables were included for analysis: the age of the subsidiary measured in years, its export propensity measured as a proportion of overall sales, and whether or not the respondent had previously worked at HQ (thought by Hofstede (1991) to be an important determinant of managerial behaviour across the HQ–subsidiary interface).

Apart from export propensity (higher for Irish subsidiaries), the above variables did not vary systematically (chi-square test) across host countries (Ireland, Scotland) or broad industrial grouping (chemicals, engineering, other manufacturing, and services.)

Data analysis

As a preliminary stage, factor analysis was used to reduce the five procedural justice variables to one dimension, where the variables loaded significantly (Cronbach alpha = 0.81). A similar procedure was carried out for the 10 autonomy variables (alpha = 0.83).

The four culture-difference variables were separated into 'low' (0) and 'high' (> 0) values. The total cultural difference variable was similarly classified. Using these five new grouping classifications, *t*-tests were carried out on performance, corporate culture, procedural justice, autonomy and other variables. Systematic differences in means were accepted at $p < 0.05$ (see Table 7.1).

Results

The research proposition (H1) and the six research questions were investigated by a series of *t*-tests, the results of which are shown in Table 7.1. So far as differences in power distance (DPD) are concerned, HQ's perception of overall performance at low DPD subsidiaries was poorer that for high DPD affiliates. The same was true of the subsidiary's own perception of its overall performance. Both HQ and affiliate perceptions of overall performance at the subsidiary were better at high individualism-difference affiliates, and this also held for the subsidiary's profitability compared to the industry norm. For low masculinity-difference firms, HQ's perception of overall subsidiary performance was poorer, as was the subsidiary's perception of its new product development programme. However, in low masculinity-difference firms the subsidiary's export propensity was higher by their own evaluation and by comparison with the industry norm. Affiliates with low differences in uncertainty avoidance had better returns on capital than the industry norm compared to those with high uncertainty-avoidance

Table 7.1 *t*-test results: $p < 0.00$

	Difference in power distance	*Difference in individualism–collectivism*	*Difference in masculinity–femininity*	*Difference in uncertainty avoidance*	*Overall cultural difference*
HQ's perception of overall performance at subsidiary	L < H	L < H	L < H		
HQ's perception of return on capital at subsidiary					L > H
HQ's perception of profit at subsidiary					L > H
HQ's perception of new product development at subsidiary					L > H
HQ's perception of export market share at subsidiary					
Subsidiary's perception of overall performance at subsidiary	L < H	L < H			
Subsidiary's perception of return on capital at subsidiary					
Subsidiary's perception of profit at subsidiary					
Subsidiary's perception of new product development at subsidiary			L < H		L > H
Subsidiary's perception of export market share at subsidiary			L > H		
Subsidiary's return on capital compared to industry norm				L > H	
Subsidiary's profit compared to industry norm		L < H			
Subsidiary's new product development compared to industry norm					
Subsidiary's export market share compared to industry norm			L > H		
Group culture predominates at subsidiary	L > H			L < H	
Procedural justice at subsidiary			L > H		
Level of autonomy at subsidiary				L > H	
Age of subsidiary					L < H
Export propensity of subsidiary					L > H
Respondent has worked at HQ (yes = 0, no = 1)	L < H	L < H		L > H	L > H

Note: L = lower cultural difference; H = higher cultural difference.

differences. Looking at overall cultural distance between HQ and affiliate, low distance firms had better return on capital and higher profitability according to HQ perceptions. In the subsidiaries own view as well as HQ's, new product development was stronger.

Thus, seven of the significant results support H1 and seven contradict. Perhaps some weight should be given to the fact that four of the seven supportive results occur in the 'overall cultural difference' column (see Table 7.1), while none of the seven paradoxical results appear there. Note, also, that there are only 14 significant *t*-tests out of a total of 70 in the performance analysis.

Where group culture predominates at subsidiary level, it has higher values in low DPD firms, but lower levels where differences in uncertainty avoidance are high. This suggests a weak and mixed response to RQ1, that cultural differences between HQ and subsidiary vary with the strength of group culture, but are not systematically associated with developmental, hierarchical and rational cultures. Procedural justice is significantly linked with differences in only one index; low masculinity-difference subsidiaries have higher levels of procedural justice than high difference firms. Thus, the response to RQ2 is weak. The same conclusion may be drawn for RQ3 where there is only one significant result: subsidiaries with lower levels of uncertainty avoidance have higher levels of autonomy.

Younger subsidiaries have lower overall cultural differences than older firms (partial response to RQ4) and the same is true for affiliates with a high propensity to export (partial response to RQ5). High differences in power distance and individualism are associated with a higher likelihood of the subsidiary CEO having previously worked at HQ. Low differences in uncertainty avoidance and overall cultural distance are associated with a lower likelihood that the subsidiary CEO previously worked at HQ. This yields a mixed response to RQ6, perhaps leaning towards a tentative conclusion that that work experience at HQ is negatively linked to culture differences between HQ and subsidiary.

Discussion

According to this survey's data, national culture differences appear to have less impact on subsidiary performance than the literature seems to suggest (see for example Hofstede, 1991; Franke *et al.*, 1991; Jain and Tucker, 1995). However, the performance differentials signalled in Table 7.1 are not inconsequential. Low overall cultural distance is the most important determinant of superior performance. This finding is neither supported nor controverted by the literature, but is in line with common-sense observation. Both the Irish Development Agency and Scottish Enterprise will happily relate numerous case examples where culturally distant inward investors endured a longish time lag before satisfactory performance was achieved.

Where the uncertainty predilections of both HQ and subsidiary are close, there is a beneficial effect on return on capital compared to the industry norm. Similarly, low differences on the masculinity index are related to export market share, in terms of both the subsidiary's own expectations and by comparison with the industry norm. These results are sympathetic with Jain and Tucker's (1995) discussion. Other performance results may be interpreted only tentatively: large differences in power distance seem to lead to better performance, which means that when the power distance index for HQ is substantially larger than at subsidiary level, better performance occurs, perhaps motivated by a hierarchical push from HQ. Much the same argument may be led in respect of individualism; the more individualistic management style of HQ visited upon subsidiary managers may motivate better performance. The results in Table 7.1 for masculinity differences are mixed, and not easily interpreted.

Compared to the findings of Smith (1992) and Lau and Ngo (1996), the results presented here show a very weak linkage between national culture difference and corporate culture. Three of the four corporate culture types show no linkage at all, and group culture is significant only for differences in power distance and uncertainty avoidance. In both cases, low cultural-difference subsidiaries have stronger group cultures than high-difference firms. In other words, where HQ and subsidiary are fairly close in terms of hierarchical distribution of power and tolerance, the subsidiary's corporate culture will tend to focus more strongly on human relationships. This is broadly consonant with Hofstede's (1991) argument.

The procedural justice result implies that similar (and probably low) levels of assertiveness and competitiveness at both HQ and subsidiary will improve the chances that subsidiary management feels fairly treated by HQ. This concurs broadly with Kim and Mauborgne's (1993) discussion. An equivalent argument applies to the autonomy result. More decision-making power at subsidiary level seems to be connected with lower differences in uncertainty avoidance between HQ and affiliate, that is where attitude to risk is fairly similar. This may be a novel linkage that has not previously been commented on in the literature. That low overall cultural distance is more likely to occur in older subsidiaries reflects the discussion of Vernon's (1966) life-cycle theory, in that an MNC's initial overseas investments may more often be made in culturally similar countries. Higher export propensity is linked to overall cultural distance, reflecting the export aspects of the previous discussion of performance.

In total, 53 subsidiary CEOs had previously worked at HQ. This was more likely to happen where low overall cultural distance existed between HQ and affiliate and where there were low differences in uncertainty avoidance. In a way, these results diverge from common-sense expectation, that more intercourse between subsidiary and HQ might be needed when cultural differences were high. This is precisely what occurs where there are large differences in power distance and individualism. The converse argument, of course, is that such intercourse is eased by low cultural differences and made more difficult in the opposite circumstance.

Implications

The implications of this study are perhaps most obvious for academic researchers. Provided the results here are valid (this is discussed in the final section of the chapter), they indicate that national culture differences are less important for managers of MNC foreign subsidiaries than has been claimed in much of the literature of the last 20 years. The linkages with performance are confused and weak. Those with organizational aspects are more in line with previous results, but they are neither strong nor wholly confirmatory. Thus a clear need exists for further empirical studies on the impact of cultural distance, and perhaps more extensive conceptual analysis extending the work of Shenkar (2001).

The main proposition for policy-makers leading from this survey is that there are several, though less than expected, aspects of performance that are closely linked to cultural distance. While policy-makers are, in general, broadly aware of the significance of cultural difference, perhaps they still underestimate the extent to which the impact may be minimized by appropriate discussion with, and learning within, those foreign subsidiaries where it is a significant factor.

For managers, the principal implication is that a general awareness of cultural differences with headquarters is insufficient if the subsidiary and its interface with HQ are to be managed effectively. Cultural sensitivity at the broad level is to be praised, but the consequences of the detailed factors explored here seem to be critical to managerial success in the subsidiary. Both subsidiary and HQ managers must understand these consequences. This, in turn, should become a standard feature of both sides' attempts to manage across the HQ–subsidiary interface.

Conclusions

There are two main potential weaknesses in this survey. The first is in the measurement of cultural difference. The process adopted here was to subtract the appropriate subsidiary index number from that of the home country, allowing for a non-indigenous CEO where this occurred. The assumption here is that the responses, if not the subsidiary, will reflect the national culture of the CEO. In addition, this work was conceived and implemented before Shenkar's (2001) work was published, and subsequent surveys will benefit from a consideration of his critical review of the cultural-distance construct. The second weakness refers to Lau and Ngo's (1996) corporate culture constructs. The 16 variables did not reduce to four principal components quite as neatly as in Lau and Ngo, and this may represent a limitation in this survey.

The survey itself admits the impact of cultural distance on performance and other aspects of subsidiary management, but the results are less explanatory and less directional than allowed by theory of national culture. Nevertheless, clear lessons emerge for policy-makers, academics and managers. Most obvious, however, is the need for further research on this most sensitive and important of topics in subsidiary management.

References

Boyacigiller, N. (1990) 'The role of expatriates in the management of interdependence, complexity and risk in multinational corporations', *Journal of International Business Studies* 21(3), 357–81.

Deal, T.E. and Kennedy, A.A. (1982) *Corporate Cultures: The Rites and Rituals of Corporate Life*. Reading, MA: Addison-Wesley.

Dosoglu-Guner, B. (2001) 'Can organizational behaviour explain the export intention of firms? The effects of organizational culture and ownership type', *International Business Review* 10(1), 71–89.

Fiol, C.M. (1991) 'Managing culture as a competitive resource: an identity-based view of sustainable competitive advantage', *Journal of Management* 17(1), 191–211.

Franke, R.H., Hofstede, G. and Bond, M.H. (1991) 'Cultural roots of economic performance: a research note', *Strategic Management Journal* 12(3), 165–73.

Gates, S.R. and Egelhoff, W.G. (1986) 'Centralization in headquarters–subsidiary relationships', *Journal of International Business Studies* (Summer), 71–92.

Hofer, C. and Schendel, D. (1978) *Strategy Formulation: Analytical Concepts*. St Paul, Minn: West.

Hofstede, G. (1980) *Culture's Consequences: International Differences in Work-related Value*. California: Sage.

Hofstede, G. (1991) *Culture and Organizations: Software of the Mind*. London: McGraw-Hill.

Jackson, T. (1995) *Cross-cultural Management*. Oxford: Butterworth-Heinemann.

Jain, S.C. and Tucker, L.R. (1995) 'The influence of culture on strategic constructs in the process of globalization: an empirical study of North American and Japanese MNCs', *International Business Review* 4(1), 19–37.

Kim, C. and Mauborgne, A. (1993) 'Effectively conceiving and executing multinationals' world-wide strategies', *Journal of International Business Studies* 24(3), 419–48.

Koopman, A. (1991) *Transcultural Management*. Oxford: Blackwell.

Lau, C-M. and Ngo, H.-Y. (1996) 'One country many cultures: organizational cultures of firms of different country origins', *International Business Review* 5(5), 469–86.

Lind, E.A. and Earley, P.C. (1992) 'Procedural Justice and Culture', *International Journal of Psychology* 27(2), 227–42.

Martinez, J.I. and Jarillo, J.C. (1991) 'Coordination demands of international strategies', *Journal of International Business Studies* 22(3), 429–44.

Morrison, A.J. (1990) *Strategies in Global Industries: How US Businesses Compete*. New York: Quorum Books.

Moon, W.C. (1994) 'A revised framework of global strategy: extending the coordination–configuration framework', *International Executive* 36(5), 557–74.

Mowday, R.T., Porter, L.W. and Steers, R.M. (1982) *Employee–Organization Linkages: The Psychology of Commitment, Absenteeism and Turnover*. New York: Academic Press.

Murray, E. and Richardson, P. (2000) 'Measuring strategic performance: the case for tracking leading indicators', in Neely, A. (ed.), *Performance Measurement: Past, Present and Future*. Cranfield University: Centre for Business Performance.

O'Donnell, S.W. (2000) 'Managing foreign subsidiaries: agents of headquarters, or an independent network', *Strategic Management Journal* 21(3), 525–48.

Peters, T.J. and Waterman, R.H. (1982) *In Search of Excellence* (New York: Harper & Row).

Pillai, R., Scandura, T.A. and Williams, E.A. (1999) 'Leadership and organizational justice: similarities and differences across cultures', *Journal of International Business Studies* 30(4), 773–9.

Porter, M.E. (1986) 'Changing patterns of international competition', *California Management Review* 28(1), 9–40.

Prahalad, C.K. and Bettis, R.A (1986) 'The dominant logic: a new linkage between diversity and performance', *Strategic Management Journal* 7(4), 485–501.

Puffer, S.M. (1996) *Management Across Cultures*. Oxford: Blackwell.

Roth, K. and Morrison, A.J. (1990) 'An empirical analysis of the integration–responsiveness framework in global industries', *Journal of International Business Studies* 21(4), 541–64.

Schein, E. (1985) *Organizational Culture and Leadership: A Dynamic View*. San Francisco, CA: Jossey Bass.

Schneider, S.C. and Barsoux, J.-L. (1997) *Managing Across Cultures*. London: Prentice-Hall.

Shenkar, O. (2001) 'Cultural distance revisited: towards a more rigorous conceptualisation and measurement of cultural differences', *Journal of International Business Studies* 32 (3), 519–35.

Smith, P.B. (1992) 'Organizational behaviour and national cultures', *British Journal of Management* 3(1), 39–51.

Taggart, J.H. (1998) 'Strategy shifts in MNC subsidiaries', *Strategic Management Journal* 37(4), 663–81.

Trompenaars, A. and Hampden-Turner, C.M. (1997) *Riding the Waves of Culture*. Oxford: McGraw-Hill.

Vachani, S. (1999) 'Global diversification's effect on multinational subsidiaries' autonomy', *International Business Review* 8(4), 535–60.

Vernon, R. (1966) 'International investment and international trade in the product cycle', *Quarterly Journal of Economics* 80 (May), 190–207.

Weick, K.E. (1985) 'The significance of corporate culture', in Frost, P.J. *et al.* (eds), *Organizational Culture*. Beverly Hills, CA: Sage.

Young, S., Hood, N. and Dunlop, S. (1988) 'Global strategies, multinational subsidiary roles and economic impact in Scotland', *Regional Studies* 22(6), 487–97.

8

Institutional Context and HRM: US Subsidiaries in Europe

Paul N. Gooderham, Odd Nordhaug and Kristen Ringdal

Introduction

The purpose of this chapter is to compare the use of characteristically US human-resource management (HRM) practices in indigenous firms and subsidiaries of US multinational companies. This will be done in four European settings, the UK, Ireland, Germany and Denmark/Norway. On the basis of new institutional organization theory we shall test hypotheses concerning differences in their application between indigenous firms by country as well as differences between indigenous firms and subsidiaries by country.

Kostova and Roth (2002: 215) have argued that an important source of competitive advantage for multinational corporations (MNCs) is the utilization of their organizational capabilities on a worldwide basis through the leveraging of their management practices across their subsidiaries. However, they also point to the need subsidiaries have to achieve and maintain legitimacy in the environment in which they operate. That is, they experience pressure to adopt local practices and become isomorphic with the local institutional context. Hereby lies a tension between the need for global integration on the one hand, and local adaptation on the other. At the subsidiary level this is experienced as two sets of pressures. They are both confronted by an external host-country institutional environment and by pressures from within the organization to become isomorphic to the parent organization's norms (Harzing, 2002: 213).

The implication is that the degree of global integration should vary according to the degree to which the local institutional context that the subsidiary confronts differs from the norms of the parent organization. By extension, because these norms will be substantially derived from the parent organization's own institutional environment, the degree of local adaptation will reflect the degree of divergence between the local institutional context and the parent institutional context. The aim of this chapter is to test this proposition empirically. We do this by analysing the degree to which characteristically US HRM practices are applied by subsidiaries of US MNCs across four European settings, the UK, Ireland, Germany, and Denmark and Norway combined.

Theoretical approach

Despite their very different assumptions, both rational and institutional explanations of management practices predict similarity among firms that operate in the same industry within the context of a single country. Within a rational perspective, firms pursue economic advantage through decision-making and actions guided by unambiguous preferences and bounded rationality. Thus transaction-cost economics contends that at any one point of time there exists a best solution to organizing labour (Williamson, 1975, 1985). 'Most transaction cost theorists argue that there is one best organizational form for firms that have similar or identical transaction costs' (Hollingsworth and Boyer, 1997: 34). While one may expect differences between industries, within industries and not least within firms, firms will implement those practices that are deemed to contribute to promoting the maximization of economic goals.

Although new institutionalism in organizational theory implies a rejection of rational actor models, emphasizing instead the pressures for acquiring and maintaining legitimacy in relation to the environment (see for example DiMaggio, 1983; DiMaggio and Powell, 1983; Powell and DiMaggio, 1991), it shares the broad expectation that uniform pressures will lead to intra-industry and intra-firm uniformity of management practices. That is, they demonstrate isomorphism.

However, the two models' predictions diverge radically when the setting is broadened to comprise different national settings. While the rational model assumes a universality of management practice across the MNC regardless of national setting, institutionalism is concerned with subsidiaries' need to achieve local legitimacy. That is, it is sensitive to the possibility of significant cross-national differences in managerial practices within MNCs. Additionally, it postulates that the degree to which a subsidiary will deviate in terms of its management practices will be determined by the degree to which the institutional setting of the parent company diverges from that of the subsidiary.

As this chapter is concerned with the adaptations made by the subsidiaries of US MNCs across different national settings, we will first delineate the institutional setting of US MNCs and the resultant characteristic US HRM. Thereafter we will briefly describe the institutional contexts of the four European settings. This will form the basis from which we formulate two hypotheses, which will then be tested.

The US context and calculative HRM

Weinstein and Kochan (1995) divide US employment relations from the late 1930s to the present day into two phases: the New Deal industrial relations system, which extended from the 1930s through the 1970s, and more recent developments which we will refer to as US HRM.

In the 1970s, American mass production grappled with the persistent effects of increased international competition and a more uncertain business environment. New flexible productive techniques emerged in the wake of advances in information technology stimulating a shift in competitive strategy towards flexible specialization aimed at producing differentiated, high-value-added products (Piore and Sabel, 1984). Coupled to these changes were significant changes to the institutional environment in which unions became increasingly marginalized while management and shareholders increased their power. In this, as Weinstein and Kochan (1995: 27) observe, 'Government played an important role by weakening its enforcement of labour and employment laws and by allowing (some would say encouraging) a harder line by management in its resistance to unions'.

The new model that emerged was different in that whereas wages in the traditional system had been attached to jobs rather than individuals, in the new model there was a move to tie wages to individual performance and competency in the form of individual incentives. It is in terms of this context, characterized by substantial firm autonomy, that Tichy, Fombrun and Devanna's (1984) HRM model is to be understood: that is, a model that emphasizes the systematic use of individual performance appraisals, individual performance-related rewards and outcomes-monitored training and development.

In summary, US HRM, with its stress on the close synchronization of human-resource policies and activities with the overall business strategy through efficient reward and appraisal systems and development monitoring systems, is essentially a rational, *calculative* approach (Gooderham, Nordhaug and Ringdal, 1999). While based on an assumption of employer–employee unanimity, this is in a unitarist rather a social partnership manner (Sparrow and Hiltrop, 1994).

The European context

In his book *Capitalisme contre Capitalisme* (1991), Michel Albert, a former director of the French planning agency, distinguished on the one hand between US or 'Anglo-Saxon' capitalism and on the other a continental, West European type of capitalism which he labelled the 'Rhineland' model. The former is a 'shareholder economy' under which private enterprise is about maximizing short-term profits for investors rather than any broader harmony of interests. In contrast 'the Rhineland model may be viewed as a regulated market economy with a comprehensive system of social security. Government, employers' organisations and labour unions consult each other about economic goals in order to try to achieve a harmony of interests' (Bolkestein, 1999). In short the Rhineland model is a 'stakeholder economy' in which competition and confrontation is avoided in the belief that it undermines sustainable, stable economic growth. Patrolling this economy is the state, which variously acts as a referee, guarantor, employer and owner.

At a general level in Europe substantial firm autonomy and weak trade unions are the exception rather than the rule. Thus Pieper (1990: 8) has concluded:

> The major difference between HRM in the US and in Western Europe is the degree to which [HRM] is influenced and determined by state regulations. Companies have a narrower scope of choice in regard to personnel management than in the US.

Let us first review the archetypal Rhineland setting, Germany, and thereafter the Scandinavian setting as illustrated by Denmark and Norway, followed by the United Kingdom and Ireland.

Germany

Although unionization in German work-life has dropped considerably since the 1970s, and in 1994 was down to 30 per cent, over 90 per cent of the workforce is covered by collective bargaining agreements that are the exclusive territory of the labour unions in a system of regional, industry-wide bargaining (Scholz, 1996). In addition, attention should be drawn to the elaborate German system of codetermination, which is regulated at the plant level by the Works Constitution Act of 1972 and at the enterprise level by the Works Constitution Act of 1952, superseded in 1976 (cf. Hollingsworth, 1997). As a consequence of this legislation, employers need to maintain positive relations with the works councils. These are powerful, employee-elected bodies legally entitled to co-determination, consultation and access to important information, hence restricting the degree of managerial autonomy (Scholz, 1996; Wächter and Muller-Camen, 2002; Wächter and Stengelhofen, 1995).

This is not to say that various calculative techniques associated with the calculative HRM model are completely absent, but that their potential use has invariably been subject to the critical eye of the works councils (Lane, 1994; Marginson and Sisson, 1994). Not least, these councils have also sought to preserve the strong traditions of social welfare that have characterized employers' treatment of their human resources.

Although Hassel (1999) has claimed that German industrial relations have been eroded during the last two decades, Klikauer (2002) argues that the system remains intact and that any changes relate to unification and the public sector. In summary, it remains therefore the case that German work-life is characterized not only by powerful labour representative bodies, but also by strong work legislation. Hence, low scores on calculative HRM can be expected not only for indigenous German firms, but also for subsidiaries of US MNCs.

Denmark and Norway

In a comparison of the legislative environment for work-life in Denmark and Norway, Graver (1995) observes that in both of these countries there is a strong and pronounced framework intended to ensure that conflicts are resolved at the firm level. In both countries, in regard to issues relating to major structural changes such as downsizing, outsourcing and potential mergers, labour unions are legally entitled to be consulted. However, as Graver (1995) indicates, the legislative framework is more general than that of Germany thereby permitting experiments with novel HRM practices. In summary, we find that in Denmark and Norway labour unions generally both possess and exert considerable influence on the management of firms (Bévort, Pedersen and Sundbo, 1995). Together with the fact that individual rights of employees are strongly protected by laws and agreements, this means that the general autonomy of management is significantly restricted (Kristensen, 1992). The consequence should be that the personnel functions of subsidiaries of US MNCs as well as indigenous firms have limited latitude to apply calculative practices.

United Kingdom

Whilst the above represent two prototypical Western European stakeholder settings, within Europe the UK and Ireland form two markedly deviant national settings.

The United Kingdom is unique in the European context in that during the 1980s its employment legislation was subject to radical changes. Most notably, this legislation includes the Employment Acts of 1980, 1982, 1988 and 1990, and the Trade Union Act of 1984. Coupled to these Acts are severe civil penalties. Together, these Acts curbed the unions' right to recognition, outlawed the closed shop and secondary picketing, and narrowed the freedom of unions to call strikes (for instance, by a requirement that a secret ballot of the members is to be called first). The result was a considerable increase in general managerial autonomy (Edwards *et al.*, 1992) and the opportunity to innovate in employment and labour strategies (Mabey and Iles, 1996; Rubery and Wilkinson, 1994). In a review of trends in HRM in the UK, based on the Workplace Employee Relations Survey (1998), Richbell (2002) observes that this opportunity has resulted in a pronounced move away from standard pay scales towards systems which reflect individual performance and behaviour such as the increased use of the core calculative practice of performance-related pay.

In summary, given the change in institutional context in the UK, it is reasonable to expect that not only do indigenous firms demonstrate a propensity for the adoption of calculative practices, but also that subsidiaries of US MNCs will also freely apply their calculative HRM practices.

Ireland

The Irish context is ostensibly contiguous with that of the Rhineland context in that trade unions enjoy strong legitimacy and collective bargaining rights. The trade-union movement is a key actor in shaping economic and social policy in its role as a 'social partner' (Gunnigle, O'Sullivan and Kinsella, 2002). However, since the early 1980s Ireland may be distinguished from Rhineland Europe in that its pursuit of foreign direct investment has caused it to grant legitimacy to greenfield sites, which permit firms to decide their preferred form of industrial relations (Gunnigle and McGuire, 2001). Significantly, research has indicated that it is primarily US MNCs that have used this latitude to pursue a unitary style of management characterized by a strong level of calculative HRM practices combined with non-union agreements (Gunnigle, Morley and Turner, 1997).

Hypotheses

On the basis of the above we may hypothesize as follows:

H1 The use of calculative HRM practices will be significantly lower in indigenous German, Danish/Norwegian and Irish firms than in indigenous UK firms.

H2 The use of calculative HRM practices in US subsidiaries will be significantly lower in Germany and Denmark/Norway than in the UK and Ireland.

Methods

To test our predictions we have employed data derived from the 1999 Euronet-Cranfield survey of HRM in European countries. The overall strategy of the survey has been to mail appropriately translated questionnaires to personnel managers in representative national samples of firms with more than 100 employees (Brewster, Tregaskis, Hegewisch and Mayne, 1996). Although the response rate for the individual countries is relatively low, mostly between 20 and 35 per cent, analyses suggest that statistical representativeness has not been impaired (Brewster, Hegewisch, Mayne and Tregaskis, 1994).

Our initial sample comprised 2,946 private-sector firms located in the UK, Ireland, Denmark/Norway and (former West) Germany. After removing firms that were neither domestically-owned nor fully-owned US subsidiaries our net sample consisted of 2,546 firms. For the UK the sample comprised 988 firms, for Ireland 349, for Denmark/Norway 753, and for Germany 456. The percentage of US-owned firms varies from a low of 4 per cent in Denmark/Norway, through 8 per cent and 11 per cent respectively in Germany and the UK, to

22 per cent in Ireland. These marked national differences in the proportion of US-owned firms in our sample are not surprising given the very different shares of foreign ownership in each of the economies (OECD, 2001).

Dependent variable

In order to measure the use of calculative HRM practices we have developed a *Calc* scale based on 10 dichotomous items from the Euronet-Cranfield questionnaire: 'individual performance appraisals' (items ca1–ca4), 'individual rewards systems' (items ca5–ca8), and 'monitoring the effectiveness of training' (items ca9, ca10). The scale was constructed using Mokken's nonparametric latent trait model as implemented in the MSPWIN 5.0 computer program (Molenaar and Sijtsma, 2000). Table 8.1 shows all items, ordered by sample difficulties, that is, by their means. As all items are dichotomous (0–1), the means are the proportion of firms employing the practice in question. The cumulative nature of the items in Table 8.1 is evident; performance appraisals are more commonly used than merit pay. Within the two groups of items, the hierarchy is also evident. Merit pay for manuals is less frequent than for professionals and managers; and performance appraisals for managers are much more frequently used than performance appraisals for manuals. Taken together, this indicates that a cumulative scaling model might be appropriate.

The main output from MSPWIN is the *H* statistic displayed in the second column of Table 8.1. The *H* value for the *Calc* scale is 0.52 and indicates a strong scale. The reliability analysis also gave satisfactory results. A Cronbach alpha

Table 8.1 Scalability and reliability analysis of scales of calculative dimensions (Euronet-Cranfield data, net sample by listwise deletion, $n=1756$. Items ordered by sample difficulties, means)

		Mean	H_{wgt}*	*Corr.***
Calc	Calculative scale, 10 items, (Cronbach's alpha = 0.85)	–	0.52	0.35
Ca8	Merit pay: manual	0.24	0.47	0.39
Ca7	Merit pay: clerical	0.27	0.59	0.55
Ca6	Merit pay: professionals	0.34	0.54	0.54
Ca5	Merit pay: managers	0.37	0.45	0.47
Ca4	Performance appraisals: manual	0.50	0.47	0.53
Ca10	Formal evaluation: details	0.56	0.43	0.48
Ca9	Formal evaluation of training	0.59	0.44	0.49
Ca3	Performance appraisals: clerical	0.60	0.60	0.68
Ca2	Performance appraisals: professionals	0.65	0.63	0.68
Ca1	Performance appraisals: managers	0.67	0.61	0.63

Notes: *Estimated by MSP (Mokken Scaling Program); H_{wgt} is Loevinger's coefficient of homogeneity, weighted. **Estimated by SPSS Reliability; Mean denotes means of dichotomized items. Corr. denotes average inter-item correlations for scales and corrected item-scale correlations for items.

of 0.85 shows that the scale's internal consistency is well-above the standard minimum of 0.7. The average inter-item correlation of 0.35 is also satisfactory. On the whole, the item-scale correlations are satisfactory (that is >0.30). In conclusion, the 10-item scale of calculative HRM practices performs satisfactorily both in terms of scalability and reliability.

The *Calc* scale scores for each firm are calculated as the means values of valid scores, that is 0 or 1, on the items, and multiplied by 100 so that the resulting scale varies between 0 and 100. Cases with valid values on less than seven indicators are coded as missing. The *Calc* scale shows a mean of 49.4 in our sample, with a standard deviation of 30.4.

Independent variables

In addition to country, our study includes four additional independent variables: industry, size, the strategy or market orientation of the firm, and the date when the firm was established in its particular setting. Institutional theory assumes that industries develop along particular trajectories characterized by distinct economic and organizational dynamics that distinguish them from other industries (Hollingsworth, Schmitter and Streeck, 1993). Because of this we include a variable that distinguishes manufacturing from banking and finance, construction, transport, personal services and other industries.

As noted by Scott (1998), most studies of the relation between organizational size and structure indicate that size, in terms of the number of employees, tends to influence the methods used for controlling and coordinating employees. The evidence suggests that the larger the size of the organization, the more standardization of human-resource management procedures (Pugh and Hickson, 1969).

The strategy of the firm is measured in terms of whether its main market is local or international. It is reasonable to suppose that subsidiaries of MNCs that are oriented towards purely local markets will be more prone to adapting to local institutional conditions than those whose function is global in the sense that they are producing for international markets. Likewise it may be supposed that indigenous firms with a global orientation will be more inclined to look beyond local best practices.

Finally we distinguish between firms that have been in the institutional setting for 20 years or more and more recent creations. The latter may be supposed to be less infused by the norms of the local environment than the former.

Results

The multiple regression analysis with *Calc* as the dependent variable is documented in Table 8.2. The first set of regressors function as controls: firm size,

Table 8.2 A multiple regression analysis of the scale measuring calculative HRM practices (Euronet-Cranfield data, net sample by listwise deletion, $n = 2546$)

Regressors with description		*B*		*SE*
Constant		38.513	••••	2.978
Lnsize	The natural logarithm of firm size	3.086	••••	0.404
Industry	Manufacturing (reference category)	–		–
	Construction	−2.255		2.629
	Transport	1.700		2.446
	Banking and finance	13.224	••••	1.906
	Personal services	0.101		1.881
	Other industries	−1.839		1.369
Fmarket	Foreign vs national markets	6.884	••••	1.179
Recent	Organization established 1980–99	3.597	••••	1.284
Country	UK (reference category)	–		–
	Ireland	−13.698	••••	1.865
	Denmark/Norway	−30.815	••••	1.340
	Germany	−18.498	••••	1.576
USS	1 = US-owned firm, 0 = native-owned	6.478	••	2.705
*USS*IR*	Design variable for the *USS* by country interaction: 1 = US-owned firm in Ireland, 0 = otherwise	11.428	•••	4.286
*USS*DN*	Design variable for the *USS* by country interaction: 1 = US-owned firm in Denmark/Norway, 0 = otherwise	14.324	•••	5.494
*USS*GER*	Design variable for the *USS* by country interaction: 1 = US-owned firm in Germany, 0 = otherwise	1.135		5.124
	$R^2_{\text{whole model}}$	0.291	••••	
	$R^2_{\text{controls (1)}}$	0.111	••••	
	$R^2_{\text{country (2)}}$	0.165	••••	
	$R^2_{\text{uss,interactions (3)}}$	0.015	••••	

Notes: *B* is a metric regression coefficient; SE is the standard error of *B*. Statistical significance of *B* (two-tailed): •$p<0.10$, ••$p<0.05$, •••$p<0.01$, ••••$p<0.001$.
R^2_{controls}, R^2_{country}, and $R^2_{\text{uss,interactions}}$ are marginal increments in the R^2 ststistic by adding the regressors in the subscripts. The numbers in parentheses indicate the order in which the variables were added to the model.

industry, the strategy or market orientation of the firm, and the date the firm was established in its particular setting. Our main independent variables are the *USS*, the country indicators, and the *USS* by country interactions. *USS* is a variable with the value 1 for firms that are US-owned subsidiaries, and 0 for domestically-owned firms. *Country* is a categorical regressor represented by dummy variables for Ireland, Denmark/Norway (grouped together), and Germany with the UK as the reference category. Then follows the three *USS* by country interaction terms: *USS*IR*, *USS*Den/Nor*, and *USS/Ger*.

Let us start by describing the results for the control variables. Firm size has a positive and statistically significant effect on the use of calculative HRM practices. This means that large firms use such practices to a greater extent than small firms, controlling for the remaining variables in the model. Among the industries, only banking and finance scores significantly higher on the *Calc* scale than the reference category, Manufacturing. Firms with foreign markets and firms established the last 20 years show more extensive use of calculative practices than firms with national markets and firms established before 1980. In total, the controls explains about 11 per cent of the variation in the *Calc* scale.

The next group of variables are the main effects of the country indicators. Since, the latter are also found in the *USS* by country interaction terms, they must be interpreted as the difference in the *Calc* score from the UK (the reference category) for native-owned firms. In line with hypothesis 1 the negative coefficients for the three country-indicators indicates a less extensive use of calculative HRM practices than in native UK firms. Native firms in Denmark/Norway score on the average about 30 points lower on the *Calc* scale than native UK firms. The multiple correlation coefficients in the second panel of Table 8.2 show that the country indicators explains about 16.5 per cent of the variance that remains in the dependent variable after the control variables were introduced in the first step. This is a further indication of rather pronounced country differences in the use of calculative HRM practices.

The last set of variables in Table 8.2 is *USS*, which indicates whether the firm is US or native-owned, and the three design variables for the *USS* by country interaction. Three out of the four variables in the set have statistically significant effects beyond the .05 level. Only the interaction term for Germany is not statistically significant, which means that the increase in the use of calculative practices by US-owned firms in Germany compared to native firms is about the same in Germany as in the UK. To make for a more accessible interpretation of the results for the country indicators, the *USS*, and the interaction terms, the main results from the regression analysis, are displayed in a more intuitive way in Figure 8.1. This displays the predicted means on the *Calc* scale for the eight combinations of country and US ownership, with control variables set to their means.

The black columns show the level of the use of calculative HRM practices in domestic firms in the four countries. Use of such practices is more common in the UK than in Ireland and Germany, and much more common than in Denmark/Norway. The grey columns show the use of calculative HRM practices in US subsidiaries. Hypothesis 2 is supported in that the use of calculative HRM practices is substantially lower in US subsidiaries located in Denmark/Norway and Germany than in Ireland and the UK.

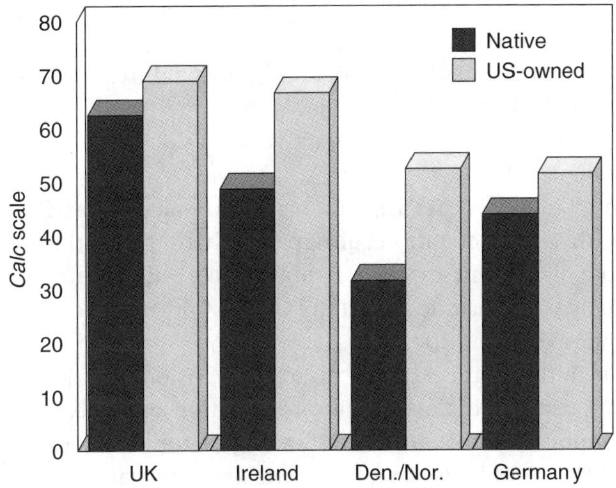

Figure 8.1 Deployment of calculative HRM practices among domestic European and US subsidiaries in the UK, Ireland, Denmark/Norway and Germany

Discussion

Our overall proposition was that the degree of local adaptation by MNC subsidiaries reflects the degree of divergence between the subsidiary and parent institutional contexts. The analysis is confined to the subsidiaries of US multinationals in four European settings and to those practices that comprise calculative HRM. Clearly future research should extend our analysis both in terms of subsidiary nationality, host countries and range of management practices. While mindful of these limitations it is reasonable to conclude that our findings are supportive of the overall proposition.

Our first hypothesis was concerned with establishing that there are significant differences by country between indigenous firms in terms of the use they are institutionally able to make of calculative HRM. Our findings support the conception that the UK represents a relatively amenable setting for calculative HRM.

Our second hypothesis focused on the degree to which US subsidiaries adapt to the four settings. The clearly lower means for US subsidiaries in Denmark/Norway and Germany compared to US subsidiaries located in the UK and Ireland indicate that US subsidiaries adapt to the local institutional setting. The effect of being a US subsidiary is, however, not uniform for these two 'Rhineland' settings, but is larger for Denmark/Norway than for Germany possibly reflecting the less legalistic nature of the Danish/Norwegian setting. In line with our institutional analysis we can observe a substantial effect of being a US subsidiary in Ireland due to the dualistic nature of the Irish institutional setting. The use US subsidiaries are able to make of calculative practices in greenfield Ireland is similar to that of the deregulated UK. This institutional latitude may represent a partial explanation for Ireland's and the UK's attractiveness as destinations for US foreign direct investment.

Our findings also indicate that in regard to calculative HRM, US MNCs diverge from their host-country counterparts. This suggests that subsidiaries of US MNCs to a significant extent attempt to take with them and apply their own, nationally idiosyncratic, repertoire of HRM practices to their subsidiaries in Western European countries.

Finally, our findings illustrate the notion of 'tension' that Kostova and Roth (2002) refer to, between the need for local adaptation and global integration. The theoretical implication for our understanding of the transfer of management practices by MNCs is that, while rational explanations have some validity, they must be supplemented with institutionalist perspectives.

References

Albert, M. (1991) *Capitalisme contre Capitalisme*. Paris: Éditions du Seuil.

Bévort, F., Pedersen, J.S. and Sundbo, J. (1995) 'Denmark', in Brunstein, I. (ed.), *Human Resource Management in Western Europe*. Berlin: Walter de Gruyter.

Bolkestein, F. (1999) 'The Dutch model', *The Economist*, 351 (8120), 115–16.

Brewster, C., Hegewisch, A., Mayne, L. and Tregaskis, O. (1994) 'Methodology of the Price Waterhouse Cranfield project', in Brewster, C. and Hegewisch, A. (eds), *Policy and Practice in European Human Resource Management*. London: Routledge.

Brewster, C., Tregaskis, O., Hegewisch, A. and Mayne, L. (1996) 'Comparative research in human research management: a review and an example', *International Journal of Human Resource Management* 7(4), 585–604.

DiMaggio, P.J. (1983) 'State expansion and organization fields', in Hall, R.H. and Quinn, R.E. (eds), *Organization Theory and Public Policy*. Beverly Hills, CA: Sage.

DiMaggio, P.J. and Powell, W.W. (1983) 'The iron cage revisited: institutional isomorphism and collective rationality in organizational fields', *American Sociological Review* 48(1), 147–60.

Edwards, P., Hall, M., Hyman, R., Marginson, P., Sisson, K., Waddington, J. and Winchester, D. (1992) 'Great Britain: still muddling through', in Ferner, A. and Hyman, R. (eds), *Industrial Relations in the New Europe*. Oxford: Blackwell.

Gooderham, P.N., Nordhaug, O. and Ringdal, K. (1998) 'HRM practices of US subsidiaries in Europe', *Management International Review* 38 (special issue), 47–64.

Gooderham, P.N., Nordhaug, O. and Ringdal, K. (1999) 'Institutional and rational determinants of organizational practices: human resource management in European firms', *Administrative Science Quarterly* 44(4), 507–31.

Graver, H.P. (1995) 'Reguleringsmodeller i arbeidsretten' (Regulatory models in labor law), in Olberg, D. (ed.), *Endringer i arbeidslivets organisering* (Changes in the Organization of Work Life). Oslo: Fafo.

Gunnigle, P., MacCurtain, S. and Morley, M. (2001) 'Why Ireland? A qualitative review of the factors influencing the location of US multinationals in Ireland with particular reference to the impact of labour issues', *Economic and Social Review* 32(1), 43–67.

Gunnigle, P., Morley, M. and Turner, T. (1997) 'Challenging collectivist traditions: individualism and the management of industrial relations in greenfield sites', *Economic and Social Review* 28(2), 105–34.

Gunnigle, P., O'Sullivan, M. and Kinsella, M. (2002) 'Organised labour in the new economy: trade unions and public policy in the Republic of Ireland', in D'Art, D. and Turner, T. (eds), *Irish Employment Relations in the New Economy*. Dublin: Blackhall Press.

Harzing, A.-W. (2002) 'Acquisitions versus greenfield investments: international strategy and management of entry modes', *Strategic Management Journal* 23(3), 211–27.

Hassel, A. (1999) 'The erosion of industrial relations in Germany', *British Journal of Industrial Relations* 37(3), 483–505.

Hollingsworth, J.R. (1997) 'Continuities and changes in social systems of production: the cases of Japan, Germany, and the United States', in Hollingsworth, J.R. and Boyer, R. (eds), *Contemporary Capitalism: The Embeddedness of Institutions*. Cambridge, MA: Cambridge University Press.

Hollingsworth, J.R. and Boyer, R. (1997) 'Coordination of economic actors and social systems of production', in Hollingsworth, J.R. and Boyer, R. (eds), *Contemporary Capitalism*. Cambridge: Cambridge University Press.

Hollingsworth, J.R., Schmitter, P. and Streeck, W. (1993) *Governing Capitalist Economies: Performance and Control of Economic Sectors*. New York: Oxford University Press.

Klikauer, T. (2002) 'Stability in Germany's industrial relations: a critique on Hassel's erosion thesis', *British Journal of Industrial Relations* 40(2), 295–308.

Kochan, T.A., Katz, H.C. and McKersie, R.B. (1989) *The Transformation of American Industrial Relations*. New York: Basic Books.

Kostova, T. and Roth, K. (2002) 'Adoption of an organizational practice by subsidiaries of multinational corporations: institutional and relational effects', *Academy of Management Journal* 45(1), 215–33.

Kristensen, P.H. (1992) 'Strategies against structures: Institutions and economic organizations in Denmark', in Whitley, R. (ed.), *European Business Systems*. London: Sage.

Lane, C. (1994) 'Industrial order: Britain, Germany and France', in Hyman, R. and Ferner, A. (eds), *New Frontiers in European Industrial Relations*. Oxford: Blackwell.

Mabey, C. and Iles, P. (1996) 'Human resource management in the UK: a case of fundamental change, facelift or façade?', in Clark, T. (ed.), *European Human Resource Management*. Oxford: Blackwell.

Meyer, J.W. and Rowan, B. (1983) 'The structure of educational organizations', in Meyer, J.W. and Scott, W.R. (eds), *Organizational Environments: Ritual and Rationality*. Beverly Hills, CA: Sage.

Molenaar I.W. and Sijtsma, K. (2000) *MSP5 for Windows, User's Manual. A Program for Mokken Scale Analysis for Polychotomous Items* (Groningen, The Netherlands: iec ProGAMMA).

OECD (2001) *Activities of foreign affiliates databases*. www.oecd.org.

Oliver, C. (1991) 'Strategic responses to institutional processes', *Academy of Management Review* 16(1), 145–79.

Pieper, R. (ed.) (1990) *Human Resource Management: An International Comparison*. Berlin: Walter de Gruyter.

Piore, M. and Sabel, C. (1984) *The Second Industrial Divide*. New York: Basic Books.

Poole, M. (1986) *Industrial Relations – Origins and Patterns of National Diversity*. London: Routledge and Kesan Paul.

Powell, W.W. and DiMaggio, P.J. (eds) (1991) *The New Institutionalism in Organizational Analysis*. Chicago: University of Chicago Press.
Pugh, D.S. and Hickson, D.J. (1969) *Organizational Structure in its Context: The Aston Programme I*. Lexington, MA: Heath.
Richbell, S. (2001) 'Trends and emerging values in human resource management – the UK scene', *International Journal of Manpower* 22(3), 261–8.
Rubery, J. and Wilkinson, F. (1994) *Employer Strategy and the Labour Market*. Oxford: Oxford University Press.
Scholz, C. (1996) 'Human resource management in Germany', in Clark, T. (ed.), *European Human Resource Management*. Oxford: Blackwell.
Scott, W.R. (1998) *Organizations. Rational, Natural, and Open Systems* (4th edn). Upper Saddle River, NJ: Prentice-Hall.
Sisson, K. (1994) 'Personnel management: paradigms, practice and prospects', in Sisson, K. (ed.), *Personnel Management* (2nd edn). Oxford: Blackwell.
Sparrow, P. and Hiltrop, M. (1994) *European Human Resource Management in Transition*. New York: Prentice-Hall.
Tichy, N.M., Fombrun, C.J. and Devanna, M.A. (1984) 'The organizational context of strategic human resource management', in Fombrun, C.J., Tichy, N.M. and Devanna, M.A. (eds), *Strategic Human Resource Management*. New York: Wiley.
Wächter, H. and Muller-Camen, M. (2002) 'Co-determination and strategic integration in German firms', *Human Resource Management Journal* 12(3), 76–87.
Wächter, H. and Stengelhofen, T. (1995) 'Germany', in Brunstein, I. (ed.), *Human Resource Management in Western Europe*. Berlin: Walter de Gruyter.
Weinstein, M. and Kochan, T. (1995) 'The Limits of Diffusion: Recent Developments in Industrial Relations and Human Resource Practices in the United States', in Locke, R. Kochan, T. and Piore, M. (eds), *Employment Relations in a Changing World Economy*. Cambridge, Mass.: The MIT Press.
Williamson, O. (1975) *Markets and Hierarchies: Analysis and Antitrust Implications*. New York: Free Press.
Williamson, O. (1985) *The Economic Institutions of Capitalism*. New York: Free Press.

storage capacity is accordingly more expensive and time-consuming amid the necessary permits, such that this space is relatively fixed in the short term. When storage is nearly full, an excess supply of oil and gas can cause relatively large moves in the market. An immediate use for it will need to be found if it can't be stored away and that marginal bid might be very low. In reverse, an excess of demand when storage is running dry could cause a spike in prices as some of that demand will need to be destroyed. Many countries hold strategic energy reserves in the interests of avoiding any extreme squeezes, but by using them, the backstop shrinks and that does not always provide comfort to investors.

Power prices are much more extreme than other energy commodities in their volatility. It is a sort of case study in how others might trade if storage was not an option, even in the short term. Batteries are uneconomically expensive, and other forms of electricity storage are not in widespread use. For example, by pumping water uphill, potential energy is stored that can be utilised upon letting it flow back down through a turbine. Without scope to store an excess supply of electricity, the price can spike unusually high before enough demand is destroyed. Some companies agree subsidies to cease production if the shortfall becomes too large, while some power stations will be paid to have capacity on standby for the same reason. Such arrangements are expensive, but they constrain the size of any imbalance between supply and demand.

The government isn't always overly concerned about creating squeezes in energy-related markets. In particular, most are keen to constrain carbon emissions and the associated negative social externalities. A cap on each company's emissions would do this, but it would pay little regard to the costs of cutting emissions. A fast-growing company could find itself stunted while a vast and inefficient organisation can lumber on, even if it can make reductions at little cost. The solution of sorts has been to create a tradable market in emissions where the highest bidder potentially buys pollution permits. That means those who can reduce emissions at the lowest cost are the ones who should end up doing so. The problem is that some companies can choose to sell any permits they have and shift production to another country outside of the emissions trading scheme, which does not benefit the environment or the country losing activity. Such trades reduce demand and without a supply reduction, will lower the carbon price in the market. The same would be true of technological improvements. Otherwise, demand pressures on prices are procyclically linked to economic activity, and the supply remains a function of regulation.

8.4 Equities

Like holdings of physical commodities, equities don't have a maturity date. However, an equity holding cannot be directly consumed or invested as a productive input, so its value and trading are determined very differently. Equity holders own a share of the company and can expect to earn a portion of its future profitability. Unlike fixed income assets, there is no commitment to pay regular sums to common stockholders, though. Future cash flows nonetheless need to be discounted into assessments of fair value. Two primary valuation models exist for this, with some shortcuts pursued in practice. Particularly from a macroperspective, it is more natural to screen investments based on the sort of factors that should outperform in the anticipated environment. Exploration of such factors will end this section after addressing the valuation models.

8.4.1 Valuation Models

The current price of a share in a company should reflect its proportion of all discounted future cash flows. This theory is the essence of the dividend discount model (DDM). Most companies pay dividends in good times, and some have such well-engrained dividends that investors buy on the condition it stays. Whether the dividend is paid in cash or more shares ("scrip") doesn't matter too much, but it saves broker fees and taxes in some jurisdictions. Other companies prefer to retain earnings instead, but that is only a deferral on when that cash flow can be realised either as future dividends or a share buyback. When dividends are rare or non-existent, it might be more efficient to use discounted free cash flow instead of dividends within the DDM.

For a given expected dividend profile and future price projection, the expected return of a share can be calculated and used for asset allocation purposes. Determining future dividends is difficult, and many analysts make simplifying assumptions, like a constant growth in dividend payments. This simplifies the DDM down to the so-called Gordon model, which can, in turn, be rearranged to say that the expected return is the dividend yield plus that constant growth rate. The results remain highly sensitive to some assumed values, but it is at least easier and more intuitive to calculate when expressed this way. A less sensitive approach to estimating the expected return can be calculated from the incomes retained by the company. This method is the residual income valuation model (RIM), and it involves recognize the *reality* of institutional stability and institutional change and not just their *appearance* (Greenwood, Suddaby and Hinings, 2002). These propositions are capable of subsequent development into testable hypotheses, as German data becomes increasingly available.

Path dependence during crisis

The isomorphism and underlying stability of the distinctive patterns of large-firm CG in different countries has been attributed to national culture (Licht, 2001), and in Japan's case CG is said to be a consequence of the influence of family values at all levels of society (Bhappu, 2000).

However, national institutions embody, promote and defend national culture (Roe, 1993, 1997; Bebchuk and Roe, 1998), and top officers in large companies everywhere are embedded in social structures that link actors, and influence legislation (Davis and Thompson, 1995). Thus, banking and tax laws in the USA discourage relational investments by banks in industrial firms, and encourage them in Germany and Japan (Roe, 1997). Anti-takeover devices have been gradually eroded by shareholder activism in the USA (Davis and Thompson, 1995), while dual-board governance is allowed to obstruct takeovers in Germany. In this case, national culture and institutions become indistinguishable in their impact on CG.

Table 9.1 reports for Germany, Japan and Russia (compared with the USA and the UK) the three main national cultural attributes (Hofstede, 1997) that may influence governance institutions. Although Hofstede's cultural dimensions have been widely criticized elsewhere (for example Schwartz, 1994), they suffice here for the purpose of informing specific research propositions. A low–high spectrum can be seen to run generally from left to right in Figure 9.1, with the familiar high individualism, low uncertainty avoidance and low power distance tolerance of the USA and the UK contrasting with national culture in Russia, Germany and Japan, to be addressed separately below. These characteristics may now be considered in relation to the general shape of governance institutions.

Table 9.2 is developed from Licht (2001) and traces the implications of low US/UK levels of power-distance tolerance, collectivism and uncertainty

Table 9.1 Dimensions of national culture

	USA/UK	*Germany*	*Japan*	*Russia*
Power distance tolerance	Low	Low	Moderate	High
Collectivism	Low	Moderate	Moderate	Moderate
Uncertainty avoidance	Low	Moderate	High	High

Sources: Based on data from Hofstede (1997), pp. 26, 53, 113; Elenkov (1998).

Table 9.2 US/UK cultural dimensions and governance strategies

	Information disclosure	*Shareholder rights*	*Insider trading*	*Executive pay*	*Takeovers*
Low collectivism (high individualism)	Individual shareholders expect transparency, no suppression of information	Equal treatment of each individual shareholder	Usually permitted to encourage information disclosure to all individuals	Toleration of wide differences in individual rewards	Allowed, but minority shareholders protected by takeover codes
Low uncertainty avoidance	Transparency; open release of good and bad news	General *laissez faire* emphasis by shareholders relatively unafraid of losses	Allowed despite windfall gains for executives	Executives accept volatile rewards; shareholders accept the volatile costs of executive rewards	Generally allowed despite unforeseen gains/losses for incumbent shareholders and employees
Low tolerance of power distance	Transparency; top officers not allowed to conceal bad news	Equal; no stock pyramids or dual-class shares	Allowed but subject to rules to prevent abuse by executives for private gains	Controls on executive pay through remuneration committees, independent directors, etc.	Allowed, but controls on poison pills/shark repellents deployed by executives to protect themselves

Note: Author's own work, developed from Licht (2001).

avoidance for individual governance elements. For example, ESOs are encouraged by low collectivism and low uncertainty avoidance on the part of executives and shareholders, but low power-distance tolerance implies that shareholders may want to control executives' excesses in relation to ESO packages through remuneration committees, and so on. On the other hand, they may not wish to pay for such monitoring privately.

With legal, fiscal, social, political and economic institutions embedded in the distinctive national cultures of the USA and the UK, one can understand the resistance of prevailing governance structures to proposed reforms that purport to advance collectivism, hierarchical control by executives, or insurance against risks for stakeholders. In these circumstances, interest groups from all sides tend to defend the *status quo* (Davis and Thompson, 1995). Data corresponding to Table 9.2 and commentaries could be produced for Russia, Japan and Germany.

Thus, UK governance has been resistant to EU attempts to impose works councils on large UK firms to advance employee participation and collectivism. By way of contrast, in the case of Germany, higher levels of collectivism and uncertainty avoidance manifest themselves in governance institutions that are said to comprise a community, or *Gemeinschaft*, of stakeholders (Schneider-Lenné, 1992). With moderate levels of collectivism, trust is an important feature of German firms, where incumbent employees and managers form coalitions and each party forego individual opportunities for short-term gain in favour of longer-term collective gains (Pistor, 1998). This means, for example, that banks and employees, fearing the uncertainty of takeover and liquidation, are strongly represented on upper-tier supervisory boards, and encourage the accumulation of labour and financial reserves by firms (Macey and Miller, 1997). EU efforts to construct a takeover code that would force German firms to permit takeovers according to the democratic wishes of individual shareholders have been blocked.

Although traditional governance patterns are deeply embedded in local culture and institutions and have tended to withstand proposed reforms, certain historical episodes of upheaval (Newman, 2000), however, may comprise the most propitious circumstances for CG change. Business history (Aldrich, 1999) and case-studies over long periods (Greenwood and Hinings, 1996) have been advocated for applications of institutional theory, and in this context archival data may be used to develop cases that investigate the introduction of governance reforms that inevitably clash with prevailing national culture and institutions. Although Williamson (2000: 597) asserts as an economic institutionalist that 'insular societies often take measures to protect themselves against "alien values"...', examples of the survival of 'alien' governance reforms have been found, but in most cases successful transplants followed very long periods of French or British colonization (Berkowitz, Pistor and Richard, 2000).

Transplants are alleged to have the most chance of survival as a result of 'conquest or revolution' (North, 1990: 89). In the case of economic institutions, Williamson observes that (2000: 598):

> occupations (following World War II), perceived threats (the Meiji Restoration), breakdowns (Eastern Europe and the former Soviet Union), a military coup (Chile) or a financial crisis (New Zealand) – will, however, occasionally produce a sharp break from established procedures. Rare windows of opportunity to effect broad reforms are thereby opened.

In this spirit, therefore, in order to examine the possibility of transplanted institutional change in the most propitious circumstances, three historical episodes from Germany, Japan and Russia are briefly considered. The vulnerability of these three societies during the chosen episodes, with an external reforming power not embedded in local culture and institutions, may have been expected to promote institutional change. In each case, however, the path dependency and inertia predicted by conventional institutional theory substantially stood unrefuted as governance structures still resisted convergence on internationally isomorphic forms. Each case is now considered, with the Russian case developed at greater length than those for Japan and Germany, as the secondary literature is less well-developed for contemporary Russia.

Russia (1991–2001)

Russia is first considered as a case study in which pressures for Anglo-American governance reforms were strong but a political and economic revolution was not accompanied by military occupation. Nevertheless, massive Russian debts with Western states, private financial institutions and public institutions meant that Russia was virtually 'held captive' by the World Bank and International Monetary Fund. The approval of these institutions, widely seen as being essentially controlled by the US government, was needed for governance reform packages. In consequence, a team from the US Agency for International Development advised the Russian cabinet minister charged with privatization, a major plank of governance reforms (Blasi *et al.*, 1997).

These reforms were staged from 1991 in the context of national institutions founded on, and mutually supporting, a national culture of high tolerance of power distance, moderately high levels of collectivism and high uncertainty avoidance (see Table 9.1). These cultural attributes favour the preservation of local institutions that protect jobs in the context of high levels of distrust of distant, though powerful, authority. This distrust became evident during the US-influenced reforms of CG in the former Soviet Union (FSU), and particularly Russia, after 1991.

Before 1991, Russian industrial CG may be characterized as state bureaucracy, and not just during the period after the Revolution of 1917. The first attempts at industrialization in Russia were made by Peter the Great before 1725 in the form of state factories that requisitioned serf workers and managers for their operation. Licensed private operators were to supply consumer goods to meet state procurements at fixed prices (Pipes, 1995: 209). State railways, state banks and state-licensed monopolies prevailed until the end of the nineteenth century. Foreign investors gradually gained access to the oil industry and some manufacturing, but by 1905 . . . 'any company in Russia could have their authority to operate withdrawn by the administration at will' (Crisp, 1976: 183). The national emergency created by the First World War was an excuse to formalize state regulatory controls, and State Councils were formed, again for product procurement at fixed prices (Gatrell, 1986: 185).

From regulation it was a small step in 1916 to the pre-Revolutionary branch ministries, *glavki*. Already, according to Blackwell (1970: 61), 'by the end of 1916, a degree of state control of industry unprecedented in Russian history had been attained', and

> seventy *glavki* were run by boards consisting in many cases of the old factory managers and technicians, but including a preponderance of trade union members, workers' representatives and party officials. In turn, the *glavki* appointed similarly composed boards, as well as directors and inspectors, for local plants (p. 70).

Of course, the *glavki* were later (in the 1930s) to become a significant feature of Stalin's central planning.

In the case of Russia, a different kind of dual economy from the large-firm/small-firm dichotomy in Japan and Germany, noted below, was to emerge, with the manufacturing sector (minus high-tech firms usually associated with the military-industrial complex) being allowed to develop a CG framework quite distinct from that in primary sectors, banking groups, utilities and in high-tech firms.

In a manufacturing sector characterized by obsolete technologies, bloated workforces and employees' anxieties concerning downsizing after privatization, the political clout of employees in state enterprises was perceived to constitute an effective veto on reforms. They desired a privatization programme that did *not* permit US-style outside shareholdings and hostile takeover threats, and so the authorities, anxious to achieve privatization that would be quick and irreversible, reluctantly agreed to voucher distributions that effectively gifted controlling stakes in firms to incumbent managers and employees (Boycko *et al.*, 1993). The outcome was 'employee-owned, manager controlled' firms (Earle and Estrin, 1996), generally without share listings and therefore safe from takeover.

While the US-dominated international financial institutions understood that this outcome was quite different from US-style capitalism, they expected that outside investors would ultimately be able to acquire shares and replace ineffective managers. Years later, however, employee-owned, manager-controlled firms continue to be the dominant governance feature of this sector (Estrin and Wright, 1999), and, in practice, incumbents were able to avoid capital-market listings for their firms and to obstruct over-the-counter stock sales to outsiders by controlling access to share registers (OECD, 1999). Of course incumbents have been unable to provide investable funds for enterprise restructuring, but some import protection for domestic markets has enabled many firms to survive. In any case, a peculiarly Russian form of relational governance has evolved, with dual-role shareholders comprising managers and other employees.

In the rest of Russia's industrial economy, primary producers (metals, oil, gas and so on), banking groups, utilities (for example telecoms) and high-tech firms were excluded from the centralized privatization programme. In these sectors, the disengagement of the state bureaucracy has often been incomplete. In 1995, a Russian government anxious to raise funds before a Presidential election arranged for Russian banks to hold large amounts of shares in 28 of Russia's large, 'blue-chip' companies in a loans-for-shares arrangement (Blasi *et al.*, 1997: 74), to culminate in open auctions in 1996 intended to accommodate foreign bidders. In practice, however, only 12 companies were auctioned (some to the banks themselves) and banks held on to the shares as security for loans never to be repaid. These holdings ultimately formed the basis for Russian financial-industrial groups.

The outcomes of these and other *ad hoc* cash auctions for some of Russia's best companies were very unsatisfactory, and the state continued to influence their activities through its personal contacts with industry and their links with the media and banks. For example, Boris Berezovsky was in charge of LogoVAZ, a conglomerate focused around car distribution, while he was deputy secretary of the Security Council, with access to files on politicians and businessmen. In many cases the state held on to a 'golden' share guaranteeing continued state control, and with Surgutneftgaz, the company's incumbent pension fund (under the control of enterprise managers) was allowed to win the auction. In the case of Norilsk Nickel, the auction was organized by Oneximbank, which itself won the contest with a bid of $170.1m when the reserve price was $170m. (Indeed, the whole loans-for-shares scheme was designed by Minister of Finance Vladimir Potanin, who was also chairman of Oneximbank, though he nominally resigned upon joining the government.) With Russian regional telecom monopolies, the state held on to large packets of shares through its Svyazinvest holding company, United Energy Systems, which is substantially the old Ministry of Power Generation.

In the case of Gazprom, the Russian gas monopolist with oil interests, together valued at around 8 per cent of Russia's GDP, the Russian Federation still holds 38 per cent of shares. The Chairman of Gazprom is Rem Vyakhirev, who was First Deputy Minister of the FSU for the gas industry 1986–91, and the government's representative on the Gazprom board is former Russian Prime Minister, Viktor Chernomyrdin.

In the 'commanding heights' of Russian industry comprising these 'blue-chip' companies, it is difficult to quantify any continuing state influence since many of their private owners have strong personal links with the government, and many large groups of companies still incorporate the old ministerial structures they were supposed to replace. In quantitative terms, despite the privatization of most manufacturing (that is, loss-making) firms, 'the Ministry of State Property still remains a majority shareholder in over 12,000 SOEs and a minority shareholder in over 3,800 companies with no coherent set of goals to exercise ownership rights. Assets are managed mostly via state boards composed of 2,000 members of ministries and agencies' (OECD, 1999: 5).

Beyond formal state ownership and board representation, many of the old state structures survive. For example, the world crisis early in 2000 in the supply of the precious metal palladium was attributed to the bureaucratic procedures necessary for Russian exports of palladium. The metal is produced by Norilsk Nickel, stocked by the Central Bank of Russia and by Gokhram, the State Precious Metals Agency, while export quotas and licences are issued by the President's Office and by Almaz, the exporting arm of the Ministry of Finance.

The participation of foreigners in privatization auctions was in practice seriously restricted, but where genuine outsiders have succeeded in obtaining shares, their ownership rights have often been severely weakened by insiders (OECD, 1999). Outsiders' stakes have been diluted by new holding structures (Maddy and Ickes, 1998) and by new share issues authorized by company meetings organized with insufficient notice. There have also been serious deficiencies in Russian accounting standards and in the disclosure of information to outsiders, and enterprises have often been stripped of their best assets by incumbents in a number of ways. These include transfer pricing that appropriates value away from subsidiaries and their outside investors to a manager-controlled holding structure (OECD, 1999).

The outcome for genuine outside investors, therefore, is a capital market quite different from that in the USA. Nevertheless, in 2001 the Russian Trading System (RTS) boasted 60 regularly traded stocks, and 27 of them have American Depository Receipt (ADR) quotations in New York, as a means of... 'escaping the weakness of their home country's institutions' (Black, 2000). Despite the barriers to free float in Russia, however, only four of these ADR stocks in 2001 traded at a substantial premium on the US market, indicating substantially lower shareholder risks and trading costs than on the Moscow RTS market.

However, in firms privatized in the central programme, outside ownership has apparently increased gradually, from around 20 per cent in 1994 to 39 per cent in 1997 (Estrin and Wright, 1999: 409).

Other signs suggest, however, that outsiders are still facing cultural and institutional barriers set up by enterprise incumbents. For example, although there are 60 regularly traded stocks on the RTS, this number is down from over 220 in early-1998, and included only three companies from manufacturing industry. The bulk of traded stocks came from primary extractive industries, banking, telecoms and electricity utilities. Furthermore, it is rare for any company to have more than 20 per cent of its shares in 'free float' and available for purchase, and this is quite typical of countries characterized by relational shareholders, that is most countries outside the USA and the UK (Blasi *et al.*, 1997: 153). Although 27 companies had ADRs late in 2001, all of these were at level 1, involving just the same information disclosure in New York as in Moscow. (Two years earlier, two Russian companies had full, level-3 ADRs involving full information disclosure to US GAAP standards.) After the collapse in Russian share prices in August 1998, four of the Russian ADRs on the US market had prices below 10 cents, and were essentially dormant. Outsiders' minority shareholder rights continue to be abused. For example, in late 1999, British Petroleum was invited to tender for the purchase of Chernognyeft, a subsidiary oil company of Sidanco (TNK) that it already substantially owned.

Although enormous changes have been achieved since 1991, therefore, it seems that privatizations achieved before 1997 had a limited impact. Modern Russian CG arguably still bears less resemblance to US capitalism and more to the default mode of historical antecedents, where a state bureaucracy and enterprise incumbents had substantial voices. In a context of high levels of uncertainty avoidance and moderately high collectivism that are characteristic of Russian national culture, and embedded in her institutions, a tendency to retain a Russian flavour to CG is evident.

Although the US government had a powerful influence on Russia's reforms after 1991, of course no military occupation was involved. Perhaps, therefore, it should not be surprising that top officers in the Russian government and in key industrial firms were able to obstruct and in some cases reverse the intentions of the reformers. In this context, therefore, a consideration of Japan and Germany after the Second World War provides cases with more powerful outside reformers and more vulnerable indigenous institutions, thus favouring the absorption of 'alien' reforms and the refutation of traditional institutional theory.

Japan (1946–52)

Japan in this period probably falls between Russia (1991–2001, see above) and Germany (1945–54, see below) in terms of the extent of crisis and the governmental power behind reforms. In Japan's case, the Supreme Command for the

Allied Powers (SCAP, effectively under the control of the US government) did not formally replace Japan's civilian government, but was able to use more informal channels to impose its will. SCAP communicated with the indigenous Japanese government through a Central Liaison Office, transmitting instructions and reporting back on implementation. In some cases, SCAP issued directives, but in practice the Japanese could dilute US instructions and delay implementation (Schaller, 1985).

Japan's resistance to governance reform must be understood in the context of institutions founded on a national culture, with high uncertainty avoidance and moderately high levels of both collectivism and power-distance tolerance as dominant traits (Hofstede, 1997; and Table 9.1). Indirect influence through an established Japanese parliament made it easy for top officers in Japanese government and industry to frustrate and reverse US-style, exit-based CG reforms. The consensus-style decision-making implied by moderately high collectivism, together with high levels of uncertainty avoidance, constituted major barriers to establishing US-style capital-market disciplines. As with Germany and Russia, high uncertainty avoidance supports CG institutions that help to preserve employment levels. In the case of Japan, however, relational investors and managers in large firms often collude to protect employees, using a paternalistic style rather than consensus. Apart from these exceptions, it is no surprise to learn that Japan resembles Germany. Indeed, Japan modelled its corporate laws on Germany after the Meiji restoration of 1868.

Like pre-Second World War Germany, CG in prewar Japan featured the ownership and control of large firms by families, but in Japan family *zaibatsu* comprised pyramidic stock holdings in diversified groups, each embracing banks that were to become a prominent postwar phenomenon. The 'fifty-six families versus seventy-two million people' (Hadley, 1979: 23) developed close links with government (Hadley, 1970: 4), helping to facilitate legislation that reinforced this structure. Family members often served in government, particularly in the Ministry of Munitions, that subsequently became the Ministry of Commerce in 1945, and after 1949 the influential Ministry for International Trade and Industry (MITI).

Zaibatsu family holdings evolved from the master–servant culture of feudalism that was relatively recently overthrown in Japan. In the villages, people had formed communities, joining forces to plant rice and distribute water. 'The landlords and the village head were the unquestioned authorities who would exploit the tenant but not actually expel him or let him down completely when he faced hard times' (Hirschmeier and Yui, 1981: 204). This culture viewed Western competitive firms as alien, but *zaibatsu* firms were made palatable by characterizing themselves as family groups attracting traditional loyalties. As today, Japan developed an extreme form of dualism, with large firms supported by a large informal sector with tiny workshops and frequently day-labour systems. In the large firms in the 1920s, however, males who were skilled or office workers enjoyed the now-familiar features of permanent employment and seniority wages (Hirschmeier and Yui, 1981: 205). In the first two *zaibatsu* firms, Mitsui was organized around a bank from the outset, and Mitsubishi, beginning as a shipping firm, gave prominence to its banking activities after 1880.

Upon assumption of direct rule over Japan, the US military government concerned with removing the perceived causes of war, designated 83 of the old holding companies that constituted the *zaibatsu* for liquidation. However, an indigenous Japanese plan, called the Yasuda Plan after the *zaibatsu* family member who authored it, with the approval of the other 'Big Four' *zaibatsu* firms (Mitsui, Mitsubishi and Sumitomo), recommended that the holding companies themselves should volunteer for dissolution and detail the means of doing this. Stock was to be sold by a Holding Company Liquidation Commission (Schaller, 1985).

Unsurprisingly, only 16 (not 83) holding companies were in fact liquidated. A brief interlude of US-style capital markets was, however, achieved, reinforced by an Anti-Trust Act that forbade corporations (including banks) from holding industrial shares (Berglöf and Perotti, 1994). Consequently, by 1949, 69.1 per cent of all industrial shares were held by individuals (Scher, 1997: 65) and the Commercial Code for Illinois was adopted, requiring minority shareholder protection, a Securities Exchange Commission (SEC) on the US model, standards of information disclosure and independent accountancy bodies (Cooke and Kikuya, 1992). In addition, the Glass–Steagall Act imposed by the US authorities was designed to weaken the power of banks in industry by requiring the separation of commercial and investment banks (Roe, 1993: 1930).

Besides capital-market reform, the USA also attempted to promote employee voice as a barrier to any reemergence of concentrated shareholdings, giving preferential treatment to employees' purchases of shares in the liquidation of holding companies. However, trade-union militancy in the form of a proposed national strike in 1947, together with US fears concerning the spread of communism, caused a switch in policy that allowed docile enterprise unions to emerge, and any prospect of German-style employee voice in CG disappeared.

US-style capital markets also did not last long. Japanese regulators effectively forced savings into the banks and they began to accumulate industrial shares (Roe, 1993: 1930). Just three months after the US handover of governmental power back to the Japanese in May 1952, the SEC was abolished, along with many shareholder rights. AGMs quickly became exercises in tokenism, and *keiretsu* began to coalesce around banks and trading companies, rather than around the old family holding companies. Indeed, three of the old *zaibatsu* (Sumitomo, Mitsui and Mitsubishi) were allowed to reemerge as *keiretsu*, and the Yasuda bank-based *zaibatsu* simply changed its name to Fuji. Stable cross-holdings, cross-directorships and Presidents' Clubs replaced the family holdings as the coordinating mechanisms of the new conglomerates. By 1991, Sheard (1994: 333) estimated that 91 per cent of listed industrial stock was tied up in interlocks.

In other words, a form of relational CG emerged in large firms after the US departure that was consistent with Japanese cultural and institutional antecedents, and not very dissimilar from prewar structures. For example, the 'new', bank-based structure of *keiretsu* groups was an echo of the earlier *zaibatsu*. Stable shareholdings in industrial firms by banks as relational investors facilitated the permanent employment and seniority wages of modern firms, but these were also used earlier by *zaibatsu* as an incremental variation of feudal village culture.

Institutional embeddedness and path dependence were the distinct outcomes for large Japanese firms after the Second World War, though, as in Germany, see below, an important small and medium-sized business sector continued to operate virtually unaffected by occupation.

Germany (1945–54)

In the case of Germany, occupying military governments faced less local resistance to reforms and had unprecedented power to impose governance changes during the most severe national crisis. While more indirect methods were used in Japan after the Second World War, see above, in W. Germany the Allies opted for direct military rule in 1945 through a central Control Council (CC) employing large numbers of bureaucrats in four zones, for example 20,000 British civil servants in the British sector alone (Turner, 1989). The British and US zones of occupation subsequently combined into a Control Commission for Germany (CCG) that was effectively under US control from Frankfurt after 1947.

In the face of a German culture of low tolerance of power-distance and moderately high levels of uncertainty avoidance and collectivism (Table 9.1), a number of early attempts, motivated by US demands for de-Nazification, were made after the Second World War to introduce US-style, market-based CG into Germany, to replace the old system of network-based CG that involved family, bank and inter-firm ownership and control. For example, vigorous attempts were made to disperse the blocks of shares held by families, banks, suppliers and competitors (through cartels), and so on, to break the strong links between industrial firms and the state. Over 1,000 cartels were broken up, family-held shares were sequestered and new share issues involved maximum holdings and loans for employees and small shareholders to acquire shares (Stolper, 1967). Nationwide banks were restricted, on the model of state banks in the USA, to single *Länder*, with limits on their holdings of industrial shares (Kindleberger, 1984).

These attempts to deconstruct *Gemeinschaft* and facilitate the construction of market-based CG in Germany (with associated high stock liquidity, takeovers, stock-based pay for executives and open information disclosure) foundered, however, on the rocks of existing national institutions and a national culture that underpinned them. In the early years of the occupation, this was a result of informal German pressures on the military governments, which gradually became more formal with the creation of the Federation of German Industry (BDI) in 1949. Under informal German pressure, the CC and CCG were responsible for regulations that provided the cornerstone of 'new', network-based CG in Germany, with significant elements of employee control. *Mitbestimmung* (co-determination) was gradually introduced from 1945, with supervisory boards in the coal and steel firms, and was the subject of CCG legislation in 1949 (CCG *Monthly Report*, 1949). The CC enacted a regulation in 1946 requiring large firms to arrange works councils in each plant (*Official Gazette*, 1946).

However, works councils already existed in many German firms immediately after reunification in 1871, they resurfaced during the flirtation with Communism in 1918, and were prominent in Hitler's German Labour Front (Bureau of Business Research, 1969). Similarly, Supervisory Boards were a feature of Hitler's Corporation Law of 1937, and certainly many large German companies already had dual-board governance in the nineteenth century (Charkham, 1995). Effectively, the post-Second World War dual boards and works councils were only minor modifications of prewar relational structures.

Under influence from German pressure groups, these network-promoting cornerstones of modern German CG were introduced after the Second World War, with the support of the US military government anxious to dilute the power of dynasties associated with Nazism. At the same time, its early attempts to dissolve networks were gradually reversed to a large degree. For example, the largest three national banks (Deutsche, Commerz and Dresdner) were slowly reunited. They began to collect places on the supervisory boards of industrial firms again and, even without the ownership of controlling blocks of shares, banks learned how to control firms through bearer stocks deposited with them (Kindleberger, 1984). Many family firms managed to reinstate their founding families, for example Alfried Krupp replaced his purged father as Chairman, and by 1970 three of the old steel firms (Krupp, Thyssen and Klöckner) had reformed. The BDI opposed deconcentration and by 1970 large block holdings were again the norm in large German firms, as competitors and suppliers accumulated firms in related areas. Even today, few modern German firms employ international or US accounting conventions and stock liquidity is low, even in DAX 30 firms (Franks and Mayer, 1997).

In Germany, it would appear that moderately high levels of collectivism (implying the wide participation of stakeholders in CG), and moderately high levels of uncertainty avoidance together produced a community of stakeholders unwilling to expose itself to the discipline of volatile stockmarket prices. Arguably, German national culture and the legal, social and political institutions that underpin that culture, reasserted itself after attempts by the US military government to establish directly enforced elements of US-style, exit-based governance. This outcome reflects the institutional embeddedness and path dependence already noted in the Russian and Japanese episodes reviewed above.

So, if CG patterns are deeply embedded in national culture and institutions, how can one explain the prevalence in Germany of one important element of US-style governance, the ESO?

Neo-institutionalism and governance evolution

The previous section demonstrated, at a national level within three quite different countries and cases, that isomorphic governance institutions withstood alien transplants in circumstances of extreme crisis. The convergence of governance institutions (Coffee, 1999) emphatically did not occur in the most propitious of circumstances, as imposed governance reforms (Aldrich, 1999) foundered on hostile national culture and institutions. In the language of innovation theory (Mowery and Rosenberg, 1993), governance innovations can be demand-induced and/or supply (or knowledge)-driven. In the three cases, on the demand-side, serious economic crisis could have been expected to induce governance reforms. On the supply-side, the strengths of Anglo-American governance innovations were already widely transmitted and appreciated.

However, Rogers (1995) clearly demonstrated the importance of national culture to innovation adoption, and the local absorptive capacity (Zahra and George, 2002) for 'alien' structures was quite low. Prevailing governance forms in the three episodes chosen above continued to conform closely to institutionally prescribed templates inherited from the past (Davis and Thompson, 1994).

To this point, therefore, institutional theory has been depicted not as a theory of organizational change, but as an explanation of the isomorphic similarity and stability of nationally established organizational arrangements. Yet institutional change *does* occur periodically, and this section will be concerned with a consideration of the circumstances conducive to institutional change. This will lead to a discussion of the power of institutional theory to explain and predict actual changes in the German economy since 1990.

The focus of recent institutional theory is not on the single state nor the single organization, but rather on different organizations or sectors within the state (Greenwood and Hinings, 1996), and the purpose of this focus is to take theories of organizational change beyond ideas of inertia and persistence (Greenwood and Hinings, (1996). Also, the emphasis here is on induced rather than coercively imposed change (Aldrich, 1999).

Institutional change tends to occur when external contingencies change (DiMaggio and Powell 1983; Aldrich, 1999). Oliver (1992) identified three main drivers of institutional change: *functional* pressures arising from perceived performance shortcomings, *political* pressures from shifts in the interest and underlying power distributions that have underpinned existing institutions, and *social* pressures from fragmented interest groups with discordant views. The influence of each of these drivers is undoubtedly related to resource dependency (Pfeffer and Salancik, 1978), and Greenwood and Hinings (1996) propose that researchers track the effects of changes in crucial market pressures on power dependencies within and between organizations.

In these circumstances, equilibrium can be punctuated (Tushman and Romanelli, 1985) by the absorption of governance innovations, depending on the tightness of coupling across institutional sectors (Greenwood and Hinings, 1996) and thus compliance with existing templates. Top officers in government and in large industrial firms play a crucial role here, embedded in social structures that link actors and influence legislation (Davis and Thompson, 1994). For example, senior executives may drive change after participating in international executive labour markets, and some firms may need to develop global product strategies to compete on world markets for goods and services (Davis and Thompson, 1994). Executive influence on institutions may be strongest when strategies are capital-intensive, that is when external financial capital is the resource upon which firms are most dependent, and where local supplies are inadequate. New laws (for example changes in takeover legislation, corporate taxation) may now be influenced by senior executives (Davis and Thompson, 1994), facilitating convergence on previously alien structures.

These circumstances for institutional change processes are consistent with the limited convergence experienced in South Korea (Mishaupt, 1998) and Taiwan (Seo and Creed, 2002), where established isomorphism conflicted with divergent executive interests. In the case of modern Germany, it is argued that large industrial firms with significant exporting levels and/or facing import competition felt obliged as a divergent sector to attract American financial capital. As suppliers of the dominant resource upon which firms depended, American investors were able to insist upon institutional change, involving changes in laws influencing the liquidity of company stock, and upon revisions in the incentive packages offered to executives.

An analysis of governance in modern Germany, in particular the reward packages of senior executives, is therefore the focus of the next section which crucially considers the relevance of the analysis to the development of institutional theory itself.

Modern German governance and institutional theory: some hypotheses

On the face of it, the convergence on 'Americanization' of the German economy progressed rapidly and spontaneously in the 1990s, in contrast to the fate of the imposed reforms after the Second World War.

Traditionally, in large German firms managers (and especially Chief Executive Officers, CEOs) have been controlled mainly through the participation of other stakeholders in decisions: banks and employees impose their influence through the upper-tier board (*Aufsichtsrat*) and shareholders are usually tied to the firm in the long term. This all suits the German national culture of moderately high levels of uncertainty avoidance and collectivism. As in Russia and Japan, share price has been fairly unimportant in disciplining managers, and in 1990 total German stockmarket capitalization was only 23 per cent of GDP, with few hostile takeovers to discipline managers (Bernhardt, 2000). Share prices can have had only a weak impact on managerial decisions and firms are quite secretive in the matter of disclosing company information to the public.

But by 1997, total German stockmarket capitalization had risen to 40 per cent of GDP (Megginson, 2000), and therefore share price movements are now likely to play a stronger role in the discipline and motivation of senior managers. However, this 40 per cent was still well-short of market capitalization in the USA (144 per cent of GDP) and the UK (155 per cent). In the USA and the UK, information disclosure is relatively open and executives are strongly disciplined by share price movements. Share price reductions increase the threat of takeover and executive dismissal and also influence executives' total rewards. Nevertheless, with rising share liquidity, German CG in general, and important corporate strategies concerning executives' rewards in particular, may be *converging* on the American model (Coffee, 1999).

The design of executives' reward packages represents a key strategic decision to be made in relation to CG, and US-style reward packages relying significantly on equity-related elements of course rely on a general environment of US-style CG, with stock prices fluctuating on liquid markets, offering extensive information disclosure to individual shareholders. This environment in turn corresponds with the low levels of uncertainty avoidance and the high levels of individualism that are distinctive features of American national culture (see Table 9.1 and the first column of Table 9.2).

Specifically, executive stock options (ESOs) are a major influence on the decisions of CEOs in the USA. Although CEOs are in powerful positions, they are subject (almost exclusively) to the discipline of the firm's share price. Perhaps for this reason, the average US CEO salary in firms with sales of $500 m or more averaged $1,932,000 in 2000 (Towers Perrin, 2002). Of this, only $530,000 was in base salary with the rest made up of bonus, benefits and ESOs, mostly the latter. ESOs in the USA are mostly 'plain vanilla', that is without performance conditions, and executives automatically benefit if share prices rise. Typical of an individualistic culture, average CEO total rewards in large US firms in 2000 were on average 531-times the average wages of hourly employee.

At the other end of the spectrum, however, stand large German firms, with consensus-based decision-taking leading to an egalitarian sharing of the power and wealth of the CEO with others. CEO power is subject to all kinds of pressure from stakeholders such as employees and banks, mostly through upper-tier boards. A typical German large-firm CEO salary in 2000 was only $230,000, plus $225,000 in bonus and so on (Towers Perrin, 2002). ESOs were rare until recently. Total CEO pay was on average only 11-times average wages, and disclosure levels required by German accounting standards have been low. For example, under German accounting rule 285/9 of the HGB (German Commercial Code), firms must disclose only aggregate pay for executive board members in total, with nothing on the mix of rewards or on the pay of individual directors.

But this situation is said to be changing as governance reforms are induced, taking advantage of American pay innovations. German firms in sectors that are adopting global product strategies, resource-dependent upon financial capital in amounts too large for 'friendly' German providers of funds, are being forced into the arms of US investors. US investors look for executive pay packages in German firms that will attract and retain senior managers capable of pushing through a global strategy, and they demand high levels of disclosure of these packages. German tax laws have now been changed to remove the disincentives for share sales by long-term, relational investors like banks, so the shares of large firms are becoming generally more liquid, a necessary condition for ESOs as effective incentives. In 1998 the German Stock Company Law (*Aktiengesetz*) was changed to make ESOs easier, without the need for convertible bonds. Before this, ESOs at Continental Tyres in 1986 and Deutsche Bank and Daimler Benz (in 1996) had attracted criticism, but were complex combinations of convertible bonds and shares.

Press reports suggest that since the 1998 Aktiengesetz, most large German companies have been 'Americanized' in terms of one important governance strategy for firms: executive pay packages. By 2001, all DAX 30 companies reported at least the existence of ESOs in AGM notices to their shareholders. This all suggests rapid convergence on American CG in terms of the important institution of executive pay, and appears to fly in the face of German culture. It also appears to be consistent with neo-institutional theory that predicts the ability of institutions to change to adjust to circumstances.

But there are fundamental contradictions between US-style executive pay and relational governance in large German companies, creating a dialectic (Seo and Creed, 2002). Despite some relaxation of the legal institutions that underpin German national culture, ESOs imply a philosophy of individualism, are essentially inegalitarian, and create uncertainties for executives with uncertain future rewards and for shareholders faced with uncertain future executive labour costs. Above all, they increase the power of executives to control their own reward packages through the possible manipulation of performance conditions, exercise prices and the timing of announcements in a way that is inconsistent with Germany's low tolerance of power distance.

It seems important, therefore, to investigate at a deeper level the innovation of German ESOs to develop research propositions that recognize the *reality* of institutional stability and institutional change and not just their *appearance* (Greenwood *et al.*, 2002). Such research propositions can contribute significantly to the development of institutional theory.

We assume for the moment that traditional institutional theory, with its emphasis on embeddedness, isomorphism and inertia, *is* appropriate for German CG. This approach is justified by (a) previous experience with path-dependent German CG and a lack of real convergence, even under US military occupation, 1945–54 (Buck and Tull, 2000); and (b) previous evidence on general human-resource strategies in German firms – of which executive pay strategies are a subset – that emphasize their embeddedness in antecedent German culture and institutions (Ferner, 1997). If traditional institutional theory is provisionally accepted for the moment, it could be expected that American-style ESOs may be manipulated by German firms to produce an instrument that, in its details, is more consistent with long-term relational CG based on voice rather than stockmarket exit. Therefore, certain propositions are advanced on the presumption that German CG will *resist* Americanization. With German firms as communities of stakeholders favouring egalitarian outcomes, variations in the extent to which ESO schemes cascade down through the organization may now be hypothesised. Thus:

> H1 ESOs in German firms may be expected to be more egalitarian, extending to a larger numbers of senior managers and other employees than equivalent schemes in the USA and the UK.

Similarly, a community of stakeholders imposing tight, collective 'voice' control of managerial decisions may be uncomfortable with the wide variations in the dispersion of income and wealth that ESOs imply. Despite any more extensive coverage of schemes in terms of their wider membership, German ESO schemes may still be expected to offer lower rewards in total. Therefore:

> H2 German ESO schemes may be predicted to involve smaller proportions of firms' total issued capital under option in ESO schemes than in the USA and the UK.

With relatively low tolerance of power-distance in Germany, besides a concern to extend less valuable ESO schemes (H2) to wider constituencies of employees (H1), influential stakeholders may want to ensure that ESO-based rewards are 'earned' by managers. This could imply more numerous and tighter performance conditions rather than 'soft' ESO schemes designed by executives to suit their own pockets. Two propositions are therefore generated:

> H3 With low levels of executive power in Germany subject to a degree of collective control, the attachment of quantitatively more performance conditions to ESO awards can be predicted compared with the USA and the UK.

> H4 Following H3, the use of qualitatively more demanding German performance indicators can be proposed compared with the USA and the UK.

With a general German CG regime founded on the collective influence of stakeholders with arguably longer time-horizons than shareholders in the USA and the UK, this 'long-termism' may also be reflected in specific ESO schemes:

> H5 CG in Germany will produce ESO schemes of longer duration, with longer qualification periods imposed before option exercise, and longer holding periods for shares after option exercise, than in the USA and the UK.

It can be seen that these five propositions implicitly favour traditional institutional theory and the adoption of an American pay innovation such as the ESO by large German firms in a way that, in its detail, does not constitute substantial Americanization. The development of concrete hypotheses from these propositions and the conduct of empirical tests must await the fuller disclosure of pay information by German firms, and, of course, fuller disclosure is itself an indicator of Americanization.

Disclosure levels are increasing slightly in German firms. For example, of the 43 DAX 100 firms declaring at least the existence of ESOs by 2002 in shareholder AGM invitations, only 11 companies disclose details of ESO schemes because they have voluntarily adopted US 'Generally Accepted Accounting Principles' (GAAP) accounts. A further 10 companies provide information on executive pay in their proxy statements to the US Stock Exchange Commission as a result of their level-2 or 3 American Depository Receipts (ADR) listings. With some firms using GAAP *and* ADRs, even fairly rudimentary ESO information is only available for 14 of the 43 large German firms disclosing the existence of ESOs.

Discussion

What conclusions can be drawn from this predominantly historical analysis for policy and theory-building? In relation to policy, it seems clear that no one form of CG, certainly not US-style, market-based CG, is appropriate in all contingencies. In particular, national culture and antecedent institutions are important contingencies, different CG structures bring their own strengths and weaknesses in different circumstances, and it may be an illusion that governments can 'pick and mix' the optimum CG package.

In relation to theory, the analysis of three historical episodes in Germany, Japan and Russia confirms the resilience of national cultures and institutions to imposed legislative change, even at vulnerable stages of their history. From this perspective, therefore, researchers within the governance–strategy–performance paradigm, especially in transition economies (see for example Thomas and Waring, 1999; Filatotchev *et al.* 2000) should not be surprised at the statistical insignificance of many of their regression coefficients. Change is emphatically path-dependent, and key actors have low absorptive capacity and an inability to unlearn embedded routines and templates quickly.

However, neo-institutional theory does contemplate the contingencies that promote institutional change, and major spontaneous governance changes have become evident since 1990 in Russia, Japan and Germany. These changes represent a new opportunity for institutional theory, offering progress towards the final stage of social science, and the most important stage for Popperians, that of empirical testing. The possibility of genuine institutional change is real. Apparent cases of convergent institutional change in relation to business strategies such as takeovers and equity-based executive pay should, however, be analysed in depth before equivalence across national cultures is assumed. If convergence in governance forms is found, the intriguing possibility arises that convergence on market-based governance may be just a special case of the predicted convergence of transactions in general, as economic systems mature (Peng, 2003).

References

Aldrich, H.E. (1999) *Organizations Evolving*. London: Sage.

Berglöf, E. and Perotti, E. (1994) 'The governance structure of the Japanese financial *Keiretsu*', *Journal of Financial Economics* 36(2), 259–84.

Bebchuk, L. and Roe, M.J. (1998) 'A Theory of path dependence in corporate ownership and governance', in *Corporate Governance Today*: 575–99. The Sloan Project on Corporate Governance at Columbia Law School. New York: Columbia Law School.

Berkowitz, D., Pistor, K. and Richard, J.-F. (2000) 'Economic development, legality, and the transplant effect', William Davidson Institute Working Paper no. 308. Ann Arbor: University of Michigan Business School.

Bernhardt, W. (1999) 'Stock options for or against shareholder value? New compensation plans for top management and the interests of shareholders', *Corporate Governance: An International Review* 7(2), 123–35.

Bhappu, A.D. (2000) 'The Japanese family: an institutional logic for Japanese corporate networks and Japanese management', *Academy of Management Review* 25(2), 409–15.

Black, B.S. (2000) 'The legal and institutional preconditions for strong stock markets', Stanford Law School Working Paper no. 179. Stanford: Stanford Law School.

Blackwell, W.L. (1986). *The Beginnings of Russian Industrialization*, Vol. 1. Princeton: Princeton University Press.

Blasi, J.H., Kroumova, M. and Kruse, D. (1997) *Kremlin Capitalism: Privatizing the Russian Economy*. Ithaca: Cornell University Press.

Boycko, B. Shleifer, A. and Vishny, R. (1993) 'Privatizing Russia', Brookings Papers on Economic Activity Vol. 2; 139–81.

Buck, T. and Tull, M. (2000) 'Anglo-American contributions to Japanese and German corporate governance after World War Two', *Business History* 42(2), 119–40.

Bureau of Business Research (1969) *Labor Relations and the Law in West Germany and the United States*. Ann Arbor MI: Bureau of Business Research.

CCG (British Element) (1949) 'Monthly Report', in von Oppen, B.R., *Documents on Germany During Occupation, 1945–1954*. Oxford: Royal Institute of Economic Affairs/ Oxford University Press.

Charkham, J.P. (1995) *Keeping Good Company: A Study of Corporate Governance in Five Countries*. Oxford: Oxford University Press.

Coffee, J.C. Jr. (1999) *The Future as History: The Prospects for Global Convergence in Corporate Governance and its Implications*. Working Paper no. 144. New York: Columbia Law School Center for Law and Economic Studies.

Cooke, T.E. and Kikuya, M. (1966) *Financial Reporting in Japan: Regulation, Practice and Environment*. Oxford: Blackwell.

Crisp, O. (1976) *Studies in the Russian Economy Before 1914*. London: Macmillan – Palgrave.

Dacin, M.T., Goodstein, J. and Scott, W.R. (2002) 'Institutional theory and institutional change: introduction to the special research forum', *Academy of Management Journal* 45(1), 45–57.

Davis, G.F. and Thompson, T.A. (1994) 'A social movement perspective on corporate control', *Administrative Science Quarterly* 39(1), 141–73.

DiMaggio, P.J. and Powell, W.W. (1983) 'The iron cage revisited: institutional isomorphism and collective rationality in organizational fields', *American Sociological Review* 48(1), 147–60.

Earle, J.S. and Estrin, S. (1996) 'Employee ownership in transition', in Frydman, R., Gray, C.W. and Rapaczynski, A. (eds), *Corporate Governance in Russia: Vol 2, Insiders and the State*: 1–61. London: World Bank/CEU Press.

Elenkov, D.S. (1998) 'Can American management concepts work in Russia: a cross-cultural comparative study', *California Management Review* 40(4), 133–56.

Estrin, S. and Wright, M. (1999) 'Corporate governance in the former Soviet Union: an overview of the issues', *Journal of Comparative Economics* 27(3), 398–421.

Evans, R.E. Jr. (1970) 'Evolution of Japanese system of employer–employee relations, 1868–1945', *Business History Review* 34(1), 110–25.

Ferner, A. (1997) 'Country of origin effects and HRM in multinational companies', *Human Resource Management Journal* 7(1), 19–37.

Filatotchev, I. Buck, T. and Zhukov, V. (2000) 'Downsizing in privatized firms in Russia, Ukraine and Belarus: theory and empirical evidence', *Academy of Management Journal* 43(3), 286–304.

Franks, J. and Mayer, C. (1997) 'Corporate ownership and control in the U.K., Germany and France', *Journal of Applied Corporate Finance* 9(4), 30–45.

Gatrell, P. (1986) *The Tsarist Economy 1850–1917*. London: Batsford.

Granovetter, M. (1985) 'Economic action and social structure: the problem of embeddedness', *American Journal of Sociology* 91(3), 481–510.

Greenwood, R. and Hinings, C.R. (1996) 'Understanding radical organizational change: bringing together the old and the new institutionalism', *Academy of Management Review* 21(4), 1022–54.

Greenwood, R., Suddaby, R. and Hinings, C.R. (2002) 'Theorizing change: the role of professional associations in the transformation of institutionalized fields', *Academy of Management Journal* 45(1), 58–80.

Hadley, E.M. (1970) *Anti-Trust in Japan*. Princeton NJ: Princeton University Press.

Hirschmeier, J. and Yui, T. (1981) *The Development of Japanese Business*. London: George Allen & Unwin.

Hofstede, G. (1997) *Cultures and Organizations*. Beverly Hills: Sage.

Kindleberger, C.P. (1984) *A Financial History of Western Europe*. London: George Allen & Unwin.

Licht, A.N. (2001) 'The mother of all path dependencies: toward a cross-cultural theory of corporate governance systems', *Delaware Journal of Corporate Law* 26(1), 147–205.

Macey, J.R. and Miller, G.P. (1997) 'Universal banks are not the answer to America's corporate governance "problem": a look at Germany, Japan and the U.S.', *Journal of Applied Corporate Finance* 9(4), 57–73.

Maddy, C.G. and Ickes, B. (1998) 'Russia's virtual economy', *Foreign Affairs* 77: 53–68.

Megginson, W.M. (2000) 'Corporate governance in publicly-quoted privatized companies', presented at the OECD conference, Corporate governance of state-owned enterprises in China. Beijing: OECD.

Mishaupt, C.J. (1998) 'Property rights in firms', in *Corporate Governance Today*: 601–638. The Sloan Project on Corporate Governance at Columbia Law School. New York: Columbia Law School.

Mowery, D. and Rosenberg, N. (1993) 'The influence of market demand on innovation: a critical review of some recent empirical studies', *Research Policy* 22(2), 107–8.

Newman, K.L. (2000) 'Organizational transformation during institutional upheaval', *Academy of Management Review* 25(3), 602–19.

Noorderhaven, N.G. (1999) 'National culture and the development of trust: the need for more data and less theory', *Academy of Management Review* 24(1), 9–10.

North, D.C. (1990) *Institutions, Institutional Change and Economic Performance*. Cambridge: Cambridge University Press.

Noteboom, B. (1999) 'Voice- and exit-forms of corporate control: Anglo-American, European, and Japanese', *Journal of Economic Issues* 3(4), 845–60.

Official Gazette, Central Council (1946) *Control Council Law 22: Works Councils*, in von Oppen, B.R., *Documents on Germany During Occupation, 1945–1954*, p. 118. Oxford: Royal Institute of Economic Affairs/Oxford University Press.

Oliver, C. (1992) 'The antecedents of deinstitutionalization', *Organization Studies* 13(4), 563–88.

Organization for Economic Co-operation and Development (1999) *Corporate Governance in Russia*. Conference Synthesis Note. Moscow: OECD.

Peng, M.W. (2003) 'Institutional transitions and strategic choices', *Academy of Management Review*.

Pfeffer, J. and Salancik, C.R. (1978) *The External Control of Organizations*. New York: Harper & Row.

Pipes, R. (1995) *Russia Under the Old Regime*. Harmondsworth: Penguin.

Pistor, K. (1998) 'Co-determination in Germany: a socio-political model with governance externalitites', in *Corporate Governance Today*: 387–414. The Sloan Project on Corporate Governance at Columbia Law School. New York: Columbia Law School.

Roe, M.J. (1993) 'Some differences in corporate structure in Germany, Japan and the United States', *The Yale Law Journal* 102(8), 1927–2003).
Roe, M.J. (1997) 'The political roots of American corporate governance', *Journal of Applied Corporate Finance* 9(4), 8–22.
Rogers, E. (1995) *The Diffusion of Knowledge*. New York: Free Press.
Schaller, M. (1985) *The American Occupation of Japan*. Oxford: Oxford University Press.
Scher, M.J. (1997) *Japanese Interfirm Networks and Their Main Banks*. Basingstoke: Macmillan – Palgrave.
Schneider-Lenné, E. (1992) 'Corporate control in Germany', *Oxford Review of Economic Policy* 8(3), 11–23.
Schwartz, S.H. (1994) 'Beyond individualism/collectivism: new cultural dimensions of values', in Kim, U., Triandis, H.C., Kagitcibasi, Ç., Choi, S.-C. and Yoon, G. (eds), *Individualism and Collectivism: Theory, Method and Applications*: 88–99. California: Sage.
Seo, M.-G. and Creed, W.E.D. (2002) 'Institutional contradictions, praxis, and institutional change: a dialectical perspective', *Academy of Management Review* 27(2), 222–47.
Sheard, P. (1994) 'Interlocking directorships and corporate governance', in Aoki, M. and Dore, R. (eds), *The Japanese Firm; the Sources of Competitive Strength*: 310–49. Oxford: Oxford University Press.
Shleifer, A. and Vishny, R. (1997) 'A Survey of Corporate Governance', *Journal of Finance* 52(1), 737–83.
Stolper, G. (1967) *The German Economy 1870 to the Present*. London: Weidenfeld & Nicolson.
Thomas, L.G. III and Waring, G. (1999) 'Competing capitalisms: capital investment in American, German and Japanese firms', *Strategic Management Journal* 20(8), 729–48.
Towers Perrin (2002) *Worldwide Total Remuneration, 2001/02. http://www.towers.com/towers publications/*
Turner, I.D. (1989) *Reconstruction in post-war Germany*. Oxford: Berg.
Tushman, M.L. and Romanelli, E. (1985) 'Organizational evolution: a metamorphosis model of convergence and reorientation', in Cummings, L.L. and Straw, B.M. (eds), *Research in Organizational Behavior*, vol. 7: 171–222. Greenwich, CT: JAI Press.
Williamson, O.E. (2000) 'The new institutional economics: taking stock, looking ahead', *Journal of Economic Literature* 38(3), 595–613.
Zahra, S.A. and George, G. (2002) 'Absorptive capacity: a review, reconceptualization and extension', *Academy of Management Review* 27(2), 185–203.

Part III

Internationalization by Small and Medium-Sized Enterprises

10

Internationalization Factors and Firm Size: An Empirical Study of the East of England*

Habte Selassie, Brian Mathews, Lester Lloyd-Reason and Terry Mughan

Introduction

The role of small and medium-sized enterprises (SMEs) in helping to deliver growth in export activity is clearly recognized, and is explicit within the strategy document of the East of England Development Agency (EEDA, 2002). It is stated that the growth in the global economy offers tremendous opportunities for SMEs within the East of England, but successfully exploiting these opportunities will not be easy, particularly as the international business environment becomes increasingly competitive. The East of England is an economically dynamic region with a record of success in recent years in both exporting and inward investment. However, its continued success will depend on the ability of its companies increasingly to adopt an international approach to business. A number of important weaknesses in the data currently available can be identified. With respect to company internationalization there has been a lack of consolidated, reliable, quantitative data on the region's companies, and furthermore the data available do not allow identification of the extent of SME involvement in export activity in a manner that would enable policy-makers accurately to target and allocate resources.

This chapter aims to contribute towards the provision of consolidated and quantitative information on the type of companies in the region that may help to measure progress in internationalization activities. Of particular interest are

* This research was funded by the East of England Development Agency and this chapter presents parts of the results of an ongoing research project concerning competitiveness in international markets of SMEs in the East of England. The authors wish to acknowledge the contributions of Professor Christos Kalantaridis for participating in the early stage of the project involving preparation of the project proposal and the questionnaire, Jane Dix who managed the project; and Zografia Bika and Annette Ulrich for their role in data collection and management.

the differences, if any, between the export behaviour of micro, small and medium-sized firms, their activities and needs, in comparison with large firms in the East of England.

Literature review

Research results examining the relationship between size and export behaviour are mixed (Buckley, 1999; Calof, 1994; Bonaccorsi, 1992; Kalantaridis, 2000; Boter and Holmqvist, 1996). One body of literature suggests that... 'the size of firm is merely a point of time view of a dynamic process of growth and that it is the growth process which is critical' (Buckley 1999: 100). Nevertheless, Calof (1994) found that size was positively related to a firm's propensity to export; there was a positive and significant relationship between firm size and the number of markets exported to, specific markets served, export stage, export intent and years exporting. Boter and Holmqvist (1996) also conclude that company size correlates to international activities, while Poutziouris *et al.* (2000) identify that there is considerable evidence, within the UK SMEs and micro-enterprising sector, for a relationship between certain demographic variables and export development. According to Poutziouris *et al.* (2000), the profile of export-active SME was: sizeable, established, and mainly production-based companies.

On the other hand, Bonaccorsi (1992) claims to falsify the proposition that firm size is positively related to export intensity, and challenges some widely held assumptions in the export marketing literature. Kalantaridis (2000) found that there was only a weak relationship between the incidence of strategy and the size of the firm; his findings implied that on the whole SMEs (as well as large firms) engaging in exchange relations beyond national boundaries adopt a strategic approach. With regards to entry-mode choice, for example, the findings of Brouthers *et al.* (1996) tend to indicate that ownership and locational advantages influence the entry-mode choice of SMEs in a manner similar to that of larger firms.

Interestingly, there appears relatively little in the literature exploring competitive advantage in export markets at the firm level; that is, what firms see as their 'edge'. The analyses by Katsikeas and Al-Khalifa (1993) and Piercy *et al.* (1998) centre round the issues of cost, product features and service, although neither gives any breakdown by company size. In terms of competitive disadvantage, that is what overseas competitors do well, there seems to be little guidance other than from the general competitiveness or internationalization literature which tends to focus on macro issues.

While the stage theory of internationalization (see Crick 1995 for a review of approaches) which proposes that firms expand to international markets in an incremental stepwise manner is credited for providing useful frameworks for the analysis of international growth patterns of firms, it may not adequately explain SME internationalization (Coviello and Munro, 1999). Nevertheless, the stages approach does emphasize physical and 'psychic' distances to be important with more advanced exporters being more adventurous in their choice of export destinations, using more complex channels and more advanced forms of internationalisation, for example overseas production.

Literature abounds that SMEs face problems unique to their characteristics (Westhead *et al.*, 2002; Buckley, 1999; Crick and Chaudhry, 1997; Karagozoglu and Lindell, 1996). Among other things, SMEs are impeded by lack of resources to exploit competitive advantages beyond domestic markets (Westhead *et al.*, 2002). Often key barriers faced by SME internationalization are categorized as: *internal* (lack of information, lack of finance, insufficient managerial skills and so on), and *external* (home-country and target-country characteristics and environments for example) (Szabo, 2002; Buckley, 1999; UN/ECE, 1997). The shortage of managerial skills is seen as a very serious liability for smaller firms. While availability of finance is among the important constraints, in most cases these constraints are secondary to managerial ones (Buckley, 1999). Baird *et al.* (1994) conclude that the distinctive challenge of the international strategy of small firm is to overcome the conditions unique to small companies and develop international strategies such as exporting or joint ventures that are effective in their situations. Karagozoglu and Lindell (1996) studied the barriers and motives that drive US small and medium-sized technology-based firms' internationalization, and found that there were more individual differences than uniform patterns.

The issue of support given to exporters is one that complements the identification of problems faced. Government agencies have been charged with the responsibility for providing effective support for exporters and have developed extensive programmes (see, for example, Diamantopoulos *et al.*, 1993; Crick, 1997; Crick and Chaudhry, 2000). In addressing the various obstacles SMEs face and to put in place an enabling environment, however, most literature has been sceptical of generic approaches. According to recent research (Crick and Chaudhry, 1997; Karagozoglu and Lindell, 1996) offering generic programmes to motivate SMEs to undertake exporting appeared to be inappropriate, and if export growth was to be encouraged certain behavioural characteristics of firms must be taken into consideration. If not, the authors argue, limited resources for assistance may be inefficiently utilized.

Even though there have recently been advances in the empirical research addressing SME export behaviour, serious shortcomings have also been noted. Leonidou (1995) points out that much remains to be done beyond the 'identification and conceptualisation' stage, and in carrying out in-depth studies, capturing recent developments, in applying a better and consistent classification of size (among SMEs), and in adopting comparative approaches with large firms.

In summary, identification and examination of the key factors that determine the pace and pattern of internationalization of SMEs is an important step in devising policy and support regimes. The key factors identified from review of the literature and examined in this study for the four groups of firms categorized by size (micro, small, medium and large) are: patterns of international activity, experiences in exporting, export destinations, export modes, decision-makers, competitive advantages and disadvantages, obstacles faced, and sources of support.

Methodology

A survey was designed to determine the extent and nature of international activity within the region, explored in terms of the issues identified above. Another key aspect of the design was in identifying the differences between the export behaviour of micro, small and medium-sized firms, in comparison with that of large firms in the region. A questionnaire was used to collect data. The questionnaire was fully structured, with response categories defined prior to the study informed by literature relevant to internationalization, although many questions contained an 'others' category, which could be post-coded subsequent to the survey. The questionnaire was pilot-tested on a small number of respondents to ensure understandability prior to the main survey. A telephone interviewing technique was used to collect data due to its quick turnaround time, accuracy and efficiency.

The sample frame used were databases that listed known exporters and non-exporters broken down by county obtained from Business Link. The listings were a random sample of organizations but, with repeated sampling, in the final event nearly all organizations recorded as exporters were approached during the survey. The telephone interviews began in June 2002 and were completed by the end of August 2002. Interviewers requested to speak with a senior executive within the organization, usually at Director level. The 12-page interview took between 5 to 30 minutes to complete depending on which of the sections were relevant to the respondent.

Many of the questions allowed, or requested, multiple responses and so percentages are presented relative to the number of respondents rather than the number of responses given (which could be up to three). Adopting this approach imposes a limitation since SPSS, the software package used, does not report statistical significance on multiple-response tables. Size categorization used in the analysis complies with the definitions the Department of Trade and Industry (DTI) usually use for statistical purposes, that is micro fewer than 10 employees; small from 10 to 49 employees; medium from 50 to 249 employees; large 250+ employees.

Response rates varied considerably, but within the exporter group these were at a very creditable 22 per cent overall; mail surveys of this nature often only achieve 12 to 15 per cent response rates. Respondents always had the option of refusing to answer questions in the survey, for example if they felt uncomfortable revealing certain information, or did not remember (or know) some of the specific details. All 'don't know/refused' responses were treated as missing values and are not presented in any of the tables. As a result, the number of responses for each question will vary.

Findings and discussion

The findings from the survey are analysed and discussed under 10 headings:

1. International activity
2. Export intensity
3. Experience of exporting
4. Export destinations
5. Export modes
6. Decision-makers
7. Firm's competitive advantages
8. Competitor's competitive advantages
9. Obstacles to exporting
10. Use of support mechanisms

International activity

The first area of analysis is to examine the penetration of international activity within our total sample of internationalized firms. This is important because apparently anomalous results in terms of exporting may be explained by engagement in other international activities, for example international production. Looking at the different sizes of organizations, Table 10.1 indicates that, overall, SMEs' international activities appear to have centred on exporting and

Table 10.1 Internationalization of firms

	All firms (% cases)	*Micro (% cases)*	*Small (% cases)*	*Medium (% cases)*	*Large* (% cases)*
Exporting	77	71	77	80	70
Importing	62	65	61	64	52
International production	14	13	9	24	38
Sample base *N*=	560	76	347	137	101

* Large firms excluded from 'All firms' total.

importing compared to large firms. The proportion of SMEs engaged in exporting and importing is 77 per cent and 62 per cent respectively, while the corresponding percentages for large firms are 70 per cent and 52 per cent. Of particular interest is that many organizations are involved in multiple forms of internationalization; for example, nearly 60 per cent of SME exporters also import, while about 7 per cent are also involved in international production.

The evidence suggests that size has some impact on the degree of internationalization among SMEs; the proportion of firms engaged in exporting increases with size. Though not that distinctly, the medium-sized firms appear to be more internationalized with regard to other modes of internationalization. While the margin is rather narrow, micro-enterprises are less internationalized than their small-firm counterparts. On the other hand, large firms fare much better regarding the other forms of internationalization; that is, international production (including subsidiaries, joint ventures, licensing, and so on). Overall, however, it would seem that micro and small enterprises are involved in fewer modes of internationalization than the medium and large organisations.

Export intensity

Table 10.2 shows the change in the proportion of export to sales for different sizes of firms. Looking at the figures for the EU between 1997 and 2001, while there is an increase for both the large firms (3 per cent) and SMEs (2 per cent), large firms appear to rely more on export to the EU than SMEs. Within the SME groups micro-enterprises reported higher proportions of their exports to the EU compared to the other two size groups, a somewhat perplexing finding given that intuitively one would expect that the larger firms, given their greater resource base, would be better able to support high export penetration. One explanation might be that micro enterprises are exploiting niche markets supported by a low overhead structure (see Table 10.7). All firms depend less on export to wider international markets compared to that of the EU. The figures for the international markets between 1997 and 2001 increased for the

Table 10.2 Exports to sales (1997–2001)

	All Firms (% cases)	*Micro (% cases)*	*Small (% cases)*	*Medium (% cases)*	*Large* (% cases)*
EU sales 2001	20.5	25.5	20.1	19.1	30.9
EU sales 1999	19.9	25.0	19.7	17.9	29.8
EU sales 1997	19.4	24.5	19.5	17.0	27.5
Other int'l sales 2001	17.8	25.1	16.4	17.8	19.1
Other int'l sales 1999	17.3	21.7	16.4	17.4	18.6
Other int'l sales 1997	17.6	23.6	16.3	18.2	17.0

* Large firms excluded from 'Firms' averages.

large firms (2 per cent), but remained stable at about 18 per cent for SMEs. However, within the SME groups, micro-enterprises appear to have a higher proportion of exports to international markets and this is shown to increase from 24 per cent in 1997 to 25 per cent in 2001.

The rate and growth of the proportion of exports to total sales (1997–2001) of SMEs in the region appeared to be low and slow for the EU countries, while there were almost no changes for other international markets. The proportion of exports to sales to both markets (EU and other international) have shown a higher growth for large firms compared to those of SMEs in the region. The rate of increase is somewhat disappointing given the long-term focus that has been given to the promotion of exports. On the other hand, given the relatively disadvantageous exchange rate of the pound in recent years the figures could be interpreted as encouraging. Looking at the levels overall, within the exporting firms over one-third of turnover is accounted for by exports. In their study of internationalization of firms in seven European countries, Boter and Holmqvist (1996) report an export intensity of 31 per cent for 'smaller firms' (under 50 employees) and 41 per cent for 'larger firms' (50 and over employees). If we regroup the firms in this study into two for comparison, that is 'smaller' (micro and small firms), and 'larger' (medium and large firms), the average export intensity (1997–2001) rate is about the same for both groups at 42 per cent. This appears a strong performance for firms in the region, particularly for the 'small' firms. Further, Crick (1995) uses 5 per cent as a threshold value to denote progress towards the higher stages of internationalization. Clearly, while overall percentages mask individual cases, the bulk of exporters could be described as experienced according to this measure.

Experience of exporting

A further dimension to experience in exporting is given by the length of time that firms have been engaged in this activity. Table 10.3 shows that more than half of

Table 10.3 Years' experience of exporters

	All firms (% cases)	*Micro (% cases)*	*Small (% cases)*	*Medium (% cases)*	*Large* (% cases)*
0–5 years	11	8	14	6	5
6–10 years	17	17	17	16	12
11–15 years	22	27	22	18	6
16–20 years	15	19	15	14	17
21–30 years	19	21	19	20	15
30+ years	16	8	13	26	45
Sample base *N*=	417	52	260	105	65

* Large firms excluded from 'Firms' total.

SMEs have less than 15 years of experience, while for large firms this is about 22 per cent. A marked difference is that 45 per cent of large firms have 30 years or more experience while the corresponding percentage for SMEs is 16 per cent.

The number of SMEs that have entered the export market in recent years appears modest. The results from the survey suggest that in the early 1990s there was a significant move to internationalization, which has slowed down to a growth of 2 per cent per annum. Nevertheless, given that Crick (1995) denotes experience of exporting of over two years as a prerequisite to attaining to the highest stages of internationalization, these results indicate a potentially high level of sophistication in exporting for many if not most of the respondents. It must be pointed out, however, that there are potential sample-frame errors present insofar as recent exporters may have not been included in our lists and so the proportion in the under-five-years category may well be underestimated.

Export destinations

Table 10.4 shows the distribution of export destinations by size of firms. Again for all sizes of firms the top destinations are France, Germany and the USA. On

Table 10.4 Export destinations

	All firms (% cases)	*Micro (% cases)*	*Small (% cases)*	*Medium (% cases)*	*Large* (% cases)*
France	25	23	24	27	49
Germany	29	30	32	24	47
Italy	7	9	8	4	6
Spain, Portugal, Greece	10	6	12	7	11
Belgium, Netherlands, Luxembourg	16	11	17	16	10
Denmark, Sweden, Norway, Finland	6	6	6	7	4
Other EU	9	8	9	10	0
Central and Eastern Europe	6	6	8	2	9
Other Europe (non EU)	3	6	3	3	1
USA	23	17	22	26	32
Canada, Australia, New Zealand	6	6	5	7	6
Russia	1	2	1	1	0
Africa	8	19	6	6	4
China	3	4	2	6	4
Japan	5	0	5	6	1
Other Asia	20	23	16	26	9
Other America	2	2	2	3	0
Sample base *N*=	425	53	264	108	71

* Large firms excluded from 'Firms' total.

a closer look, it appears that the large firms have concentrated their export operations on two EU countries, France and Germany (96 per cent), while the corresponding percentage for the SMEs is 54 per cent. Overall, the export destinations of SMEs are more diversified than those of the large firms. For example, large firms have no presence in such markets as Russia, Other America, and Other EU as principal export markets, while SMEs have reached all corners of the globe.

Overall, the major export destinations are Germany, France and the USA; suggesting that geographic as well as psychic factors are major determinants. Other Asia is also an important market. It is interesting to note, however, that the incidence of depending on closer markets is consistent across all sizes of firms, including large ones. This is somewhat paradoxical, in that according to incremental theory, over time and through experience, firms increase foreign market commitment and expand to more 'psychically-distant' markets (Coviello and Munro, 1999). As large firms are more experienced in foreign markets it would be logical to expect large firms to venture into distant and culturally diverse markets. The wide reach of SMEs to 'psychically-distant' markets observed in this study, however, may be explained by such factors as close relationships with customers, inter-firm relationships, and in general by their network relationships (Coviello and Munro, 1999).

Export modes

Table 10.5 shows that the use of a certain export mode varies with size. Large firms mostly use their own sales-office mode, while SMEs may use agents, distributors or export houses. The rationale could be that large firms have the resources and the required experience to invest in offices and facilities in overseas

Table 10.5 Mode of export

	All firms (% cases)	*Micro (% cases)*	*Small (% cases)*	*Medium (% cases)*	*Large* (% cases)*
Agents, distributors or export houses	35	37	31	42	18
Own sales office	21	13	21	26	45
Direct sales	13	11	16	7	10
Network of reps	9	6	9	10	23
Internet/website	6	9	6	3	3
Through current customers	4	4	5	5	0
Word of mouth	4	6	5	0	0
Other	8	15	7	7	2
Sample base *N*=	428	54	266	108	71

* Large firms excluded from 'Firms' total.

markets. This view is strengthened as the incidence of use of the own-sales-office mode declines with firm size: large firms (45 per cent), medium (26 per cent), small (21 per cent) and micro-enterprises (13 per cent). The same trend is observed with regard to networking of representatives, where the incidence of use declines with size. It is interesting to note that the reverse is true for internet/website use.

The use of agents and distributors is associated with the middle ranges of stages models of internationalization (see Crick, 1995, for a review). The most advanced stage, international production, is not shown in Table 10.5 but was covered in Table 10.1, confirming the view that export sophistication increases with size. The relatively higher incidence of orders received via websites and through word of mouth exhibited by micro and small firms suggests that there may be a small but significant incidence of unsolicited export orders, characteristic of firms in the early stages of internationalization.

Decision-makers

The issue of who makes the decisions in exporting is important since it facilitates the targeting of services to the correct individual. Table 10.6 shows that decision-making varies by size. The incidence of owner/manager as the decision-maker declines as the size of firms increases: micro-enterprises (80 per cent), small (70 per cent), medium (50 per cent) and large (42 per cent). This implies that the larger the firm becomes the more decision-making is delegated to specialist section of the organization. The percentage of firms where the sales manager makes decisions increases with size within the SMEs, but does not feature that strongly in the large firms. In the large firms, a team/department of specialist managers (31 per cent) or a specialist export manager (14 per cent) are notable decision-makers. On the other hand, the percentage of SMEs where these play a decision-making role are insignificant. These results are as expected

Table 10.6 Decision-makers

	All firms (% cases)	*Micro (% cases)*	*Small (% cases)*	*Medium (% cases)*	*Large* (% cases)*
Owner/manager	66	80	70	50	42
Sales manager	15	6	15	20	11
A team/department of specialist managers	9	9	5	18	31
Specialist export manager	5	2	5	7	14
Other	5	4	5	5	1
Sample base *N*=	423	54	261	108	71

* Large firms excluded from 'Firms' total.

since with an increase in size specialization is likely to occur, and indeed this is the case with exporting.

Firms' competitive advantages

Examining the reasons behind exporting success can give clear leads as to which aspects of a firm or its products can form the best basis for promotion of other firms in exporting (Table 10.7). Better quality tops the advantages that firms have both in the SME and large categories in equal measure (52 per cent). Where large firms do have an increased competitive advantages over SMEs is in improved technology (29 per cent to 18 per cent), and better marketing and distribution (22 per cent to 9 per cent). Also, large firms appear to have greater advantages in terms of economies of scale, and lower production costs, which is to be expected. Where SMEs seem to score, even though marginally, are in access to information and niche market/specialization. It is interesting to note that improved technology and, though not to the same level, economies of scale as advantages increase with size. Within the SME sector, certain patterns emerge. Access to information, and lower production costs as advantages decrease as firm size increases. However, better quality and improved technology as advantages increase along with firm size. Exporter SMEs in the region recognize that the quality of their products and services, and their technologies, are the most valued competitive advantages.

Looking at the overall profile, product-related features of quality and technology are prominent and consistent with the findings of Katsikeas and

Table 10.7 Firm competitive advantages

	All firms (% cases)	*Micro (% cases)*	*Small (% cases)*	*Medium (% cases)*	*Large* (% cases)*
Better quality	52	48	52	55	52
Improved technology	18	10	16	25	29
Access to information	14	27	14	8	12
Lower production costs	13	19	14	10	16
Better marketing and distribution	9	12	9	10	22
Niche market/specialization	9	12	7	12	3
Flexibility	5	2	5	5	4
Economies of scale	4	2	2	8	9
Relationship building	1	0	2	2	0
Government support	1	2	1	1	0
Macroeconomic advantages	1	0	0	3	0
Other	12	12	15	7	1
No advantages	3	0	4	1	1
Sample base *N*=	424	53	264	108	71

* Large firms excluded from 'Firms' total.

Al-Khalifa (1993), but other product-related aspects identified by Piercy *et al.* (1998) such as packaging, style and brand image do not figure in these results. This may be because of differences in research design. The Piercy *et al.* (1998) study presented the additional items on the questionnaire rather than the current study, which gave no such direction and simply recorded respondent's answers (presumably the most salient issues). In terms of service, again there are considerable differences with Piercy *et al.* (1998), with no real prominence of service-related aspects identified in the current study; presumably for the same reasons.

Competitors' competitive advantage

The counterpart to competitive advantage is the challenges firms perceive in competing with other players in export markets (Table 10.8). Compared to SMEs, large firms see more disadvantages in lower production costs, and government support. On the other hand, SMEs see more disadvantages in economies of scale. In fact, the importance of economies of scale as a disadvantage decreases as firm size increases. SMEs and large firms' assessment of some disadvantages appear the same; for example access to information (12 per cent), better marketing and distribution (11 per cent). For those stating 'no advantage' there is a clear decrease from micro to medium, but the large firms report a much higher value than any other group. This may be related to the economies of scale being a material concern for SMEs, but not so for larger companies. Overall, they consider economies of scale and lower production costs as the most important competitive disadvantages.

Table 10.8 Competitors' competitive advantages

	All firms (% cases)	*Micro (% cases)*	*Small (% cases)*	*Medium (% cases)*	*Large* (% cases)*
Economies of scale	35	39	35	34	15
Lower production costs	26	23	23	37	35
Access to information	12	9	12	11	12
Better marketing and distribution	11	14	11	9	11
Government support	4	0	5	5	14
Macroeconomic advantages	4	0	4	6	0
Better quality	3	2	3	2	2
Improved technology	2	0	3	0	0
Other	12	14	14	8	2
No advantages	17	23	18	14	39
Sample base *N*=	386	44	244	98	66

* Large firms excluded from 'Firms' total.

Obstacles to exporting

Table 10.9 shows that, on the whole, SMEs appear to face more obstacles than do large firms. While 32 per cent of large firms reported that they do not face any obstacles, the corresponding figure for SMEs is just 16 per cent. For the large firms, obstacles are reported to be exchange rate fluctuations (32 per cent), government policies abroad (25 per cent) and need to improve price competitiveness (20 per cent). On the other hand, SMEs reported exchange rate fluctuations (27 per cent), communications difficulties (19 per cent) and red tape (14 per cent). Though there are differences in terms of degree and importance, both categories of firms appear to face the same types of obstacles.

Table 10.9 Obstacles to exporting

	All firms (%cases)	*Micro (%cases)*	*Small (%cases)*	*Medium (%cases)*	*Large* (%cases)*
Exchange rate fluctuations	27	19	28	27	32
Communication difficulties (including language)	19	19	18	22	10
Red tape	14	20	14	10	3
Government policies abroad	13	11	13	15	25
Need to improve price competitiveness	13	13	11	17	20
Access to distribution channels	12	11	11	12	13
Insufficient finance	10	13	10	8	0
Sector-specific	9	13	7	11	6
Lack of or limited information	8	11	8	4	1
Freight cost	7	2	8	8	1
Local infrastructure	5	0	4	9	1
Lack of time	4	0	4	5	9
Need to improve product/service quality	3	4	2	5	1
Risk of non-payment	3	2	2	4	0
Insufficient production capacity	2	0	3	2	0
Customs/excise tariff	2	0	2	3	1
Poor management information systems	1	4	1	1	0
Insufficient managerial expertise	1	0	1	1	1
Management commitment and motivation	1	0	0	2	0
Political instability	1	2	0	0	1
Other	17	20	19	12	0
No obstacles	16	9	20	10	32
Sample base *N*=	424	54	263	107	69

* Large firms excluded from 'Firms' total.

However, some patterns emerge indicating that some obstacles vary along with size. For example, though not consistently, need to improve price competitiveness increases with size. Insufficient finance is a relatively important obstacle for micro-enterprises, and the problem declines as size of firms increases. This becomes more apparent as no firm in the large category reported finance as a problem. Lack or limited information becomes less of a problem with size of the firm, whilst Lack of time as an obstacle tends to increase with size. It appears that while lack of time is not an obstacle at all for micro-enterprises, it is at its highest, albeit low at 9 per cent, for large firms.

Obstacles under the 'other' category decline with size, indicating that smaller firms have peculiar problems inherent to their sizes. For example, no large firm expressed any problem classified as 'other', while 20 per cent of micro-enterprises mentioned areas allocated to this category.

The top five obstacles experienced by exporting SMEs are largely external to the firm and originate mainly in the overseas markets. Those obstacles that can be described as internal, and within the domestic business environment, that is those that can be tackled by the management of the firm, are fewer and appear low in relative importance. Obstacles that may be described as external to the firm but originate within the domestic environment are also few, reflecting positively on the UK business environment. Finance is mentioned by one in ten of the respondents and is ranked seventh; much lower than might be expected.

It is worth reflecting that a number of obstacles cited within the literature do not figure prominently within our results. For example, according to Fillis (2001) the most important obstacles faced by craft micro-enterprises are not enough production capacity, business being too small and lack of time (internal), and sufficient business in domestic market, lack of export enquiries and complicated export regulations (external). Karagozoglu and Lindell (1996) put the top three obstacles as difficulties in forming international relationships, lack of managerial experience, and difficulties in gathering information. Others emphasize lack of managerial skills (Buckley, 1999), and lack of resources (Westhead *et al.*, 2002). Some of the variations could be explained by the nature and context of the study undertaken; overall, however, the findings support Leonidou's (1995) conclusions that the pattern of obstacles faced by exporting SMEs tend to be operational and experiential in nature, and relate to external factors.

Use of support mechanisms

Table 10.10 presents use of support mechanisms by size of firms. While both SMEs and large organizations agree that the greatest source of support is internal assistance, the importance of the other two sources varies slightly among size categories. After internal assistance, a network of suppliers, customers, etc., is important for one in four of large firms, while those that used business support

Table 10.10 Use of support mechanisms

	All firms (*% cases*)	*Micro* (*% cases*)	*Small* (*% cases*)	*Medium* (*% cases*)	*Large** (*% cases*)
Internal assistance	88	87	88	86	91
Business support organizations	32	21	33	35	19
Network of suppliers, customers, etc.	23	13	20	35	25
Sample base *N*=	289	38	171	80	32

* Large firms excluded from 'Firms' total.

organizations is about 19 per cent. Within SMEs a pattern emerges: the use of a network of suppliers, customers, etc. and business support organizations increases with size. It is interesting to note that, relatively speaking, though the differences are not that distinct, micro-enterprises use the business support organizations the least.

A very high proportion of exporters use internal sources to overcome their obstacles, at a level slightly higher than the 79 per cent recently reported by Pollock and Bussell (2003). Business support organizations came second. Of those exporters that did take up external assistance this came from Business Link and the DTI. This profile is also similar to Pollock and Bussell (2003). The low take-up of external assistance found in this research concurs with other findings such as those of Anderson *et al.* (2001) and Sheikh and Durand (2003), who found that participation of small businesses in support services in the UK and EU countries, respectively, is low. The fact that relatively few exporting SMEs seek external assistance indicates that either the supports available are perceived as inappropriate or the awareness of the services is poor, the latter point being supported by research by Crick and Chaudhry (2000) and PricewaterhouseCoopers (2002). Anderson *et al.* (2001: 215) maintain that 'Management learning in SMEs frequently occurs in an informal and often unplanned way through a process of interaction within social and business networks'. However, the results from the current study indicate that 'networks' is the least used form of support.

Conclusion

The study had the main aim of examining the impact of size on the internationalization behaviour of firms categorized into four groups by size. Compared to large firms, SMEs as a group appear to be more focused on exporting and importing while larger firms have a somewhat more diversified profile of international activities. Within the SMEs group, the proportion of firms engaged in exporting increased with firm size. The larger the firms the higher the export intensity and the more the experience in internationalization. Export destinations appear to be concentrated in psychically and physically close markets, and, contrary to expectations, large firms have not ventured further afield than SMEs, although this might be a reflection of larger firms possibly using international production to service more distant markets. The smaller the firm the lesser the use of 'own sales office' and 'network of suppliers and customers, etc.'. The larger the firm the more the use of specialists and the more structured are the international activities. While SMEs and large firms consider 'better quality' as the mainstay of their competitive advantages, large firms also count on technology and better marketing expertise. On the other hand, the smaller the firm the higher the use of the internet. Key obstacles faced by firms in their international operations are similar, though the importance is seen to vary a little by firm size.

In order to facilitate exporting assistance in overcoming obstacles, capitalizing on advantages and reducing disadvantages would appear to be central to further develop policy. As Diamantopoulos *et al.* (1993) point out, indirect export assistance comes from a variety of sources including support for R&D, technology support and the development of productivity. These aspects tie in well with the competitive advantages and disadvantages identified in this study and so should be considered within internationalization policy. While these are generic issues concerning firms and typically not explicitly linked to exporting, they serve the dual purpose of both assisting firms secure or maintain their position within export markets and also assisting indigenous industry in staving off the threat of overseas competition.

Policy implications coming from the analysis of obstacles are somewhat problematic since neither SMEs nor most national governments have much control over exchange rate fluctuations (in the short term at least) and the policies of overseas governments (ranked 1 and 4 respectively). Communication difficulties represent a perennial problem of UK firms and poor foreign language skills are claimed seriously to undermine competitiveness (Packard, 1999). However, as the EU is by far the major export market for firms in the region, the imminent decision on whether the UK will join the euro is likely to have a significant impact. While many language programmes are on offer, as with many other support services awareness and take-up are likely to be low. Indeed, making the best use of existing support provision by increasing awareness and perceived relevance among client groups may have more impact than adding new services since, as PricewaterhouseCoopers (2002: 31) point out, ...'many of those interviewed expressed a desire for services that were already in existence'. Therefore, creating awareness and installing a continuous evaluation of effectiveness for the support provided appear to be among the urgent tasks.

Among weaknesses observed in the export behaviour literature is the focus on small to medium-sized firms, with only a minority of studies examining large firms also as a basis for comparison. There also seems to be a great deal of ambiguity among researchers with regard to firm-size classification. The majority of studies also have manufacturing industry as the principal focus despite the predominance of service industries within the economy (Leonidou, 1995). This study has addressed some of the shortcomings identified in the literature. A standard firm classification framework has been used, a control group of large firms was included for comparison, and manufacturing firms as well as firms in the service sector (in a representative proportion) were also included.

While the findings reported help in mapping out the internationalization patterns of firms in the East of England, they are based on descriptive analysis and the differences observed have not been tested for significance. In research terms, these conclusions can serve as a base upon which a set of hypotheses can be developed for future studies to consider using more robust statistical tests.

The findings reported in this study support the literature that implies that factors and obstacles faced by SMEs during internationalization are varied and complicated, and generic approaches may not be appropriate. The literature also highlights the inadequacy of current theory in explaining the internationalization behaviour of small firms (Fillis, 2001; Coviello and McAuley, 1999; Leonidou and Katsikeas, 1996). Therefore, one way to take these issues forward in terms of theory development and the identification of specific needs for devising effective support regimes would be to direct research in a more qualitative direction through case studies, participative observations and in-depth interviews, to gain a better understanding of the dynamics of the internationalization activities of SMEs.

References

Anderson, A., Boocock, G. and Graham, S. (2001) 'An investigation into the learning needs in internationalising small and medium sized enterprises', *Journal of Small Business and Enterprise Development* 8(3), 215–32.

Baird, I.S., Lyles, M.A. and Orris, J.B. (1994) 'The choice of international strategies by small businesses', *Journal of Small Business Management*, January, 48–59.

Bonaccorsi, A. (1992) 'On the relationship between firm size and export intensity', *Journal of International Business Studies* 23(4), 605–36.

Boter, H. and Holmqvist, C. (1996) 'The impact of size, industry, and nation on internationalisation in small and medium-sized enterprises', Research in Entrepreneurship and Small Business, Brussels.

Brouthers, K.D., Brouthers, L.E. and Werner, S. (1996) 'Dunning's eclectic theory and the small firm: the impact of ownership and locational advantages on the choice of entry-modes in the computer software industry', *International Business Review* 5(4), 377–94.

Buckley, P. (1999) 'Foreign direct investment by small- and medium-sized enterprises: the theoretical background', in Buckley, P. and Ghauri, P. (eds), *The Internationalisation of the Firm*. London: International Thomson Business Press, 99–113.

Calof, J.L. (1994) 'The relationship between firm size and export behaviour revisited', *Journal of International Business Studies* 25(2), 367–87.

Coviello, N. and McAuley, A. (1999) 'Internationalisation and the smaller firm: a review of contemporary empirical research', *Management International Review* 39(3), 223–56.

Coviello, N. and Munro, H. (1999) 'Network relationships and the internationalisation process of small software firms', in Buckley, P. and Ghauri, P. (eds), *The Internationalisation of the Firm*. London: International Thomson Business Press, 114–35.

Crick, D. (1995) An investigation into the targeting of UK export assistance, *European Journal of Marketing* 29(8), 76–94.

Crick, D. (1997) 'UK SMEs' awareness, use, and perceptions of selected export assistance programmes: an investigation into the effect of the internationalisation process', *The International Trade Review* XI(1), 135–67.

Crick, D. and Chaudhry, S. (1997) 'Small businesses' motives for exporting: the effect of internationalisation', *Journal of Marketing Practice: Applied Marketing Science* 3(3), 156–70.

Crick, D. and Chaudhry, S. (2000) 'UK SMEs' awareness, use, and perceptions of selected export assistance programmes: an investigation into the effects of ethnicity', *International Journal of Entrepreneurial Behaviour and Research* 6(2), 72–89.

Diamantopoulos, A., Schlegelmilch, B.B. and Ste, K.Y.K. (1993) 'Understanding the role of export marketing assistance: empirical evidence and research needs', *European Journal of Marketing* 27(4), 5–18.

EEDA (2001) *East of England 2010: The Regional Economic Strategy*. Cambridge: East of England Development Agency.

Fillis, I. (2001) 'Small firm internationalisation: an investigative survey and future research directions', *Management Decision* 39(9), 767–83.

Kalantaridis, C. (2000) 'Internationalisation and strategic behaviour: a comparison between SMEs and large organisations, Conference on National Small Firms Policy and Research, Aberdeen.

Karagozoglu, N. and Lindell, M. (1996) 'Internationalisation of small and medium-sized technology-based firms: an exploratory study', *Journal of Small Business Management* 36(1), 44–70.

Katsikeas, C.K. and Al-Khalifa, A. (1993) 'The issue of import motivation in manufacturer – overseas distributor relationships: implications for exporters', *Journal of Marketing Management* 9(1), 65–77

Leonidou, L.C. (1995) 'Empirical research on export barriers: review, assessment, and synthesis', *Journal of International Marketing* 3(1), 29–43.

Leonidou, L.C. and Katsikeas, C.S. (1996) 'The export development process: an integrative review of empirical models', *Journal of International Business Studies* 27(3), 517–51.

Packard, J. (1999) 'UK competitiveness hit by language skills shortages', *People Management* 5(17), 11.

Piercy, N., Kalika, S. and Katsikeas, C.S. (1998) 'Sources of competitiveness in high performing exporting companies', *Journal of World Business* 33(4), 378–93.

Pollock, M.R. and Bussell, L.J. (2003) '"Help! We need somebody": a study of exporters in the North East of England and an evaluation of support networks', CD ROM Proceedings of ICSB 48th World Conference: Advancing Entrepreneurship and Small Business, Belfast.

Poutziouris, P., Soufani, K. and Michailas, N. (2000) 'On the determinants of exporting in UK small medium sized enterprises: evidence from company panel data', Proceedings of Small Business and Enterprise Development Conference, Manchester.

PricewaterhouseCoopers (2002) 'Trade partners UK: customer needs review', PricewaterhouseCoopers, *http://www.tradepartners.gov.uk/files/customer_needs.pdf*

Sheikh, S. and Durand, F. (2003) 'Support services for micro, small, and sole proprietors businesses', CD ROM Proceedings ICSB 48th World Conference: Advancing Entrepreneurship and Small Business, Belfast.

Szabo, A. (2002) 'Internationalisation of SMEs', *http://www.UNECE.org/indust/sme/internat.htm*
UN/ECE (1997) 'SMEs – their role in foreign trade', *http://www.sme/foreignt.htm*
Westhead, P., Binks, M., Ucbasaran, D. and Wright, M. (2002) 'Internationalisation of SMEs: a research note', *Journal of Small Business and Enterprise Development* 9(1), 38–48.

11
Regional Products and Internationalization Processes in the Internet Era: Does Location Still Matter?

Giulio Cardilli, Fabrizio Cocciola, Luciano Fratocchi and Luca Giustiniano

Introduction

This chapter aims critically to analyse the relevance of location for small and medium-sized enterprises (SMEs) producing regional products (RPs) and selling them internationally by e-commerce. This type of product is important for the Italian economy, as Italy is the most important country in the world for RPs (4,120 food specialties, data on craft products are not available) and the second for European Union (EU) protected designations with 19.51 per cent of Protected Designation of Origins (PDO), Protected Geographical Indication (PGI) and Traditional Specialty Guaranteed (TSG) designations. With respect to these designations, the total turnover of Italian food having a EU designation is €7.6 billion of which €1.4 billion are exports.

With respect to opportunities offered by e-commerce to SMEs internationalisation, two ideas seem to be generally accepted. Firstly, internet and electronic transactions are supposed to provide SMEs and bigger companies with the same access to global markets (Zwass, 1998). Secondly, it is assumed that e-commerce may reduce boundaries of distance among markets and make location not so relevant. In other words, both production and market areas become bigger and bigger, thereby allowing manufacturers to produce and sell products everywhere (Quelch and Klein, 1996). This chapter focuses attention on business opportunities that the internet offers to SMEs, especially in terms of internationalization strategies.

The chapter is structured into two main sections. In the first a series of reflections regarding the definition of RPs are presented and a short literature review on the internationalization processes of such products is conducted. More specifically, this introductory section tries, first of all, to define the concept of RPs, taking into consideration the relevant categories defined by the EU, and showing how the 'certification' may influence the internationalization process. Further, the literature review discusses the contradictory impact of the internet on the internationalization process of SMEs. This aspect is particularly significant given the wide majority of small firms involved in the manufacture and distribution of RPs. The search for a theoretical background with respect to such a peculiar field is then completed by the analysis of the characteristics of RPs as internet-deliverable goods. This section is completed with the identification of the possibilities for 'virtual internationalization'. In the second section, empirical findings related to manufacturers selling by e-commerce in a specific region (Abruzzo) are presented and discussed. Finally, some concluding remarks and suggestions for further research are presented.

Literature review

Our literature review is split into three sections:

1 An operational definition of regional products (RP).
2 The internet and the internationalization process of SMEs.
3 Regional products and the internet.

An operational definition of regional products

In order to analyse the relevance of location for RPs, it is necessary to clearly define them. Different notions are used in the literature such as: typical or traditional products; foods with territorial or regional associations; place-identified foods, and so on. Moreover, the same word (for instance, traditional product) is often used with very differentiated meanings. Notwithstanding this terminological confusion, different authors seem to agree on the relevance of the following three elements for defining RPs (Sodano, 2001):

(a) Geographic specificity of raw materials and/or manufacturing processes.
(b) Historical tradition.
(c) Cultural and social specificity.

At the same time, EU Regulations (2081/1992 and 2082/1992) define the following types of origin-labelled products: PDO (Protected Designation of Origins), PGI (Protected Geographical Indication), TSG (Traditional Specialty Guaranteed) and DOC-DOCG (Controlled Origin Denomination and Guaranteed Controlled Origin Denomination).With respect to these designations, it must be noted that DOCG and DOC are utilized only for wine, while the other three are used over a broad range of food products. At the same time, it must be considered that in the wine industry the use of appellations is governed by the country that issues them to group wines by geographic origin, alcohol content, grape variety and so on. As regards food products other than wine, the Italian Law D. Lgs. 173/1998 introduced the concept of 'Food Traditional Products', which must be produced with manufacturing processes older than 25 years. However, there are still a lot of products having earlier defined elements which are not certified either by the EU or by Italian law, such as in the Italian cases of Sulmona's confetti (Jordan almonds) and L'Aquila saffron. To overcome such a problem, in this chapter a RP is defined as a product:

> associated spatially with a geographical area and culturally with the latter's customer or modes, with a minimum permanence in time or history... [having] particular qualitative characteristics which differentiate it from other products. (Caldentey Albert and Gómez Muñoz, 1977: 77)

As a consequence, EU designations are not essential, even if they represent the most relevant certification of RPs. At the same time, the definition concerns not only food products, but also craft products such as jewels or carved woods.

The internet and the internationalization process of SMEs

The literature on the effects of the internet on foreign market expansion by firms is disputable and far from obvious. Petersen *et al.* (2002) note that internet-based strategies may reduce one of the most relevant barriers to foreign market expansion: the uncertainty connected with managing business activities abroad (Johanson and Vahlne, 1977). Bakos (1997), Barua *et al.* (1997) and Lal and Savary (1999) emphasize internet opportunities in reducing search costs for both customers and firms. At the same time, however, it is still disputed whether the internet may facilitate tacit knowledge-creation, transfer and retention (Petersen *et al.*, 2002), elements extremely critical for firms' market expansion abroad.

Evaluation of the internet's potential for internationalization by SMEs is still more difficult. In this respect, Giustiniano (2001) notes that in recent years many SMEs opted for the internet assuming it was 'the thing to do'. However, some of them could not appreciate its potential, while others activated e-commerce tools without adequately planning the new distribution infrastructure they would have to face at a worldwide level. Finally, a small percentage of SMEs adopting e-commerce strategies succeeded in using real and exact internet marketing strategies (Hofacker, 2001), which at times significantly influenced their degree of internationalization. Considering the threats and opportunities hidden in the use of electronic commerce, the possibilities for SMEs to increase their degree of internationalization by participating in the global marketplace must be critically evaluated (Rockwell, 1998; Fariselli *et al.*, 1999). On the one hand, it seems that e-commerce increases business opportunities by providing the means to overcome disadvantages of scale and geographic position. On the other hand, compared to bigger firms, SMEs do not generate the resources (human, technological and financial) to invest in the construction and management of sales systems via the internet. From this fact stems the consideration that although entry to on-line markets might theoretically pose very few problems (Zwass, 1998), effective competition needs further investment: to acquire computer infrastructure, for advertising and promotion, or to widen the product range offered, and eventually their prices (Tiessen, Wright and Turner, 2001). Furthermore, the adoption of internet-based strategies involves a traumatic passage from the consideration of reference target markets to the consideration of global niches, which implies a rethinking of management logic, as well as of the acquisition of resources and the development of competencies based on this logic (Giustiniano, 2001).

The fact that using electronic commerce may force SMEs to internationalize emerges from a critical evaluation of factors that can feed or negatively affect such a development (Poon and Swatman, 1999). The possibilities offered by the internet must be analysed and evaluated in the light of the problems that could result from focusing on the new competencies – managerial and organizational – that SMEs must develop. It should be borne in mind that e-commerce can be a useful tool for them better to implement their strategies for foreign development. In this respect, Giustiniano (2001) states that e-commerce alone is not a source of competitive advantage if SMEs do not have a definite strategy nor the necessary competencies. In these conditions the use of the internet will most probably have negative effects, rather than offer an effective solution. As a consequence, the processes of internationalization by SMEs, based on the internet, should be developed in two phases. First, a radical change in the business logic is required to assimilate – with varying degrees of intensity – the potential of web tools and to evaluate the risks involved. Second, firms should consent to a process of creation and development of the suitable organizational competencies to confront the new managerial logics.

To sum up, resorting to the internet – and to e-business in general – can be a step forward for SMEs, in terms of conquering foreign markets, only if the conditions for the development of 'devoted' organizational competencies within the same firm are fully considered. Therefore, use of the internet can allow SMEs to 'expand' the market niches in which they operate by increasing the critical mass of potential buyers at an international level. This is mainly possible if the web is used as a means of integrating individuals associated with specific common interests, although geographically dispersed. Thus, by taking advantage of virtual communities, SMEs could find interesting opportunities for developing foreign markets. Moreover, SMEs with strong craftsmanship connotations could further exploit electronic commerce and the potential expansion of market niches by customizing the products they sell, achieving mass personalization (Peppers and Rogers, 2000).

Lastly, Petersen *et al.* (2002) recently proposed three predictions with respect to the effects of the internet on foreign market expansion by exporting firms in the early stages of internationalization:

1 It will have a modest effect on the internationalization process of such firms.
2 It will dramatically speed up the expansion of foreign markets.
3 It will generate rapid, diversified international expansion as a dominant, but mostly unsuccessful strategy.

Such predictions are not necessarily complementary, therefore it is necessary to understand which of them is more consistent with specific business and marketing attributes of RPs.

Regional products and the internet

Traditionally, RPs were sold to people living in the production area or in the closest urban areas. Emigrants, wishing to maintain their traditions, represented another relevant market niche. More recently, tourists – and especially so-called 'eco-gastronomic' ones – have become a relevant market segment. Finally, in the last years, RPs' sales have been dramatically improved due to consumers' concerns about food quality (see, among others, Smeets and Baretton, 1990; Raven and Lang, 1994; Henson, 1995; Gilg and Battershill, 1998).

Research conducted by INRA (1998) pointed out two main consumption models with respect to food. The so-called continental model (common in Germany, Netherlands and the United Kingdom) where price is considered the most important element for customer choice; and the so-called Mediterranean approach where consumers are less price-sensitive and pay more attention to traditional aspects. However, in recent years it seems that Northern European customers are becoming more concerned with quality than quantity, and look for healthier products, such as may be found in RPs.

The consequent enlargement of their market area may represent a tremendous strategic opportunity for RP manufacturers, often living in rural and less-developed areas. In this respect, internet technologies may represent a useful tool to promote local economies, being an innovative form of direct marketing and selling. In fact, according to several authors the so called *vente directe* represents the most effective strategy of adding value to RPs (see, among others, Sylvander, 1993; Gilg and Battershill, 1998). More specifically, such a distribution policy assures large margins to producers and the most complete information on product quality and traceability to customers. More specifically, direct selling may be realized in two different ways (Gilg and Battershill, 1998): the 'true *vente directe'* where the producer sell directly to the final customer (for example farm or marketplace sales, home delivery, distance orders – also by the internet on trade fairs); and the 'short-circuit *vente directe'* where products are sold to one-step distributors (sales to local restaurants, small shops and supermarkets for example).

Even if the internet is the most innovative tool for *vente directe* of RPs, it seems little attention has been paid to this topic, especially with respect to so-called 'virtual internationalization'. Here a useful insight comes from May and Ness (1997), which states that mail order (that is, the internet ancestor) may represent a useful basis for RP manufacturers' internationalization, although the number of foreign customers is often quite small. At the same time, is widely accepted that such products may be easily sold on the internet, as they are often difficult to buy outside their specific production area. Moreover, RPs may be sold almost everywhere with any adaptation thus creating a global niche market.

Notwithstanding these elements, data collected with respect to Italian wine and olive oil industries (Giustiniano and Fratocchi, 2003) clearly show that the internet is not yet a real tool to promote the internationalization process of SMEs. Four main factors seem to explain this failure:

1 The only recent adoption of such a business model.
2 The importance of logistic costs that dramatically increase in the case of exports.
3 A lack of customer relationship management (CRM) tools.
4 The ineffective use of consortia of manufacturers, especially those having the same EU protected-origin indication.

This raises a number of interesting questions:

- Do e-commerce systems influence the internationalization strategies of Italian SMEs manufacturing RPs?
- What is the importance of e-commerce competences for successful internationalization by Italian RP manufacturers?
- How can traditional and virtual solutions be complemented in order to implement better internet strategies?

The study

With the purpose of analysing opportunities for market area enlargement offered by e-commerce to RP manufacturers, field research was conducted on internet sites of companies located in Abruzzo, a region in the centre of Italy. In Abruzzo, 92 RPs are produced, 16 of which have EU-protected designations.

Table 11.1 Abruzzo origin-labelled products

	PDO	*PGI*	*TSG*	*DOCG*	*DOC*	*IGT*	*Food traditional products*	*Total*
Abruzzo	3	1	0	0	3	9	76	92
Italy	79	40	1	22	301	119	3.558	4.120
% from Abruzzo	3.8	2.5	0.0	0.0	0.99	7.56	2.13	2.23

Although the region is small (3.5 per cent of national surface and 2.2 per cent of national inhabitants), its relevance for RPs is interesting, especially for olive oil (8 per cent of national PDO) and wine (2.7 per cent) (Table 11.1). However, it must be pointed out that several products have the required characteristics to be protected by EU laws, but did not receive recognition mainly because of local administration inactivity.

A database 'Abruzzo Regional Products on Internet 2002' was created using research engines, links, banners, specialized press and commercial-fairs databases. It contains 225 internet sites, both of first and second-level, related to RPs and registered before November 2002 in Abruzzo (Cardilli, Cocciola and Fratocchi, 2002) (Table 11.2). A first-level site is defined as being completely independent as a top-level domain (for example *www.amazon.com*). A second-level site is defined as being contained within a wider internet site (for example *http://www.thevirtualmall.co.uk/Shops/WHSmith.asp*). Analysing the database led to the identification of five different types of players:

1 Producers, that decided to complement traditional distribution channels with the internet.
2 Virtual and physical distributors, that is traditional sellers (with physical points of sales) who also sell products by e-commerce methods.
3 Virtual distributors, that is sellers who sell chosen products only by the internet.
4 Virtual shops, more or less specialized to sell RP by the internet.
5 Organizations promoting RPs and eco-gastronomic tourism.

Our interest is focused on the first type of player, since the research aims to investigate the relevance of localization. At the same time, three different strategies of internet presence were found:

(1) Window sites: internet sites that contain only news about a company and its products, that do not allow customers to order goods.

Table 11.2 Internet sites of firms in regional product industries in Abruzzo

Type of player	*First-level internet site Strategy*				*Second-level internet site Strategy*			
	Window site	*Off-line e-commerce*	*On-line e-commerce*	*Total*	*Window site*	*Off-line e-commerce*	*On-line e-commerce*	*Total*
Producers	91	14	4	109	61	6 + 1**	29	96 + 1**
Virt. and Phys. distributors		3	2	5		1	1	2
Virtual distributors		3 + 1*	1	4 + 1*				
Thematic virtual shops	1 (e-comm. under construction)		3	4				
RPs & tourism promotion	3			3				
Total	95	20 + 1*	10	125 + 1*	61	7 + 1**	30	98 + 1**

Notes: *A company registered the same site with two different extensions (.it, .com). ** A company has two second-level internet sites (in two virtual shops) but offered the same products.

(2) Off-line e-commerce sites: allow customers to order products on-line, but payment is subsequently made off-line by traditional tools (for example cheques, postal orders).
(3) On-line e-commerce sites: here the entire order and delivery cycle is performed on-line, including payments made by credit cards, debit cards, smart cards and other electronic tools.

Our interest was focused on the last two types of internet presence, since our research aims to investigate the support of internet strategies to exporting activities.

A large number of window sites are available, which confirms the view that SMEs often create a site just because they believe it is 'the thing to do'. With respect to e-commerce sites, it must be pointed out that they are used more in the second-level group than the first-level one. This is because it is easier to be present in a virtual shop, where skilled technicians may manage technical and often even commercial aspects. In this respect it may be assumed that second-level internet sites are less risky than first-level ones for SMEs at the beginning of their internet presence.

The analysis presented is based on the total population of 18 first-level and 35 second-level internet sites belonging to Abruzzo RP manufacturers (available on November 2002). While no first-level site offers products, six second-level sites (that is 17.1 per cent of this type of companies) do. This evidence is consistent with the situation depicted in the whole database, where 188 sites belong to foodstuffs and only 18 to craft products.

In order to investigate the role of the internet for the enlarging market area of Abruzzo RP manufacturers, a questionnaire was sent to the 53 firms in the population. The response rate was 88.8 per cent for the first-level and 94.2 per cent for the second-level sites.

Results and discussion

As expected considering the investigated industry, respondents were mainly very small companies, with just four of them having sales of more than €2.5 million (Table 11.3). Moreover, in two cases the number of employees is also small (less than 50).

With respect to internationalization strategies, respondents were mainly involved in domestic operations. Specifically, 50 per cent of the first-level and 75 per cent of the second-level internet site operators export less than 5 per cent of their total sales. However, it is interesting to note that two companies (both in the olive oil industry) export more than 50 per cent of their turnover, showing that RPs may be extremely successful at the global level (Table 11.4).

Table 11.3 Classification by firm dimensions (total sales and number of employees)

	Number of employees									
	First-level internet site					*Second-level internet site*				
Total sales	1–5	6–49	50–249	250–	*Total*	1–5	6–49	50–249	250–	*Total*
0–50	5				5	8				8
51–250	2				2	13	2			15
251–500	2				2	4	1			5
501–2,500	2	3			5	1	2			3
2,501–5,000		2			2					0
5,000–					0		2			2
Total	11	5	0	0	16	26	7	0	0	33

Another important result is the correlation between total turnover and export propensity ($r=0.57$ for first-level internet sites, but not available for second-level sites). A similar positive correlation was found between number of employees (generally accepted as a proxy of firm size) and sales abroad ($r=0.51$). As a consequence, it may be concluded that, among the respondents, total exports are strictly related with firm dimensions.

The data reveal that more than 80 per cent of companies with a first-level site and more than 90 per cent of those with a second-level site began their internet presence in 2000 or after. With respect to second-level sites, it must be noted that the majority belong to the same virtual shop, which was created in 2000 by the regional agency supporting companies in the agro-food industry (ARSSA, Regional Agency for Support Service to Agriculture, *www.terrabruzzo.it*). Again the data confirm the view that most Italian SMEs have adopted an e-commerce strategy – and more generally created Internet sites – thinking it was 'the thing to do'.

With respect to the strategic aims pursued by e-commerce activities, market enlargement is considered the most relevant in nearly 75 per cent of first-level sites and 90 per cent of second-level sites. Less importance (25 per cent in both groups) is given to improvements in operating efficiency. This confirms the idea that the internet is not conceptualized as a distribution channel cheaper than traditional channels, but as a good tool for commercial expansion, and also at the worldwide level. As a consequence, e-commerce is often conceptualized as a mere adjunctive distribution channel. This appears to be confirmed by the evidence that only one firm (operating in the wedding-gifts industry) sells different goods via the internet than it sells via non-internet means. At the same time, nearly all companies (respectively, 81 per cent and 88 per cent) sell their entire range on-line. Moreover, 75 per cent and 82 per cent of firms operating by first and second-level sites, respectively, state that they do not make

Table 11.4 Export propensity (as a % of total sales)

	Export as % of total sales													
	First-level internet site							*Second-level internet site*						
Total sales	0–5	6–10	11–20	21–30	31–50	51–100	*Total*	0–5	6–10	11–20	21–30	31–50	51–100	*Total*
0–50	3	1	1				5	8						8
51–250	1		1				2	11	2	1	1			15
251–500	2						2	3	1		1			5
501–2,500	1	1	1	1	1		5	1		1			1	3
2,501–5,000	1					1	2							0
5,000–							0	2						2
Total	8	2	3	1	1	1	16	25	3	2	2	0	1	33

Table 11.5 The contribution of internet-based exports to total sales

% exports to total sales	*First-level internet site, no. of companies*	*Second-level internet site, no. of companies*
<5	5	4
5–10	0	2
11–20	1	0
21–50	1	1
>50	0	0
Total	7	7

any adaptation to products offered to virtual customers. This may be explained by the fact that we are discussing RPs, that is products whose value is strictly connected with ancient local traditions. However, even though adaptations regarding raw materials and production processes may be unacceptable, modifications of packaging may be requested for shipment in some cases. However, only 1.8 per cent of companies with independent sites and 15 per cent of those with second-level sites make such variations.

The main aim of this chapter is to investigate the support of e-commerce strategies to RP manufacturers' developments in foreign markets. Consequently, the number of customers was investigated and the contribution of internet-based sales abroad was evaluated. With respect to the first aspect, it must be taken into account that among the investigated RP manufacturers very few are internationalized (Table 11.4), and therefore it is likely that the contribution of the internet to market-area enlargement is quite marginal. In fact, the data collected clearly show that only a minority of companies have overseas customers buying via the internet (Table 11.5). More specifically, the percentage is bigger in the case of first-level sites than far second-level sites. This finding is unexpected since one might have expected that to be involved in a virtual shop would increase the possibilities of selling in global markets. In other words, it might have been assumed that managers who were internet players would have more appropriate competences to attract overseas business. Moreover, in the very few companies which do export by the internet, the relevance of sales abroad realized by e-commerce is generally less than 5 per cent. However, in two cases (one for each type of site and both belonging to the oil industry) more than 5 per cent of sales were from exports.

As regards the foreign customers' countries of origin, the evidence indicates the importance of countries with a high number of Italian emigrants. In fact, in both cases the USA and Germany are among the three main markets for the majority of exporting firms. However, it must be pointed out that customers of these countries are quite used to buying foodstuffs made in Italy.

In order to investigate why the internet does not play a positive role in supporting the internationalization processes of the investigated companies, a deeper analysis was conducted. First of all, the availability of site pages in foreign languages was assessed. In this respect, 43.7 per cent of companies with independent sites and 93.9 per cent of those with second-level sites listed items in a foreign language. Several of the interviewed entrepreneurs candidly admitted that their site's English version was proposed and created by the virtual shop's technical staff. This indicates the advantages for SMEs to be involved in such collaboration. Moreover, the data show a positive correlation ($r = 43.7$) between the number of languages and the export level in the case of companies with autonomous internet sites. Here, the olive-oil manufacturer had the biggest percentage of foreign sales by internet (21–50 per cent of total sales), with his site translated into three foreign languages.

To understand the limited virtual internationalization of RP manufacturers, an examination of the effectiveness of their own sites was made. Several scholars have proposed key success factors which may influence the performance of e-commerce systems (for example Tiessen *et al.*, 2001), and the following elements seem to assume special relevance:

1 Know-how and competences owned by the firm with regard to e-commerce and e-business (Giustiniano, 2001).
2 Tools to achieve higher site accessibility.
3 Business intelligence activities related to competitors' websites and own-site internet users.
4 Use of customer relationship management (CRM) tools in order to increase customer retention.
5 Use of accepted payment systems.

As regards the first element, scholars and practitioners cite the critical role of 'learning by doing' in order to create and preserve a sustainable competitive advantage. As a consequence it is often suggested to establish an e-commerce site only after having acquired adequate experience with e-business, through managing a windows site, for example. The data clearly show that the firms generally do not respect such a 'golden rule'. More specifically, 50 per cent of those with independent sites and 55 per cent of the others had not used the internet for any other purpose before starting electronic commerce. For some of these cases the evidence might be explained by the fact that, because of a total absence of previous skills and competences in internet use, they trusted virtual-shop capabilities; thus most of the second-level sites are within the virtual shop of the Regional Agency supporting companies in the agro-food industry (*www.terrabruzzo.it*). It may also be noted that some of the interviewed entrepreneurs asserted that on the basis of experience within the virtual shop they were deciding to activate completely independent first-level sites. It must also be taken into account that many of the sites in the virtual shop were mere window sites, composed of only a homepage. Finally, with regard to companies with independent sites, only two of them created a window site before starting to sell by the internet.

As regards policies aimed at increasing site visibility, all firms with independent sites used promotion activities, whilst only about 20 per cent of those with second-level sites considered this as an important part of their activities. For the latter group, this may be explained by a lack of competences with internet tools, trusting in the ability of the virtual shop to create traffic. The data clearly show that while first-level sites are generally promoted with internet-based means, mainly banner and ranking on search engines, the others prefer more traditional policies such as commercial fairs. Finally, it must be noted that among different electronic promotion tools, ranking on search engines is the most adopted (Table 11.6).

Business intelligence strategies related to competitors' websites and own-site visitors were analysed. In both cases the evidence is rather surprising, since only a modest part of the sample carries out such activities and uses their outcomes. The same dramatic situation was found with respect to CRM policies, focused on already acquired customers in order to promote their retention. However, it is really unpardonable that some of investigated companies collect data but do not use them to derive useful information for their own on-line strategies (Table 11.7).

Lastly, referring to payment systems a distinction was made between traditional systems (for example cheque, transfer orders, postal orders) and payment systems that can be used electronically (such as credit cards, debit cards,

Table 11.6 Promotion techniques*

Promotion type	*First-level sites*		*Second-level sites*	
	Tot. num.	*%*	*Tot. num.*	*%*
Traditional promotion				
Advertising on traditional media	6	37.50	8	24.24
Commercial fairs	6	37.50	17	51.52
Outdoor advertising	4	25.00	4	12.12
Mailing	4	25.00	6	18.18
e-promotion				
Banners	5	31.25	4	12.12
Ranking on search engines	12	75.00	13	39.39
Link exchange	1	6.25	9	27.27
No promotion	0	0.00	6	18.18

*More than one answer allowed.

Table 11.7 Use of business intelligence and CRM tools

	Data on competitors		*Data on visitors*		*Data on customers*	
	First-level site	*Second-level site*	*First-level site*	*Second-level site*	*First-level site*	*Second-level site*
No	50%	45%	62%	85%	56%	82%
Only collected	18%	25%	19%	9%	25%	0%
Collected and used	32%	30%	19%	6%	19%	18%
Total	100%	100%	100%	100%	100%	100%

Table 11.8 Accepted payment systems*

	First-level internet site		*Second-level internet site*	
	Num.	*%*	*Num.*	*%*
Traditional systems				
Voucher	10	62.5	20	60.6
Fund transfer	3	18.7	13	39.4
Bank transfer	6	37.5	10	30.3
Innovative systems				
Credit card	7	43.7	12	36.3

* More than one answer allowed.

smart cards). The data clearly show that the use of traditional payment systems is higher in both groups of enterprises (Table 11.8). Such evidence is typical of the Italian entrepreneurial culture that has an aversion to credit-card acceptance because of high transaction fees and the risk of tailed payment. Such a cultural position may represent a huge obstacle for foreign customers who are generally used to electronic means of payment.

Using the five elements outlined above (p. 206) an index was derived in order to estimate the coherence between the strategies supporting e-commerce as effectively adopted by the selected enterprises, and those described as more appropriate by scholars and practitioners. Each of the five elements has the same weight because it is assumed that all of them have the same influence on the performance of the whole site. The index ranges from 0 to 100, where 0 means absolutely no coherence with best practice related to e-commerce activities, and 100 the most effective use of the site. The average value of the index for first and second-level sites was 31.4 with a standard deviation of 13.9, and 24.1 with a standard deviation of 15.6, respectively. In just one case, a first-level site, was the index greater than 50. These results indicate that the companies investigated have a poor e-commerce strategy. The analysis shows that the main problems are related to payment systems, and developing knowledge of how to use the internet at an early enough stage. The former result is quite consistent with previous researchers' findings (see for instance Giustiniano, 2001).

However, it is interesting to point out that more than 30 per cent of companies with a first-level internet site gave a positive judgment of their experience with the internet. Firms with second-level sites expressed less satisfaction, mainly because of overestimation of the ability of the virtual shop to create traffic on the firms' sites. At the same time, 71.4 per cent of the analysed companies with first-level sites and 85.7 per cent of those with second-level sites are firmly convinced that the number of internet-based foreign customers will increase in the future.

Conclusion

The study outlined in this chapter has tried to bridge the gap between theoretical business-strategy constructs for the on-line world, and practical implementation in a competitive real-world environment, with a particular focus on typical food products.

The results show how some SMEs have tried to develop a marketing-oriented approach to website development, as well as a systematic integration of on-line business with existing traditional business models. At the same time, the results show how this approach to on-line business is often not very effective. It seems that the entrepreneurial culture is the main obstacle to the successful adoption of e-commerce strategy in the RP industry in Italy, and the predictions proposed by Petersen *et al.* (2002) are consistent with the results of this study. Further cross-sectional and longitudinal studies on the effect of the internet on the internationalization of SMEs in different industries and countries are required to help us to understand this important issue.

References

Bakos, Y.J. (1997) 'Reducing buyer search costs: implications for an electronic marketplace', *Management Science* 43(12), 1676–92.

Barua, A., Ravindran, S. and Whinston, A.B. (1997) 'Efficient selection of suppliers over the internet', *Journal of Management Information Systems* 13(4), 117–37.

Caldentey Albert, P. and Gómez Muñoz, A.C. (1977) 'Typical products, technical innovation and organizational innovation', Proceedings of the 52nd EAAE Seminar, Typical and Traditional Productions: Rural Effect and Agro-industrial Problems, Parma.

Cardilli, G., Cocciola, F. and Fratocchi, L. (2002) 'Abruzzo regional products on internet 2002 report', Unpublished Research Paper, School of Engineering, University of L'Aquila.

Fariselli, P., Oughton, C., Picory, C. and Sugden, R. (1999) 'Electronic commerce and the future for SMEs in a global market-place: networking and public policies', *Small Business Economics*, 12(3), 261–76.

Gilg, A.W. and Battershill, M. (1998) 'Quality farm food in Europe: a possible alternative to the industrialised food market and to current agri-environmental policies: lessons from France', *Food Policy* 23(1), 25–40.

Giustiniano, L. (2001) 'SMEs, the internet and internationalisation processes: a critical analysis', in Giustiniano, L., Guido, G. and Marcati, A. (eds), *SMEs, International Markets and the Internet: Opportunities and Challenges*. Roma: Luiss Edizioni.

Giustiniano, L. and Fratocchi, L. (2002) 'The virtual internationalisation process of Italian SMEs in the food industry', accepted for publication in Tonchia, S. (ed.), *e-Business Strategic Planning and Development*, Special Issue of the *International Journal of Business Performance Management*, 4(2/3/4), 69–81.

Henson, J. (1995) 'Consumer willingness to pay for reductions in the risk of food poisoning in the UK', *Journal of Agricultural Economics* 47(3), 403–20.

Hofacker, C.F. (2001) *Internet Marketing*. New York: John Wiley & Sons.

Institut National de la Recherche Agronomique-France (INRA) (1998) 'Les Européens et les labels de qualitè', *Eurobaromètre* 50(1), 23–35.

Johanson, J. and Vahlne, J.E. (1977) 'The internationalisation process of the firm: a model of knowledge development and increasing foreign market commitments, *Journal of International Business Studies* 8, Spring/Summer, 23–32.

Lal, R. and Savary, M. (1999) 'When and how is the internet likely to decrease price competition?', *Marketing Science* 18(4), 485–503.

May, L.W. and Ness, M. (1997) 'Consumers' perception of specialty foods and the rural mail order business', Proceedings of the 52nd EAAE Seminar, Typical and Traditional Productions: Rural Effect and Agro-industrial Problems, Parma.

Peppers, D. and Rogers, M. (2000) *Enterprise One to One. Tools for Competing in the Interactive Age*. New York: Doubleday.

Petersen, B., Welch, L.S. and Liesch, P.W. (2002) 'The internet and foreign market expansion by firms', *Management International Review* 42(2), 207–21.

Poon, S.P.H. and Swatman, P.M.C. (1999) 'An exploratory study of small business internet commerce issues', *Information and Management* 35(1), 9–18.

Quelch, J. and Klein, L.R. (1996) 'The internet and international marketing', *Sloan Management Review* 37(1), 60–76.

Raven, H. and Lang, T. (1994) *Off of Our Trolleys?* London: Institute for Public Policy Research.

Rockwell, B. (1998) *Using the Web to Compete in a Global Marketplace*. New York: John Wiley & Sons.

Smeets, J. and Baretton, F. (1990) 'From the farmer to the consumer', *Green Europe* 1, 90.

Sodano, V. (2001) 'Competitiveness of regional products in the international food market', Proceedings of the 77nd EAAE Seminar / NJF Seminar No. 325, Helsinki.

Sylvander, B. (1993) 'Quality products: an opportunity for rural areas', *Leader Magazine* 3, Spring, 8–21.

Tiessen, J.H., Wright, R.W. and Turner, I. (2001) 'A model of e-commerce use by internationalizing SMEs', *Journal of International Management* 7(2), 211–33.

Zwass, V. (1998) 'Structure and macro-level impacts of electronic commerce: from technological infrastructure to electronic marketplace', in Kendall, K.E. (ed.), *Emerging Information Technologies*. Thousand Oaks, CA: Sage. URL: *http://www.mhhe.com/business/mis/zwass/ecpaper.html*

12

The Internationalization Process and the Role of Learning in Small Service Firms

Sue Bridgewater, Bridgette Sullivan-Taylor, Robert Johnston, Jan Mattsson and Bruce Millett

Introduction

Research into the internationalization process of small firms (SMEs) presents contradictory models. The process has been modelled both as a stage-wise, incremental process (Sullivan and Bauerschmidt, 1990; Chang and Grub, 1992; Calof and Viviers, 1995) and as a more rapid, even simultaneous process (Erramilli and D'Souza, 1993; Oviatt and McDougall, 1994, 1995; Jones, 1999). As well as differing as to the expected pattern of internationalization, these two schools of literature diverge in their theoretical assumptions about how firms overcome uncertainty to operate successfully in international markets.

Furthermore, the internationalization of services literature shows that service firms may have both different modes and strategic imperatives than those facing product firms (Erramilli, 1991; Välikangas and Lehtinen, 1994). As service excellence often relies on an ability to adapt to cultural specifics, the need to 'learn' about specific international markets rises to the top of the strategic agenda.

The primary aim of this chapter is to generate a deeper understanding of how small, service firms expand within and across international markets, and the nature of the learning that underpins this process. Its main argument is that the apparent contradiction between incremental and simultaneous models of SME internationalization lies in the assumptions of knowledge accumulation and transfer upon which they are predicated. By exploring this process, useful insights can be gained that will make a contribution to the field of SME internationalization.

We analyse the cases of four small, service firms as these represent a good vehicle for the study of the internationalization process and of the ways in which learning and knowledge transfer impact upon this process. Accordingly, we analyse:

- the way in which knowledge is accumulated;
- the way in which knowledge is transferred; and
- the way in which this influences the internationalization process in four small, service firms.

Our secondary aim is to use an inductive research method that explores respondent-driven incident data on the internationalization process. In so doing, we allow respondents to determine the key issues and key incidents rather than deducing these *ex ante* and testing their validity.

Literature review

In this section we explore the divergent contributions to understanding the internationalization process of small firms offered by sequential and simultaneous ('born-global') models, together with the contributions from the services internationalization literature. These differing strands of the literature present different models of the stages and speed of internationalization in small firms. The apparently divergent expectations of these approaches are, to a large extent, based on their differing assumptions of the ways in which firms learn about international markets. We start this review by exploring the expectations of each of these strands of the literature.

Sequential models of small-firm internationalization

One of the most frequently used models of the internationalization process is the 'Uppsala' or 'stages' model. This model, closely associated with the Nordic studies of Johansson and Wiedersheim-Paul (1975) and Johansson and Vahlne (1977), describes an incremental progression to successively higher commitment modes of operation and, geographically, into markets with progressively higher levels of psychic distance. Whilst the initial empirical evidence came from Nordic multinational firms, the Uppsala model has subsequently been validated for firms in other markets and industries (Dichtl, Köglmayer and Müller, 1990; Sullivan and Bauerschmidt, 1990; Calof and Viviers, 1995).

Whilst this model has been criticized for being overly deterministic (Reid, 1983; Turnbull, 1987), a number of studies suggest its applicability as a descriptor of the internationalization of SMEs (Sullivan and Bauerschmidt, 1990; Hakam *et al.*, 1993; Calof and Viviers, 1995). Other studies propose amendments to the precise stages and progression, but concur that SME internationalization is likely to be incremental and stage-wise (Rao and Naidu, 1992; Chang and Grub, 1992).

A frequent explanation of incremental internationalization in SMEs is that of the financial and managerial resource constraints facing these firms. Additionally, incremental models are also supported by the 'gambler's earnings' hypothesis (Penrose 1956), among the implications of which are (Buckley, 1989) that: 'the risk averse firm is likely, initially to underinvest and to begin with a small stake', and 'rather than scanning the world for further, possibly more profitable opportunities, the firm will reinvest in its safe bet – the existing subsidiary'. Accordingly, small firms might be expected to expand within one market before entering the next.

Simultaneous models of small-firm internationalization

Since the mid-1990s, the literature has highlighted a number of trends that favour a more rapid internationalization process, even in small, resource-constrained firms. Firstly, there is the suggestion of an increasing number of global niche opportunities (Bonaccorsi, 1992; Chang and Grub, 1992), and indeed in some sectors the ability to capitalize on this type of niche may be key to survival:

> competitive advantage may be vested in their ability to develop and exploit new innovations, carve out narrowly defined and defensible niches, and adapt rapidly to change. (Jones, 1999: 19)

Buckley (1989) suggests that small firms may be at no disadvantage compared to larger rivals in serving specialized markets with few economies of scale.

Secondly, the opportunities for raising external finance, or cooperating with other firms to gain access to scarce resources, have increased (Bonaccorsi, 1992; Hansen *et al.*, 1994; Kaufmann, 1995). Thirdly, and most significantly, the entrepreneurship literature has seen the emergence of a number of studies (D'Souza and Erramilli, 1993; Oviatt and McDougall, 1994; Jones, 1999; Crick and Jones, 2000) which suggest a more rapid and even simultaneous process of internationalization. This 'born-international' school suggests that the barriers to the internationalization of small firms have reduced to the point where small firms may even be international from inception.

One of the key arguments underpinning the 'born-international' school highlights a fundamental difference in the theoretical assumptions underpinning incremental and simultaneous models of small-firm internationalization. Oviatt and McDougall (1994) suggest that advances in technology mean that:

> An internationally-experienced person who can attract a moderate amount of capital can conduct business anywhere in the time it takes to press the buttons of a telephone.

The most striking part of this argument is the assumption that the requisite knowledge for international success is presumed to exist within individuals, and can therefore be transferred between organizations. This contradicts the assumptions and represents a central theoretical debate in the area of SME internationalization.

Learning and entrepreneurial networks

The internationalization literature bases its arguments on the generally accepted principle that operation in international markets exposes firms to higher levels of uncertainty than does domestic operation (Miller, 1992; Mascarenhas, 1992). However, the way in which firms learn about international markets and overcome uncertainty is subject to considerable debate. The Uppsala model (Johanson and Vahlne, 1977; Johanson and Wiedersheim-Paul, 1975) contends that uncertainty – or specifically psychic distance – can only be overcome by direct, experiental knowledge of each market. This type of knowledge, it is argued, cannot readily be transferred but is specific to each market and to each firm. This contention has prompted criticism of the Uppsala model, yet it remains unclear exactly how knowledge affects the decision to commit further resources (Andersen, 1993).

Subsequent work has suggested revisions to the assumptions of the Uppsala model. Millington and Bayliss (1990) and Clark *et al.* (1997) suggest that general and transferable knowledge exists alongside market-specific knowledge and that this can help to facilitate more rapid internationalization. Born-international studies go a step further in suggesting that this general, transferable knowledge exists within entrepreneurial individuals and can be used in successive international ventures (Oviatt and McDougall, 1994). A key question that remains is whether all of the knowledge needed to operate successfully in international markets exists within these entrepreneurial individuals? Oviatt and McDougall (1995, p. 35) suggest that:

> some understanding of the nuts and bolts of cross-border business conduct... and most important, potential communication and cultural conflicts seem necessary. Without that experience small problems can become disasters.

This type of knowledge is clearly specific to different markets and must be gained locally. Is it necessary, however, that the knowledge is gained directly or can it be acquired with key individuals or collaborative partners?

A growing body of small-firm internationalization studies are based on network theories (Coviello and Munro, 1992; Coviello and Martin, 1995; Blankenburg, 1995), and suggest that in addition to the knowledge that exists within the entrepreneurial founders, SMEs need to access networks that are specific to each market. Networks exist at the macroorganizational, interorganizational and intraorganizational levels, and provide access to local market knowledge and contacts. Entrepreneurial networks also often involve networks of personal contacts (Dubin and Aldrich, 1994), providing important information for SMEs (Tyrri, 1994; Jones, 1999). Existing network connections and those that can be built in new international markets play a vital role in successful international operation. Indeed, successful operation of small businesses has been described as the process of leveraging a network of networks (Hara and Kanai, 1994).

Internationalization in service firms

Research also highlights specific challenges facing service firms in their internationalization process. Firms increase their commitment from shared-control or contractual modes, such as franchise, towards foreign direct investments as they become more experienced (Erramilli, 1990, 1991). Some differences should, however, be noted between the challenges facing providers of services and products.

Firstly, Erramilli (1990, 1991) highlights the fact that inseparable services, such as hotels or restaurants, cannot be exported. Franchise is the minimum level of involvement and involves higher levels of investment than does export. Secondly, the challenge of implementing service excellence in international markets may dictate the mode of operation used.

Both product and service firms gain higher control from foreign direct investment than from shared control modes such as franchise (Simyar and Argeyd, 1987). Välikangas and Lehtinen (1994) suggest that the levels of control required by service providers may differ depending on the competitive positioning of the service. Process-based service firms can be internationalized via low control modes, such as franchise, provided a standard set of procedures can be created and transferred to the partner. More specialist or differentiated services may require higher levels of control as service excellence is intangible and highly culturally-specific (Dahringer, 1991).

Methodogical and conceptual development

The literature argues that small service firms need to adapt successfully to local market conditions in order to succeed internationally. Consequently, learning about international markets is particularly important for this type of firm and they are considered a good vehicle through which to study knowledge accumulation and transfer in the internationalization process. Accordingly, we analyse:

- the ways in which knowledge is accumulated;
- the ways in which knowledge is transferred; and
- the ways in which this influences the internationalization process for four small service firms.

Choice of research method

A case-based research methodology was adopted as it allows for the study of decisions in their context (Yin, 1983). Moreover, use of a fine-grained, theory-building methodology is believed to be most appropriate for this exploratory research (Harrigan, 1983; Bonoma, 1985). Yin (1990) contends that case-study research should not aim to generalize on a numerical basis, but rather that it should use 'analytic generalization' by means of replication, where each replication seeks:

> convergent evidence regarding the facts and conclusions for the case; each case's conclusions are then considered to be the information needing replication by other individual cases. (*Ibid.*: 15)

Of the four service firms that we study, the first two, Northtel (A) and Teleserve (B), are telecommunications service providers; the third firm, Compute (C), provides education for children in using computers; whilst the fourth, Tempsearch (D), provides temporary employment services. The first three firms are in high-technology sectors. Cases A and B provide specialist services, whilst cases C and D are more readily standardized, or process-based (Välikangäs and Lehtinen, 1994).

Accordingly, the cases can be differentiated both in respect to high-tech versus low-tech, and level of specialization. This sample frame provides literal replications (the same on key dimensions of level of technology) and theoretical replications (different on key dimensions of level of technology and level of specialization). It is hoped that this will provide insights into the generalizability of the 'born-international' literature – currently restricted to high-technology firms – and service literature – which differentiates on the basis of type of service. The cases can be classified as in Figure 12.1.

Respondents

We interviewed the senior managers from the founding market firm together with respondents from subsidiaries in other international markets. Whilst the broader international expansion of the firm was studied, specific attention was

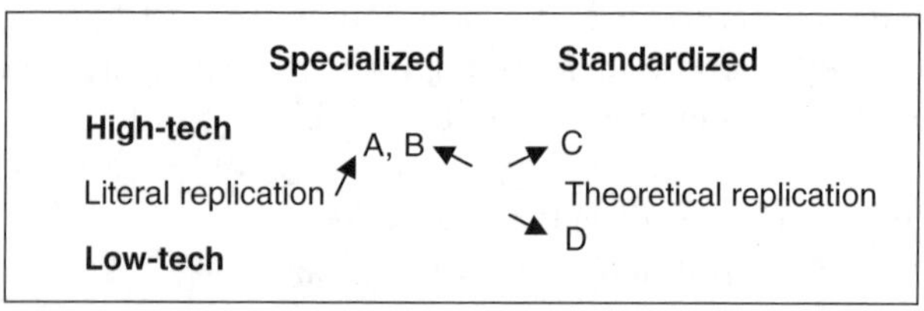

Figure 12.1 Classification of firms A–D

paid to the establishment of international operations in England, Australia and Sweden. Cases were selected where:

1 we could have total access to all key informants;
2 the international ventures were of significant size; and
3 English could be used and understood by all respondents.

Contacts with senior managers of these ventures led to other key informants who all agreed to participate.

Critical event analysis

A secondary aim with this research has been to develop data-collection procedures that bridge the gap between the standard case-study approach (Yin, 1990), using a set of semi-structured questions during interview, and the much less-structured and respondent-driven critical-incident technique (CIT). The former aims at a global case description and understanding of the behaviour of firms over time, whereas the latter is used to map micro-level incidents as they are perceived by individual respondents.

Flanagan (1954) developed CIT to study actual behaviour with the purpose of finding behaviours critical for the success or failure in a given situation. Recently, CIT has been used in a number of studies related to service quality (see for example Bitner *et al.*, 1990; Edvardsson, 1992; Johnston, 1995; Mattsson, 1993). The approach was considered important in our research as it allows respondents to decide which were the critical incidents in their internationalization processes. This inductive technique is less likely to bias the responses than a deductive data-collection technique.

Case analysis

The cases are assessed in four sections:

1 Incremental or simultaneous internationalization.
2 The process of increasing commitment within each market.
3 Proactive and reactive internationalization.
4 Learning and the internationalization process.

A summary of case histories and the events associated with internationalization is provided in the appendix.

Incremental or simultaneous internationalization

The most rapid internationalization process is found in the cases A (Northtel) and C (Compute). Northtel both incorporated and began to internationalize in

1994. It was international from inception as its concept was designed to be transferred to international markets, and by 1997 Northtel operated in 10 EU countries with further international expansion planned. Compute was founded in 1983, decided to franchise its concept in 1987, began this process in 1989 and – by the mid 1990s – had expanded into 40 countries.

Cases B (Teleserve) and D (Tempsearch) showed a slower internationalization process. B incorporated in 1989 and only began to consider international expansion in the late 1990s. Tempsearch began the process relatively early after the firm was taken over by the founder's son and his partner (1987), but after one foray into international markets chose a different route and formed an alliance with an international partner, who would take responsibility for further expansion.

As rapid – indeed simultaneous – internationalization occurred in specialized and standard firms (A and C) and did not occur in one of the high-tech firms (B), it appears that neither sector nor type of service alone can fully explain the nature of the internationalization process in small service firms.

The process of increasing commitment within each market

Two of the firms (C and D) began international operations by franchising their concepts, whilst the other firms (A and B) began with higher levels of investment. The latter both opted for a small, wholly-owned subsidiary. The choice of mode appears, therefore, to relate to the type of service provided. Both firms that chose to franchise their concepts internationally provided an inseparable, process-based service (Välikangäs and Lehtinen, 1994). The more specialist firms, in contrast, offering value-added telecommunications services, internationalized using higher control modes.

The choice of second or subsequent mode of operation within each market and that used to enter subsequent markets varied. Firm C (Compute) operated successfully using franchise and continues to use this mode to expand within and across international markets. Firm D (Tempsearch) used franchise initially, but seemingly with less success. It later opted to enter a strategic alliance with an international partner that would reduce its need to internationalize under its own initiative.

Similarly, firm A (Northtel) considered a range of higher commitment modes (joint venture and acquisition) for entry into subsequent markets. It has also made further commitments within its initial market in order to enhance its service proposition. Firm B (Teleserve) has been hindered in its further international expansion by the size of the investment this involves. Based on its successful growth in the Australian market, it does plan, however, to expand into other international markets.

The progression in mode found in our study provides partial support for the contentions of incremental models of internationalization. Firm A expanded to higher control modes as it gained in resources and international experience. Firm B is likely to follow this path when it has gained sufficient resources, and firm D has entered a strategic alliance as it does not feel that is has sufficient resources and experience to expand on its own. Firm C – in contrast – continues to expand into successive markets without diverting from its initial choice of franchise.

Proactive and reactive internationalization

Two patterns of internationalization are found; rapid internationalization (cases A and C), and slower internationalization (cases B and D). Within each pattern, the firms differ with respect to how and why internationalization occurs. In case A (Northtel), rapid expansion is attributable to the ambitions of the founders and their proximity to multiple countries and markets within Europe. The service (high-tech and relatively low-cost) means that this is feasible even with limited finance. Firm C created a service with international appeal, and rapid internationalization is dictated by high levels of interest by potential international partners. This is reactive rather than proactive internationalization, as it is largely dictated by the partners rather than the founding firm.

In the cases of slower international expansion (B and D), case B began to internationalize following opportunistic behaviour of an individual previously employed by a larger and more conservative parent. The opportunity was seized upon quickly but the internationalization process is as yet at an early stage of development.

A key finding of our study relates to the ways in which firms learn to expand within and between markets. Although they are new ventures, three of the cases (A, B and D) involve firms where the founder has previous international experience, and it is clear that this experience plays a valuable role in their internationalization. To this extent, there is support for the suggestions of Oviatt and McDougall (1994, 1995) that knowledge can be transferred between firms with individuals. Thus the knowledge that provides learning in our study is transferable.

Learning and the internationalization process

The key characteristics of the sources of knowledge, and how – and if – they are transferred are summarized in Table 12.1.

The successful expansion of firms A and C suggests that learning about international markets has taken place but, given their different mode choices, that this impacts on their decisions in different ways. That these firms have expanded into successive markets with such rapidity suggests that knowledge resides with the individual – rather than has to be gained within each enterprise before the firm can process. The knowledge of the founders is evidently a key strategic

Table 12.1 Types and sources of knowledge

Type of knowledge	*Where is knowledge gained?*	*Whay knowledge is gained?*
General international	From experience; from parent company; from local partner	Issues when individual leaves; knowledge is transferable but it is not always transferred
Market-specific characteristics	By exposure to market From partner	Slow process More rapid, but can be little listening and no learning
Need for service adaptation	By exposure to market; from partner	Some partners do not listen or accept
Contacts	By exposure to market From partner	Gained by trial and error Hands over book, but introductions are useful
Networks	By exposure to market From partner	Builds up relationships Access by introductions and meetings. Gains from reputation of partner

asset. Hence, analysis of these cases provides strong support for the idea that knowledge is transferable and does not have to be firm-specific to enhance learning about how to operate in international markets.

It is clear that the business contacts of firm A, the experience of working with the investing firms for case B, and the working background in East Asia for the partners in firm D provide sufficient confidence to internationalize into markets in which they have not always had direct experience. Case C, however, provides an example where the founders' previous experience is not a strong determinant in international expansion; perhaps it is not surprising, therefore, that this is the one firm which does not internationalize proactively.

The connection into relevant international networks seems to be an important differentiator between cases A and C. Case A shows that learning via international networks facilitates entry and successful operation in markets. Case C, in contrast, provides interesting insights into how firms may achieve this learning if it is not part of their direct experience. Firm C gains this knowledge via its franchise partners, who – in turn – have sufficient understanding of their market to make some necessary adjustments to an otherwise fairly standard service proposition. To this extent, firm C is reliant on its partners to use their knowledge of individual markets. There are, however, different views between the founding firm and the Australian franchisee on the extent to which adaptation is necessary or difficult. It is likely that the internationally inexperienced founders have underestimated what is required to succeed in individual international markets. As this persists, despite its operation in 40 countries, it appears that firm C has not 'learned' from the knowledge of its franchisees.

Case D shows parallels with firm C. The firm has decided that it does not have the knowledge or resources to internationalize on its own, and therefore takes the radical step of surrendering its responsibility for this process to a strategic alliance partner with international experience. Likewise, although firm A does have an understanding of the international markets it is entering, it recognizes that the most valuable resource that it can gain from a joint-venture partner or acquiree is its 'book of contacts', in other words the firm's knowledge of how to gain business in the market and its local networks.

An additional dimension of the founder's impact on increasing international involvement is that of leveraging business connections to access finance and other necessary resources for expansion.

Discussion

The cases presented above offer a number of insights into the internationalization process of small, service firms. Firstly, the pace of internationalization is rapid, especially in cases A and C, who have expanded within a relatively short time frame into a large number of markets. Much of the internationalization is in parallel, which supports the patterns suggested in the 'born-international' literature (Oviatt and McDougall, 1994; Jones, 1999; Crick and Jones, 2000) with respect to the expansion across geographic markets.

Not all of the firms we have studied are international from inception. Firms B and D internationalized more slowly given constraints on resources and international experience respectively, providing support for the contentions of incremental models (Johanson and Wiedersheim-Paul, 1975; Johanson and Vahlne, 1977). The existence of resource constraints supports arguments that incremental models are most applicable to small firms (Buckley *et al.*, 1988; Coviello and Munro, 1992; Hakam *et al.*, 1993; Calof and Viviers, 1995).

An interesting codicil to the debate on the impact of resource constraints on internationalization centres on the fact that firms A and C – of similar if not smaller size than the other – have been able to expand despite resource constraints. In the case of firm A, this has been achieved by effective leveraging of business contacts and an aggressive acquisition/finance-generating strategy. For firm C, the possibility of franchising the service has meant that the firm could expand using a network of franchisees who put up the finance for their own operations. Hence it is apparent that while resource constraints do inhibit the internationalization of these firms, such difficulties can be overcome via external funding and alliances as suggested by Bonaccorsi (1992), Hansen *et al.* (1994) and Kaufmann (1995).

The ways in which firms expand relate to the types of services they offer (Välikängas and Lehtinen, 1994). Whilst the process-based services of firms C and D can readily be franchised, higher control is preferred by the providers of value-added specialist services such as A and B. There is also some evidence of the U-shaped control experience curve suggested by Erramilli (1990). Firm A moves from wholly-owned subsidiaries to shared control joint ventures and mergers as it gains in experience; likewise firms C and D move from sole control to joint operations as they expand via franchises. The extent to which shared control is effective – there are suggestions that firm C passes over too much control to its franchisees and may be failing to learn about its international markets – raises the key area of learning and internationalization.

A key finding of our study relates to the way in which firms learn about international markets and overcome uncertainty. Although they are new ventures, three of the cases (A, B and D) involve firms where the founder has previous international experience, and it is clear that this experience plays a valuable role in their internationalization. To this extent, there is support for the suggestions of Oviatt and McDougall (1994, 1995) that knowledge can be transferred between firms via individuals. Thus the knowledge that provides learning is to some extent transferable.

The differences in the success of firms A and C relates to their ability to leverage networks of contacts internationally (Tyrri, 1994; Blankenburg, 1995; Coviello and Martin, 1995; Jones, 1999). The experience of firm A, in particular, shows that personal networks provide market-specific knowledge, contacts and even finance. Indeed, firm A states that the most valuable resource gained by an acquisition is the 'book of contacts' that the business owner may have for his market. Thus, although firms can learn from general international experience accumulated by individual entrepreneurs (Oviatt and McDougall, 1994, 1995), it is clear that specific knowledge and network connections are required to develop within each market.

In case D, where the founders have experience of Southeast Asia, this knowledge is not sufficiently specific that it can be used to gain insights into other regions. In sum, general transferable knowledge plays a role in internationalization (Millington and Bayliss, 1990; Clark *et al.*, 1997), but it is not, in itself, sufficient for international expansion. Our findings support Johansson and Vahlne's (1977) contention that market-specific knowledge is essential to overcome uncertainty. This does not, however, need to be gained directly, but may be accessed via networks in individual markets (Blankenburg, 1995; Coviello and Martin, 1995).

Conclusions on case studies

The pace of internationalization varies between the firms studied such that there is support for both simultaneous and incremental models. It is also clear that the minimum mode of operation required for use in international markets differs with the type of service provided. Thus, franchise can be used effectively for the more process-based standardized services, but higher control modes are preferred, even initially, for services that are more specialized.

Although the slower internationalization process of firms B and D relates to resource constraints – both financial and in the international experience of managers – it is clear that these difficulties can be overcome. Firms A and C have managed to access resources via cooperative ventures to complement their own ability to internationalize. The international experience of the founder played a key role in firm A's ability to access these resources. As this has been transferred into the firm – in three cases – it is apparent that this knowledge is transferable. That the knowledge of the founders in firm D has been insufficient to allow successful internationalization, indicates that knowledge should be market-specific and preferably provide a good understanding of the business networks within each market if it is to provide the necessary learning for continued internationalization.

Practioner implications

The ability to internationalize small, service firms rapidly and successfully relates to certain key competencies of the founders. Firstly, they should be able to raise external finance, either via their business connections, or other sources such as joint ventures. Secondly, previous international experience of each market in which they wish to operate seems essential to successful operation. Specifically, a good understanding of the business networks and key players in each market seems vital to successful international operation. Without this specific knowledge, firm D has been unable to put their general international experience to good effect. Firm C, which does not have previous experience seems to have underestimated the requirement to tailor its offer to the needs of customers in each market. It is uncertain whether they will succeed in growing their business within each market without this understanding, nor is it clear that they have learned much from franchisees who do have this understanding of each market.

Learning about how to operate effectively in each market, therefore, appears a central ability for international managers. With a good understanding of the business networks, even financial and other constraints can be overcome. This knowledge can be bought in, by employing key individuals or entering franchise, joint-venture or other cooperative agreements with those who have the knowledge. The disparity in views on the need to tailor the service offering of firm C, however, points to the importance of benefiting from this knowledge – of learning from partners – to promote further international development.

Appendix: summaries of case histories

Case A, Northtel, a high-tech, specialized firm

A cost efficient and customer-oriented provider of competitive telecommunications through a combination of high quality, low-cost and value added services to small and medium-sized customers.

Event 1: investigation of opportunities in Norway

In early 1994, Northtel investigated the possibility of setting up a fixed network in Norway but discovered that this would require more capital than they had available: 'They told us we can't use 1 billion [German] marks to invest in the infrastructure in a country with 4 million inhabitants'. The high cost of entry into Norway in landlines stems from the costs of setting up base stations in this large geographic area.

Not deterred by this setback, the two entrepreneurs involved in this investigation realized that they had had a good discussion of the opportunities emerging in the European telecommunications market more broadly.

Event 2: incorporation of Northtel as a company to serve the EU telecommunications market

The above discussion prompted further investigation into ways of benefiting from the forthcoming EU deregulation of the telecommunications sector. A meeting was held in Luxembourg to discuss the formation of the company to serve this new market opportunity. As there was some uncertainty whether Sweden and Norway – the home markets of the business associates interested in involvement in this company – it was decided to base the company in Luxembourg. This was felt to be an appropriate location for a truly European company. The company was incorporated in August 1994.

Event 3: gathering information in Europe

Market research into the telecommunications trends in Europe revealed that a major phase of telecommunications deregulation was scheduled for 1 January 1998. Furthermore, there was significant overcapacity in telecommunications, which sparked the idea to lease capacity and provide routing to the cheapest operator.

Event 4: visit to USA

Two of the founder members of Northtel went to the USA to make contacts that might provide the key strategic assets needed to set up the service that Northtel wanted to provide. One of the smaller players in the market has an FFC242 payments system and a suitable billing system, which was essential to their plan. Northtel subsequently acquired this company.

Worthy of discussion here are the learning implication of the advantages accrued over time, in particular the technological advantage of the acquired billing system.

Event 5: setting up in Sweden

Once the strategic assets were in place, Northtel began the process of expanding to serve the market opportunity in Europe. In August 1995 it set up in Sweden. This market was selected because some of the founding members of the Northtel organization were Swedish and had good knowledge and contacts in the market. The General Manager of Northtel moved to Sweden for a year to get the business up and running. Growth was rapid.

Northtel moved from gaining its first customer (November 1995) to 300 customers within the first four months.

Event 6: setting up in Norway

As a further step in anticipating EU deregulation of telecommunications, Northtel began a planned expansion into 10 European countries during 1997. These were Norway and Austria in March, Switzerland at the end of April, Italy in early May and then Greece. Entry was also planned into France, Spain, Portugal, Benelux and possibly Eastern Europe.

In each of these markets, the most appropriate entry mode was considered. In Norway, Northtel initially considered a joint venture with a Swedish partner, but the potential partner – which had considerable financial resources – turned the offer down. Norway was interesting as it is outside the EU and may be comparable with other markets.1000 + signed up from direct mail approach.

Event 7: Germany

Began working on this in January 1996, and used consultancy to help with set-up. Lack of knowledge of market?

Looked at 80 potential representatives and then identified one – 'suddenly we find a little tiny operation with no turnover with not really a good structure but they had something we needed', local node-switching capacity and an efficient distribution network. The company chose this mode to speed up entry compared with starting from scratch. The company was acquired in October 1996. Turnover increased from DM 100,000 in December 1996, to DM 1 million in to April 1997, and was projected to double.

Event 8: setting up in Austria

Because this had to happen fast, they bought into an existing company.

Start-up was different in each country: 'Well, two years ago I was in Florida; I was negotiating for the first partnership in the US and they had, by coincidence, been invited by some Austrian guys that needed to buy some American traffic and we were meeting for breakfast at the hotel and Mr A [the person associated with the Austrian company] was sitting there'.

A follow-up phone call to see how it was going a few months later revealed that the Austrian's deal had broken down, with an Ericsson switch coming in that couldn't be paid for. A quick meeting offered 85% equity ($150,000): 'He was looking at me and I said alright, I know you for two years and you always keep your word so I'm going to consider it.'

One month later operating in Austria with Mr A as general manager, 'he's maybe not the right guy to be a managing director in the long-term and he knows it. But for the time being he is important because he is the power for sales and marketing . . . But for the time being what we need is someone who could be very entrepreneurial . . . '.

The above highlights the value of having a 'book of names constituting potential relationships'. In sum, Northtel entered four markets in 1997 but had been preparing the ground for a year. 'It takes 9–10 months to find the mix of local investors, management and resource . . . Normally it is based on individual relations. You need to have the right people that you have trust in and they have confidence in you. That could mean that we could buy a company, we could buy a customer base, we could build it up around an individual etc. It is not a fixed story. There is not one way to put it together.'

Case B, Teleserve

Event 1: involvement in the Australian bid

Formed in 1990, the founder of Teleserve was a business development consultant for a US firm in the Asia-Pacific region. The parent organization bid for a tender in the Australian market, on which the Teleserve founder was employed. If the bid were successful, it would make the US firm the second carrier in the Australian market. At one point the team had 140 people working on the bid for the second carrier licence including people from America, France and Hong Kong. The founder recalls:

> we spent one big bucket full of money putting together the business case. I took it back to [the American parent company] and [they] decided not to make the investment...we spent probably $10 million evaluating the whole process. Came back and said it looks OK but it's not something that we can make money out of. There's not enough people in the country.

Eventually, however, the US firm decided to withdraw from the bid as they had more attractive options in South America, Asia-Pacific and Eastern Europe.

Event 2: formation of Teleserve

In the belief that Australia and New Zealand would become one telecommunications market, the New Zealand subsidiary of the firm, Teleserve, was formed as a separate company to investigate these opportunities in mid-1991. Teleserve focused on the potential for non-carrier opportunities, particularly in value-added areas. Teleserve has two major investors: the US parent and the New Zealand subsidiary of the original firm. Hence it was a separate small firm, but backed by larger, more resource-rich companies.

Event 3: bid for New South Wales (NSW) and Queensland contracts

Soon after incorporation, Teleserve put in bids for facilities management services to the NSW and Queensland governments. Teleserve was unsuccessful in the first of these, but succeeded in the latter:

> The business case for the business at that point was really with the Queensland government contract, that's what the shareholders invested in and we had a mission to build a business and use that as the basis but I've got to say a that point we weren't really clear on what would be the shape or structure of the business beyond the Queensland government contract.

Event 4: the experience of the Teleserve founder

The potential success of the Teleserve operation is clearly linked to the experience of its founder, who had a history of developing several small companies as a young entrepreneur. One of the more successful ventures had been sold to the American investing firm. He had experience in sales, developing and introducing new technologies and negotiating new contracts. He sums this up as: 'The long and the short of it is that my background kind of [allows me to] work through many issues that we were going to face here.' He also adds: 'I think companies are... coming into markets through one vehicle or another to learn their way around the market before the big investments come.'

Event 5: planned international expansion

Although Teleserve began with low initial equity, it went through a period of high growth (100% in 1994–95). Even by its second year, Teleserve had returned sufficiently good results to be able to develop a plan to expand into other international markets. Targets included fax and electronic mail services in New Zealand, and cable plant management in Indonesia. Teleserve management sum up their position as follows: 'while in the first three years we grew to a critical mass, now we're going to use that to leverage it into the size of the business that telecommunications companies are interested in.'

Case C, Compute

Event 1: setting up the business

Compute is a computer education firm set up in the USA in 1983. The MD is from South Africa but moved to the United States as he wasn't particularly keen on going into the army. The founder's wife was an educational researcher at UCLA. Together they established a Learning Centre in Los Angeles where children would learn mathematics and English using computers.

Over the first five years, Compute continued to purchase hardware and software and a set of teachers were trained to teach children 'on the road'. Compute had now expanded to a point where it had 40 teachers servicing 400 locations up and down the West Coast of the USA.

Event 2: redefining the service

The MD relates an incident that helped to shape the focus of Compute. One woman was very emphatic that she did not want her child to be taught the typical academic subjects on a computer, but rather that the child should learn how to use a computer. This focus on technological literacy inspired the MD to re-focus on computer science and technology. This incident shows the importance of listening to customers about the needs in particular markets.

Event 3: deciding to franchise the concept

In 1987–88, the founders of Compute were considering ways of expanding the concept across the USA. With the aid of a marketing franchise consultant, they decided in 1989 that franchising was the best was forward as it would: 'expand the business without having to raise too much additional capital'. Moreover, it would 'encourage highly motivated people who would hopefully operate – in their self-interest – at a high level so that we would be able to extend our presence.'

In the first year of franchising, 10 outlets were franchised. By the second year, 50. The business how has over 200 franchises in the USA.

Event 4: the decision to internationalize

The significant aspect of the internationalization of Compute is that the Americans were not looking to take their programme overseas. The idea to do so came from potential franchisees that saw adverts aimed at the US market: 'here were some internationals knocking at their door saying "we think its a goer, we want to take it to our own countries"'.

Event 5: entry into Japan

A Japanese group purchased the franchise from Compute in 1990, but progress was slow; business in Japan only really began to get off the ground in 1993. There was reluctance on the part of Japanese parents to enrol their children in a programme that was not approved by their government. Indeed, as internationalization was not planned, nor had the Americans made any cultural adaptations to their products or systems.

Event 6: starting up in Australia

The Australian franchisee explains that he and his wife were looking for a business opportunity. He was involved in adult education in the professional body for stock-brokers, merchant bankers and analysts. His wife was a teacher. In 1990, the Australian couple saw an advert for someone willing to set up a Learning Centre to teach children how to work with computers. After 15 months investigating the business area, travelling to the USA and trying to sort out the finance and negotiations, an agreement was made in Indonesia.

Event 7: relationship between Australian and US franchisor

The founder of Compute and his Australian franchisee found that they had an affinity because they shared many characteristics. They were of similar age, has similar upbringing, ethnic backgrounds and both had wives who were educationalists. The Australian franchisee says: 'we got on very well from day one . . . there were a lot of similarities – our own relationship clicked'. The franchisor says: 'From the beginning it was as much a developing of a personal relationship as it was a business relationship'.

Event 8: franchises set up in Argentina and Mexico

Together with the expansion into Australia, expansion into these further two countries pushed the Americans to set up an international office that could understand the implications of trying to handle international variations in customer needs. Although Compute had stumbled into international markets initially, it soon began to realize that there was a potential market everywhere that had computers and electricity. At this point: 'There was definitely, a very definite strategic commitment on our parts to pursue international operations.'

The international manager of Compute lists the difficulties of international operation as including issues of adaptation, finding the right partners to work with, and securing an appropriate legal arrangement. He goes on to say that the cultural issues proved not to be significant as: 'Technology is universal, and so, from that stand point . . . technology transcends culture, religion and politics etc.'. Some adaptations were, however, made to account for differences in educational systems and for doing business in different countries.

A different perspective is gained from the Australian franchisee who says that cultural differences are, in fact, 'significant and variable and need to be managed effectively'. He comments that people from non-English-speaking backgrounds not only have to translate the programme themselves, but need to adapt it to meet cultural, learning, teaching and customer-relationship issues.

Event 9: managing relationships between franchisor and franchisee

The MD views the relationship as open and up-front and based on the percentages that franchisees are receiving. Common difficulties are around cultural differences and may have a detrimental effect on communication. There is a classic tension in the relationships: 'The franchisor provides a certain level of service and the franchisee is obliged to execute this. [The] franchisee always believes that the franchisor can do more for him . . . There are great challenges but none that can't be overcome.'

Event 10: leveraging the international infrastructure

Now that franchises exist in more than 40 countries, it wishes to use its international base to exploit its existing resources further. The intention is to expand the service offer to meet the needs of adults who wish to learn about computers. This will form a platform for entry into the information highway. The MD realizes that though the basic infrastructure exists to allow this expansion, the organizational structure and support will need to develop to make it possible to capitalize on the opportunities.

Case D, Tempsearch

Set up in Sweden in 1953 to offers temporary employment services. Bought by son and his partner in 1987. Sales volume doubled each year until Tempsearch had a one-third share of the Swedish market.

Event 1: economic depression in Sweden

In 1990–91, the volume of business had declined as a result of economic depression in the home market. This forced the partners to look for an international business partner who could provide a strategic alliance that would help the business to grow further and succeed in the face of growing competition.

Event 2: entry into a franchise agreement with US franchisee

The Swedish market had a unique 'no fee if not satisfied' clause in the temporary services market. To reduce the number of occasions on which this would happen, Tempsearch did extensive skills-testing and matching with client needs, with a focus on accounting, secretarial and sales personnel. This formula was unusual in other markets and therefore had value as a franchise concept. The franchise was licensed to the US partner in 1992.

Event 3: strategic alliance with US competitor

In 1996, the Swedish firm entered a strategic alliance with a US competitor that had set up in the Swedish market. The motive behind the sale of equity to the partner was to gain capital and the extensive international network of the US partner who wished to gain access to the Scandinavian market. When the managers of the two firms met at a congress in Hawaii, the US firm made a good impression on its potential partner from the beginning: 'we made good friends with them because they were easy to know . . . communicated easily with us . . . and seemed generally well-liked'.

In the Swedish market, the Tempsearch brand would be used although the competences of the US partner would be used to improve performance. The US brand was used to expand into other markets jointly as it was better known.

References

Andersen, O. (1993) 'One the internationalisation process of firms: a critical analysis', *Journal of International Business Studies* 24(2), 209–31.

Andersson, B.-E. and Nilsson, S.-G. (1964) 'Studies in the reliability and validity of the critical incident technique', *Journal of Applied Psychology* 48(6), 398–403.

Bitner, M.J., Booms, B.H. and Stanfield Tetrault, M. (1990) 'The service encounter: diagnosing favorable and unfavorable incidents', *Journal of Marketing* 54(1), 71–84.

Blankenburg, D. (1995) 'A network approach to foreign market entry', in Möller, K. and Wilson, D. (eds), *Business Marketing: An Interaction and Network Perspective.* London: Kluwer.

Bonaccorsi, A. (1992) 'On the relationship between firm size and export intensity', *Journal of International Business Studies* 23(4), 605–25.

Bonoma, T. (1985) 'Case research in marketing: opportunities, problems and a process', *Journal of Marketing Research* 12(3), 99–208.

Buckley, P.J. (1989) 'Foreign direct investment by small and medium-sized enterprises: the theoretical background', *Small Business Economics* 1(2), 89–100.

Calof, J.L. and Viviers, W. (1995) 'International note: internationalisation behaviour of small- and medium-sized South African enterprises', *Journal of Small Business Management* 23(3), 71–9

Chang, T. and Grub, P.D. (1992) 'Competitive strategies of Taiwanese PC firms in their internationalisation process', *Journal of Global Marketing* 6(3), 5–27.

Clark, T., Pugh, D.S. and Mallory, G.R. (1997) 'The process of internationalisation in the operating firm', *International Business Review* 6(6), 605–9.

Coviello, N. and Martin, K.A.-M. (1999) 'Internationalisation of service SMEs: an integrated perspective from the engineering consulting sector', *Journal of International Marketing* 7(4), 42–63.

Coviello, N. and Munro, H. (1997) 'Network relationships and the internationalisation process of small software firms', *International Business Review* 6(4), 361–86.

Crick, D. and Jones, M. (2000) 'Small, high-technology firms and international high-technology markets', *Journal of International Marketing* 8(2), 63–85.

Dahringer, L.D. (1991) 'Marketing services internationally: barriers and management strategies', *The Journal of Services Marketing* 5(3), 5–17.

Dichtl, L.E.M. Liebold, M., Köglmayr, H.G. and Müller, S. (1984) 'The foreign orientation of management as a central construct in export centred decision-making', *Research for Marketing* 23(2), 34–45.

Dubini, P. and Aldrich, H. (1991) 'Personal and extended networks are central to the entrepreneurial process', *Journal of Business Venturing* 6(5), 305–14.

Edgett, S.J. and Cullen, C. (1993) 'Service organization selection: a cross-cultural analysis of the role of involvement', *European Journal of Marketing* 27(2), 33–45.

Edvardsson, B. (1992) 'Service break-downs – a study of critical incidents in an airline', *International Journal of Service Industry Management* 3(4), 17–29.

Erramilli, M.K. (1990) 'Entry mode choice in service industries', *International Marketing Review* 7(5), 50–61.

Erramilli, M.K. (1991) 'The experience factor in foreign market entry behaviour of service firms', *Journal of International Business Studies*, Fall, 479–501.

Erramilli, M.K. and D'Souza, D.E. (1993) 'Venturing into foreign markets: the case of the small service firm', *Entrepreneurship Theory and Practice* 17(4), 29–39.

Flanagan, J.C. (1954) 'The critical incident technique', *Psychological Bulletin* 51(4), 327–57.

Hakam, A.N., Lau, G.T. and Kong, S.B. (1993) 'The export behaviour of firms in singapore: an application of the stage of internationalisation model', *Asia-Pacific Journal of Marketing and Logistics* 5(1), 1–20.

Hansen, N. Gillespie, K. and Gencturk, E. (1994) 'SMEs and export involvement: market responsiveness, technology and alliances', *Journal of Global Marketing* 7(4), 7–27.

Hara, G. and Kanai, T. (1994) 'Entrepreneurial networks across oceans to promote international strategic alliances for small businesses', *Journal of Business Venturing* 9(4), 89–507.

Harrigan, K. (1983) 'Research methodologies for contingency approaches to business strategy', *Academy of Management Review* 8(3), 398–405.

Johansson, J. and Vahlne, J.-E. (1977) 'The internationalisation of the firm: a model of knowledge development and increasing foreign market commitments', *Journal of International Business Studies* 8(1), 23–32.

Johansson, J. and Wiedersheim-Paul, F. (1975) 'The internationalisation of the firm – four Swedish cases', *Journal of Management Studies*, October, 305–22.

Johnston, R. (1995) 'The determinants of service quality: satisfiers and dissatisfiers', *International Journal of Service Industry Management* 6(5), 53–71.

Jones, M. (1999) 'The internationalisation of small, high-technology firms', *Journal of International Marketing* 7(4), 15–41.

Kaufmann, F. (1995) 'Internationalisation via co-operation – strategies of SME', *International Small Business Journal*, Jan.–March, 27–32.

Mascarenhas, B. (1982) 'Coping with uncertainty in international business', *Journal of International Business*, Fall, 87–98.

Mattsson, J. (1993) 'How bank loan officers evaluate persons applying for credit', *International Journal of Bank Marketing* 11(2), 25–34.

Miller, K.D. (1992) 'A framework for integrated risk management', *Journal of International Business*, Summer, 311–31.

Millington, A.I. and Bayliss, B.T. (1990) 'The process of internationalisation: UK companies in the EC', *Management International Review* 30(1), 51–161.

Nyquist, J.D., Bitner, M.J. and Booms, B.H. (1985) 'Identifying communication difficulties in the service encounter: a critical incident approach', in Czepiel, J.A., Solomon, M.R. and Surprenant, C.F. (eds), *The Service Encounter*. New York: Lexington Books.

Olsen, M.J.S. and Thomasson, B. (1992) 'Qualitative methods in service quality research', paper presented at the QUIS III Conference, Karlstad, Sweden.

Oviatt, B.M. and McDougall, P. (1994) 'Toward a theory of international new ventures', *Journal of International Business Studies*, Spring, 45–64.

Oviatt, B.M. and McDougall, P. (1995) 'Global start-ups: entrepreneurs on a worldwide stage', *Academy of Management Executive* 9(2), 30–43.

Oviatt, M. and McDougall, P. (1997) 'Challenges for internationalisation process theory', *Management International Review* 2(2), 85–99.

Penrose, E.T. (1956) 'Foreign investment and the growth of the firm', *Economic Journal* 66(2), 230–5.

Rao, T.R. and Naidu, G.M. (1992) 'Are the stages of internationalisation empirically supportable?', *Journal of Global Marketing* 6(1/2), 147–70.

Reid, S. (1983) 'Firm internationalisation: transaction costs and strategic choice', *International Marketing Review* 2, Winter, 45–56.

Simyar, F. and Argeyd, K. (1987) 'Export entry and expansion strategies' in Rosson, P.J. and Reid, S.D. (eds), *Managing Export, Entry and Expansion*. New York: Praeger.

Sullivan, D. and Bauerschmidt, A. (1990) 'Incremental internationalisation: a test of Johanson and Vahlne's thesis', *Management International Review* 30(1), 19–30.

Turnbull, P.W. (1987) 'A challenge to the stages theory of the internationalisation process', in Rosson, R.J. and Reed, S.D. (eds), *Managing Export Entry and Expansion*. New York: Praeger.

Välikangas, L. and Lehtinen, U. (1994) 'Strategic types of services and international marketing', *International Journal of Service Industry Management* 5(2), 72–84.

Yin, R.K. (1990), *Case Study Research*. California: Sage.

13
Pricing Strategies of Born-Globals

*Mika Gabrielson and Zuhair Al-Obaidi**

Introduction

A research programme was initiated at the Helsinki School of Economics in 2001 to examine the phenomenon of 'born-global' firms. It was observed that the number of small and medium-sized Finnish start-up firms that rapidly moved to a global stage was increasing (Kirplani and Luostarinen, 1999; Autio *et al.*, 2000). Similar developments have also been identified in other countries such as Denmark (Madsen *et al.*, 1997), Ireland (Knight *et al.*, 2001), Israel (Almor, 2000), Australia (Rennie, 1993) and the USA (Knight and Cavusgil, 1996; Oviatt and McDougal, 1994). As this was seen to be of significance to the Finnish economy and was also becoming acknowledged by many researchers, it was considered important to identify and understand the globalization process and global marketing strategies of such firms (Luostarinen and Gabrielsson, 2001). Rapid globalization was considered to include tremendous challenges for such small firms with limited resources – be they human or capital – originating in a small country like Finland.

Various researchers have put forward different suggestions as to how born-globals can cope with these challenges. Rennie (1993) suggests that success stems from their ability to adapt to the requirements of the global environment and achieve cost-effectiveness. Kirpalani and Luostarinen (1999) emphasize that,

> in today's world, since the global business environment is changing so rapidly, marketing has again become the leading function. What one knows is that

*We acknowledge the contribution of the Born Globals II research group (Lavikkala 2001, Mattila 2001, Ratia 2001, Sankari 2002, Viljanen 2002), headed by Professor Reijo Luostarinen, colleagues and researchers, as well as students of the export marketing course, for the definitions, examples of born-globals, and discussions on pricing strategies.

> a market-oriented corporate culture is increasingly being considered a key element of superior corporate performance.

Thus, given the urgency, complexity and enormous pressures of globalization, and limitations faced by born-globals, it would seem valuable to understand how they decide upon marketing strategies. Although the international/global marketing literature has contributed much to our understanding of the marketing strategies of large globalizing firms (see for example Buzzell, 1968; Keegan, 1969; Levitt, 1983; and Jain, 1989), little has been written on specific born-globals marketing strategies (see for example Knight, 1997; Gabrielson and Gabrielson, 2003a), and few of these studies are related to the challenges facing born-globals in their endeavours to price their products (see McDougall *et al.*, 1994; Luostarinen and Gabrielsson, 2002).

In light of the research gap identified, the objective of this chapter is firstly to explore the viability of the alternative global generic pricing strategies (that is market differentiated, dual, globally standardized) suggested by the pricing literature (Al-Obaidi and Gabrielson, 2002) in the case of born-globals, and secondly to find out how such strategies can be further developed into individually applicable and usable pricing strategies at the target market and customer level (for example skimming, penetration, leader, follower, bundling, and so on), and finally to identify what factors influence the strategic choices made by born-globals.

It is assumed that such research objectives would contribute to our general understanding of the characteristics of born-global firms and the factors that influence their marketing behaviour in general and pricing strategies in particular. This requires integration of two streams of literature: international business and domestic marketing, both of which have developed distinctive concepts and definitions for pricing strategies. The nature of our approach is conceptual-analytical as we intend to develop a conceptual framework and generate propositions for future quantitative studies. In order to make our point, we also intend to include empirical illustrations of eight Finnish born-globals. Hence, to achieve the objectives, the following research questions were formulated:

1. On the basis of current literature, what factors influence born-globals' pricing behaviour and what pricing strategy alternatives do they adopt?
2. On the basis of empirical cases, which strategies do born-globals select and what factors influence this pricing behaviour?

In this way we hope to generate interest in researching born-globals' pricing behaviour and its contribution to their success. Furthermore, such studies will enable future research to dispel some of the myths surrounding the increasing number, importance, and failure of these firms.

Literature review on pricing

The literature review below outlines the general characteristics of price and born-global firms and then proceeds to examine in detail the main factors that influence the pricing decisions of born-global firms.

Characteristics of price

For many managers, price can ultimately mean a number that more than anything captures the costs involved in providing a market offering to a customer. But for a born-global manager, in the final analysis, it is a tool to compete successfully by generating a long-term sales volume at a profit. In this sense, it is more than the break-even point of costs and revenues.

Schindehutte and Morris (2001) argue that a number of factors influence the prices charged by marketing-oriented managers. Thus, price is a statement by a customer of the value perceived when buying. This value may sometimes be difficult to estimate, as the born-globals' products are often unique but not yet proven or tested. However, the payment (that is price) made in exchange for this perceived value is often negotiable, which makes it variable. These ways are commonly referred to as terms of payment, mode of payment and time of payment. Prices also give variety to the means used by managers to accomplish different aims related to the overall product and marketing offering, for instance by influencing the sales of other products, bundling and unbundling sets of products, and eventually influencing intermediary behaviour.

From the customer's point of view, a price is also highly visible, though they may not always consider all the components of the price that they pay and certainly not all the benefits in full. Consequently, prices usually send messages and signals about value, image, quality, exclusivity, uniqueness, and the capabilities of the firm. This may be particularly important for born-globals, whose products have not yet proven their functionality and developed global brand awareness. Such signals can have a significant effect on market share and profits. Finally, pricing is the only marketing mix variable that is not a cost but rather a means of generating the revenues desperately needed to help born-globals meet their high-growth expectations. Because of these pricing characteristics, managers tend to find it easier to adjust or change the price rather than other of the marketing mix variables (Simon, 1992).

Recognizing such price qualities and the best way to use them may be easy for experienced marketing managers, but can often be beyond the skills of the born-global founders, who may lack proper business education or/and experience in global business and marketing management. Such decisions are also quite interrelated with many other strategic decisions and are heavily influenced by a large group of factors. This we will examine in the next section with respect to pricing by born-globals. However, it is important to say a few words about the general characteristics of these firms.

Characteristics of born-global firms

The born-globals can be defined in many ways. These definitions vary from very strict to relatively loose, depending on the school of thought. Some of the earlier studies have used revenues and export percentage as measurement criteria (Knight and Cavusgil, 1996), whilst others have emphasized the elements of an international venture, which 'seeks to derive significant competitive advantage from the use of resources and the sales of outputs in multiple countries' (Oviatt and McDougall, 1994). Generally speaking, born-globals have been associated with small size, entrepreneurship and few employees; limited resources and experience in international business; small domestic markets and global niche products intended for global markets.

The latest global business research has insisted on a strict interpretation of the concept 'global' and taken up strategic perspectives whereby born-globals (1) start international operations even before or simultaneously with domestic ones, (2) base their visions and missions mainly on global markets and customers from the inception, (3) plan their products, structures, systems and finances on a global basis, (4) plan to become global market leaders as part of their vision, (5) utilize different product, operation and market strategies as firms have traditionally done, (6) follow different global marketing strategies, and (7) grow exceptionally fast on global markets (typically over half of their sales are generated from markets outside the home continent) (Luostarinen and Gabrielson, 2002).

Factors influencing born-globals' pricing decisions

The literature dealing with pricing decisions are full of references to factors influencing managers in their efforts to decide and innovate in price-setting approaches and strategies (Cateora and Graham, 1999; Czinkota and Ronkainen, 1998; Nagle and Holden, 1995; Toyne and Walters, 1993; Walters, 1989). In this section we categorize them into three major groups: macro, meso, and micro.

General global market forces

These factors include the general macro environmental factors that characterize the global marketplace, often referred to as political, economical, sociocultural, and technological factors. At the political level, the world has become a freer context for conducting business; liberalization of markets and encouragement of small business around the world have created a better atmosphere for global business conducted by SMEs. However, firms are still subject to changes in the political and regulatory environments of individual target markets.

As lower barriers to trade and investment have led to growth in international trade during the last 20 years, a process involving the integration of national economies was triggered. The phenomenon known as the globalization of world markets has been characterized by increased globalization of production and trade as technological development made it possible for firms to produce and export wherever profitable. The end result is intensified competition. However, this has provided many entrepreneurs and SMEs with enormous opportunities. For small countries such as Finland (five million inhabitants) this was particularly significant, as a huge market space was opened up, often a hundred times larger than their domestic markets. Under such global competitive pressures and in the face of vast opportunities for global market expansion, development of the right strategic decisions regarding pricing issues becomes crucial.

At the sociocultural level, the global environment presents many opportunities, but also many constraints. Nations across the globe have certain specific characteristics, values and traditions that influence economic behaviour. However, globalization trends viewed from the sociocultural dimension point to the rise of a global culture, making many aspects of sociocultural life universal (Knight and Cavusgil, 1996; Madsen *et al.*, 1997). Some writers have even suggested a creeping homogenization in lifestyle, products, production, various processes, institutions and consumer behaviour (Levitt, 1983). However, born-globals need to recognize that the trends towards homogeneity in the aspects referred to earlier are not necessarily equally distributed across world communities. Hence, although new global segments and niches may appear, pricing strategies may not be easily implemented as one would assume on the basis of the above trends. This challenge to born-global managers is real, given their limited human resources, brands that are still unknown and short-term experience in dealing with different sociocultural environments.

At the technological level, R&D activities and the speed of new technological development have a great impact on corporate strategies. Advancements in information technology and transportation are making it easier, quicker and cheaper to move or transfer goods, equipment, people, data and payments around the world (Jeannet and Hennessy, 1998). These developments influence the business of born-globals (Knight and Cavusgil, 1996; Madsen *et al.*, 1997). Both firms and customers can, through the worldwide web, stay in touch with developments in world markets, production, logistics, consumer attitudes and the activities of other firms. Productivity in many industries has been constantly rising, aided by technological development, which has created an exponential growth of expectations and valuations by some dot.com companies (up to Autumn 2000) which, however, proved unrealistic. Regardless of the overspills, the fact remains that computer technologies have increased the competitiveness of born-globals by reducing the cost of reaching and serving a global customer base. Being innovative, most born-globals have used the latest technologies to enable them to communicate directly with customers and even to bypass channel members when entering markets. Use of advanced information technologies helps in reducing the costs of production and makes it possible to pass savings to customers. The extent to which firms and their customers are able to use and benefit from technological changes can have tremendous impact on many of the strategic decision areas closely related to pricing, such as dot.com marketing.

Globalization drivers

Finnish born-global firms come from a small and open-economy (SMOPEC) country, and are located at the periphery of the international business triad (Ohmae, 1985). According to Luostarinen (1994), when such a small nation of 5 million population opens its borders for international trade, the push and particularly pull forces for internationalization in the case of born-globals become considerably stronger and the slogan 'globalize or die' becomes an urgent call. Thus, the born-globals soon find themselves in the global business game, struggling with the forces of globalization if they wish to survive. They should be able to find a small niche that major MNCs have either not bothered to identify or are not interested in serving. Such a small niche can be a great segment for a born-global. Their entrepreneurial approach allows them to move swiftly, sometimes unnoticed by the big MNCs, to seize new markets and to develop new global products. The products must be differentiated from those of competitors. A good example is the Finnish biotech company Biohit, which sells multi-channel pipettes to laboratories and hospitals all around the world. Another example is Woodnotes, which sells carpets made out of paper yarn to 50 foreign countries. The market factors are closely related to the competitive pressures exerted at the firm and the convergence and homogeneity of the global demand and technological standards. To be viable, in such tough market conditions, a competitive strategy also needs to address the cost efficiency issue in scale and scope. Thus, born-globals need to view the whole world as their market, serving similar segments across the world through a standardized marketing mix strategy whenever possible, but adapted when necessary (Cateora and Graham, 1999).

Many forces have also been working towards the globalization of industries. Managers of born-globals can benefit from examining these forces, assessing the degree of industry globalization in their businesses, and attempting to design their marketing strategies to capitalize on the opportunities offered by such conditions. Four sets of factors drive industry globalization: market-drivers, cost-drivers, government-drivers, and competitive-drivers. In the following section we examine these drivers and suggest some of their impact on the pricing considerations of born-globals.

Product factors

Most born-global firms are suppliers of products that have been the outcome of a long process of R&D. The products are often new innovations; may contain a high degree of intangible aspects and can be part of a system that solves a particular techno-economic problem facing potential customers. Hence, these products and their suppliers are not usually widely known; neither do the product's technologies and brands have full legal protection through patents and trademarks.

The product lifecycle literature suggests that a firm's ability and pricing flexibility decline as a product moves along its lifecycle. As most born-globals are suppliers of new products located in the innovation/introduction stage with very few substitutes and inelastic demand, a high (skimming) price strategy may be followed. Nagle and Holden (1995) suggest that a skimming strategy can be used for only a certain period of time, and thus a sequential pricing strategy should be adopted. But product newness implies that it may not have a brand name yet or its brand equity is not yet substantial. Furthermore, potential customers are reluctant to use it since it has not yet proven itself in terms of value, fit and quality. The intangibility often associated with many of the born-global products makes them vulnerable in many respects. They require legal protection and a lot of pre- as well as post-purchase advice and service. In such circumstances, suppliers find themselves engaged in various adaptations or modifications to meet the special needs of customers. Although this may add to the uniqueness and novelty of a product, adaptations will also introduce some extra costs that lead to pursuing price differentiation. The above aspects form the core of product characteristics recognized as important by the literature when making strategic pricing decisions (Toyne and Walters, 1993).

Customer factors

Demand and its analysis is an important aspect in the process of setting prices, but born-global management may not use such a sophisticated, systematic and demanding approach. Instead, they may prefer the comfort of a simpler way of pricing given their circumstances: small size, lack of resources, especially human resources, and the pressures of time. Thus, they turn their attention to potential customers and in many cases there might not be a well-established customer base due to the novelty of their product offering. These potential customers have most likely been identified earlier at conferences and trade fairs or through feasibility and market studies estimating market potential at the firm's establishment or product commercialization phase. In some cases, the management may have previous experiences and contacts with potential customers due to their earlier assignments in the field.

Moore (2002) has classified customers in high-technology firms as enthusiasts (group 1), visionaries (group 2), pragmatists (group 3), conservatives (group 4) and sceptics (group 5). The enthusiasts (innovators) are technology-driven, and willing to try new products and to be seen using the latest state-of-the-art technology. Basically, they would also be willing to pay. Pricing, however, is difficult, as such customers are often used to getting demo versions free of charge. The visionaries (early adopters) are opportunities-driven and expect to be the first to adopt a new innovation that differentiates them from the competition. The customer may be expected to pay for their products, without being too price-sensitive, enabling value-based or skimming pricing. The pragmatists (early majority) are those who wait until the innovation has been tried and its success proved. Since they form the majority of the customers they see no reason to pay a premium price for their product that may not distinguish them from others. Pricing for this group is important to generate a profitable market share and make innovative products the standard in the marketplace. A bundling or penetration pricing strategy may be followed for this market segment. Conservatives (late majority) and sceptics (laggards) are the last groups during the lifecycle of the innovation, and are normally of little interest to born-global firms as they will have embarked on a new innovation or be upgrading their products to reach other more profitable groups discussed earlier.

Furthermore, the pricing strategy to be followed can be influenced by the number of customers to be served, their other characteristics such as country, nature of business (business-to-business or business-to-consumers), size, purchasing volume, and operation modes and channel arrangements. A further important aspect of customer-related factors is closely connected with the need to develop relationships. Born-globals, whose customers are mainly other manufacturing firms, may find that their products are passive items that can only be activated when the firm interacts with other firms (Ford and Saren, 2001) that place some value on them. In most cases, particularly in business-to-business marketing, the perceived value of a new innovation is specific to other firms and will be related to these firms' own technologies, technological requirements, and their views of the technological landscape of other firms in the network of business relationships (Ford and Saren, 2001; Tsai and Ghoshal, 1998). This interdependence influences the business-generation potential and can become an important factor impacting pricing strategy.

In this kind of market situation, the born-global firm can pursue a customer-relationship marketing approach to develop close, long-term relationships that create mutual benefits or win–win solutions. For born-globals, it is easier and cheaper to keep current customers happy than to search for new ones. Developing trust, commitment and interdependence with key customers has many implications for a firm's ability to understand their customers' price-sensitivity and design its pricing strategy. A price should reflect the value or quality that the customer expects or derives from using the product (Nagle and Holden, 1995). The born-globals' product characteristics make price-sensitivity measurement rather difficult. Thus, consideration of both the product characteristics and the customer relationships may reveal that there could be no single 'global customer group' with consistent attitudes, expectations, demand characteristics and income level.

Channel factors

The born-globals need to consider how to deliver, sell and market their products to end customers. The number of layers or length of their channel often influences end-user pricing, as each middleman wants to receive a margin for the functions performed. This naturally depends greatly on the functions they are performing and the bargaining power they exercise. When the resulting channel arrangement is similar from country to country, a more standardized pricing strategy may be applied. In contrast, a longer channel in some countries than others, without adding value to the end product, may very easily lead to differentiated-market pricing. To avoid this, the producers may consider cutting their own profits for markets where longer or more expensive channels are used in order to keep end prices similar.

Another problem is that channel members often behave opportunistically and may cheat their suppliers. Also, the fact that the born-globals' products and brands are often not well-recognized by the end customers make their selling and marketing very hard and time consuming. This would require producers to grant exceptionally large margins to channel members to make them interested, which in most cases is not possible. The born-globals have two means to solve the above problems. One way would be to bypass the channel members by using modern technologies such as the internet. This would lead to increasingly standardized pricing as the internet is global by nature and prices, and hence sales, can seldom be effectively market-restricted. Another approach is to develop close and trustworthy relationships with channel members, which would safeguard them from cheating. This would enable a functional division between the producer and channel members based on their competences and skills in the partnership. In the end-customer market this would be reflected in differentiated pricing as each partnership would be likely to differ from another. Only if the born-global could find a global channel partner with a global reach could standardized pricing be achieved.

Firm factors

Born-global firms are characterized by several features. They are mainly new start-ups launched by a single entrepreneur or small team of founders with limited financial resources and few employees (Madsen *et al.*, 1997). Typically, among them there can be one or two innovators in the high-tech, high-design, high-service or high-systems fields (Kirpalani and Luostarinen, 1999; Luostarinen and Gabrielson, 2002). They usually produce leading-edge products in their respective fields. Their products have required enormous resources and efforts from the founders; they have been developed to render value appreciated highly by a global niche segment, for which domestic clientele would be too limited (Rennie, 1991; Oviatt and McDougall, 1994; Cavusgil, 1997).

Because of the extremely tough context in which they are born, such firms try to capitalize on their strengths: entrepreneurial spirit, quick response, flexibility, and the leading-edge quality of products. Their products often feature high added value and are therefore based on innovative technology, design, flexibility and sometimes customization. Although born-globals do not always possess the necessary experience needed for globalization, they may hire experienced and qualified managers or invite some to participate in decision-making through various arrangements ranging from business angels to advisory boards (Luostarinen and Gabrielson, 2003). Some of these firms rely on hybrid structures for their international expansion activities such as partnerships, joint ventures, personal connections and network relationships of some form of another (see Oviatt and McDougal, 1994). However, the founders, personnel and cooperative partners can be important in shaping the pricing strategies and policies of these firms.

Strategic decisions

The factors presented earlier in this literature review pointed to certain strategic decisions relevant to pricing that the born-global firm needs to address. Their nature, the factors that make them vital, and the outcome of their deliberation (that is consideration) have an impact on pricing strategy. Generally, the literature suggests the following decision areas of strategic importance to pricing: market segmentation and choice of customers, other marketing mix variables, competitive strategy, pricing objectives, and price-setting approaches (Barker and Kaynak, 1989; Toyne and Walters, 1993; Nagel and Holden, 1995; Nagle, 1987; Czinkota and Ronkainen, 1998).

The segmentation of born-globals differs significantly from that of conventionally internationalizing firms. Whereas traditionally companies have started their segmentation from country-market analysis and proceeded towards customer segmentation, born-globals reverse the process. They start their segmentation by looking for global customer segments, whose sales potentials' lead to country segmentation coming second (see for example Luostarinen and Gabrielson, 2003). The global niche or segment served by the born-global firm and its customer characteristics exert important pressures on its price strategy. As mentioned earlier, the main customers of born-globals are mainly enthusiasts and visionaries. Although the first group is not very important in terms of revenue, it is the key to accessing the second group and even the third group (pragmatists), where the bulk of revenues originate. The decision concerning which market to serve can have an impact on the use of the other marketing-mix elements and also on decisions regarding pricing strategy. Serving all market customers may require price differentiation as their price sensitivity and requirements differ. The pragmatists are customers who are used to other products and technologies; it is not so easy to convert them (that is to compete with established firms) to the new products without incentives that affect price. In addition, this may make price-listing difficult. Further, what the born-global may aim at when pricing the product during different periods of time and to different countries can vary based on the pricing objectives: profit-maximization, highest return on investment, market penetration, meeting specified sales goals, and so on (Barker and Kaynak, 1989). However, to meet such objectives, the born-global needs to consider a strategic decision concerning price-setting: whether to use a cost or market approach (see Al-Obaidi and Gabrielson, 2002).

Standardization of the marketing mix is often the objective of a globalizing company. Hence, the extent to which a company applies a globally standardized or adapted marketing strategy may also influence the pricing strategy. However, it has been argued that pricing has been one of the most difficult elements to standardize (Gabrielsson and Gabrielson, 2003b), and, furthermore, the earlier empirical research on pricing strategies used by born-globals is scarce and also conflicting. McDougall *et al.* (1994) suggest that born-global products are 'specialty products... often associated with premium pricing policies', but this proposition was not supported in their empirical study. In contrast, Luostarinen and Gabrielson (2002) have suggested that penetration pricing and customer-value-based pricing are common and propose that the born-globals pricing strategy should be examined against a two-dimensional matrix consisting of (1) generic pricing strategies (market-differentiated, dual, globally standardized), and (2) specific market and customer strategies (e.g. skimming and penetration). By dual pricing we mean a pricing strategy in which the international price level is standardized, but differs from the domestic-country price level (Al-Obaidi and Gabrielsson, 2002). The other strategies are well-documented in most of the international marketing books (for example Toyne and Walters, 1993; Czinkota and Ronkainen, 1998; Cateora and Graham, 1999). In the empirical part of our study the conceptual framework presented in Figure 13.1 is used for investigating eight Finnish born-global cases.

Pricing strategies applied by Finnish born-globals

We interviewed managers from eight Finnish born-global companies that had been established after 1985 and had rapidly expanded to global markets to the extent that in every case the sales derived from markets outside Europe in 2002

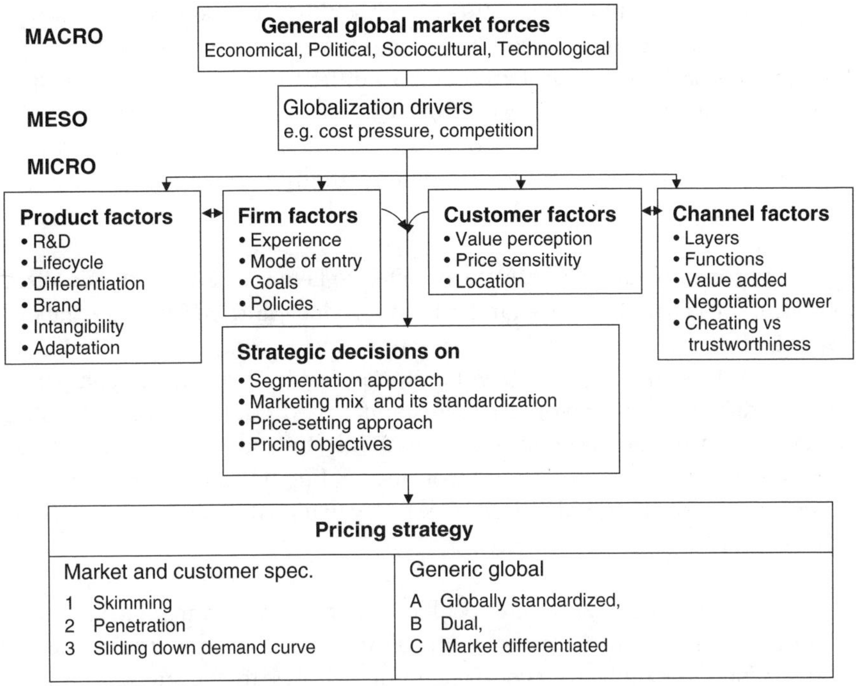

Figure 13.1 A conceptual framework for born-global pricing strategies: influencing factors and strategic alternatives

accounted for more than 30 per cent of total sales and in many cases more than 50 per cent. In addition, each company had a global vision and intended to expand outside Europe from the very beginning.

The companies examined can be divided into the following product groups, based on whether they served business-to-business (b–b) or business-to-consumer (b–c) customers:

- High-tech (b–b components, b–b investment goods, b–b equipment);
- High-biotech (b–b bio equipment);
- High-quality services (b–c services);
- High know-how (b–b software);
- High-design (b–c and b–b/c design products).

Generic pricing strategies

Our first interest was to find out whether the generic pricing strategies were market-differentiated or standardized across countries. We found that there were basically three different levels of standardization:

1 Country-market differentiated (b–b components, b–c services, b–c design products; and besides b–b equipment and b–b software in the early phase).
2. International prices standardized, but differ from domestic ones (b–b investment goods b–b/c design products).
3 Globally standardized pricing process which result in minor variations in end prices (b–b bio equipment, high-tech b–b equipment, b–b software).

The born-globals would naturally be expected to favour a globally standardized approach, given their often-standardized product and marketing strategy. However, this was not common. In fact, none of the companies utilized globally standardized pricing at the end-customer level. At most, the companies had introduced global pricing lists and standardized pricing processes, which, however, allowed for modifications based on the market situation. When enquiring about the reasons for favouring a differentiated market strategy rather than a globally standardized one, many explanations were given. These are discussed below:

- Comparison between prices is difficult due to the nature of high-tech products or high-services, or to the nature of the business relationship. Service prices are in general more difficult to compare. In many cases, the business-to-business products were part of larger systems, which made price comparisons difficult. In fact, many born-globals reported that business-to-business customers wanted the relationship to remain confidential. Further, distribution-channel members were said in many cases to be unwilling to reveal their margins, which prevented overseas comparisons and thus made price discrimination possible across customers located in different markets.
- Grey markets do not develop even though price differences exist due to the product nature or size of the business. For example, services in most cases cannot be re-exported and it may not be economically wise to arbitrate luxury design products that are sold through trusted channels in limited volumes.
- Also, it was reported that in many cases the export costs for born-globals vary based on the country to which they are exporting (product requirements, channel structure, marketing costs, exchange rates). Born-globals often transfer these additional costs to the price in order to maintain or secure profitability. All in all, born-globals have started to emphasize costs more after the financial difficulties encountered in autumn 2000. Until then, costs were often secondary.
- Further, country markets differ in terms of income levels, preferences and channel structures. For instance, Japanese markets were often priced higher than those of other countries. In some cases the Finnish market had been priced lower because there were fewer channel layers there. This kind of price distortion may take a long time to rectify.

Specific pricing strategies

Next we turn to an investigation of the specific pricing strategies used by the Finnish born-global companies. The question whether born-globals are able to charge premium prices for their often highly-specialized and unique products is interesting. However, it has become evident in the financial crisis witnessed since the late 1990s that many born-globals also fail. The rate of bankruptcy for Finnish born-globals between autumn 2000 and 2002 is estimated to be above 10 per cent (Luostarinen and Gabrielson, 2002) and this may only be the tip of the iceberg. These failures at least partly relate to the fact that they have been unable to generate enough revenue and often failed to charge the correct price for their products and services.

The specific pricing strategies applied by the interviewed case companies are listed below:

A Penetration pricing strategy, to secure entry into a new market, or building trust in the eyes of new customers in terms of references, functionality of the product or brand (b–b investment goods, early stage of product lifecycle of b–b equipment, b–b software).

B Skimming pricing strategy, aiming at generating a high return on investment, profit goal, or image on the market. It could take the form of premium pricing as long as the competition was non-existent (b–b bio-equipment, b–c design, b–b/c design products).

C Customer-value-based pricing or revenue sharing (b–b components, b–c services).

D Competitive pricing, based on position in the market, either leader or follower (b–b equipment, b–b software).

We started with the assumption that the specific price strategies would be influenced by the factors identified in the theoretical framework presented in Figure 13.1. While reviewing the above selected pricing strategies, one can clearly see how various sets of factors may have an influence on the pricing: the company itself, its products and respective strategies, customers, channels, and competition. The findings are consistent with product lifecycle pricing, although each company does not necessarily observe each stage. It is interesting to observe how their company- and product-related characteristics match a particular stage in the model. In a few cases, we were able to identify a clear development along their lifecycle, although in many cases the products were in some of the early stages. We will next briefly review the pricing decisions in terms of product lifecycle stages:

- In the entry stage of the product lifecycle, gaining a reference customer is a key to success. Furthermore, as the product functionality and brand are often unknown to the world, market prices must be low to generate trials. It is obvious that cost-plus pricing would be suicidal under these circumstances. Skimming pricing in the entry stage only seems possible when the product includes an exceptional innovation or is a design product (for example building on a famous designer). This is consistent with our earlier finding, where specialty channel members in the design business insist on high margins (Gabrielson and Al-Obaidi, 2002).

- In the growth stage, customer value and revenue sharing between cooperation partners, such as channel members, were important in determining the price level. The decisive factor is the extent to which there are strong competitors and to what extent prices are comparable with those of other producers. The cases analysed revealed that larger customers or channel members often had the resources needed to seek price knowledge and also the bargaining power to negotiate prices with the born-global companies, whereas smaller customers were less price-sensitive.
- When the product lifecycle entered the maturity stage, the born-globals examined followed the pricing of the market leader. Also, many other case companies not yet facing tough price competition foresaw this development. Hence, they invested in continuous product innovations and considerable branding efforts. Perhaps the nature of the industry and the newness of the born-global firms explain why none of the case companies had products that could have been positioned within the decline stage.

Generic and specific pricing strategies

Turning to an examination of the generic pricing strategies in relation to the specific pricing strategies, the matrix displayed in Figure 13.2 can be drawn, and we now turn to an examination of the factors that lead to the selection of any of the seven price strategies presented in this matrix.

A1: Market-differentiated penetration pricing

Some of the companies selected market-differentiated penetration pricing, although their market segment was global and the drivers to globalize were high. However, due to their newness, their product functionality had not yet been proven, and hence their only possibility was to gain recognition in order to increase prices. It was typical that their channel strategy differed strongly from country to country. Typically they were dependent on a particular party; in one of the cases, their distributors also acted on certain markets as themselves. In another, their role was that of a subcontractor to larger firms. The internet was not used for pricing, which effectively prevented customers from comparing their pricing in different markets.

A2: Dual pricing based on standardized international pricing

In the case company, the brand awareness was low, which therefore prevented them from charging premium prices. Also, the industry's globalization drivers were so high that only through aggressive growth and a leading position could profitability be maintained. A global strategy would have called for an even more standardized approach. However, the home market was priced lower than the foreign markets due to the shorter channel and because that had been the previous practice. Grey markets were not seen as a problem due to the fact that the products are heavy industrial investment goods, and their pricing is not available on internet.

B1: Market-differentiated skimming pricing and B2: Dual pricing based on standardized international pricing

Design is universal. High-quality handcrafted products can be sold at premium prices. High price contributes to the image. One of the case companies that sells to the business-to-business segment was standardizing the international pricing whereas the one targeting consumers alone differentiated its pricing. The differentiation was justified based on export-cost and market differences. Grey markets were not reported to be a problem due to small volumes and trusted channel members.

B3: Globally-standardized skimming pricing process with minor variation in end-customer prices

The company is already relatively large and has a global strategy. It operates in a segment, which is highly influenced by improvements in the standard of living

Specific/generic strategies	1 Country market-differentiated pricing	2 Dual pricing	3 Globally standardized pricing
A Penetration pricing strategy	**A1** b–b equipment and b–b software (in the early stage)	**A2** b–b investment goods	
B Skimming pricing strategy	**B1** b–c design products	**B2** b–b/c design products	**B3** b–b bio equipment
C Customer-value-based pricing	**C1** b–b components; b–c service.		
D Competitive pricing			**D3** b–b equipment and b–b software (in the mature stage)

Figure 13.2 Pricing strategies of born-globals

and health conditions. Profitability is an important objective, which is regarded as a requirement for market entry. The products are global and sold through exclusive channel arrangements, which guarantee skimming pricing. The pricing lists are global and the pricing process is standardized, although purchasing volume and the strategic importance of the customer may qualify for minor discounts leading to small differences in end-customer pricing levels.

C1: Customer-value and market-differentiated pricing

The customer-value-based pricing strategy is applied here. In the case companies, price discrimination was based on the readiness of customers to compare and seek the right price level. Also, privatization of one of the business sectors has led to the existence of both private and governmental channels. Markets were selected on the basis of the location of cooperation partners and customers rather than on any other factors. Co-branding was important. Competition was limited when the companies were established and they have acted as market leaders ever since. SME customers were charged higher prices than MNCs because they did not have similar resources to compare and bargain. Customer-value-based pricing has been applied on the basis of expected revenue or then revenues have been shared on the basis of a division agreed on in advance. Grey markets were not possible due to the nature of products (service, unique components) and their short lifecycles; prices were not put on the internet, and pricing-related terms and agreements were kept confidential. One problem encountered has been that the partners and channels have exercised their higher bargaining power, which has led to pricing that has hindered sales growth.

D3: Globally-standardized competition-based pricing

As the product functionality of the case companies using market differentiated penetration pricing (same case companies as in A1) was proven and the companies were recognized on the market, the standardization of pricing increased. The market differentiation started to turn towards a more standardized approach as global competitors that became important price-setters entered the industry. Also, the companies have been able to obtain global customers that required equal treatment. For the future, the company managers identified two alternative strategies; either to increase volumes substantially to compensate for low price, or build brand recognition to enable further price increases.

Discussion and conclusion

Based on the above pricing behaviour of the born-global case companies and observed patterns some interesting results may be identified. It seems that the

Pricing strategies/Born-global stage	1 Country market-differentiated pricing	2 Dual pricing	3 Globally standardized pricing
Early	**Penetration** b–b equipment and b–b software **Skimming** b–c design products	**Penetration** b–b investment goods **Skimming** b–b/c design products	X
Development	**Customer value-based** b–b components; b–c service.	X	**Competitive pricing** b–b equipment and b–b software **Skimming** b–b bio equipment

Figure 13.3 Born-globals' pricing strategies based on development stage

pricing behaviour of born-globals is heavily influenced by their development stage. In their early stage, when product functionality has not yet been proven and their brand is still unknown, born-globals price differently compared to the development stage of the product (see Figure 13.3).

Market-based price differentiation may be more useful and perhaps the only viable alternative in the early phase of globalization when competition has not yet developed to any great extent. At this early stage, the company, its products and brand, and relations with potential customers and channels are decisive in determining the appropriate specific pricing strategy, be it penetration or skimming pricing. At the development stage, companies that have earlier penetrated the markets have proved the functionality of their products and gained brand recognition, can try to upgrade their pricing to match the value perceived by their customers. This is often associated with following the market expansion of their initial customers or with utilizing them as references. For those companies that have started off by skimming the markets, the only possibility to continue this approach is through continuous investments in product innovation, protection of their technology, and development of a global brand. In many of the born-global industries the high globalization drivers will eventually lead to increased global competition that will force all the companies that are to survive to race for global leadership or first-tier positions. Eventually only a few will succeed.

On the basis of analysing the pricing literature and the actual behaviour of eight Finnish firms that have been successful so far, we can suggest the following tentative propositions, which we think would be interesting for future research:

> ***Proposition 1:*** The pricing of born-globals is influenced at the macro level by general global market forces, at the meso level by globalization drivers, and

at the micro level by product, firm, customer and channel factors, and how the strategic importance of these factors is perceived in the pricing process.

Proposition 2: The born-globals' pricing at the generic and market-specific levels are different, depending on the stage of globalization of the firm:

- *early stage:* pricing strategy is either (a) market-differentiated penetration/ skimming strategy, or (b) dual -penetration/skimming strategy;
- *developed stage:* pricing is either (a) market-differentiated, customer-value-based pricing, or (b) standardized –skimming/competitive pricing.

We believe that the results of this study include some important theoretical contributions and managerial implications, which we will now address briefly. Born-global research has to date focused on the characteristics of such firms and the globalization processes associated with them (Oviatt and McDougall, 1994; Kirpalani and Luostarinen, 1999; Luostarinen and Gabrielson, 2001). No doubt this research is important. However, research examining the marketing strategies of born-globals is desperately needed; only a very few studies have touched upon this area (Knight, 1997; Luostarinen and Gabrielson, 2002). Our research selected pricing, one of the marketing mix elements that has perhaps been studied least, for examination. The conceptual framework and empirical illustrations of Finnish born-globals, and the suggested propositions, should be valuable for future research, and for born-global managers the pricing strategy dimensions that have been developed should be valuable. These inform them that it is not enough to select either from generic globally standardized and market-differentiated pricing alternatives or from specific pricing strategies alone; as Levitt (1983) once put it, the born-global manager needs to 'think globally and act locally'.

References

Al-Obaidi, Z. and Gabrielson, M. (2002) 'Price setting approaches of Finnish exporting SMEs', 28th Annual Conference of the European International Business Academy (EIBA), Athens.

Almor, T. (2000) 'Born global: the case of small and medium sized, knowledge-intensive, Israeli firms', in Almor, T. and Hashai, N. (eds), *FDI, International Trade and the Economics of Peacemaking, A Tribute to Seev Hirsch*. Rishon LeZion, Israel: School of Business Administration, Academic Division, The College of Management.

Autio, E., Sapienza, H.J. and Almeida, J.G. (2000) 'Effects of age at entry, knowledge intensity, and imitability of international growth', *Academy of Management Journal* 43(5), 909–24.

Barker, T. T. and Kaynak, E. (1989) 'Cost-based pricing in global markets: practices of New Zealand firms', in Kaynak, E. and Lee, Kam-Hon (eds), *Global Business: Asia-Pacific Dimensions*, London: Routledge.

Buzzell, R.D. (1968) 'Can you standardize multinational marketing', *Harvard Business Review*, November–December, 46(6), 102–13.

Cateora, P.R. and Graham, J.L. (1999) *International Marketing*, 10th edn. Boston: Irwin-McGraw-Hill.

Czinkota, M.R. and Ronkainen, I.A. (1998) *International Marketing*, 5th edn. Orlando: Harcourt Brace & Co.

Craig, C.S. and Douglas, S.P. (1996) 'Developing strategies for global markets: an evolutionary perspective', *Columbia Journal of World Business*, Spring, 31(1), 71–81.

Gabrielson, M. and Al-Obaidi, Z. (2002) 'Multiple sales channel strategies in export marketing of small and medium sized design companies', in McDonald, F. Tüselmann, H. and Wheeler, C. (eds), *International Business: Adjusting to New Challenges and Opportunities*. Basingstoke: Palgrave.

Gabrielson, M. and Gabrielsson, P. (2003a) 'Global marketing strategies of born globals and globalising internationals in the ICT field', *Journal of Euromarketing* 12 (3–4).

Gabrielsson, P. and Gabrielson, M. (2003b) 'Globalizing internationals – standardization of product and marketing strategies in the ICT field', in Wheeler, C. McDonald, F. and Greaves, I. (eds), *Internationalization – Firm Strategies and Management*. Basingstoke: Palgrave.

Jain, S.C. (1989) 'Standardization of international marketing strategy: some research hypotheses', *Journal of Marketing* 53(1), 70–9.

Jeannet, J.-P. (1995) *Global Marketing Strategies*, 3rd edn. Boston: Houghton Mifflin.

Keegan, W.J. (1969) 'Multinational product planning: strategic alternatives', *Journal of Marketing* 33(1), 58–62.

Kirpalani, V.H. and Luostarinen, R. (1999) 'Dynamics of success of SMOPEC firms in global markets', 25th EIBA Conference, Manchester.

Knight, G.A. (1997) *Emerging Paradigm for International Marketing: The Born Global Firm*. Doctoral dissertation, Department of Marketing and Supply Chain Management, Michigan State University.

Knight, J., Bell, J. and McNaughton, R. (2001) 'The "born global" phenomenon: a re-birth of an old concept?'. 4th McGill Conference on International Entrepreneurship; Researching New Frontiers, 2, Glasgow.

Knight, G.A. and Cavusgil, S.T. (1996) 'The born global firm: a challenge to traditional internationalization theory', in Cavusgil, S.T. (ed.), *Advances in International Marketing* 8, 11–26.

Lavikkala, L. (2001) *Customer Strategies of Born Globals – Globalization Challenges and Current Practices*, Born Globals Pilot Study/Master's thesis, Helsinki School of Economics.

Levitt, T. (1983) 'The globalisation of markets', *Harvard Business Review*, May–June, 99–102.

Luostarinen, R. (1994) *Research for Action: Internationalisation of Finnish Firms and their Response to Global Challenges*. Forssa: UNU Wider.

Luostarinen, R. and Gabrielson, M. (2001) 'Born globals of SMOPEC – what, where, when, why and how', 27th Annual Conference of the European International Business Academy, Paris.

Luostarinen, R. and Gabrielson, M. (2002) 'Born globals of small and open economies (SMOPECs) – globalization and marketing strategies', 28th Annual Conference of European International Business Academy (EIBA), Athens.

Luostarinen, R. and Gabrielson, M. (2003) 'Born globals of small and open economies (SMOPECs) – a new entrepreneurial challenge', in Léo-Paul Dana (ed.), *Handbook of Research on International Entrepreneurship*. Cheltenham: Edward Elgar.

Mattila, J. (2001) *Promotion Strategies of B2C Born Globals*, Born Globals Pilot Study/Master's thesis, Helsinki School of Economics.

McDougall, P.P., Covin, J.G., Robinson, R.B. and Herron, L. (1994) 'The effects of industry growth and strategic breadth on new venture performance and strategy content', *Strategic Management Journal* 15(7), 537–54.

Moore, G.A. (2002) *Crossing the Chasm: Marketing and Selling Technology Products to Mainstream Customers*, 2nd edn. New York: Capstone Publishing Ltd.

Morris, M. and Joyce, M. (1988) 'How marketers evaluate price sensitivity', *Industrial Marketing Management* 17(2), 169–76.

Nagle, T.T. (1987) *The Strategy and Tactics of Pricing*. Englewood Cliffs, NJ: Prentice-Hall.

Nagle, T.T. and Holden, R.K (1995) *The Strategy and Tactics of Pricing*. Englewood Cliffs, NJ: Prentice-Hall.

Noble, P.M. and Gruca, T.S. (1999) 'Industrial pricing: theory and managerial practice', *Marketing Science* 18(3), 33–45.

Ohmae, K. (1985) *Triad Power: The Coming Shape of Global Competition*. New York: Free Press.

Oviatt, B.M. and McDougall, P.P. (1994) 'Toward a theory of international new ventures', *Journal of International Business Studies*, First quarter, 25(1), 45–64.

Oxenfeldt, A. (1975) *Pricing Strategies*. New York: American Management Association.

Ratia, L. (2001) *Pricing Strategies of Born Global Companies*, Born Globals Pilot Study/Master's thesis, Helsinki School of Economics.

Rennie, M.W. (1993) 'Global competitiveness: born global', *The McKinsey Quarterly* 4(2), 45–52.

Sankari, P. (2002) *Distribution Strategies of Born Global Companies*, Born Globals Pilot Study/Master's thesis, Helsinki School of Economics.

Schindehutte, M. and Morris, M.H. (2001) 'Pricing as entrepreneurial behavior', *Business Horizon*, June–August, 44(4), 41–8.

Simon, H. (1992) 'Pricing opportunities: how to exploit them', 2nd Global Conference on Marketing, Paris.

Toyne, B. and Walters, P. (1993) 'Dimensions of global pricing strategy', in Toyne, B. (ed.), *Global Marketing Management: Strategic Perspective*. Massachusetts: Allyn & Bacon.

Tsai, W. and Ghoshal, S. (1998) 'Social capital and value creation: the role of intrafirm networks', *Academy of Management Journal* 41(4), 464–76.

Viljanen, H. (2002) *Promotion Strategies of B2B Born Globals*, Born Globals Pilot Study, Helsinki School of Economics.

Part IV

The Impact and Policy Implications of Foreign Direct Investment

14

Economic Growth, Inward Direct FDI and Trade Policy in Four ASEAN Countries: Evidence from Simultaneous-Equation Panel-Data Estimation

Hang Le and Ali Ataullah*

Introduction

Based on the Keynesian–Kaleckian approach, this chapter studies the relationship between inward direct foreign investment (FDI) and economic growth in four ASEAN countries. Following Keynes (1936) and Kalecki (1954, 1970), we assume that economic growth of a country is demand-driven and constrained by its productive capacity, and investment is dependent on the marginal efficiency of investment. Within this framework we hypothesize that inward FDI could contribute to economic growth by generating demand and enhancing the productive capacity of a host country. This economic growth, in turn, attracts FDI by positively influencing investors' profitability and confidence. Moreover, an export-oriented regime (EOR) could strengthen the relationship between economic growth and FDI: if an EOR is implemented in a host country, this could enhance the attractiveness of the country to FDI and the impacts of FDI on its growth. This two-way relationship between FDI and economic growth and the influence of an EOR on the relationship, however, has not attracted much attention in the existing literature on FDI.

This chapter fills this gap by putting forward hypotheses about the relationship between economic growth and FDI, and empirically testing these hypotheses using data on four ASEAN countries: Indonesia, Malaysia, Singapore and Thailand[1] during 1975–95. These countries are chosen for the test because they have been among the largest FDI hosts among developing countries, and they

* Hang Le wishes to thank Professor Tony Cockerill, Professor Mark Casson, the editors of this book, and anonymous referees and participants at the 2003 AIB UK Chapter Conference for useful comments. She also wishes to thank the University of Durham for financial support from the Research Studentship Fund. Support from colleagues at Nottingham Trent University, especially Steve Heasell, is gratefully acknowledged.

also achieved high economic growth rates, higher than most other developing countries, in the last few decades, especially during 1975–95. It is therefore interesting to examine whether the two-way relationship between FDI and economic growth exists in these countries. Key findings from the simultaneous-equation estimation for fixed-effects panel data are strongly consistent with our hypotheses: during 1975–95 inward FDI contributed to high economic growth in the ASEAN countries, and the high growth of these economies was a key factor to attract FDI. Also, the two-way relationship between economic growth and inward FDI in the ASEAN countries was conditional upon the implementation of an EOR in these countries.

The rest of this chapter is structured as follows: in the next section I discuss the hypotheses about the relationship between FDI and economic growth in the ASEAN countries. This is followed by specification of the model, methodology, and data sources. The results of the empirical test are then interpreted, followed by a final concluding section.

Economic growth, inward FDI and trade policy

The literature on economic growth and internationalization is reviewed in four sections which provide the basis for deriving hypotheses to be tested using data on FDI in ASEAN countries.

Contribution of inward FDI to economic growth

The contribution of FDI to economic growth is examined in three sub-sections:

1 Obstacles to economic growth in developing countries.
2 Inward FDI, demand and productive capacity.
3 EORs and the contribution of FDI to economic growth.

Obstacles to economic growth in developing countries

Following Keynes and Kalecki, we assume that producers' output decisions depend on domestic and foreign demand: expected demand determines firms' decisions to produce, while actual demand generates profits that enable firms to continue and expand their production (Keynes, 1936; Kalecki, 1954, 1976). Domestic demand is largely composed of domestic consumptions and investment, while foreign demand is demand for export products of the country. Insuff[illegible] in demand is an obstacle to economic growth in developing coun-
[illegible]omestic markets are small and the majority of people have low
[illegible]ping countries also face another obstacle to economic growth,
[illegible] in productive capacity (Kalecki, 1976, chapter 2). These two
[illegible]mic growth in developing countries – insufficiency in demand

and inadequacy in productive capacity – interact and form a vicious circle in which inadequate productive capacity hinders job-creation and income-generation, keeping domestic demand at a low level, and low demand constrains the expansion of productive capacity. A deficiency in productive capacity to produce for exports, for example the lack of capital equipment or an efficient management system, is also a key factor keeping foreign demand at a low level, thus holding back economic growth in developing countries.

Inward FDI, demand, and productive capacity

In the Keynesian and Kaleckian approach, investment is a key determinant of economic growth (see for example Kalecki, 1954, and Robinson, 1962). An increase in investment raises demand not only because investment is an element of demand itself, but also because it generates other elements of demand such as consumption. Increases in investment also build up a country's productive capacity. Like other types of investment, FDI could tackle the two major obstacles to economic growth in host developing countries, that is raising demand and improving productive capacity. Considering the shortage of financial resources in developing countries (see for example Fry, 1995), the role of FDI could be crucial in the economic growth process of these countries.

Inward FDI affects domestic demand through its direct and multiplier effects. The former occurs when FDI raises demand for inputs for its own production and generates income by creating employment within itself. The latter occurs when other firms operating in the country, in order to meet demand from FDI, raise demand for their production and create employment. It should be noted that the direct and multiplier effects of FDI on domestic demand are highly dependent on the degree of linkages between FDI and the domestic economy. The contribution of FDI to economic growth is presumably small when direct and multiplier effects are limited.

FDI, especially export-oriented FDI, can increase exports of a country, that is increase foreign demand, because foreign firms normally have internationally recognized brand names, established marketing channels and knowledge about consumer taste in export markets. Increases in international production and intra-firm trade of multinational corporations also enable foreign firms to export their products (see for example UNCTAD, 1992). Endowed with such factors, FDI tends to be at an advantage over domestic investment in accessing foreign markets.

The impact of FDI on productive capacity is quite straightforward. It is argued that FDI brings technology, capital equipment and entrepreneurial skills, which contribute to the productive capacity of host countries (see for example UNCTAD, 2002). The impacts of FDI on productive capacity not only help in satisfying domestic demand that was previously unfilled, but also influence and raise domestic demand by changing consumers' tastes and demand. More importantly, FDI may improve the productive capacity of export-oriented industries. Besides intangible assets such as understanding of foreign markets, marketing expertise and networking relations, FDI also possesses capital equipment and management systems that enable them to meet the requirements of export products.

EORs and the contribution of FDI to economic growth

Export expansion can be a path for developing countries to promote high economic growth because an export potential allows firms to increase output and productive capacity without being constrained by small domestic markets. Inward FDI, with its specific advantages discussed above, can make important contributions to economic growth through improving export performance. In this context, the implementation of an export-oriented trade policy may facilitate the contribution of FDI to economic growth.

In developing countries, export-oriented regimes (EORs) are designed to encourage exports and include at least one of the following: (1) import barriers (tariff and non-tariff) are eased to enable exporters to import needed technology and raw materials; (2) financial and fiscal incentives are granted such as tax exemptions and subsidized export credit; and (3) export processing zones (EPZs) are set up, normally in major port areas, and provide favourable terms to export-oriented foreign investors (see for example UNCTAD, 2002). It is important to note that import liberalization is not necessarily an essential element of EOR. Protective barriers for the importation of products other than for inputs of export production may not be dismantled when a country moves towards export-orientation. A country could be relatively protective and yet export-oriented at the same time.[2] Increases in imports of capital goods and inputs for the export production enable a country to improve its export performance. Without increases in such imports, export expansion may not occur. Accordingly, we suggest that it is the degree of openness – an indicator relevant to both exports and imports – as a result of an EOR that affects growth, rather than export expansion alone.

Under an EOR, foreign firms may import needed capital goods and materials to expand their export capacity. FDI boosts foreign demand and productive capacity, and thus contributes more to economic growth.[3] The contribution of FDI to economic growth can be enhanced further under EOR if there are linkages between export-oriented FDI and the domestic sector. There is evidence of such linkages in some more developed Asian countries. For example, it is reported that in Korea the emphasis on an export-led growth strategy and the welcoming of FDI enabled foreign firms to facilitate the technological upgrading process in several key Korean industries (see, for example, Hill and Athukurala, 1998).

Economic growth as a determinant of inward FDI

Economic growth as a determinant of inward FDI is investigated in three subsections:

1 Determinants of FDI.
2 Economic growth as a determinant of FDI.
3 EORs and the impact of economic growth on FDI.

Determinants of FDI

The Keynesian and Kaleckian investment function depends crucially on the 'marginal efficiency of investment'. Under this approach, expected profitability and confidence about the future influence the 'marginal efficiency of investment', which, in turn, determines investment decisions. The expected profitability of investment is essentially dependent upon expected growth in sales and costs. Following the Keynesian and Kaleckian investment theory, expected growth of sales, costs and confidence about the future are assumed to be key determinants of inward FDI. It should be noted here that different kinds of FDI might value these factors differently.

FDI to developing countries may be broadly categorized as 'domestic-market-seeking FDI' and 'efficiency-seeking FDI'. For domestic-market-oriented FDI, the expected growth of domestic sales and cost factors are important although the former could be more important. Efficiency-seeking FDI is chiefly concerned with factors that enable producers to reduce costs, such as cheap labour or incentives provided by host government. This type of investment tends to use the host developing country as a platform to produce and export to home or third countries, and thus domestic sales might not be a primary objective. Confidence about the future, which not only deals with the host country's economic prospects but also the government's attitude toward FDI, is important for both types of FDI.

The decision to make new FDI to a host developing country could be negatively affected by existing inward FDI in the country. This negative relationship exists because the presence of other FDI in the same industry could easily saturate the limited domestic market. More importantly, the operation of existing FDI might fully utilize skilled labour, infrastructure and other supporting facilities in the host country. Such factors are important for both types of FDI but might not be easily and quickly upgraded and expanded in a developing country.

Economic growth as a determinant of FDI

Economic growth, *inter alia*, is a crucial factor that determines how much FDI a developing country could attract. This is because rates of economic growth influence the expected growth of sales, cost factors and confidence of investors. Overall, a rapidly growing economy is assumed to provide a relatively better opportunity for making profits than those growing slowly or not growing at all (Lim, 1983). For market-seeking FDI, high rates of economic growth may indicate a growing domestic market, and thus higher than expected growth of sales. For both types of FDI, high economic growth rates may promise a certain level of infrastructure development that is cost-beneficial. High economic growth may also signal a country's good development potential and deliver the pro-business and pro-growth message of the government more efficiently than many other policy instruments. This function of high economic growth enhances the confidence of foreign investors. Furthermore, high economic growth is a factor that could offset the negative impact of existing inward FDI discussed above; the domestic market is less likely to be saturated when it is growing rapidly. Domestic resources are also less likely to be fully utilized if high economic growth is accompanied by the host country's effort to develop its physical and human infrastructure.

It should be noted here that high and consistent economic growth, rather than high and fluctuating growth, positively influences inward FDI. High and sustained growth not only promises a better prospect of doing business in the country, but also indicates a long-term prospect, which is always praised by far-sighted investors. This persistency of high economic growth might also reveal sound and stable macroeconomic conditions, which is a priority in the checklist of foreign investors.

EORs and the impact of economic growth on FDI

When a developing country implements an EOR, the country's attractiveness for FDI due to high economic growth is enhanced because such a regime generally provides more profitable opportunities for FDI. Under an EOR, foreign firms find it more cost-beneficial to export and get involved in the trend of globalized production. It allows efficiency-seeking FDI to import capital goods and needed inputs at lower tariff rates, and financial and fiscal incentives are also offered. For market-seeking FDI, an EOR might reduce high competition in the domestic market and raise expected sales because more domestic income is generated. Without an EOR in practice, even if a developing country could manage to have consistently high economic growth, firms – domestic and FDI – would sooner or later face high competition. The expected growth of sales and thus expected profitability might start falling.

The two-way relationship between economic growth and FDI

The above arguments suggest the possibility of a two-way relationship between economic growth and inward FDI. High and sustained economic growth of a host developing country may positively influence inward FDI because it promises foreign investors a growing market in terms of size and prosperity and indicates a certain level of physical and human infrastructure development. Inward FDI, in turn, may promote economic growth in host countries by raising demand and improving the productive capacity of the country. The implementation of an EOR in the host country can enhance the contribution of inward FDI to economic growth and make the country more attractive to FDI.

Economic growth and FDI in ASEAN countries

The four ASEAN countries – Indonesia, Malaysia, Singapore and Thailand – are among the few developing economies that were comparatively dynamic and, to some extent, experienced impressive economic growth during the second half of the twentieth century. During 1960–95, economic growth rates for these countries were among the highest in the developing world, and relatively stable.[4] These four ASEAN countries, in addition, have been among the largest FDI hosts among the developing countries. FDI inflows started increasing rapidly from the mid-1980s, and by 1995 the total stock of inward FDI in these countries was more than US$156 billion accounting for 18 per cent of the total FDI stock located in the developing world (UNCTAD, 2002). Table 14.1 provides some key indicators of the ASEAN economies.

Until the early 1980s, FDI to the four ASEAN countries was concentrated in natural-resource-based and domestic-market-oriented industries. Export-oriented FDI firms mainly used unskilled workers for simple assembly tasks, and were located in free-trade zones to enjoy tariff incentives. Since the mid-1980s, FDI has concentrated in manufacturing, especially the electronics and electrical

Table 14.1 Key indicators of four ASEAN economies, 1995 (1990 US$ prices)

	GDP (US$ millions) (Singapore = 100)	*GDP per capita (US$) (Singapore = 100)*	*Export volume (US$ millions)*	*Exports/GDP*
Indonesia	161,457 (290.2)	832 (4.4)	46,168	26.3%
Malaysia	64,871 (116.6)	3,147 (16.6)	72,337	95.4%
Singapore	55,635 (100)	18,963 (100)	128,706	177.4%
Thailand	128,655 (231.2)	2,165 (11.4)	60,929	41.8%
	Stock of inward FDI (current US$ millions) (% of GDP)	*Pub. spending on education per capita (US$)*	*MVA per worker (US$)*	*(Exports + imports)/ GDP*
Indonesia	50,601 (25.0%)	5.54	4,181	53.9%
Malaysia	28,732 (32.9%)	150.75	13,522	194.8%
Singapore	59,582 (70.0%)	568.34	44,447	339.1%
Thailand	17,452 (10.4%)	77.7	9,393	89.75%

Sources: Compiled and calculated by the authors from World Bank (2000), Asian Development Bank (various issues) and UNCTAD (2002).

products, located outside free-trade zones. FDI has also gradually shifted towards more value-added, skill- and technology-intensive and export-oriented manufacturing activities in Singapore and Malaysia, and to some extent in Thailand and Indonesia, although a large share of FDI still goes to import-substituting activities such as automobile production (Thomsen, 1999).

The inflows of FDI to the manufacturing sector and the intra-firm trade strategies of multinational corporations have played an important role in the surge of manufacturing exports in the ASEAN countries since the mid-1980s (Chia, 1999). Since FDI firms play a dominant role in manufacturing production and exports of the four ASEAN countries, it could well be argued that FDI has participated in the structural changes from agriculture-based to manufacturing-based economies, and from import-substitution towards export-oriented strategies in these countries.

Hypotheses

Based on the arguments above, the following hypotheses are made regarding the relationship between high rates of economic growth and large inflows of FDI in the four ASEAN countries during 1975–95:

> *Hypothesis 1*: There was a two-way relationship between FDI and high economic growth in the four ASEAN countries during 1975–95. Inward FDI contributed to economic growth, and high economic growth was a positive determinant of FDI.
>
> *Hypothesis 2*: EORs implemented in the ASEAN countries were positive factors in the relationship between FDI and economic growth; that is, EORs enhanced the contribution of FDI to growth and enabled the countries with high growth to attract more FDI.

Methodology

In testing the two-way relationship between economic growth and FDI in the ASEAN countries, we have estimated a simultaneous-equation system of two equations: the growth equation (1) and the FDI equation (2). Based on the arguments above, equation (1) models the dependence of economic growth on factors that influence domestic demand, foreign demand and productive capacity, and equation (2) models the dependence of growth rates of FDI on factors that influence the expected profitability of investment and the confidence of investors. The expected sign of influence of each variable is in brackets. The growth rate of GDP per capita (*GDPPC*) is used as an indicator of economic growth, while proxy for the growth of FDI is the growth rate of real FDI stock (*FDIStock*).[5] The growth rate of GDP per capita and the growth rate of real FDI stock are two endogenous variables of the system.[6]

$$\Delta\ln(GDPPC) = f(\underset{(+)}{\Delta\ln(FDIStock)}, \underset{(+)}{\ln(Invest/GDP)}, \underset{(+)}{\Delta\ln(ConsPC)}, \underset{(+)}{\ln(Open)}, \underset{(+)}{\Delta\ln(Labour)}) \quad (1)$$

$$\Delta\ln(FDIStock) = f(\underset{(+)}{\Delta\ln(GDPPC)}, \underset{(+)}{\ln(GDPPC_{-1})}, \underset{(-)}{\ln(FDIStock_{-1})}, \underset{(+)}{\ln(OECD_{-1})}, \underset{(+)}{\ln(Open_{-1})}) \quad (2)$$

where Δln(GDPPC) is the growth rate of real GDP per capita; (Δln(FDI*Stock*) is the growth rate of real FDI stock; ln(Invest/GDP) is the log of gross domestic investment as a share of GDP; Δln(ConsPC) is the growth rate of real consumption per capita; ln(Open) is the log of the sum of exports and imports as a share of GDP. In equation (1), the log of exports as a share of GDP – ln(Export/GDP) – is used as an alternative for ln(Open); Δln(Labour) is growth of the labour force; $\ln(GDPP_{-1})$ is the log of real GDP per capita of the previous period; $\ln(FDI\mathit{Stock}_{-1})$ is the log of real FDI stock in the previous period; $\ln(OECD_{-1})$ is the log of the sum of real GDP of 22 high-income OECD countries in the previous period. In equation (2) log of real exports of the previous period – $\ln(Export_{-1})$ – is used as an alternative for $\ln(OECD_{-1})$.

In equation (1), the growth of FDI stock and the growth of domestic capital stock, proxied by gross domestic investment as a share of GDP,[7] represent the influence of investment on economic growth. They are expected to have a positive relationship with growth of GDP per capita because, as discussed above, an increase in capital stock, that is investment, contributes to economic growth by increasing demand and productive capacity. As economic growth is influenced by domestic consumption, another element of domestic demand, the growth rate of consumption per capita is included in the model. This variable is also expected to have a positive relationship with the growth of GDP per capita. As discussed earlier, the implementation of an EOR is expected to have a positive relationship with economic growth. In this chapter we assume that levels of openness and exports reflect the implementation of an export-oriented (EO) policy, and alternatively use the openness degree, that is the sum of exports and imports as a ratio of GDP, and the ratio of export over GDP as indicators of the EO policy.[8] These two variables are expected to affect the growth of GDP per capita positively. Following the practice of growth empirics, we also include the growth rate of the labour force in the equation.

In equation (2), the growth of GDP per capita and the level of GDP per capita of the previous period represent the influence of growth and size of the domestic market on the growth of FDI. These two variables are expected to affect the growth of FDI positively. The stock of FDI of the previous period is used as an indicator of the existing stock of FDI and is expected to be a negative determinant of FDI growth. To take into account the fact that a large part of inward FDI in the ASEAN countries is export-oriented, we include a variable for the size of the foreign market in the equation. We assume that high-income OECD countries are the main exporting market of FDI firms located in the ASEAN countries.[9] The sum of the real GDP of 22 high-income OECD countries of the previous period (*OECD*) is used as the proxy for the size of the foreign market. We also use the country's exports in the previous period (*Export*) as an alternative proxy for the foreign market. In this equation, the sum of exports and imports as a ratio of GDP (*Open*) is used as a proxy for the EOR. The foreign market and EOR variables are expected to have positive relationships with FDI growth.

The major sources of data are the *World Development Indicators* CD-ROM (World Bank, 2000), *International Financial Statistics* (IMF, various issues) and *Key Indicators of Developing Asian and Pacific Countries* (ADB, various issues). Variables expressed in monetary units are converted into real terms of US dollars at 1990 prices. Most variables are in the form of a ratio of GDP or per capita to standardize the size of the economy and population. All variables are used in logarithmic form. The rate of growth is calculated as the first difference, that is $y_t = \log Y_t - \log Y_{t-1}$. Table 14.2 presents statistical features of the data.

Among the variables, data on FDI stock are not available and are thus calculated in two steps: first, annual FDI inflows are converted into constant 1990 US dollar prices; second, FDI stock is accumulated from FDI inflows at constant prices starting from the year 1970 with the assumption that the inflows of FDI to the four ASEAN countries before 1970 were trivial.[10]

The system specified in equations (1) and (2) estimated by simultaneous-equation regression for fixed-effects panel data. We use the two-stage-least-square procedure (2SLS), with country dummy variables and exogenous variables of the system as instruments. This technique may detect the two-way relationship between economic growth and FDI growth and provide unbiased and consistent results. Single-equation methodologies are not applicable to each equation individually, for example ordinary least-square (OLS), because they would lead

Table 14.2 Statistical description of data

Series	*No. of observations*	*Mean*	*Std error*	*Minimum*	*Maximum*
Δln(*FDIStock*)	80	0.129	0.062	0.029	0.279
Δln(*GDPPC*)	80	0.051	0.026	−0.038	0.108
ln(*Invest/GDP*)	84	3.464	0.205	3.143	3.881
Δln(*ConsPC*)	80	0.034	0.078	−0.195	0.157
ln(*Open*)	84	4.658	0.820	3.707	6.085
ln(*Export/GDP*)	84	3.970	0.823	2.910	5.372
Δln(*Labour*)	80	0.029	0.011	0.012	0.051
ln(*GDPPC*)	84	7.542	1.144	5.845	9.850
ln(*FDIStock*)	84	9.114	0.935	7.102	11.000
ln(*Export*)	84	10.215	0.631	8.757	11.765
ln(*OECD*)	84	16.294	0.217	15.977	16.653

to bias and inconsistent estimates due to the problem of endogeneity with economic growth and FDI growth variables. The pooling of four countries increases the number of observations significantly, giving more information and more degrees of freedom, and making the regressions more efficient. Panel-data analysis is also better at detecting issues that would be undetectable through time-series or cross-sectional analysis. The simultaneous-equation system is estimated under the assumption that the errors from the two equations are dependent, or there is no autocorrelation in the regression.[11]

Findings

This section presents results from the simultaneous-equation estimation for fixed-effects panel data of the four ASEAN countries during 1975–95. Our findings are strongly consistent with the main hypotheses, and most variables have significant coefficients with the expected signs. Results from Tables 14.3 and 14.4 do not reject the first hypothesis that there exists a two-way relationship between economic growth and inward FDI. Growth of real FDI stock is an important determinant of growth of GDP per capita (Table14.3), and growth of

Table 14.3 Economic growth, inward FDI and trade policy: the growth equation
Dependent variable: growth rate of real GDP per capita

	(1)	*(2)*	*(3)*	*(4)*	*(5)*	*(6)*	*(7)*
ln(*Invest/GDP*)	0.012	0.010	–0.025	–0.024	–0.020	–0.026	–0.028
	(0.75)	(0.62)	(1.13)	(1.05)	(1.04)	(1.32)	(1.43)
Δln(*FDIStock*)	0.068	0.094	0.144	0.137	0.143	0.192	0.205
	(0.89)	(1.17)	(1.98)*	(1.74)*	(1.97)*	(2.49)**	(2.85)***
Δln(*ConsPC*)	0.174	0.172	0.139	0.142	0.134	0.123	0.119
	(5.51)***	(5.07)***	(4.18)***	(3.96)***	(4.02)***	(3.41)***	(3.51)***
ln(*Open*)			0.037	0.037			
			(2.05)**	(2.02)**			
ln(*Export/GDP*)					0.039	0.042	0.042
					(2.50)**	(2.64)**	(2.67)***
Δln(*Labour*)		0.097		0.063		0.030	
		(0.43)		(0.28)		(0.14)	
R^2	0.437	0.438	0.463	0.458	0.480	0.450	0.447
t-value (Hausmann)[a]	1.606	1.558	2.055**	1.979*	1.735*	1.912*	3.039***
F-value[b]	1.791	1.842	2.785**	2.757**	3.297**	6.234***	5.108***
x^2(Hausmann)[c]	994.2***	282.02***	388.25***	149.93***	11.043**	13.752***	1024.0***

Notes: Absolute value of *t*-statistics in parentheses; *, ** and *** denote statistical significance at the 10, 5 and 1% levels. Coefficients of constant and dummy variables are not reported.
[a] the Hausmann test for simultaneity *effect*: the hypothesis of a simultaneous effect is not rejected if the *t*-value is significant.
[b] the *F*-test for joint significance of dummy variables: the hypothesis of unequal country-specific effects is not rejected if the *F*-value is significant.
[c] the Hausmann test for misspecification: the hypothesis that the regression is not misspecified is rejected if the chi-square value is significant.

Table 14.4 Economic growth, inward FDI and trade policy: the FDI equation
Dependent variable: growth of real stock of inward FDI

	(1)	(2)	(3)	(4)	(5)	(6)	(7)
$\ln(FDIStock_{-1})$	−0.142	−0.155	−0.155	−0.145	−0.158	−0.140	−0.054
	(3.07)***	(3.50)***	(3.50)***	(3.09)***	(3.89)***	(3.03)***	(2.64)***
$\Delta\ln(GDPPC)$	1.556	1.125	1.131	1.531	0.959	1.446	1.162
	(3.88)***	(2.63)***	(2.64)**	(3.90)***	(2.50)**	(2.61)**	(2.18)**
$\ln(GDPPC_{-1})$	0.314	0.318	0.318	0.302	0.325	0.291	
	(2.55)**	(2.73)**	(2.73)***	(2.41)**	(3.03)***	(2.03)**	
$\ln(Open)$		0.089	0.089		0.099		
		(1.88)*	(1.87)*		(2.65)**		
$\ln(OECD_{-1})$						0.028	0.128
						(0.28)	(1.49)
$\ln(Export_{-1})$				0.014			
				(0.44)			
R^2	0.289	0.363	0.363	0.285	0.372	0.297	0.300
t-value (Hausmann)[a]	1.606	1.558	2.055**	1.979*	1.735*	1.912*	3.039***
F-value[b]	3.463**	5.680***	5.645***	3.790**	5.444***	5.055***	9.699***
x^2(Hausmann)[c]	225.2***	34.29***	46.48***	41.59***	42.007***	47.33***	35.24***

Notes: See Table 14.3.

real GDP per capita is also significantly and positively related to growth of real FDI stock (Table 14.4). We also find that an EOR plays an important role in this two-way relationship. When variables that represent the EOR are excluded from the growth equation – specifications (1) and (2) – inward FDI exerts no significant impact on growth, and there is no interdependence between economic growth and inward FDI. When we reestimate the simultaneous-equation system for two sub-periods, 1975–85 and 1986–95, we find that in 1975–85 the two-way relationship between inward FDI and economic growth is weak and mostly insignificant. During 1986–95, when the ASEAN countries actively pursued export-led and FDI-led growth strategies, this relationship becomes strong and significant.[12] These findings confirm the second hypothesis that EORs played a crucial role in the two-way relationship between economic growth and inward FDI in the ASEAN countries. The impacts of EORs on economic growth and FDI will be discussed in more detail below.

Determinants of economic growth

Table 14.3 shows that growth of real stock of FDI, growth of consumption per capita and EOR are the main determinants of GDP per capita growth. Nevertheless, FDI growth has positive and significant coefficients only when a variable that represents EO policy, either the openness degree or the share of exports over GDP, is introduced into the regression. Our findings suggest that growth of FDI stock contributed to economic growth of the ASEAN countries when an EOR was implemented. This is consistent with the results from a study by Balasubramanyam, Salisu and Sapsford (1996) that FDI is a potent driving force in the growth process of export-promoting countries and it exerts no significant influence upon growth of import-substituting countries. It is also consistent with the proposition that some other large FDI recipients, such as Latin America, lagged behind East Asian countries in promoting high growth and attracting FDI due to the absence of, *inter alia*, policies for export-led and FDI-led growth (Nunnenkamp, 1997).

Our results suggest that FDI and EOR contributed to economic growth of the ASEAN countries by improving export performance. Since the mid-1980s, along with EOR implementation and FDI promotion, the export performance of the ASEAN countries improved substantially. Table 14.5 shows that the annual average growth rates of exports in these countries are much higher between 1985 and 1995, that is after the export-led and FDI-led strategy was pursued. The export structure shifted increasingly away from traditional primary products such as agro- and resource-based, toward manufactures as the share of manufacturing exports in total exports increased rapidly. FDI played an important role in these changes since FDI firms were major exporters of textile, garment and electronic products, which were main components of these countries' exports in this period. In 1992 for example, exports by foreign firms accounted for 74 per cent of Singaporean manufacturing exports; in 1995, exports of electronic goods by FDI firms accounted for 94 per cent of total exports of the industry. In Thailand, the share of exports by foreign firms in total non-oil manufacturing exports rose from 15 per cent in 1986 to 33 per cent in 1990, largely due to exports in electric machinery, non-electric machinery (mainly office and computing machinery) and food. The share of exports by foreign

Table 14.5 Exports in the ASEAN countries, 1975–85 and 1986–95 (by %)

	Annual average growth of exports		*Manufacturing exports as share of total exports*		
	1975–85	*1986–95*	*1981*	*1985*	*1995*
Indonesia	1.3	6.4	3	13	51
Malaysia	6.2	17.4	20	27	75
Singapore	5.0	12.7	48	51	84
Thailand	2.9	23.5	26	38	73

Source: Compiled and calculated by the authors from World Bank (2000). Annual average growth of exports is calculated with exports at 1990 prices.

firms in office and computing machinery in total exports of the industry was 74 per cent in 1990. Foreign firms in electric machinery exported 82 per cent of total exports of the industry in 1992.[13]

Our findings about the roles of FDI and EORs in the economic growth of the ASEAN countries are not consistent with the existing literature about sources of growth in those countries.[14] Collins and Bosworth (1996), for example, claim that the extraordinary growth of East Asian countries, including the four ASEAN countries and Korea, Philippines and Taiwan, has been driven by factor accumulation, while gains in technological progress have been modest, and this outcome is not encouraging for the view that their performance reflects the benefits of trade openness. As FDI is often seen as a means of technology transfer, such a finding about the modest growth of technology progress also seems to question the technological contribution of FDI and thus the effectiveness of FDI promotion strategies of those countries. The empirical findings of this chapter, however, confirm the hypothesis that FDI and the higher degree of openness resulted from EO policies, including increases in exports, have played critical parts in the economic growth of the ASEAN countries. Although this chapter does not detect a direct link between FDI and technological progress, the fact that in the ASEAN countries during 1985–95 FDI increased rapidly along with higher economic growth and a surge in manufacturing exports dominated by FDI firms, especially in relatively more technological-intensive industries such as electronics and electrical goods, suggests that an association between FDI and technological progress exists. Our view is supported by a closer look at the findings of Collins and Bosworth (1996), a distinctive study that carefully estimates sources of growth in East Asian countries. According to their estimate (1996, table 6), total factor productivity (TFP) growth accounted for more or less a quarter of the growth in output per worker between 1960 and 1994 in Indonesia, Malaysia and Singapore, and for one-third in Thailand. These are, however, averages over more than three decades. Between 1973 and 1984, TFP growth accounted for 11 per cent of growth in Indonesia and Malaysia; during 1984–94 it was 24 per cent in Indonesia and 36 per cent in Malaysia. During 1984–94, TFP growth accounted for around half of output growth in Singapore and Thailand, compared with 23 per cent in Singapore and 30 per cent in Thailand during 1973–84. According to Collins and Bosworth's study, then, the period when TFP growth contributed most to output growth in the ASEAN countries was 1984–94; this was the period during which FDI and EOR policies were largely promoted.

There seem, however, several problems with this FDI-led and export-led growth of these countries. The presence of foreign firms in the ASEAN countries has created so-called dualistic industries, especially in electronics and electrical products, where foreign firms, though small in number of establishments, have much more advanced technologies and dominate the value-added and export shares of the industries. Most domestic firms are small- and medium-sized with laggard technologies, mainly serving the local market (Thomsen, 1999, and Chia, 1999). Improvements in export performance in the ASEAN countries tend to be attributed to FDI firms, the dominating players in exports, especially manufacturing exports. The less-prominent role of the domestic sector in the export-led and FDI-led growth of these countries could, to some extent, explain the insignificant impact of domestic investment as a share of GDP, a proxy for growth of the domestic capital stock in all specifications. Our finding that inward FDI has a large positive impact on economic growth, while domestic investment has no significant impact, is consistent with the findings of Balasubramanyam *et al.* (1996).[15]

Growth of consumption per capita has a positive and significant relation with economic growth, which is consistent with our hypothesis that growth is demand-driven. The growth rate of the labour force does not have significant impacts on economic growth, which indicates that in the ASEAN countries during 1975–95 the size of the labour force might not have been important in promoting high economic growth. Observations about human-capital development and productivity improvement in the ASEAN countries (Hill and Athukurala, 1998, and Chia, 1999) suggest that the quality of labour – rather than the quantity – could be influential in the growth process.

Determinants of inward FDI

Table 14.4 shows that the growth of real GDP per capita is an important determinant of FDI growth; the coefficients of this variable are highly positive and statistically significant in all specifications. Our result is consistent with the finding of Jackson and Markowski (1994) that high economic growth is the most prominent factor that attracts FDI to the Asian and Pacific countries. This also confirms the finding of Goldar and Ishigami (1999) that Japanese FDI has moved from utilizing cheap labour in Asia to produce for exports to the USA and EU markets, to taking advantage of growing Asian markets and producing final consumer goods for those markets. We find that GDP per capita growth exerts a significant impact on FDI growth regardless of the appearance of the openness variable, which is consistent with our earlier proposition that a country with high economic growth rates could attract FDI with or without the presence of an EO policy; however, along with high economic growth, an EOR enhances the attractiveness of a country to FDI. The coefficients of GDP per capita of the previous period are positive and highly significant, but smaller than that of GDP per capita growth. This indicates that the growth and size of the domestic market are important determinants of inward FDI, but the former seems to have a larger impact.

Results of Specifications (4), (6) and (7) in Table 14.4 show that two proxies for the size of the foreign market have no significant impact on growth of inward FDI. This reflects the globalized production strategy of multinational corporations and the position of FDI firms located in these ASEAN countries in the global production chain, where intra-firm trade rather than direct trade plays a dominant role (see Hill and Athukurala, 1998). The openness variable, on the other hand, has a statistically significant and positive impact on the growth of FDI. Our results indicate that although the location decision of FDI might be unrelated to the size of the foreign market, the implementation of an EOR in the host country is of paramount importance. This is consistent with the findings of Singh and Jun (1995) that export orientation is the strongest variable for explaining why a country attracts FDI.

The coefficients of the existing stock of FDI are highly significant and have the expected negative sign in all specifications, which strongly supports our hypothesis that the existing stock of inward FDI adversely influences growth of FDI. As a considerable part of FDI inflows serve the domestic markets of the ASEAN countries, the negative relationship between existing FDI and the growth of FDI stock might indicate that the domestic market was still rather limited. It might also indicate that the infrastructure, human resources and other supporting facilities in these countries constrained their absorptive capacity to new FDI.

Conclusion

This chapter has hypothesized that there is a two-way relationship between inward FDI and economic growth, which may be strengthened by the implementation of an EOR. Inward FDI may contribute to the economic growth of a developing country by generating demand and improving the productive capacity of a country. High economic growth can improve profitability and confidence of investors, thus attracting more FDI. Results from the simultaneous-equation estimation for fixed-effects panel data find that in four ASEAN ountries, Indonesia, Malaysia, Singapore and Thailand during 1975–95, inward FDI and high economic growth were interdependent: inward FDI was an important growth-enhancing factor, and high economic growth was a positive determinant of inward FDI. We also find that this relationship was conditional upon the implementation of export-oriented policies. Besides the growth of FDI stock, the growth of domestic consumption and the implementation of an EOR are other key determinants of economic growth. The growth and size of the domestic economy, and the implementation of an EOR affect the growth of FDI stock positively, while the existing stock of FDI in the host country is negatively related to FDI stock growth.

This chapter has made two contributions to the existing literature. First it has studied the two-way relationship between economic growth and FDI, which, although recognized in some studies, has been mainly dealt with by econometric techniques of instrument variables (see for example Balasubramanyam *et al.*, 1996). This chapter points out the possibility as well as the mechanism of this two-way relationship. Our second contribution is in the analysis of economic growth and FDI in the four ASEAN countries using an econometric methodology suitable to the hypotheses. The existing literature about FDI and its impacts on economic growth in the ASEAN countries seems inadequate considering their roles as among the largest FDI recipients.

The empirical exercise of this chapter, however, does have some limitations. First, the proxy for EOR used in this chapter is rather simple, and a more accurate measure to capture different aspects of EOR such as the reduction of tariff and non-tariff barriers is needed. Second, we have not assessed the role of the economic and social environment in the relationship between economic growth and FDI. It might well be that the overall economic and social environment, along with government commitment to growth and supporting policies, rather than the implementation of EOR *per se*, enabled FDI to contribute to growth and for high growth to attract FDI in the ASEAN countries during 1975–95. Among the four countries, it is widely recognized that Singapore has a pro-FDI and pro-growth environment; the other governments have also carried out different programmes to promote a favourable environment. The impact of the economic and social environment on economic growth and FDI could be assessed if suitable measures of those influences could be constructed. Finally, our sample ends at the year 1995, that is before the Asian crisis of 1997. Further research on the relationship between economic growth and FDI in these countries is needed due to the new challenges that these countries face in the post-crisis period.

Notes

1 ASEAN stands for the Association of Southeast Asian Nations. In this study the ASEAN countries refers to four countries, Indonesia, Malaysia, Singapore and Thailand. Other members of ASEAN – Brunei, Cambodia, Laos, Myanmar, the Philippines and Vietnam – are not considered.

2 See e.g. Chia (1999) about the coexistence of export promoting and protective measures in ASEAN countries.

3 Balasubramanyam *et al.* (1996) argue that FDI is much more efficient in promoting growth when it is allowed to operate in a distortion-free environment, which is defined as efficient with fair play of market forces and competition. They consider the environment created by the export-promoting policy as the one that has those characteristics. We believe that the implementation of the export-promoting policy could create inefficiency and distortion in the form of government intervention such as incentives and export credits, and in the form of dualism, i.e. the coexistence of the technology-advanced foreign sector and the laggard domestic sector.

4 Author's calculation from Pen World Table for annual average growth of GDP and its standard deviation for 87 developing countries, see also Collins and Bosworth (1996).

5 Some empirical studies have used the ratio of FDI inflows over GDP and it is suggested that the results could be improved significantly if some proxies on FDI stocks could be built up (Balasubramanyam *et al.*, 1996).
6 See Gujarati (1995) for further details on simultaneous-equation estimation.
7 Most empirical studies for developing countries have used this ratio for the growth rate of capital stock, e.g. Thirlwall and Sanna (1996) and Balasubramanyam *et al.* (1996).
8 These two indicators are not included in the regression at the same time in order to avoid the problem of multicollinearity, because they are highly correlated.
9 In the ASEAN countries exports to OECD countries account for around half of total exports (ADB, various issues).
10 Our constructed data on FDI stock in the ASEAN countries are also adjusted with the 5-year interval data from UNCTAD (2002).
11 In order to test for autocorrelation in simultaneous-equation panel-data estimation, a test procedure should consider the correlation of the residuals of each equation and the correlation of the residuals across equations. The existing tests in the literature, which take into account only one dimension of the issue, Baltagi's (1995) tests for the fixed-effect panel-data model, are inapplicable in our model. Moreover, these tests for panel data are normally based on the assumption that typical panel data contain large individual observations and small time observations. Our assumption is supported by the implicit assumption in the 2SLS estimation that the disturbances in the structural equations are not contemporaneously correlated.
12 These results are available from the author.
13 See Dobson and Chia (1997) for various studies about the role of inward FDI in trade and manufacturing production in ASEAN countries.
14 See Collins and Bosworth (1996) and their references.
15 Our results are inconsistent with empirical results of the growth literature, which suggest that growth is positively and significantly related to domestic capital. Most studies in the growth literature, however, do not include any trade or openness variable (see Thirlwall and Sanna, 1996, for a review on empirical results).

References

Asian Development Bank, *Key Indicators of Developing Asian and Pacific Countries* (various issues).

Balasubramanyam, V.N., Salisu, M. and Sapsford, D. (1996) 'Foreign direct investment and growth in EP and IS countries', *The Economic Journal* 106(1), 92–105.

Baltagi, B.H. (1995) *Analysis of Panel Data*. Chichester: John Wiley.

Chia, Y.S. (1999) 'Trade, foreign direct investment and economic development of Southeast Asia', *Pacific Review* 12(2), 249–70.

Collins, S. and Bosworth, B. (1996) 'Economic growth in East Asia: accumulation versus assimilation', *Brookings Papers on Economic Activity* 2, 35–205.

Dobson, W. and Chia, S.Y. (1997) *Multinationals and East Asian Integration*, edited, Institute of Southeast Asian Studies, Singapore.

Fry, M.J. (1995) *Money, Interest, and Banking in Economic Development*, 2nd edn. Baltimore and London: The Johns Hopkins University Press.

Goldar, B. and Ishigami, E. (1999) 'Foreign direct investment in Asia', *Economic and Political Weekly* 34, 22, M50–M60, 29 May.

Gujarati, D.N. (1995) *Basic Econometrics*, 3rd edn. New York and London: McGraw-Hill.

Hill, H. and Athukurala, P.C. (1998) 'Foreign investment in East Asia: a survey', *Asia-Pacific Economic Literature* 12(2), 23–50.
International Monetary Fund, *International Financial Statistics* (various issues).
Jackson, S. and Markowski, S. (1994) 'The attractiveness of countries to foreign direct investment, implication for the Asia-Pacific region', *Journal of World Trade*, 159–79.
Kalecki, M. (1954) *Theory of Economic Dynamics: An Essay on Cyclical and Long-Run Changes in Capitalist Economies*. London: Unwin University Books.
Kalecki, M. (1976) *Essays on Developing Economies*. Humanities Press.
Keynes, J.M. (1936) *The General Theory of Employment, Interest and Money*. London: Macmillan – Palgrave.
Lim, D. (1983) 'Fiscal incentives and direct investment in less developed countries', *Journal of Development Studies* 19(2), 23–42.
Nunnenkamp, P. (1997) 'Foreign direct investment in Latin America in the era of globalised production', *Transnational Corporations* 6(1), 51–81.
Robinson, J. (1962) *Essays in the Theory of Economic Growth*. London: Macmillan – Palgrave.
Singh, H. and Jun, K.W. (1995) 'Some new evidence on determinants of foreign direct investment in developing countries', World Bank Working Paper, no. 1531.
Thirlwall, A.P. and Sanna, G. (1996) 'The macro determinants of growth and "New" growth theory: an evaluation and further evidence', in Arestis, P. (ed.), *Employment, Economic Growth and the Tyranny of the Market, Essays in Honour of P. Davidson*, Vol. 2. Cheltenham, UK: Edward Elgar.
Thomsen, S. (1999) *Southeast Asia: The Role of FDI Policies in Development*, OECD Working Papers on International Investment.
World Bank (2000) *World Development Indicators*, CD-ROM 2000.
UNCTAD (1992) *World Investment Report 1992: Transnational Corporations as Engines of Growth*. New York and Geneva: United Nations publication.
UNCTAD (2002) *World Investment Report 2002: Transnational Corporations and Export Competitiveness*. New York and Geneva: United Nations publication.

15
Employment and the Embeddedness of German Subsidiaries in the UK

*Frank McDonald, Heinz Josef Tüselmann, David Williams and Ulrich Hoppe**

Introduction

Attracting and retaining foreign direct investment (FDI) to boost regional development and thereby employment in host locations has been identified as a major policy priority in the UK and elsewhere in Europe (Brown and Raines, 2000; Wren and Taylor, 1999). There has also been an increasing focus on the benefits of foreign-owned subsidiaries that are rooted or embedded into their host location (Birkingshaw and Hood, 1998a; Enright, 2000). This has led to expectations that the more subsidiaries are embedded the greater will be their contribution to regional and local development. The boost to regional development from such embeddedness in host locations should lead to beneficial employment effects both by foreign-owned subsidiaries and, via spillovers, by other firms in the same locations (Driffield and Taylor, 2000).

A study of German FDI into NW England has cast doubt on this outcome in terms of direct employment by foreign-owned subsidiaries as it found evidence that German investment into this part of England was predominantly related to export-enhancing activities and they tended to have low levels of local sourcing. Moreover, many German firms in NW England had been primarily engaged in export-enhancing activities for over 10 years (Heise *et al.*, 2002b; McDonald *et al.*, 2003a). The study suggested that even in the long term, German FDI into the UK is motivated by the desire of parent companies to supply and develop the UK market, and this implies that the employment effects of German FDI are likely to be small. The study was not large enough to obtain an accurate picture of the employment effects of FDI, it did not examine

*This study was funded by the Anglo-German Foundation for the Study of Industrial Society and the German–British Chamber of Commerce and Industry.

the impact on the skill level of the jobs connected to German investment and it did not focus on embeddedness factors.

To remedy these defects, this chapter reports on a survey of all known German subsidiaries in the UK and is centred on the importance of embeddedness factors, such as linkages to local suppliers and local networks. We also investigate the strategic autonomy of subsidiaries and the number of foreign markets supplied by them. In addition, the link between embeddedness and strategic autonomy factors and employment, including the type of jobs, is examined.

The chapter begins by outlining the background to German FDI into the UK. This is followed by a review of the existing macroeconomic and microeconomic studies of the impact of FDI on employment in host countries. The review provides the basis for the construction of a conceptual framework and a set of hypotheses on the relationship between embeddedness and the employment characteristics of subsidiaries. The hypotheses are tested using the results of the survey, and finally a future research agenda is outlined that might help to improve our understanding of the links between the strategic development of subsidiaries and employment in host economies.

Background to German FDI into the UK

Germany is a significant investor in the UK providing the second largest source of FDI into the UK in terms of both stock and flow of such investments (Office of National Statistics, 2002). The UK is the destination of a significant proportion of outward FDI from Germany: about 14 per cent of outflows and 10 per cent of stocks (Bundesministerium für Wirtschaft und Technology, 2002; Deutsche Bundesbank, 2002). The size of these flows suggests that German FDI may be induced by labour-market advantages in the UK; however, a study on German and British labour-market flexibility and FDI found that labour-market flexibility differences between Germany and the UK tended to be exaggerated. Moreover, the study did not find any evidence that German FDI flows to the UK were significantly influenced by labour-market conditions (Raines *et al.*, 1999).

The evidence suggests that Germany has not lost significant numbers of jobs due to FDI outflows, and it is possible that jobs have been created, or safeguarded, in the home country because of these flows. Moreover, the main motivations for these flows appear to be to develop markets and to shift labour-intensive manufacturing to lower labour-cost countries (Beyfuss and Eggert, 2000; Tüselmann, 1998). This may indicate that German FDI is at an early stage of internationalization (Johanson and Vahlne, 1977). If this were the case it would be expected that German FDI should become more linked to diversifying the activities of their subsidiaries, thereby leading to a change in employment. This type of development is predicted by resource-based theories of multinational corporations that suggest that foreign-owned subsidiaries become more rooted (embedded) in their host locations as they build up locally-based assets that aid in the process of creating value. This type of development is based on increasing the embeddedness of subsidiaries in their host region leading to growing specialization within multinational corporations that requires a change in the pattern of employment as different parts of the firm specialize in particular functions and operations (Birkinshaw and Hood, 1998a, b).

This literature points towards the development of subsidiary operations that include expanding activities such as high value-added production, product development, and R&D in countries that provide suitable environments. Developments of this kind are thought to be more likely between developed economies that have similar but slightly different types of economic and social systems (Dunning, 2000). In the context of FDI from Germany to the UK, this should lead to changes in the patterns of employment. Thus, as German subsidiaries in the UK become more embedded in their local area as they develop linkages to local suppliers and local networks of firms and agencies that aid in the process of creating value, they should become more specialized in high value-added operations based on the development of desirable assets that are only available, or are available at lower cost, in the host region. The result would be a change in the pattern of employment in the UK with an increase in skilled jobs in those functions and operations in which subsidiaries have become more focused.

FDI and economic development

It has long been recognized that FDI has the potential to facilitate trade of goods, services, capital and knowledge (Georgiou and Weinhold, 1992; Dunning, 1992; UNCTAD, 1994). These flows permit host and home countries to reap the advantages of comparative advantage and to develop internal economies of scale. External economies of scale arising from spillovers into host economies further boost the benefits of foreign investments (Barrell and Pain, 1997; Blomström and Kokko, 1998; Engelbrecht, 1997). In recent years there has been an increasing emphasis on FDI and the development of clusters based on the network linkages with firms and supporting agencies in host locations in order to obtain benefits from agglomeration economies (Driffield and Munday, 2000; Enright, 2000).

The benefits from FDI flows have been found to increase productivity, improve competitiveness and thereby boost growth in home and host economies. However, these positive effects are at least partially offset by the loss of market share by domestic firms in host economies and potential problems with balance of payments from the repatriation of profits, and there is also the possible loss of technological leadership to foreign-owned firms (Bailey *et al.*, 1993; Sachs and Warner, 1993). Moreover, there are adjustment costs associated with the reaping of comparative advantage and internal and external economies of scale (Rodriquez and Rodrik, 1999).

The evidence from the many studies conducted on the impact of FDI on economic development in host countries suggests that there are net benefits but there are questions about the extent and on the main characteristics of these net benefits. The impact of FDI on the growth of both the quantity and quality of employment has been investigated by macroeconomic studies, but the focus has been on the growth in the quantity of jobs. The relationship between the strategic development of subsidiaries and other microeconomic factors and employment has received little attention.

Macroeconomic studies on FDI and employment

A number of econometric studies (based on regional and national data on wages, productivity and employment) have established that FDI leads to positive employment effects (Barrell and Pain, 1997; Driffield, 1999a; Fingini and Görg, 1999; UNCTAD, 1994). These studies find evidence that FDI stimulates demand for labour but that this has a large and beneficial impact on employment in host regions only if the enhanced technology that accompanies FDI is effectively transferred to domestic firms within the region. If this does not happen and if subsidiaries obtain much of their labour from existing domestic firms and from the use of expatriates, FDI will have only a marginal impact on employment in host regions (Driffield, 1999b). Other studies have found a tendency for FDI to boost the employment of skilled workers in host countries and that this spills over to wage levels in domestic firms (Aitkin *et al.*, 1996; Driffield and Taylor, 2000; Machin and van Reenen, 1998; Wakelin *et al.*, 1999).

The employment effects from spillover benefits to domestic firms from FDI activities arise from demonstration effects and the transfer of knowledge to suppliers and other firms that are connected to foreign subsidiaries. There is also evidence that FDI leads to spillover benefits that improve the general level of productivity in host countries (Blömstrom and Kokko, 1998; Engelbrecht, 1997; Liu *et al.*, 2000). In the UK, the evidence is mixed on the extent and significance of spillovers. Driffield (1999b) found that they were small and restricted to the areas near centres of FDI and that they did not benefit the industries that had experienced large FDI inflows. This would imply that FDI leads to indirect job losses in the domestic firms that experience high FDI inflows into their industry, and that adjustment to this requires the channelling of released resources into other or new industries. However, other studies have found that the spillover effects are large and benefit both industries that experience large FDI flows and other industries (Hubert and Pain, 1999). Another study found that the employment effects in host regions arising from

FDI spillovers are positive but small and normally take a long time to materialize (Gillespie *et al.*, 2000)

Some econometric studies have found conflicting evidence on the beneficial impact of FDI on employment (Aitken and Harrison, 1999; Blonigen and Slaughter, 1999; DeMello, 1999). These studies find that the spillover effects are often small and the displacement of domestic firms by more competitive foreign entrants combined with the transfer of labour from domestic to foreign-owned firms reduces the productivity of large parts of the national or regional economy and thereby, in the long-run, undermines the positive employment effects of FDI inflows.

Most macroeconomic studies suggest that FDI between developed economies has a positive impact on employment in host economies and that the main impact is on the skills composition of employment with a tendency for FDI to boost the skills content of jobs in both home and host economies. This result stems from the move towards greater intra-firm specialization generated by horizontal FDI that requires higher-skilled workers (more specialized workers). However, complementary FDI flows connected to trade flows, especially FDI in sales and distribution and low-level manufacturing and services provision connected to exporting, may lead to job losses in host economies as less-efficient domestic producers are displaced with consequent job gains in home countries as they experience an increase in exports, often with high value, to the host countries. This type of FDI may undermine the skill and technology base of host economies unless effective adjustment processes are at work to shift resources to those areas where the host economy has competitive advantages.

Microeconomic studies on FDI and employment

In contrast to the macroeconomic studies on the impact of FDI there has been relatively little attention to the role of the development of foreign-owned subsidiaries in the process of national and regional development and therefore on employment. The studies that have been carried out provide mixed evidence on the impact of FDI on growth and employment. Some, such as Segal and Quince (1985), have suggested that the subsidiaries of MNCs do not encourage the process of cumulative development, whereas others, such as Del Monte and De Luzenberger (1989), have suggested that foreign-owned subsidiaries may help to encourage the growth and further development of local firms. These studies have focused on entry mode, organizational aspects of foreign-owned subsidiaries, benefits of locations and stages theories of internationalization (Ashcroft and Love, 1993; Young *et al.*, 1994; Taggart, 1996).

More recently attention has been focused on resource-based theories of subsidiary development (Bartlett and Ghoshal, 1989) that have sought to highlight the benefits of locating and developing subsidiaries that are firmly embedded in their host regions thereby yielding high-level benefits to the MNCs as a whole by exploiting assets that are only available (at least at reasonable cost) in particular locations. These subsidiaries are called centres of competence or centres of excellence (Birkinshaw and Hood, 1998a,b). These theories suggest that in some cases embeddedness in host regions can lead to the emergence of centres of competence that lead to the development of such subsidiaries, thereby boosting the growth and employment impact in host locations (Heise *et al.*, 2002a). Moreover, the development of such centres of competence, because of the beneficial effects on the overall operations of the MNC, can boost or at least defend jobs in the home country. The benefits of investing in clusters or industrial districts have also increased interest in embbeddedness (Enright, 1998 and 2000; Driffield and Munday, 2000). However, most of these studies have not focused on the employment effects of subsidiary development, neither have they explicitly considered the effects of such development on employment by the parent company.

The microeconomic factors traditionally associated with the development of host economies have been entry mode (greenfield or brownfield), type of activity (manufacturing, services, sales and distribution, R&D and so both), size and age of subsidiaries, and technology transfer. More contemporary literature has focused on the development of local sourcing (the development of local supply chains), the use of local networks (formal and/or informal connections between firms and supporting organizations) and the development of the strategic autonomy of subsidiaries. The contemporary literature is focused on the concept of embeddedness or the level at which subsidiaries are rooted into their local base in terms of aspects of their strategic decisions and operations.

Embeddedness factors and employment

The degree of embeddedness is influenced by local sourcing (local intra-firm connections with suppliers in the supply chain), local networks (networks of firms and supporting organizations that aid in the operations of the subsidiaries), and the strategic development of subsidiaries in terms of granting high-level autonomy that is useful to exploit locally available resources. The supply of a variety of markets is also connected to embeddedness because subsidiaries that supply foreign markets as well as their domestic market are likely to require closer links to their local area to provide the inputs and knowledge base that enables effective supply to a number of different countries.

Local sourcing

Hirschman (1958) argued that the development of local sourcing could lead to the cumulative expansion of industry, and many studies have attempted to measure the impact of local sourcing on the domestic economy. Scott (1983) and Ó hUallacháin (1986) provide summaries of these studies. The studies reveal no consensus on the outcome of local sourcing effects except that the character of the local economy will greatly influence the nature of the effects. This is further confirmed by studies undertaken on the Scottish economy by Ashcroft and Love (1989) and on the German economy by Schachmann and Fallis (1989). These studies indicate that employment should be positively related to the level of local sourcing. A recent study on the link between employment growth and the use of local sourcing has confirmed the view of the pioneering research on this issue (Williams, 2003)

Local networks

The importance of MNCs locating within local networks for international competitiveness has been highlighted in work investigating the role of geographical factors in the internationalization process (Dunning, 2000; Krugman, 1991; Porter, 1990, 1994). This literature indicates that the use of local networks composed of other firms, R&D agencies such as universities and government research bodies, local authority agencies, chambers of commerce and other organizations can help subsidiaries to attain their objectives. These local networks enhance the ability to attain collective learning and innovation benefits (Lundvall, 1999) and to acquire spillover benefits associated with proximity (Porter and Sölvell, 1999). These network benefits, together with the benefits from effective local supply chains, form the basis for agglomeration benefits. Local networks that provide such benefits are at the core of clusters or industrial districts that have been shown to deliver competitive advantages to foreign-owned subsidiaries that locate in these geographical concentrations (Benito, 2000; Enright, 1998, 2000; McDonald and Vertova, 2002). In principle, membership of locally-based networks should boost productivity and thereby enhance employment in terms of the number and skill level of jobs because collective learning and innovation, that is enabled by such networks, allows for expansion of both the size and complexity of operations.

Strategic development of the autonomy of subsidiaries

Resource-based theories of the strategy of MNCs regard them as international networks of subsidiaries that blend firm-specific resources into an effective unit capable of conferring competitive advantages to MNCs (Bartlett and Ghoshal, 1989; Doz and Prahalad, 1993). Therefore, MNCs take advantage of the different cultures and business environments in which their subsidiaries operate to develop intra-firm networks that make the best use of the resources available to them (Birkinshaw, 2000). Some subsidiaries can be selected to be centres of competence where subsidiaries are granted autonomy to provide outputs that are used in all parts of the MNC or substantial parts of the operations of the MNC (Birkinshaw *et al.*, 1998; Holm and Pedersen, 2000).

Market supply mandates

There are a number of typologies that categorize the ability of subsidiaries to take decisions on matters connected to the supply of markets (Etemad and Dulude, 1986; Birkinshaw and Morrison, 1995; Taggart, 1996). The mandates given to subsidiaries in areas such as the geographical spread of supply and the types of products offered for sale in these markets have been developed within the 'international management tradition' (Young *et al.*, 1994), in order to devise a conceptual framework to facilitate the study of the management of organizations rather than as a means to investigate the ways in which different subsidiary types affect the host economy. However, in general it is expected that the higher the level of mandates that are granted, the more subsidiaries will need to employ highly-skilled labour in order to carry out specialized and high-value-added operations. Moreover, mandates that restrict subsidiaries to low-level assembly or low-level processing of services and/or that are primarily connected to sales and distribution are likely to create fewer and less skilled jobs than subsidiaries that have mandates to supply a wide range of markets with a variety of complex products.

Summary of embeddedness and employment

Embeddedness is a complex phenomenon that is influenced by the extent of local sourcing, local networks, the strategic development of the autonomy of subsidiaries, and the extent of foreign market supply. In terms of employment, the creation of more extensive local sourcing, local networks, strategic autonomy, and the increased supply of foreign markets should be accompanied by the need to employ both more workers and also more highly skilled workers. The development of local sourcing requires supply-chain management systems that are organized at the subsidiary level. This implies a need for staff capable of effectively operating such supply chains. Moreover, high levels of local sourcing are likely to increase the required skill level of workers who will be engaged in more complex operations compared to the skill levels required to assemble products from supplies that comes largely from sister companies in the home base. By the same token, networks will only be developed if the workers at a subsidiary level are able to develop relationships with universities, trade associations, quality clubs and other forums. Membership of such networks should stimulate higher-valued operations that require additions to the labour force and more skilled jobs. High-level mandates are unlikely to be granted to the subsidiary unless it has the capability of managing the process. Thus, the development of strategic autonomy is likely to boost employment, especially of skilled workers. Subsidiaries that supply more than their domestic market are likely to be more embedded because they will be involved in more complex operations connected to foreign market supply that requires linkages with locally based suppliers of inputs and knowledge that is essential for effective supply of foreign markets. This will also require more skilled labour. Therefore, subsidiaries that are embedded in their local economy are likely to have a high demand for labour, especially skilled labour. Similarly, subsidiaries that have high levels of embeddedness are likely to have lower levels and lower growth of semi-skilled and unskilled jobs.

Model of FDI and employment

The review of the literature provides the basis for the construction of a conceptual framework on the relationship between traditional and embeddedness factors and employment (see Figure 15.1). The traditional and embeddedness factors outlined above influence the employment effects of foreign-owned subsidiaries in host economies. In this study, traditional factors (entry mode, type of activity, size, age and technical transfer) were used as control variables and the embeddedness factors (local sourcing, local networks, strategic development and autonomy of subsidiaries, and marketing mandates) were used as independent variables to explain the employment effects of FDI inflows.

Hypotheses

The conceptual framework outlined in Figure 15.1 highlights positive relationships between embeddedness factors and employment growth and the growth

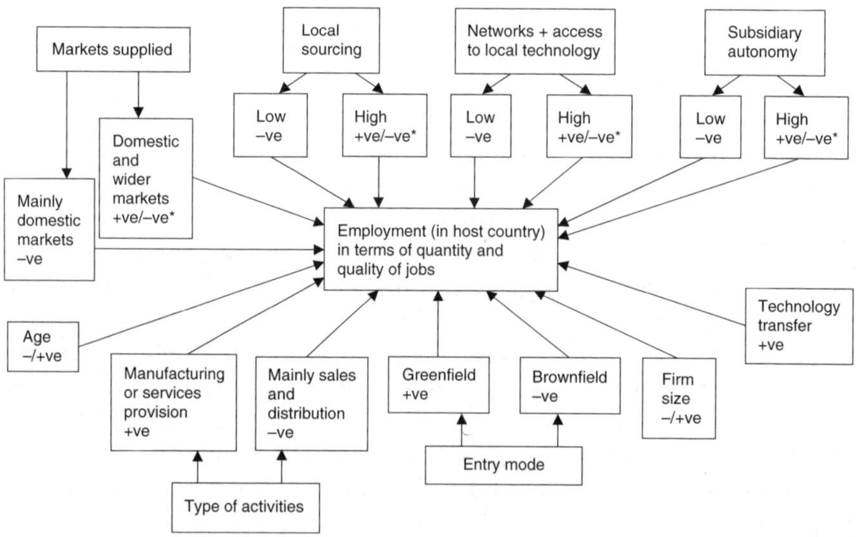

Figure 15.1 Factors affecting employment in host economies

Notes: +ve denotes a positive effect on employment/skilled jobs; –ve denotes a negative effect on employment/skilled jobs; and –ve* denotes a negative effect on semi and low skilled jobs.

of skilled jobs, and negative relationships with the growth of semi-skilled/unskilled jobs. Three hypotheses were constructed on the links between the embeddedness factors and employment effects:

H1 Growth of employment is positively related to embeddedness factors and to increases in embeddedness factors.

H2a The level of skilled jobs is positively related to embeddedness factors and to increases in embeddedness factors.

H2b The percentage change in skilled jobs is positively related to embeddedness factors and to increases in embeddedness factors.

H3a The level of semi-skilled/unskilled jobs is negatively related to embeddedness factors and increases in embeddedness factors.

H3b The percentage change of semi-skilled/unskilled jobs is negatively related to embeddedness factors and increases in embeddedness factors.

The study

To test the hypotheses a survey of all known German subsidiaries in the UK was carried out in 2002, using the database of the German–British Chamber of Commerce and Industry to identify the subsidiaries. The questionnaires were piloted and amended in the light of the comments from respondents. The database identified the names of the managing directors of the subsidiaries, and therefore the questionnaires were sent to those named heads of subsidiaries. This led to 275 responses (24.2% response rate). The returns compared to the total population revealed that there were no significant differences between the respondents and non-respondents in terms of sector and region.

The data to assess the hypotheses for the subsidiaries were analysed by ordinary least-squares (OLS) regressions in three ways. All subsidiaries in all sectors using both level and change variables; all subsidiaries excluding establishments where the main activity was sales and distribution; and all subsidiaries in traditional and/or slow-growing industries (hereafter referred to as traditional industries) and new industries and/or fast growing industries (hereafter referred to as new industries). Traditional industries were defined as mechanical and electrical engineering, automotive, chemical and chemical engineering, retailing, wholesaling and logistics, energy and utilities, textiles, and wood and construction products. New industries were defined as pharmaceuticals, IT and telecommunication equipment, business services, and financial services.

Regressions were run with and without sales and distribution to check if the large number of establishments that specified this activity as their main area of business masked significant evidence of embeddedness and employment effects among subsidiaries centred on manufacturing or services. The split into traditional and new industries was used to see if traditional industries were more likely to have low levels of embeddedness compared to new industries, and therefore to be less likely to have beneficial employment effects.

The Appendix provides definitions of the variables. The traditional factors of age, size (turnover), entry mode and technology transfer were used as control variables; change in employment and the number and increase in skilled and semi-skilled/unskilled jobs were the dependent variables; and embeddedness factors were the explanatory variables. Change in employment was measured for the period 1997 to 2001. The definition of skilled and semi-skilled jobs was based on the standard classification of the skill level of jobs used by the UK government. The explanatory variables for employment and type of jobs regressions used stock (level) and change variables. This was done on the basis that the employment effects are likely to be influenced not only by the level of, but also change in embeddedness variables. The dependent variables for type of jobs were also considered for stock and change categories.

Most of the categorical non-metric variables are dichotomous and are denoted by dummy variables. Where they are significant and positive, the 'yes' version of the variable is significant; where they are significant and negative, the 'no' version of the variable is significant. The exception to this is for the sectoral dummies, that is manufacturing, service and sales and distribution. If, for example, the manufacturing dummy is significant and negative it is not possible to infer that one of the other dummies is positive and significant. In all the regressions the manufacturing and service dummies are used as the default dummies and the estimation has then been run with the sales and distribution dummy with the services dummy dropped to see if it is significant. Size and change in size (turnover) and age use metric data, and a positive significant variable indicates that the variable has a positive influence on the dependent variable. In the case of age a negative sign implies that relatively younger firms have a greater influence on the dependent variable than older firms.

The results were tested for heteroscedasticity (Cook–Weisberg test), omitted variables (Ramsey Resit test) and multicollinearity (variance inflation factor test). None of the regressions displayed multicollinearity, but some tested positive for heteroscedasticity and for omitted variables. In the cases where the tests proved positive, remedial action was taken to correct the problems (Hair *et al.*, 1998; Weisberg, 1985). The adjusted R^2 and F statistics reveal that few of the regressions have high levels of goodness of fit. The regressions that excluded sales and distribution provided the best fit, and those for traditional industries the worse fit (see Table 15.1). No significant variables were found in the regressions for new industries.

Table 15.1 Summary of significant explanatory variables

Level and change variables	*All subsidiaries*	*Excluding sales and distribution*	*Traditional industries*
Change in employment (*demploy*)	*dsto****	*–dsto**** *dscope** *age*** *–dhcs*** *aut** *–man****	*dhcs** *dsto**
	Adjusted R^2 0.3434 *F* statistic 3.09	Adjusted R^2 0.7361 *F* statistic 8.77	Adjusted R^2 0.1665 *F* statistic 1.71
Level of skilled jobs (*hskill*)	*sto*** *expat**** *–dsto**** *–em*** Adjusted R^2 0.2846 *F* statistic 3.69	No significant variable	*expat**** *man*** *–net*** *–sdist*** *sto**** Adjusted R^2 0.3618 *F* statistic 4.12
Level of semi–skilled/ unskilled jobs (*lskill*)	*expat** *man**** *sto*** *–sdist**** *–dsto**	*–net**** *man**** *sto****	*expat**** *–age** *–serv** *daut*** *–sdist****
	Adjusted R^2 0.3698 *F* statistic 4.67	Adjusted R^2 0.6275 *F* statistic 5.15	Adjusted R^2 0.3882 *F* statistic 4.68
% change in skilled jobs (*dhskill*)	*dnet*** *dsto**** *dhcs**	*dsto**	*dhcs*** *dsto***
	Adjusted R^2 0.3670 *F* statistic 3.39	Adjusted R^2 0.5716 *F* statistic 4.47	Adjusted R^2 0.1807 *F* statistic 1.66
% change in semi-skilled/unskilled jobs (*dlskill*)	No significant variables	*–dsto**** *aut** Adjusted R^2 0.5072 *F* statistic 3.87	No significant variables

Note: A negative and significant sign for *expat* (proxy for parental control) indicates that parental control is not strong and indicates embeddedness.
Level of significance is denoted by: *(1% level), **(5% level), and ***(10% level).

Results

Increase in host-country sourcing (*dhcs*) is positively related to employment growth in traditional industries, but is negatively associated with employment growth for those firms not primarily engaged in sales and distribution. Decision-making autonomy (*aut*) and change in scope (*dscope*) are positively associated with employment growth for subsidiaries whose main activity is either manufacturing or services (Table 15.1). Therefore, there is some support for H1.

The positive sign for the *expat* variable (at the 10% level) indicates that skilled jobs are not associated with autonomy from the parent company. The negative sign for networks (*net*) for firms in traditional industries suggests that high network connections have a harmful impact on the level of skilled jobs. No other embeddedness variables are linked to the level of skilled jobs. Thus, there is no support for hypothesis H2a.

The percentage increase in skilled jobs is positively related to increased use of networks (*dnet*) and increased use of host-country sourcing (*dhcs*). Hence, there is support for H2b. The link between change in these embeddedness factors and the percentage change in skilled jobs highlights the importance of growing embeddedness for the growth of skilled jobs.

There is some support for H3a as networks (*net*) and high autonomy from parent companies (measured by the positive *expat* variable) are negatively associated with the level of semi-skilled/unskilled jobs. However, increase in decision-making autonomy (*daut*) is positively related to the level of semi-skilled/unskilled jobs in traditional industries.

Decision-making autonomy (*aut*) is positively related to the percentage change in semi-skilled/unskilled jobs for firms whose main activity is not sales and distribution and no other embeddedness variables are related to this dependent variable. Hence, H3b is not supported.

Restricting significance to the 1 per cent and 5 per cent levels reveals that change in host-country sourcing (*dhcs*) is the only embeddedness variable that is frequently associated with beneficial employment effects. In terms of the regressions with the best goodness of fit (that is those excluding sales and distribution), decision-making autonomy (*aut*), and increase in the scope of activities (*dscope*) are positively related to good employment effects, but change in host-country sourcing (*dhcs*) has the wrong sign. The only dependent variables that are positively related to at least two embeddedness variables are change in employment (*dhcs, dscope* and *aut*) and percentage change in skilled jobs (*dnet* and *dhcs*).

The control variables show no significant relationship between technical transfer and employment effects, and only one with entry mode. The later indicates that greenfield entry is negatively associated with high-skilled jobs. Age is only related to employment effects in two cases. Size, especially change in size, is related to most of the tested employment effects. The controls for main type of activity generally showed the expected signs.

Summary of evidence

The results do not provide strong support for the view that German FDI, which is embedded, has led to the creation of a large number of jobs or of skilled jobs.

Table 15.2 Summary of evidence on hypotheses

Hypotheses	*Support*	*Comments*
H1 Employment growth	Some support	Embeddedness factors *dhcs, aut* and *dscope* have a positive impact on the growth of employment. But *dhcs* has the wrong sign for firms not primarily engaged in sales and distribution and this is in the regression with the best fit (excluding sales and distribution)
H2a Level of skilled jobs	No support	No embeddedness factors are positively associated with the level of skilled jobs
H2b % change in skilled jobs	Some support	Embeddedness factors *dhcs* and *dnet* have a positive impact on the percentage change in skilled jobs. But no embeddedness factors are significant in the regression with the best fit (excluding sales and distribution)
H3a Level of semi-skilled/ unskilled jobs	Some support	Embeddedness factors *net* and *expat* are negatively related to the level of semi-skilled/unskilled jobs. But *daut* has the wrong sign for firms in traditional industries and the *net* variable is only significant at the 10% level
H3b % change in semi-skilled/ unskilled jobs	No support	No embeddedness variables are negatively associated with the percentage change in semi skilled/ unskilled jobs. Moreover, *aut* is positively related to this dependent variable in the case of firms that are not primarily engaged in sales and distribution and this is the only regression that had significant variables

There is some evidence of an association between increase in host-country sourcing and beneficial employment effects. Weak evidence was found for positive relationships between subsidiary autonomy, and networks, and favourable employment effects. No evidence was found for a link between markets supplied and employment effects. Furthermore, no evidence for a link between embeddedness factors and employment effects was found for new industries. The findings also do not lend much support to the argument that high levels of embeddedness are related to less emphasis on employment of semi-skilled/ unskilled workers. A summary of the results is provided in Table 15.2.

Discussion

The results indicate that there is no strong evidence that the employment effects of German FDI into the UK are heavily influenced by embeddedness factors, although there appear to be some minor effects on the growth of employment and for the change in skilled workers. Therefore, the results of this study extend and confirm similar results from studies on the impact of German FDI on employment in the UK. These studies indicate that German FDI has had little impact on the number of jobs in the UK (Hood and Taggart, 1997; Heise *et al.*, 2002b; McDonald *et al.*, 2003a,b). The main factor influencing employment is increasing host-country sourcing, a result that has also been found in other studies (Williams, 2003).

The study found little to support the literature on the resource-based view of the strategic development of subsidiaries based on developing access to desirable assets in host locations (Birkinshaw and Hood, 1998a,b; Holm and Pedersen, 2000). It appears that German FDI into the UK has not been significantly driven by a desire to obtain assets that are embedded in host locations. Similarly, the granting of strategic autonomy to subsidiaries appears to have had little impact on employment. The number of markets supplied also does not influence the growth of employment or of skilled jobs by German subsidiaries.

The results for the control variables suggest that traditional factors such as entry mode, main activity of business, technology transfer and age have only very marginal impact on the employment characteristics of German subsidiaries. Only size had a consistent impact on employment effects. It is not surprising that size measured by the growth of turnover will influence both the growth of employment and the type of jobs, given that higher output is normally associated with more and often higher-skilled jobs. However, the orthodox theories of FDI (for example, Dunning, 1993; UNCTAD, 1994) would suggest that traditional factors should have a pronounced affect on employment. The failure to find any relationship between technical transfer, and only one case where entry mode affected employment, also runs counter to some of the literature (Ashcroft and Love, 1989, 1993; Young *et al.*, 1994).

Policy implications

The results suggest that the current emphasis on policies to attract FDI to make a significant contribution to regional development and to boost skilled employment (Brown and Raines, 2000) may not be wise, especially as FDI has become a crucial component of regional development policy in Western Europe (Wren and Taylor, 1998). Policies that focus on the attractiveness of local sourcing, qualities of the labour force and beneficial networks in host regions are unlikely to be attractive for much of German FDI into the UK unless the current dominant motive for such investment moves away from a desire to develop UK supply channels for German exports.

Clearly, some German FDI is attracted by embeddedness factors, for example the supply of skilled labour and access to effective networks for international financial services in London. However, these embeddedness factors, that are clearly present in the cluster of international financial services in London, are attractive (and well-known) to most MNCs in this industry. Thus, these MNCs, including German MNCs, will have strong motives to locate in such clusters to remain competitive. The most effective policies in these cases would be to ensure that such clusters are able to develop without excessive increases in input prices and congestion costs. Policies in these circumstances should not be based on promoting embeddedness factors to potential investors, but should focus on improving housing, social and transport infrastructures to boost the supply of labour and to reduce congestion costs in the cluster, thereby lessening the incentive for firms to disperse from high-cost clusters (DETR, 2000). Policies to promote embeddedness factors in regions that do not have clear cluster advantages are likely to have to provide overwhelming evidence of the attractiveness of embbeddedness factors relative to other potential locations.

In many cases the attractiveness of a location for German FDI will be the ability to enhance supply channels for German exports. In this case, the emphasis should not be on backward linkages to potential suppliers, but on forward linkages to potential customers. The importance of local networks in this case is also to promote the customer base rather than to focus on improving the effectiveness of supply chains. Such policies may help to attract German FDI, but will be very unpopular among UK suppliers who will be displaced by such German FDI. Moreover, policies of this type are unlikely to generate substantial numbers of jobs in the host location.

In host locations that currently do not have obvious and clear cluster advantages based on existing strong and effective local sourcing and networks, it may better to avoid policies with a heavy reliance on FDI to boost development. Locations in these conditions may be better placed to seek to develop international, national or regional excellence by local firms by fostering the development of industries where the location grants benefits associated with the geographic, historical and institutional characteristics of the area (McDonald and Vertova, 2002). Such policies will attract FDI because of increasing income levels and the emergence of effective local sourcing and networks that enable enhanced learning and innovation. Even German FDI that is motivated by the desire to develop the UK market will be attracted by successful regional development of this type in order to supply the growing and dynamic local market.

Policies to enhance regional development, primarily by FDI, should focus on firms that are likely to require high and growing levels of skilled labour. However, the results of this study suggest that even if subsidiaries are embedded, the link to high and growing demand for skilled labour is not strong. Thus, careful targeting of potential investors will be required to identify those most likely to demand skilled labour. However, such policies are likely to attract footloose investments motivated by cost advantages arising from low wages and tax/subsidy benefits. This type of investment is unlikely to promote a high demand for skilled labour. Such policies may also attract sales and distribution outlets with small-scale host-based operations to enhance supply channels for exports from the parent company's home base. These type of FDI are unlikely to make a major contribution to regional development.

Conclusion

This study found evidence that assets and resources that are available in host locations are not important for the employment effects of German FDI into the UK. Moreover, strategic autonomy for subsidiaries and the number of markets supplied are also not strongly related to beneficial employment effects. Thus, it would seem, embeddedness factors are not very important for the impact of German FDI on employment. Indeed, even some of the traditional factors such as technical transfer, age and entry mode are not particularly important for either the growth of employment or for the type of jobs that are connected to German subsidiaries. German FDI into the UK is largely driven by a desire to take advantage of core German competencies and advantages by expanding the UK market for German exports. This is not necessarily disadvantageous for host and home countries as it permits the development of comparative advantage (Heise *et al.*, 2002a), however the results also imply that German FDI is unlikely to be a significant driver of high-quality employment in the UK.

This work requires development in terms of the gathering and analysis of data and the conceptual framework needs to be refined to enable more robust hypotheses to be derived. Different techniques to test hypotheses from improved data would also enhance the reliability of results obtained from a more developed conceptual framework. Comparison with non-European MNCs in the UK would also help to identify the importance of embeddedness for MNCs that are geographically and psychically distant from Europe. Gathering more data, particularly qualitative data from in-depth interviews, would also help to unravel many of the unresolved and unexplained relations between embeddedness factors and employment. Such qualitative work would be particularly useful to assess the importance of clusters for attracting FDI that is embedded and closely linked to high and growing demand for skilled labour. Studies of the relationships between FDI and employment in other European countries would also help to discover if embeddedness factors are more or less important for employment effects in different economic, institutional, cultural and industrial structures across Europe. Such a research agenda would provide better information that could be used to improve policy formation that is seeking to use FDI as a major means of enhancing regional development and employment.

Appendix: definition of variables for subsidiaries

Stock (level) embeddedness variables

Variables	*Definition*
Importance of foreign Markets (*mkt*)	Yes – if the subsidiary has a foreign market as a main market or if the UK is a main market as well as two foreign markets as secondary markets
Presence of expatriate managers (*expat*)	Yes – if the subsidiary has expatriate managers
Decision-making autonomy (*aut*)	Yes – if the subsidiary has decision-making autonomy within its main area of business
Importance of host-country sourcing (*source*)	Yes – if the subsidiary makes purchases of 30% or greater from its local region or if it purchases 50% or greater from the whole of the UK
Importance of use of networks (*net*)	Yes – if the subsidiary engages in two or more local networks.

Dynamic (change) embeddedness variables

Variables	*Definition*
Increase in decision-making autonomy (*daut*)	If there has been an increase in decision-making in the main area of business accompanied by an increase in two other areas
Increase in scope of activity (*dscope*)	If there has been an increase in the scope of the main area of business
Increase in host-country sourcing (*dhcs*)	If the level of UK purchases has increased by more that the average for all subsidiaries
Increase in use of networks (*dnet*)	If use of local networks has increased

Control and dependent variables

Control variables	*Dependent variables*
Change in sales turnover (*dsto*)	Change in employment (*demploy*) 1997–2001
Sales turnover (*sto*)	Stock of skilled jobs (*hskill*) 1997–2001
Firm age (*age*)	Stock of semi-skilled/unskilled jobs (*lskill*) 1997–2001
Entry mode (*em*)	% change in skilled jobs (*dhskill*) 1997–2001
Manufacturing (*man*)	% change in semi-skilled/unskilled jobs (*dlskill*) 1997–2001
Services (*serv*)	
Sales & distribution (*sdist*)	
Technology transfer (*ttr*)	

References

Ashcroft, B. and Love, J. (1989) 'Evaluating the effects of external takeover on the performance of regional companies', *Environment and Planning A*, 22(3), 197–220.

Ashcroft, B. and Love, J. (1993) *Takeovers, Mergers and the Regional Economy*. Edinburgh: Edinburgh University Press.

Aitken, B., Harrison, A. and Lipsey, R. (1996) 'Wages and foreign ownership: a comparative study of Mexico, Venezuela and the United States', *Journal of International Economics* 40(3), 345–71.

Aitken, B. and Harrison, A. (1999) 'Do domestic firms benefit from direct foreign investment? Evidence from Venezuela, *American Economic Review* 89(2), 605–18.

Bailey, P., Porssotto, A. and Renshaw, G. (1993) *Multinationals and Employment: The Global Economy of the 1990s*. Geneva: International Labor Office.

Barrell, R. and Pain, N. (1997) 'Foreign direct investment, technological change and economic growth within Europe', *Economic Journal* 107(4), 1770–86.

Barrell, R. and Pain, N. (1999) 'Domestic institutions, agglomerations and foreign direct investment in Europe', *European Economic Review* 43(4), 925–34.

Bartlett, C. and Ghoshal, S. (1989) *Managing Across Borders: The Transnational Solution*. Boston, MA: Harvard Business School Press.

Benito, G. (2000) 'Industrial clusters and foreign companies' centres of excellence in Norway', in Holm, U. and Pedersen, T. *The Emergence and Impact of MNC Centres of Excellence: A Subsidiary Perspective*. Basingstoke: Macmillan – Palgrave.

Beyfuss, J. and Eggert, J. (2000) *Auslandsinvestitionen der deutschen Wirtschaft und ihre Arbeitsplatzeffekte*. Köln: Institut der deutschen Wirtschaft, Deutscher-Instituts-Verlag.

Birkinshaw, J. and Morrison, A. (1995) 'Configurations of strategy and structure in subsidiaries of multinational corporations', *Journal of International Business Studies* 26(3), 729–53.

Birkinshaw, J. and Hood, N. (eds) (1998a) *Multinational Corporate Evolution and Subsidiary Development*. Basingstoke: Macmillan – Palgrave.

Birkinshaw, J. and Hood, S. (1998b) 'Multinational subsidiary evolution: capability and charter change in foreign-owned subsidiary companies', *Academy of Management Review* 23(3), 773–95.

Birkinshaw, J. Hood, N. and Jonsson, S. (1998) 'Building firm-specific advantages in multinational corporations: the role of subsidiary initiative', *Strategic Management Journal* 19(2), 221–41.

Birkinshaw, J. (2000) *Entrepreneurship in the Global Firm*. London: Sage.

Blomström, M. and Kokko, A. (1998) 'Multinational corporations and spillovers', *Journal of Economic Surveys* 12(3), 247–77.

Blonigen, B. and Slaughter, M. (1999) 'Time series evidence on the sources of trends in wage inequality', *American Economic Review, Papers and Proceedings* 84(1), 10–16.

Brecher, R. and Diaz-Alejandro, C. (1997) 'Tariffs, foreign capital and immiserizing growth', *Journal of International Economics* 7(3), 317–22.

Brown, R. and Raines, P. (2000) 'The changing nature of foreign investment policy in Europe: from promotion to management', in Dunning, J. (ed.), *Regions, Globalization and the Knowledge-Based Economy*. Oxford: Oxford University Press.

Bundesministerium für Wirtschaft und Technologie (2002) *Wirtschaft in Zahlen*, Berlin.

DeMello, L. (1999) 'Foreign direct investment-led growth: evidence from time series and panel data', *Oxford Economic Papers* 51(2), 133–51.

Del Monte, A. and De Luzenberger, R. (1989) 'The effect of regional policy on new firm formation in Southern Italy', *Regional Studies* 23(3), 219–30.

DETR (2000) 'Planning for clusters: a research report', Department of the Environment, Transport and the Regions, London.

Deutsche Bundesbank (2002) *Kapitalverpflechtung mit dem Ausland*, Statistische Sonderveröffentlichung 10, Frankfurt.

Doz, Y. and Prahalad, C. (1993) 'Managing MNCs: a search for a new paradigm', in Ghoshal, S. and Wesney, D. (eds), *Organization Theory and the Multinational Corporation*. New York: St Martins Press.

Driffield, N. (1999a) 'Indirect employment effects of foreign direct investment into the UK', *Bulletin of Business Research* 51(2), 207–21.

Driffield, N. (1999b) 'Regional and industry level spillovers from FDI', NIESR Conference on Inward Investment, Technological Change and Growth, London.

Driffield, N. and Munday, M. (2000) 'Industrial performance, agglomeration, and foreign manufacturing investment in the UK', *Journal of International Business Studies* 31(1), 21–37.

Driffield, N. and Taylor, K. (2000) 'Foreign direct investment and labour market: a review of the evidence and policy implications', *Oxford Review of Economic Policy* 16(2), 90–103.

Dunning, J. (1992) 'The competitive advantages of nations and the activities of transnational corporations', *Transnational Corporations* 1(2), 135–68.

Dunning, J. (2000) 'Regions, globalization, and the knowledge economy: the issues stated', in Dunning, J. (ed.), *Regions, Globalization, and the Knowledge Economy*. Oxford: Oxford University Press.

Engelbrecht, H. (1997) 'International R&D spillovers, human capital and productivity in OECD economies', *European Economic Review* 41(4), 1479–88.

Enright, M. (1998) 'Regional clusters and firm strategy', in Chandler, A. Hagstrom, P. and Solvell, O. (eds), *The Dynamic Firm: The Role of Technology, Strategy, and Regions*. Oxford: Oxford University Press.

Enright, M. (2000) 'Globalization of competition and the localization of competitive advantage: policies towards regional clustering', in Hood, N. and Young, S. (eds), *Globalization of Multinational Enterprise Activity and Economic Development*. Basingstoke: Palgrave.

Etemad, H. and Dulude, L. (1986) *Managing the Multinational Subsidiary*. London: Croom Helm.

Figini, P. and Görg, H. (1999) 'Multinational companies and wage inequality in the host country: the case of Ireland', *Weltwirtschaftliches Archiv* 134(4), 594–612.

Georgiou, G. and Weinhold, S. (1992) 'Japanese direct investment in the US', *World Economy* 15(4), 761–78.

Gillespie, G., McGregor, P., Swales, J. and Yin, Y. (1999) 'The regional employment impact of foreign direct investment: an ownership-disaggregated computable general equilibrium analysis', NIESR Conference Paper, London.

Hair, J., Anderson, R., Tatham, R. and Black, W. (1998) *Multivariate Data Analysis*. Upper Saddle River, NJ: Prentice-Hall.

Heise, A., McDonald, F. and Tüselmann, H. (2002a) 'The development of pan-European industrial structures and the strategic development of subsidiaries', in McDonald, F., Tüselmann, H.J. and Wheeler, C. (eds), *International Business: Adjusting to New Challenges and Opportunities*. Basingstoke: Palgrave.

Heise, A., McDonald, F. and Tüselmann, H. (2002b) 'Foreign direct investment and employment in host regions?', *European Business Review* 14(3), 40–50.

Hirschman, A. (1958) *The Strategy of Economic Development*. New Haven: Yale University Press.

Holm, U. and Pedersen, T. (2000) *The Emergence and Impact of MNC Centres of Excellence: A Subsidiary Perspective*. Basingstoke: Macmillan – Palgrave.

Hood, N. and Taggart, J. (1997) 'German direct investment in the UK and Ireland: survey evidence', *Regional Studies* 31(3), 139–50.

Hubert, F. and Pain, N. (1999) 'Inward investment and technical progress in the United Kingdom', NIESR Conference on Inward Investment, Technological Change and Growth: The Impact of Multinational Corporations on the UK Economy, London.

Johanson, J. and Vahlne, J. (1977) 'The internationalisation process of the firm – a model of knowledge development and increasing foreign market developments', *Journal of International Business Studies* 8(1), 23–32.

Jungnickel, R. (1995) *Foreign Direct Investment, Trade and Employment – The Experience of Germany*. Paris: OECD.

Krugman, P. (1991) 'Increasing returns and economic geography', *Journal of Political Economy* 99(3), 484–99.

Liu, X., Siler, P., Wang, C. and Wei, Y. (2000) 'Productivity spillovers from foreign direct investment: evidence from UK industry level panel data', *Journal of International Business Studies* 31(4), 407–26.

Love, J., Ashcroft, B. and Dunlop, S. (1996) 'Corporate structure, ownership and the likelihood of innovation', *Applied Economics* 28(5), 737–46.

Lundvall, B. (1999) 'Technology policy in the learning economy', in Archibugi, D., Howells, J. and Michie, J. (eds), *Innovation Systems and Policy in a Global Economy*. Cambridge: Cambridge University Press.

Machin, S. and van Reenen, J. (1998) 'Technology and changes in skill structure: evidence from seven OECD countries', *Quarterly Journal of Economics* 45(4), 1215–44.

McDonald, F. and Vertova, G. (2002) 'Clusters, industrial districts and competitiveness', in McNaughton, R. and Green, M. (eds), *Global Competition and Local Networks*. Aldershot: Ashgate.

McDonald, F., Tüselmann, H.J., Heise, A. and Williams, D. (2003a) 'Employment in host regions and foreign direct investment', *Environment and Planning C*: government and planning, 21(5), 687–701.

McDonald, F., Tüselmann, H.J., Hoppe, U. and Williams, D. (2003b) *Standort UK: German DFI in the UK and Employment*. London: Anglo–German Foundation for the Study of Industrial Society.

Office of National Statistics (2002) *Annual Abstracts of Statistics*. London: HMSO.

Ó hUallacháin, B. (1984) 'Linkages and foreign direct investment in the United States', *Economic Geography* 60(3), 238–53.

Porter, M. (1990) *The Competitive Advantage of Nations*. Basingstoke: Macmillan – Palgrave.

Porter, M. (1994) 'The role of location in competition', *Journal of the Economics of Business* 1(1), 35–9.

Porter, M. and Solvell, O. (1998) 'The role of geography in the process of innovation and the sustainable competitive advantage of firms', in Chandler, A., Hagstrom, P. and Solvell, O. (eds), *The Dynamic Firm: The Role of Technology, Strategy, and Regions*. Oxford: Oxford University Press.

Raines, R., Döhrn, R., Brown, R. and Scheuer, M. (1999) *Labour Market Flexibility and Inward Investment in Germany and the UK*. London: Anglo–German Foundation for the Study of Industrial Society.

Rodriquez, T. and Rodrik, C. (1999) 'Trade policy and economic growth: a sceptic's guide to cross-frontier trade', National Bureau of Economic Research, Working Paper no. 7081, Cambridge, MA.

Sachs, J. and Warner, M. (1993) *Economic Reform and the Process of Global Integration*, Brookings Papers on Economic Activity, Washington, DC.

Schachmann, K. and Fallis, P. (1989) 'External control and regional development within the Federal Republic of Germany', *International Regional Science Review* 12(3), 245–61.

Scott, A. (1983) 'Location and linkage systems: a survey and reassessment', *Annals of Regional Science* 17(1), 1–39.

Segal, N. and Quince, R. (1985) 'The Cambridge phenomenon and the role of the Cambridge science park', in Gibb, J. (ed.), *Science Parks and Innovation Centres: Their Economic and Social Impact* London: Elsevier.

Taggart, J. (1996) 'Multinational manufacturing subsidiaries in Scotland: strategic role and economic impact', *International Business Review* 5(4), 447–68.

Tüselmann, H.J. (1998) 'Standort Deutschland: German Direct Foreign Investment – Exodus of German Industry and Export of Jobs', *Journal of World Business* 33(3), 295–312.

UN (1994) *Transnational Corporations, Employment and the Workplace,* United Nations Conference on Trade and Development, Division on Transnational Corporations and Investment. New York: United Nations.

Wakelin, K., Girma, S. and Greenaway, D. (1999) 'Wages, productivity and foreign ownership in UK manufacturing', NIESR Conference on Inward Investment, Technological Change and Growth: The Impact of Multinational Corporations on the UK Economy, London.

Weisberg, S. (1985) *Applied Linear Regression.* New York: Wiley.

Williams, D. (2003) 'Explaining employment changes in foreign manufacturing investment in the UK', *International Business Review* 12(4), 479–97.

Young, S., Hood, N. and Peters, E. (1994) 'Multinational enterprises and regional economic development', *Regional Studies* 28(4), 657–77.

Wren, C. and Taylor, J. (1999) 'Industrial restructuring and regional policy', *Oxford Economic Papers* 51(4), 487–516.

16
A Four Regional Approach to Inbound FDI Location Decisions

Grahame Fallon and Mark Cook

Introduction

This chapter seeks to add to the literature on the determinants of UK regional inbound foreign direct investment (FDI). Following a discussion of the literature on the major influences on FDI location, four regions are considered: the South-East, the West Midlands, Wales and Scotland. The sectoral pattern of FDI in these regions is investigated and interregional variations are highlighted. The construction of multiple regression models is then discussed, with reference to the four motives underlying FDI location decisions – market-seeking, resources-seeking, efficiency-seeking and strategic asset-seeking behaviour (suggested by Stopford and Strange, 1991; Dunning, 1993b, 2002). Following the development of these models, the locational determinants of inbound FDI are explored.

The findings indicate that FDI is attracted into the four regions under a common set of broad headings, yet there are differences in the specific influences which appear to draw FDI into each region. Part of the explanation for this may be the sectoral differences that exist between the predominant types of FDI the four regions attract. The chapter concludes by considering the theoretical and policy implications of the findings and an agenda for future research is also suggested.

Literature review

Although no single theory of FDI has yet emerged, Dunning's 'eclectic paradigm', (1977 and 1988) provides a widely accepted framework within which modern theoretical and empirical developments in the study of the determinants of FDI location can be examined (Dunning, 2001). For FDI to occur, transnational corporations (TNCs) must firstly possess ownership-specific advantages not shared by competing firms, and they may secondly be best-placed to exploit these advantages if they can internalize their market transactions. The third element in the eclectic paradigm, location, is also important if TNCs are to exploit their ownership advantages as fully as possible (Dunning, 1977, 1988). TNCs must choose whether to internalize their transactions at home or in a foreign country, and the choice which they make is heavily influenced by the costs and benefits of locating value-added activities in these different geographical locations (Dunning, 2002). This current chapter and the underlying research project therefore focus on identifying the factors influencing the choice of FDI location by multinational enterprise (MNE) decision-makers. Reference is made to modern resource-based, geographically-based and technologically-driven theories as well as those generally considered to be part of the eclectic paradigm.

Three current developments in the global economy are helping to focus scholarly interest on the links between FDI location and TNCs' capabilities and strategies, and on the attractions which particular locations offer to existing or potential investors (Dunning, 2002). Firstly, intellectual capital is becoming an increasingly important element in the wealth-creation process, leading to a growing emphasis on the need to access spatially immobile assets (such as skilled labour and public infrastructure) in order to exploit firm-specific knowledge-intensive assets to the full (Peck, 1996). Secondly, TNCs' abilities to shift intangible assets from country to country are becoming increasingly restricted by the existence of location-specific clusters of complementary activities, leading to the growing concentration of some industries in particular geographical areas (Storper and Scott, 1995; Markusen, 1996). Thirdly, TNCs are tending increasingly to collaborate with suppliers, customers and competitors on a global scale, leading to a growth in cross-border alliances, mergers and acquisitions and providing a motive for FDI in particular locations (UNCTAD, 1997).

Four main strategies influence the location of value-added activities by TNCs: the search for markets, resources, efficiency and strategic assets (Stopford and Strange, 1991; Dunning, 1993b, 2002). The main variables influencing the location of each type of FDI are discussed in turn in the following sections of this chapter, following which the explanatory variables used and the underlying research are summarized in Figure 16.1.

Market-seeking FDI

Market-seeking FDI may be driven by the desire to sustain or safeguard existing geographical markets or by the wish to develop new markets (Dunning, 1993b). Such FDI can be drawn to countries or regions by the population density of national, regional or adjacent markets, together with per capita income levels, market size and growth prospects (Wheeler and Mody, 1992; Billington, 1999; Ford and Strange, 1999). It may be attracted to locations which are close to the country of origin in geographical and cultural terms (Dunning, 1993b), and to those with good market access (Hill and Munday, 1992; Arpan and Ricks, 1995). It may also be drawn to countries or regions with a highly developed transport and communications infrastructure (Arpan and Ricks, 1995; Mudambi, 1995; Yeung and Strange, 2002), where leading suppliers are present (Dunning, 2002), where there are well-developed service support facilities (Dunning, 2002) or where competition from rival firms and from imports is relatively low (Milner and Pentecost, 1994). Its location may also be influenced by the fear of losing potential markets by not engaging in FDI (Dunning, 1993a), by the need to maximize familiarity with target-market conditions (Barkema *et al.*, 1997) and by the need to preserve existing foreign markets established by exporting (Dunning, 1993b).

National and regional governments may exercise a substantial impact on the attraction of market-related FDI, by the use which they make of trade policy measures (where the imposition of tariff and non-tariffs barriers to imported goods and services is likely to raise FDI levels in some sectors) (Dunning, 2002). Their ability to develop and maintain competent local institutions, pursue sound macroeconomic policies and promote inward investment may all influence the volume and value of market-related FDI, which flows into particular geographical locations (Woodward, 1992; Dunning, 2002).

Resources-seeking FDI

Resources-seeking TNCs carry out FDI in order to gain access to resources not obtainable at home or to acquire them at a lower real cost (Dunning, 1993b). The exploitation of firm-specific resources can create competitive advantage (Barney, 1991) provided that they are valuable, rare and difficult to imitate (Birkinshaw *et al.*, 1998). Some such resources are location-bound (Rugman and Verbeke, 1992) and can only add value in a particular country or region, whereas others can be leveraged by TNCs to deliver ownership advantages in a range of different locations (Birkinshaw *et al.*, 1998).

The availability of labour resources can be an important influence on the location of FDI (Arpan and Ricks, 1995; Yeung and Strange, 2002), encompassing the supply and cost of local labour, educational attainment levels, the quality of human skills capital, and local trade union strength. FDI can be attracted by the presence of a large, well-educated and trained workforce in particular countries or regions (Ford and Strange, 1999), and by the existence of positive workforce attitudes towards employment, company loyalty and continuous improvement (Mair *et al.*, 1988). High labour costs and resultant wage differentials may deter FDI (Billington, 1999), although high and growing levels of labour productivity may offset this effect (Ford and Strange, 1999). High levels of unemployment can be expected to attract FDI where it increases the availability of labour and the willingness of employees to work harder and for lower wages, but such levels can also reduce FDI in their negative impact on regional incomes and spending power (Friedman *et al.*, 1992; Billington, 1999). The impact of trade-union strength is also unpredictable, since high levels of unionization can both attract foreign investors by raising worker morale and labour productivity (Billington, 1999), and deter them due to their capacity to increase worker militancy and raise average wage levels (Ford and Strange, 1999).

Resources-related FDI can also be attracted to particular locations by the availability, price and quality of natural resources. Some such resources are location-bound (Rugman and Verbeke, 1992), and can only add value in a particular country or region, whereas others can be leveraged by TNCs to deliver ownership advantages in a range of different locations (Birkinshaw *et al.*, 1998). The presence of natural resources is most likely to attract FDI inflows where there is sufficient infrastructure for them to be exploited by TNCs and for related products to be exported. Local opportunities for processing and upgrading the quality of natural resources, and the existence of local partners with the ability to promote knowledge or exploit resources on a joint basis, can also draw in such FDI, as can government investment incentives (Billington, 1999; Dunning, 2002).

Efficiency-seeking FDI

Efficiency-seeking FDI is motivated by the desire to rationalize the geographical structure of FDI in order to take advantage of economies of scale and scope and the diversification of risks (Dunning, 1993b). The location of efficiency-seeking FDI is influenced by the ability to supply multiple markets from common locations, and to exploit differences in factor endowments and production costs. Regional economic and industrial development, the availability and quality of supporting industries and the resultant potential for building supply-chain links, cluster development and networking can all exercise an important influence on the geographical location of efficiency-seeking FDI (Dunning, 2002). Increasing host-country industrialization can act as a stimulus to such FDI, as can high geographical concentrations of manufacturing or services activity (Wheeler and Mody, 1992; Billington, 1999). FDI is also believed to be attracted to particular regions by local supply-chain linkages (Crone, 2001; Gorg and Ruane, 2001) and internationally competitive regional clusters (Enright 1995, 1996 and 1998), enabling TNCs to reduce their transactions costs by exploiting locally available externalities and agglomeration economies (Krugman and Venables, 1995; Ivarsson, 1999). Inter-firm proximity, networking and interactions in regionally-based sectoral clusters can also exert an important influence on FDI location due to their ability to help create ownership-specific advantages which can be internalized by the TNC as a whole (Birkinshaw and Hood, 1997; Anderson *et al.*, 2001; Gorg and Ruane, 2001).

Government actions can also help to increase the attraction of efficiency-seeking FDI to particular countries and regions. Such actions can include the provision of investment incentives (such as tax breaks), the promotion of industrial restructuring and the upgrading of human skills capital, the promotion of local cluster development (based for example around science parks) and inter-firm cooperation (Young and Hood, 1994; Tavares and Young, 2002). Governments can also help to maximize the potential opportunities for new TNC initiatives and for related domestic-firm start-ups and development by helping to create a business environment conducive to entrepreneurship (Dunning, 2002).

Strategic asset-seeking FDI

Strategic asset-seeking FDI is typically motivated by the desire to sustain or advance TNCs' international competitiveness by protecting or augmenting their existing ownership-specific advantages (Dunning, 1993b and 2002). The search for strategic assets is becoming an increasingly important influence on the location of FDI. Strategic asset-seeking FDI can be attracted to particular locations by the availability of knowledge-related assets and markets and by regionally concentrated technological strengths (Enright and Roberts, 2001), and TNCs are now using FDI to gain access to strategic assets such as R&D capability and human capital (Cantwell and Janne, 1999; Enright and Roberts, 2001), often utilizing collaborative joint ventures, cross-border mergers and outright acquisitions as a means to this end (Dunning, 1993b; Clarke, 2001).

The importance of strategic asset-seeking FDI is increasing over time (Grabher, 1993) owing to the growing geographical dispersion of knowledge-based assets, and to the resultant need for TNCs to exploit them from overseas locations (Dunning, 2002). The increasing integration of TNCs' subsidiaries into their host economies, leading to a growth in opportunities for the exchange of localized knowledge and ideas is helping to reinforce this trend, as is the existence of host-government policies promoting local supply-chain and cluster development (Young and Hood, 1994; Tavares and Young, 2002). The ease or difficulty with which institutional and legal arrangements allow strategic assets to be acquired by foreign firms is also an important influence on the location of FDI (Dunning, 2002).

Summary of explanatory variables

The explanatory variables used in this chapter and the underlying research to measure the importance of market-, resources-, efficiency- and strategic asset-seeking motives to the decision of whether to locate FDI in the South-East, the West Midlands, Wales or Scotland are summarized in Figure 16.1.

Changes in FDI entering the UK regions

Official government figures (*Regional Trends*, 2001) suggest that the traditional concentration of FDI in the south-eastern core of the UK economy is being broadly maintained despite the apparent breakthrough by peripheral regions such as Scotland and Wales and intermediate regions such as the West Midlands

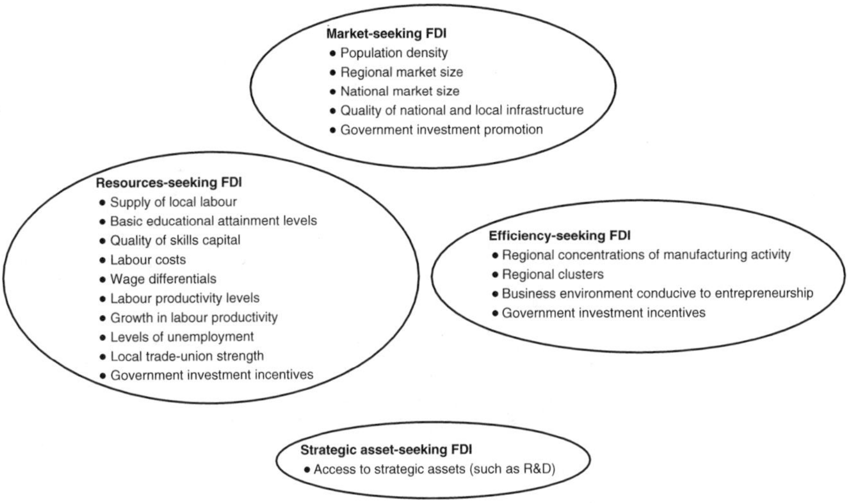

Figure 16.1 Explanatory variables used to measure the four types of FDI

suggested by recent commentators (Tewdr-Jones and Phelps, 2000). Between 1995/6 and 1999/00, the increase recorded in FDI new project terms for the UK as a whole appears to have been largely attributable to non-manufacturing activities, as Table 16.1 indicates. The South-East appears to have maintained its share of non-manufacturing FDI during this period whilst its share of manufacturing FDI would seem to have increased. In contrast, the shares of non-manufacturing FDI attracted by the West Midlands, Wales and Scotland appear to have declined, whilst these regions have been unable to strengthen their shares of manufacturing FDI over the same period.

Much of the FDI entering the West Midlands has traditionally been concentrated in a narrow range of manufacturing sectors in which the region is strong, such as the automotive sector, added-value engineering, rubber and plastics, manufacturing and food and drink. Since the late 1990s, however, the region has been successful in attracting increased FDI in absolute terms in the business services, and in particular in the information technology and software sectors (Advantage West Midlands, 2001). Nonetheless, the region's proportion of national non-manufacturing FDI has declined over recent time

Scotland's share of UK manufacturing FDI has remained relatively stable, whereas it has been particularly successful in attracting inbound FDI to its electronics and services industries (Locate in Scotland, 2001). The region is now home to a cluster of over 420 electronics companies, many of which are foreign-owned and together these make up 'Silicon Glen', arguably 'the largest concentration of electronics companies anywhere in Europe' (Invest UK, 2001). In the years since 1996, Scotland's services industry has replaced electronics as the prime

Table 16.1 Percentage of new UK FDI projects going to the four regions (1995/6, 1999/2000)

Region	*Manufacturing FDI (1995/6) (%)*	*Manufacturing FDI (1999/2000) (%)*	*Non-manufacturing FDI (1995/6) (%)*	*Non-manufacturing FDI (1999/2000) (%)*	*Total FDI (1995/6) (%)*	*Total FDI (1999/2000) (%)*
South East	7.2	9.1	16.8	16.9	10.1	13.8
West Midlands	17.9	17	10.1	9.1	15.5	12.4
Wales	12.7	12.2	10.1	7.6	10.7	5.9
Scotland	16.4	11.0	6.0	2.3	14.5	9.5
UK total no. of new projects	347	328	149	472	496	800

Source: Based on data from *Regional Trends* (2001).

target for inbound FDI in volume, value and employment terms. Services FDI covers a broad compass, including higher value-added activities such as electronics design, biotechnology, research and development, financial services and call centres. Once again Scotland's proportion of UK FDI in non-manufacturing appears to be declining over time.

The services sector continues to dominate the South-East's economy (*Invest UK*, 2002). A number of the world's leading financial and business services companies are present in the region, while it also hosts a substantial and growing number of 'significant' call centres (SEEDA, 2002). The region still has a 'strong and diverse manufacturing base', however, and it is now said to be the world's most important region outside the USA for the IT and telecommunications industry (Invest UK, 2002). The South-East's cluster of pharmaceutical and bio-technology industries is said to rank 'second to none in Europe', and the region also has substantial representation in the automotive, motorsport, electronics, avionics, aerospace, marine technology and manufacturing sectors (SEEDA, 2002).

The Welsh economy retains a substantial manufacturing base although this has tended to decline over time (*Regional Trends*, 2001). Wales has a large presence in the aerospace, automotive, IT/multimedia, biotechnology/life sciences, optoelectronics and telecommunications sectors. Services also play a part in the Welsh sectoral mix and customer-relations management and contact centres are particularly prominent in this context (Welsh Development Agency, 2002). However, as with the West Midlands and Scotland, the proportion of UK non-manufacturing FDI attracted to Wales appears to have fallen over recent years.

Methodology

The empirical research underlying this study was designed to answer the following questions:

1. Does the search for markets, resources, efficiency and strategic assets provide a statistically significant explanation for the decision to locate inbound FDI in the four UK regions?
2. To what extent can the results from the statistical analysis be used to explain the differing sectoral composition of FDI in these regions?
3. What are the implications of the overall study for government policy towards inbound FDI in the UK regions?

The basic model underlying the regression has been developed from the literature. Flows of inbound FDI (proxied by the number of *new projects* per year) were used as the dependent variable throughout the multiple regression analysis (MRA). A range of independent variables reflecting different aspects of market-, resources-, efficiency- and strategic asset- seeking FDI was added to the equation one at a time for each region in turn. These variables were subsequently incorporated in or discarded from the models for each region depending on whether they contributed significantly to the explanatory power of each regression. The explanatory variables used in regressions for each region are listed in Table 16.2, together with their expected signs.

New FDI projects are used here to proxy inflows of FDI to the UK regions (following the example of Hill and Munday, 1992). A choice has had to be made between proxies recorded in *Regional Trends* (the annual number of foreign investment project successes), and by Invest UK (the annual number of new investment projects). The latter measure is chosen for this study as it quantifies inbound FDI projects on a current-year basis rather than recording the number of project 'successes' in a particular year, the actual investment for which is likely to have taken place at least one year before.

The analysis of data in the study is based on the estimation of the empirical relationship between inbound FDI and the selected explanatory variables for the four regions between 1980 and 1999, making use of the (SPSS) package.

Findings

Table 16.3 shows the explanatory variables for each of the four regions (the South-East, West Midlands, Wales and Scotland respectively) that have the greatest explanatory power in the MRAs. Use is made of the acronyms listed and explained in Table 16.2 in all cases. For all four regions the goodness of fit statistics indicate that the models are fairly robust. The adjusted R^2 coefficients are estimated as being 0.686, 0.784, 0.716 and 0.742 for the South-East, West Midlands, Wales and Scotland respectively.

Table 16.3 also provides evidence of the statistically significant variables that are related to FDI inflows into the four regions. The results of the *t*-test suggest that the key influences on FDI vary markedly between the four regions. In the South-East region, the most important FDI-inducing factors appear to be *WAGEINEQ*, followed by *EMPLOY* and *POPN*. For the West Midlands, the results suggest that *RPAREAL* and *EDU* are the two significant explanatory variables. In the case of Wales, the most significant explanatory variable determining inbound FDI is *CLUSTERS*, followed by *CLUNEMP* and *RPAREAL*. In Scotland, however, the most important determinant appears to be *UKGDPREAL*, followed by *CLUNEMP*, *POPN* and *RPAREAL*. Taken together, these findings suggest that it is difficult to explain the regional distribution of inbound FDI in the UK regions using a common set of explanatory variables.

The signs generated by the regression equations in the main agree with the *a priori* assumptions made. In the South-East *POPN* and *EMPLOY* appear to have a positive impact on FDI inflows as expected, whereas *WAGEINEQ* has the expected negative sign implying that as relative wages fall, FDI increases.

Table 16.2 Explanatory variables used to measure FDI

Influences on FDI	*Related variables*	*Meaning of acronym*	*Expected sign*
Market-seeking FDI			
Population density	*POPN*	Size of regional population	Positive
Regional market size	*GDPPCREAL*	Real regional GDP per capita	Positive
Size of national market	*UKGDPREAL*	UK GDP in real terms	Positive
Quality of national and local infrastructure	*ROAD REAL*	Regional expenditure on roads (annual basis)	Positive
Government investment promotion	*RPAREAL*	Government spending on regional preferential assistance	Positive
Resource-seeking FDI			
Supply of local labour	*EMPLOY*	Total regional employment	Positive
Basic educational attainment levels	*BASICED*	School leavers' examination achievements	Positive
Quality of skills capital	*EDU*	Percentage of 16–17-year-olds in post-compulsory education	Positive
Labour costs	*AWCREAL*	Average wage costs per manual employee	Negative
Wage differentials	*WAGEINEQ*	Regional manual wage levels/national average	Negative
Labour productivity levels	*PRODUCTI*	Regional output per employee	Positive
Growth in labour productivity	*CHNGPROD*	Year-on-year change in output per employee	Positive
Levels of unemployment	*CLUNEMP*	Regional claimant unemployment rate	Positive/ Negative
Local trade-union strength	*DISPUTES*	Working days lost per 1,000 employees through disputes	Negative
Government investment incentives	*RPAREAL*	Government spending on regional preferential assistance	Positive
Efficiency-seeking FDI			
Regional concentrations of manufacturing activity	*MANREAL*	Share of manufacturing industry in regional GDP	Positive
Regional clusters	*CLUSTERS*	Share of top 3 clusters in regional GDP	Positive
Business environment conducive to entrepreneurship	*BUSREG*	Net annual change in small business registrations	Positive
Government investment incentives	*RPAREAL*	Government spending on regional preferential assistance	Positive
Strategic asset-seeking FDI			
Access to strategic assets (such as R&D)	RANDREAL	Total R&D spending as % regional GDP	Positive

Table 16.3 Multiple regression results

Variable	*Coefficient*	*T ratio*
The South-East		
Constant	–35.495	–0.314
POPN	0.04030	1.999**
WAGEINEQ	–898.622	–5.491*
EMPLOY	0.118	2.581*
R^2	0.735	
R^2	0.686	
The West Midlands		
Constant	–84.081	–3.093*
RPAREAL	224.881	4.446*
EDU	1.683	4.007*
R^2	0.807	
R^2	0.784	
Wales		
Constant	–123.4	–2.861**
RPAREAL	–9.465	–2.074**
CLUNEMP	4.060	3.730**
CLUSTERS	2.622	4.349*
R^2	0.716	
R^2	0.716	
Scotland		
Constant	–3818.157	–4.702*
RPAREAL	–11.913	–2.510**
CLUNEMP	11.467	5.035*
POPN	0.695	4.520*
UKGDPREAL	0.058	5.356*
R^2	0.796	
R^2	0.742	

* Significant at the 0.01 level, **Significant at the 0.05 level, *** significant at the 0.1 level.

For the West Midlands *RPAREAL* and *EDU* both have the expected positive effects on inbound FDI inflows.

In the case of Wales, *CLUNEMP* and *CLUSTERS* have positive signs as predicted, whilst *RPAREAL* has an unexpected negative sign implying that FDI falls as RPA increases. An explanation for this anomalous result could be that availability of financial incentives has not been sufficient to counteract the effect of adverse economic circumstances which may have deterred many direct investors from locating to Wales during the period studied.

For Scotland the expected signs were obtained for *CLUNEMP, POPN* and *UKGDPREAL*, suggesting that increases in all three explanatory variables were linked with increases in FDI inflows. As with Wales, an unexpected negative

Table 16.4 *F*-test results

Region	*F-ratio*	*Significance of F-values*
The South-East	14.815	0.000
The West Midlands	35.434	0.000
Wales	16.974	0.000
Scotland	14.663	0.000

sign was recorded for *RPAREAL* in Scotland, suggesting that increasing levels of government investment promotion and incentives are associated with lower inflows of FDI into the region. This result may be explained, at least in part, by the heterogeneity of the Scottish economy, which cannot be reflected by its treatment as one unified region in published official statistics. Government support may be expected to attract FDI to core areas of the Scottish economy (such as the Central Lowlands), but this effect may be masked by its inability to overcome the inherent disadvantages of peripheral areas (such as The Highlands and Islands) as locations for inbound FDI (due to their remoteness from markets, relatively poor infrastructure and lack of agglomeration economies).

The results of the adjusted R^2 tests are supported by the *F*-test for all four regions – see Table 16.4. The *F*-test results, used as a measure of significance of all the explanatory variables together within the equation, are highly significant for all four regions. The models therefore appear to be a good determinant of inbound FDI into each of the four regions.

The Durbin–Watson (D–W) test is a test for autocorrelation. It is based upon the null hypothesis that there is no autocorrelation present; if the hypothesis can be accepted then there is no autocorrelation. Autocorrelation occurs when the error terms in the regression equation are serially correlated. A two-tailed test is used where the D–W tests for both positive and negative autocorrelation. Table 16.5 shows the D–W statistics for the regression equations for each of the four regions, and the figures show that there is no autocorrelation in any of the regression equations for the four regions.

Table 16.5 Durbin–Watson test results

Region	*Durbin–Watson statistic*	*Significance of the Durbin–Watson statistic*
The South-East	2.091	No autocorrelation
The West Midlands	2.214	No autocorrelation
Wales	1.753	No autocorrelation
Scotland	2.179	No autocorrelation

Discussion

The findings reported in this chapter provide tentative support for the view that the attraction of inbound FDI into the four regions studied is related to the search for markets, resources, efficiency and strategic assets at a statistically significant level. The related explanatory variables (set out in Table 16.2) do help to identify the key (but varying) factors which appear to be influencing TNCs' FDI location decisions in these regions.

It is difficult to make use of the findings, however, to explain the sectoral composition of FDI in the four regions. Official sources suggest that the balance between manufacturing and non-manufacturing FDI varies from region to region; non-manufacturing FDI being dominant in the South-East, whereas manufacturing occupies the larger share of FDI in the West Midlands, Wales and Scotland. The results of this analysis suggest no straightforward explanation for these differences, since there is little evidence of systematic variation between the statistically significant motives for FDI identified in the equations for the South-East and those estimated for the other three regions.

There are considerable, interregional differences between the main influences which appear to be driving the location of FDI in these regions, raising issues worthy of attention from both theoretical and policy-making perspectives. Market- and resources-seeking motives explain much of the FDI entering the South-East and Scotland, but there appear to be considerable interregional differences between the specific influences, which draw both types of FDI into these two disparate regions. Resource-seeking motives would seem to underlie a significant part of the FDI attracted to both the West Midlands and Wales, yet the variables influencing the location of such FDI in these two regions are again different. Efficiency-seeking FDI would seem to be important only in the case of Wales, whilst government support for investment (*RPAREAL*) is significant and positive in the West Midlands, but significant and negative in Scotland and Wales where it might be expected to play an important role in attracting FDI.

Theoretical implications

There has been considerable development in the theoretical understanding of the locational determinants of FDI, as noted in the literature review at the beginning of this chapter. Modern theoretical sources do go a long way to explain the regional variations in the determinants of FDI found in the research underlying this paper. However, further theoretical development is now required in order to help explain the differing sectoral composition of FDI at the UK regional level noted in our findings. It would also be useful to determine whether FDI from different countries of origin is attracted to particular regions by the same or different influences.

Theoretical issues are also raised by the need to distinguish between the regional, national and international influences affecting TNCs' foreign investment location decisions. It is potentially misleading to treat issues such as location and agglomeration on a regional basis alone, at least in the context of small nations such as the United Kingdom. Regional, national and international issues are all likely to impact on TNCs' decisions to locate in UK regions, as the Scottish findings indicate. Regional economic performance, institutional, industrial and cluster developments may be sufficiently distinctive to explain some of reasons for the attraction of the four types of FDI to specific UK regions. However, TNCs' investment location decisions will also inevitably be influenced by variables which cross regional boundaries, such as the size and growth of the national or European Union (EU) markets and the impact of central government and EU policies on the availability of knowledge-related assets in all UK regions. Theoretical explanations of FDI location must take due account of all relevant variables, whether regionally compartmentalized or nationally or internationally based, if they are to provide a realistic explanation of the factors influencing TNCs' location decisions at the UK regional level.

Policy implications

The greater is the contribution that FDI makes to employment and output at the regional level, the more likely it is that policy-makers will focus their attention on identifying and meeting the needs of existing and potential foreign investors when devising regional economic development strategies. The findings presented in this chapter suggest, however, that a more discriminating approach towards the application of regional policy in the UK could help to maximize the inflow of FDI into the country's weaker regions, so helping to reduce the scale of the regional economic divide. More generous incentives could be provided for investment and job-creation in these regions as a means to this end, supported by increased levels of spending on education and on capital projects supporting cluster development. Heavier investment in business sites, premises and transport infrastructure could also be carried out in the weaker regions, helping to facilitate the attraction of FDI and so reduce the economic disadvantages from which these regions suffer in comparison with the South-East.

Regional development agencies (RDAs) may be able to increase FDI into all UK regions by identifying the key influences that attract foreign investment to them. Appropriately targeted investment promotion (and retention) strategies should be developed, incorporating a strategy for identifying key existing or potential foreign investors, and for meeting their needs (for example, by providing investment incentives prior to entry, or aftercare services aimed at keeping existing investors within the region concerned). Efforts should also be made to encourage the development of core regional strengths (such as existing and emerging clusters and workforce employability), which can attract FDI and maximize the resultant benefits for the regional economy. Effective partnership with key foreign investors, central government, local authorities, business support agencies and education and training providers will help RDAs to implement these policies effectively.

Future research agenda

There is now a need for further research in order to address the theoretical issues raised by the findings reported in this chapter. The reasons underlying the differing sectoral compositions of FDI at the UK regional level require additional exploration and clarification, focusing on how far the key influences which draw in FDI differ from sector to sector. Further work is needed in order to determine whether the same factors attract FDI from different countries of origin to the UK regions. It would also be profitable to identify and distinguish between the regional, national and international influences (including agglomeration effects), which affect TNCs' foreign investment location decisions.

The present research could therefore be usefully extended in future by carrying out a new econometric study focusing on sectoral, country of origin and agglomeration issues. Further insights could be gained from the use of an expanded study, including all UK regions simultaneously in the dataset. Alternative specifications of both the dependent and independent variables could be introduced in order to improve the reliability and value of the findings. Use could be made, for example, of a new dependent variable based on a value measure of FDI, in order to help focus on explaining the influences which draw in larger direct investments to the UK regions. Efforts could also be made to distinguish between the factors that attract new investments from those that encourage the retention of FDI at the regional level. Finally, the effectiveness of current UK government and RDA policies towards inbound FDI could form a useful focus for study at a time when the country's ability to attract and retain FDI is coming increasingly into question.

References

Advantage West Midlands (2001) *Inward Investment Annual Self Monitoring Report, April 2000-March 2001*. Birmingham: Advantage West Midlands.

Anderson, U., Holm, U. and Holmstrom, C. (2001) 'Relationship configuration and competence development in MNC subsidiaries', in Hakansson, H. and Johanson, J. (eds), *Business Network Learning*. Oxford: Pergamon.

Arpan, J. and Ricks, D.A. (1995) *Directory of Foreign Manufacturers in the United States*. Atlanta: School of Business Administration, Georgia State University.

Barkema, H.G., Shenka, O., Freek, V. and Bell, J.H. (1997) 'Working abroad, working with others: how firms learn to operate international joint ventures', *Academy of Management Journal* 40(2), 426–42.

Barney, J.B. (1991) 'Firm resources and sustained competitive advantage', *Journal of Management* 17(1), 99–120.

Billington, N. (1999) 'The location of foreign direct investment: an empirical analysis', *Applied Economics* 31(1), 100–20.

Birkinshaw, J.M. and Hood, N. (1997) 'An empirical study of development processes in foreign-owned subsidiaries in Canada and Scotland', *Management International Review* 37(4), 339–64.

Birkinshaw J., Hood, N. and Jonsson, S. (1998) 'Building firm-specific advantages in multinational corporations: the role of subsidiary initiative', *Strategic Management Journal* 19(3), 221–41.

Cantwell, J.A. and Janne, O.E.M. (1999) 'Technological globalisation and innovative centres: the role of corporate technological leadership and locational hierarchy', *Research Policy* 28(2), 119–44.

Clarke, B. (2001) Foreign direct investment in Russia: an examination of location-specific advantage, Centre for Research into East European Business, 7th Annual Conference, Buckinghamshire Chilterns University.

Crone, M. (2001) 'Local learning from multinational plants: knowledge transfers in the supply chain', *Regional Studies* 35(6), 535–48.

Dunning, J.H. (1977) 'Trade, location of economic activity and the MNE: a search for an eclectic approach', in Ohlin, B., Hesselborn, P.O. and P.M. Wijkman (eds), *The International Allocation of Economic Activity*. London: Macmillan – Palgrave.

Dunning, J.H. (1988) 'The eclectic paradigm of international production: a restatement and some possible extensions', *Journal of International Business Studies* 19(1), 1–31.

Dunning, J.H. (1993a) *The Globalisation of Business: The Challenge of the 1990s*. London and New York: Routledge.

Dunning, J.H. (1993b) *Multinational Enterprises and the Global Economy*. Wokingham: Addison-Wesley.

Dunning, J.H. (2001) 'The eclectic (OLI) paradigm of international production: past, present and future', *International Journal of the Economics of Business Studies* 8(2), 173–90.

Dunning, J.H. (2002) *Global Capitalism, FDI and Competitiveness*. Cheltenham: Edward Elgar.

Enright, M.J. (1995) 'Organisation and co-ordination in geographically concentrated industries', in Raff, D. and Lamoreux, N. (eds), *Co-ordination and Information: Historical Perspectives on the Organisation of Enterprise*. Chicago: Chicago University Press.

Enright, M.J. (1996) 'Regional clusters and firm strategy', in Staber, U., Schaefer, N. and Sharma, B. (eds), *Business Networks-Prospects for Regional Development*. New York: de Gruyter.

Enright, M.J. (1998) 'Regional clusters and firm strategy', in Chandler, J., Solvel, A.D. and Hagstrom, P. (eds), *The Dynamic Firm: The Role of Technology, Strategy, Organisation and Regions*. Oxford: Oxford University Press.

Enright, M.J. and Roberts, B.H. (2001) 'Regional clustering in Australia', *Australian Journal of Management* 26(1), 65–86.

Ford, S. and Strange, R. (1999) 'Where do Japanese manufacturing firms invest within Europe, and why?', *Transnational Corporations* 8(1), 117–42.

Friedman, J., Gerlowski, D. and Silberman, J. (1992) 'What attracts foreign multinational corporations? Evidence from branch plant location in the United States', *Journal of Regional Science* 32(4), 403–18.

Gorg, H. and Ruane, F. (2001) 'Multinational corporations and linkages: panel data evidence for the Irish electronics sector', *International Journal of the Economics of Business* 8(1), 1–18.
Grabher, G. (ed.) (1993) *The Embedded Firm*. London and New York: Routledge.
Hill, S. and Munday, M. (1992) 'The UK regional distribution of foreign direct investment: analysis and determinants', *Regional Studies* 26(6), 535–68.
Invest UK (2001–02) *UK Regional Information, Scotland and West Midlands*, http://www.Invest.uk.com/investing/uk_regional
Ivarsson, I. (1999) 'Competitive industry clusters and inward TNC investments: the case of Sweden', *Regional Studies* 33(1), 37–49.
Krugman, P.R. and Venables, A.J. (1995) 'Globalisation and the inequality of nations', *Quarterly Journal of Economics* 90(4), 857–79.
Locate in Scotland (2001) *Inward Investment Annual Review*, http://www.lis.org.uk.
Mair, A., Florida, R. and Kenney, M. (1988) 'The new geography of automotive production: Japanese transplants in North America', *Economic Geography* 64(4), 352–73.
Markusen, A. (1996) 'Sticky places in slippery space: a typology of industrial districts', *Economic Geography* 72(3), 293–313.
Milner, C. and Pentecost, E. (1994) 'The determinants of the composition of the US foreign direct investment in UK manufacturing', in Balasubramanyam, V.N. and Sapsford, D. (eds), *The Economics of International Investment*. Cheltenham: Edward Elgar.
Mudambi, R. (1995) 'The multinational investment location decision: some empirical evidence', *Managerial and Decision Economics* 16(3), 249–57.
Peck, F.W. (1996) 'Regional development and the production of space: the role of infrastructure in the attraction of new inward investment', *Environment and Planning* 28(3), 327–39.
Regional Trends (2001) Office for National Statistics, http://www.statistics.gov.uk/pdFDIr/FDI
Rugman, A.M. and Verbeke, A. (1992) 'A note on the transnational solution and the transaction cost theory of multinational strategic management', *Journal of International Business Studies* 23(4), 761–71.
South-East England Development Agency (2002) 'Inward investment in the South-East'. Reading: SEEDA, http://www.seeda.co.uk/seril
Stopford, J. and Strange, S. (1991) *Rival States, Rival Firms: Competition for World Market Shares*. Cambridge: Cambridge University Press.
Storper, M. and Scott, A.J. (1995) 'The wealth of regions', *Futures* 27(5), 5–26.
Tavares, A.T. and Young, S. (2002) 'Sourcing patterns of multinational subsidiaries in Europe: testing the determinants', UK Chapter, Academy of International Business, 29th Annual Conference, University of Central Lancashire.
Tewdr-Jones, M. and Phelps, N.A. (2000) 'Levelling the uneven playing field: inward investment, inter-regional rivalry and the planning system', *Regional Studies* 34(5), 429–40.
UNCTAD (1997) *World Investment Report 1997: Transnational Corporations, Market Structure and Competition Policy*. Geneva and New York: United Nations.
Welsh Development Agency (2002) 'Locate in Wales', http://www.invest-in-wales.com
Wheeler, D. and Mody, A. (1992) 'International investment location decisions: the case of US firms', *Journal of International Economics* 33(1/2), 57–76.
Woodward, D.P. (1992) 'Locational determinants of Japanese manufacturing start-ups in the United States', *Southern Economic Journal* 50(3), 690–708.
Yeung, P. and Strange, R. (2002) 'What attracts Japanese manufacturing investment? Evidence from the United States', Proceedings of 29th Annual Conference, UK Chapter, Academy of International Business, University of Central Lancashire.
Young, S. and Hood, N. (1994) 'Designing developmental after-care programs for inward investors in the European Community', *Transnational Corporations* 3(2), 45–72.

17

Regional Clusters between Localization and Globalization: An Empirical Investigation of a High-tech Metropolitan Cluster

Cristina Boari, Luciano Fratocchi and Manuela Presutti

Introduction

Physical boundaries seem to be less important than in the past, mainly because of reductions in transport costs (Padmore and Gibson, 1998), and innovations in information technologies (especially internet-based) make communications inexpensive, inducing a faster diffusion of knowledge. Moreover, reductions in commercial barriers give to small and medium-sized enterprises (SMEs) the opportunity to expand markets at the international level. As a consequence, the relevance of location for the creation of sustainable competitive advantage has been supposed to be diminished (Scott, 1998). More specifically, it is often assumed that financial resources and technology may be easily found everywhere in the global market.

At the same time, recent works suggest that national economies continue to develop through the emergence and the growth of regional clusters. As a consequence, the clustering phenomenon maintains its fundamental role in the economic context (Enright and Roberts, 2001). In this respect, the persistence of clusters and their critical contribution to competitive success confirms Porter's argument that 'the competitive advantage lies outside companies and even outside their industries, residing instead in the locations at which their business units are based' (2000: 15).

To sum up, the global era seems to be characterized by a paradoxical situation in which globalization and localization seem to coexist and influence firms' performances. As a consequence, managers are requested to balance global and regional forces in their decision-making processes. The same issue faces policy-makers at both national and local levels.

This chapter attempts to investigate the interplay of localization and globalization with respect to the competitive advantage of firms embedded in regional clusters. More particularly, this exploratory study wants to answer the following research questions:

1 What value-chain activities are more influenced by globalization than by localization forces?
2 Why is the internationalization process of some value-chain activities more influenced by local forces in comparison to the other activities?

In order to investigate these research objectives, a field study was conducted of a metropolitan cluster in Rome (in the Tiburtina Valley). The concentration of high-tech SMEs in this area makes the paradox between the localization and globalization forces more evident. The chapter is structured in three main sections: the first contains a brief definition of the theoretical background, based on the main attributes of clusters in a global context; research propositions and the methodology to verify them are then presented, after which we focus on data discussion. Some concluding remarks and suggestions for further research complete the study.

Theoretical background

To define the theoretical background, we analysed the literature on clusters in order to understand their origin and development. Several authors show that geographical clustering is a phenomenon diffused both in small and large economies, rural and urban areas (see, among others, Lawson and Lorenz, 1999). At the same time, it is considered a major element characterizing the economic growth of extremely different industries. As a consequence, this research topic has attracted the attention of scholars (Saxenian, 1994; Porter, 1998) and policy-makers (OECD, 2001). According to Porter (1998, 77), clusters can be defined as 'the geographic concentrations of interconnected companies, specialized suppliers and service providers; firms in related industries; and associated institutions in particular fields that compete but also cooperate'.

Several reasons seem to explain the emergence and development of clusters. Generally the concept of clusters focuses not so much on the agglomeration of a single industry but on the externalities across industries. In this respect, the economic and sociological factors seem to be the most relevant (Amin and Wilkinson, 1999), including the presence of unique natural resources, proximity to markets, economies of scale in production, labour pooling, shared infrastructure and localized externalities connected to networking. Among them, scale economies and the presence of unique natural resources are generally considered the most important (Chandler *et al.*, 1998). The main benefits deriving from the localization include an increasing degree of specialization and a rapid diffusion of know-how. This, in turn, creates an abundance of skilled workers and service firms (such as consulting and maintenance ones) and a strong utilization of specialized machinery (Amin and Wilkinson, 1999).

Cluster development has been explained on the basis of efficiency criteria; more specifically, it is assumed that firms embedded in the same industry generally decide to co-localize their activities in order to benefit from agglomeration economies (Marshall, 1920). In this regard, Harrison *et al.* (1996) propose the concept of collective efficiency. A similar theoretical position may also be found in sociological researches related to the clustering phenomenon. These works demonstrate that clustering positively influences firms' productivity. This is because personal and frequent relationships – among local actors having a similar culture and living in a narrow area – allow the emergence of cooperative and trust behaviour, which in turn facilitates the growth of tacit knowledge (Nonaka, 1991) and simplifies the diffusion of information (Ibarra, 1992).

Another interesting field of study identifies the relevance of clusters for both production and innovation activities. More specifically, clusters provide a locus for innovation activities (Krugman, 1991), especially in the case of high-tech industries. Such an innovation potential is related to firms' localization in a restricted territorial area and to their ability to create reciprocal positive relationships (Saxenian, 1994; Deeds *et al.*, 1999). Such a critical role is extremely important in the early stages of new technologies' development, as proximity is supposed to be crucial for perceiving and benefiting from new technological opportunities.

It seems that the earlier-discussed economic and sociological factors explaining firms' localization are still valid, even in the new globalized competitive scenario. In fact, we can remark that even in the global economy competitive advantage is still dependent on firm localization. Recent evidence, especially from the UK and the USA, confirms that not only the geography of economic knowledge is concentrated in a regional context but, more and more, in specific urban areas (Cooke *et al.*, 2001).

As a consequence, several authors point out that globalization and localization are two interacting forces mutually influencing the creation of firms' competitive advantage. There is little doubt that the emergence of global markets encourages the restructuring of economic competition in several industries and often local clusters emerge as a major source of competitive advantages (Keating, 1997). At the same time, several empirical studies provide clear evidence on how local and global forces can shape technical change (Brown, 2000).

Research propositions

The mutual influence of localization and globalization forces on competitive advantage development requires investigation to help to understand which activities are more influenced by local factors and which by global factors. Here, different authors have demonstrated that tacit knowledge-based activities are more influenced by localization than activities based on codified knowledge (Enright and Roberts, 2001; Scott, 2001). From an economic perspective, this means that it is possible to realize highly routinized activities based on codified knowledge at a global level. As a consequence, local-based activities are not relevant, while tacit knowledge-based activities need face-to-face relationships among actors (Dyer and Sing, 1998). Therefore, for such activities 'the costs of transacting rise greatly as distance increases, and with the geographical scattering of producers, inefficiencies rapidly set in' (Scott, 2001: 15). These works provide the basis for the first proposition:

P1 Firms embedded in clusters have the highest level of internationalisation for activities based on systematic and routinized mechanisms.

The second proposition is connected to understanding the internationalization process of activities that are more influenced by local than global forces. Several variables are considered to be linked to the globalization process (see, among others, Johanson and Vahlne, 1977), but first we point out that SMEs internationalization is strongly influenced by their domestic business environment, more than in the case of large multinationals (Reid, 1983; Johansson and Vahlne, 1977; Forsgren and Johansson, 1992). This is because their technological and managerial competencies are developed under the influence of national culture, institutions and common knowledge (Porter, 1990). As a consequence, assets and capabilities needed to promote a firm's internationalization may be developed in collaboration with other actors embedded in the local network (Anderson *et al.*, 1998; Casson, 1994). Thus localization within a cluster reinforces and simplifies the development of appropriate relations among actors, which in turn favours learning by interacting (Boari and Lipparini, 1999). The relevance of local networks for the internationalization process differs with respect to activities undertaken. More specifically, it is critical for activities based on mutual trust and common long-term interests (Anderson *et al.*, 1998), such as R&D and supply-chain operations that are complex and risky and less capable of the application of routine procedures. This leads to the second proposition:

P2 In the internationalization process, local forces are most important for activities based on tacit knowledge.

Methodology

In order to verify the propositions a field study was carried out on the Tiburtina Valley cluster, near Rome. This cluster is characterized by a relevant concentration of firms, having up-to-date technological capabilities and good performance on both national and foreign markets. It is a typical example of a metropolitan cluster in Italy, being characterized by productivity ratios higher than those at a national level. It also has a high export propensity, due to the presence of foreign multinationals.

The high-tech cluster is situated along the Tiburtina route, about 14 kilometres from the centre of Rome. It is composed of 880 SMEs employing about 20,000 workers in the information and communication industry. The Tiburtina Valley has been developed from firms that operated in the armaments industry; the downturn in demand for armaments at the end of the 1980s provoked a reduction in production and consequently a lot of dismissals of skilled workers. The presence of both experienced employees and hi-tech companies (such as Alenia, Telecom Italia and Ericsson) provided a high level of flexibility and productive specialization which in turn permitted the development of new business and the rapid diffusion of knowledge among local actors.

To investigate the propositions attention was focused on the most innovative and internationalized companies operating within the cluster. According to some literature (Audretsch and Acs, 1991; Acs and Gifford, 1996), it emerged that the characteristics under investigation were mainly diffused in firms less than eight years old (that is, start-ups, according to Covin and Slevin, 1992), and using the Rome Chamber of Commerce databank, 54 start-ups were identified.

A preliminary exploratory study through semi-structured interviews of privileged actors within the cluster permitted a qualitative prospective of the relationships among the principal actors in the area. A structured closed questionnaire was constructed and tested on three firms of the sample using face-to-face interviews. A total of 40 of the 54 firms of the identified statistical population responded to the request for information, a response rate of 75 per cent. The internationalization process on sales, purchasing and R&D value-chain activities was measured using 13 variables. The internationalization of sales-based activities was measured using the four variables:

- Foreign sales as a percentage of total turnover;
- Number of foreign customers;
- Foreign customers as a percentage of total customers;
- Number of foreign markets where companies export.

The internationalization of supply-based activities was measured using:

- Number of foreign suppliers;
- Foreign suppliers as a percentage of total suppliers;

- Value of raw materials and components imported as a percentage of total purchasing budget;
- Number of foreign markets from where raw materials and components are imported.

The internationalization of R&D-based activities was measured using:

- Total number of R&D agreements with foreign firms;
- Number of R&D agreements with foreign companies as a percentage of total R&D alliances;
- R&D expenditure abroad as a percentage of total expenditure on R&D;
- Number of foreign customers involved in R&D projects as a percentage of total customers involved in R&D projects;
- Number of foreign suppliers involved in R&D projects as a percentage of total suppliers involved in R&D projects.

In order to measure the importance of localization on the implementation of internationalization activities, the age and size of firms were used as proxies for local forces. Age was used as a proxy of the experience level acquired by a firm inside a cluster (Saxenian, 1994). The years spent by a firm inside a cluster can be a useful measure of the development of experience necessary to enter foreign markets, through the appropriate mechanisms of learning by interacting that typically occurs inside the limited territorial surroundings among different local actors (Boari and Lipparini, 1999). The size of a firm was used as a proxy of resources and competencies owned by the firm, as in the international business literature there is a general consensus that a firm's size is positively related to the firm's propensity to export (Reid, 1983; Forsgren and Johanson, 1992), based on the view that larger firms more easily develop appropriate relational competencies that allow them to obtain the resources necessary to operate in foreign markets. In this study, size is seen as an ability of the firm to be successful in the cluster thanks to the appropriate processes of growth based on beneficial local networks. Size is measured by the total sales of the firm and by the number of employees (Reid, 1983). Thus, the second proposition of research was split into two sub-propositions:

P2A Firm size is more correlated with the internationalization process of R&D and supply activities, in comparison to sales activities.

P2B Firm age is more correlated with the internationalization process of R&D and supply activities, in comparison to sales activities.

Table 17.1 The investigated sample

	No. of employees	*Turnover (€000s)*
Average	4.07	226.35
Std. dev.	2.06	110.16

Results

About 80 per cent of the total sample has fewer than five employees, while only 5 per cent has more than 10 employees. The average number of employees within start-ups is slightly more than four. The small dimension is also confirmed by total turnover; about 40 per cent of the sample has annual sales of less than €200,000, while only 7 per cent has annual sales higher than €400 million. Total sales range from a minimum of €50 million (2.5 per cent of the sample) to a maximum of €450 million (7.5 per cent) with an average of €225 million (see Table 17.1).

With respect to sales, it is interesting to note that all companies have at least one customer within the cluster that is generally also the oldest. Moreover, about 70 per cent of investigated companies have customers from within Italy but outside the cluster, while 80 per cent have customers in European countries and 24 per cent in other areas. Although a lot of customers are localized within the cluster, the international customers are more relevant in terms of contribution to total turnover. As a consequence, it seems that for start-ups the small size of a firm does not limit its possibility of selling to big foreign multinationals.

To verify the first proposition of the research, an assessment was made of data relating to sales-based internationalization, supply-based internationalization and R&D-based internationalization.

Sales-based internationalization

The four variables listed earlier (p. 317) were used to verify the level of sales-based internationalization within the cluster. The data show that about 90 per cent of the firms within the sample realize part of their total turnover in foreign markets. The value of foreign sales as a percentage of total sales ranged from 0.02 per cent (for 22.5 per cent of start-ups) to 50 per cent (for 2.5 per cent of start-ups), with an average level of 13 per cent. More specifically, each firm within the cluster has, on average, five foreign customers. The percentage of foreign customers of total customers is equal, on average, to 15%. At the same time, such companies sell on average in two different countries other than Italy (Table 17.2).

Table 17.2 Sales-based internationalization: descriptive statistics

	Per start-up			
	No. of foreign customers	*Foreign customers as % total customers*	*Foreign sales as % total sales*	*No. of foreign markets*
N	40	40	40	40
Average	5	15%	13%	2
Std. Dev.	3.8	0.13	0.14	1.5

Supply-based internationalization

Supply-based internationalization was investigated by the four variables listed earlier (p. 318). The data revealed that the investigated start-ups generally prefer suppliers within the cluster. More specifically, only 25 per cent of the companies in the sample have foreign suppliers, while the remaining firms buy only from Italian companies, both within and outside the cluster. On average, every firm has 2.8 foreign suppliers (Table 17.3), while it has around five foreign customers (see Table 17.2). At the same time, foreign purchases are a small percentage of total supply (8.3 per cent on average).

R&D-based internationalization

Focusing attention on R&D-based internationalization, the data show an insignificant relevance of this phenomenon for the investigated start-ups. However, around 30 per cent of the total sample had R&D agreements with foreign players, against 25 per cent of international purchasing relationships. On average, each company in the cluster has 0.9 R&D agreements with international firms (Table 17.4). More specifically, the percentage of R&D foreign partners of the total in R&D agreements is quite small (2.8 per cent in average).

Table 17.3 Supply-based internationalization: descriptive statistics

	Per start-up			
	No. of foreign suppliers	*Foreign suppliers as % of total*	*Foreign supply as % total supply*	*No. of foreign markets supplied*
N	40	40	40	40
Average	2.8	8.3	6.8	0.2
Std. Dev.	8.5	1.8	1.8	0.4

Table 17.4 R & D-based internationalization: descriptive statistics

	Per start-up				
	No. of foreign partners	*Foreign partners as % of total*	*Foreign investments in R & D as % total*	*No. of foreign customers involved in R & D as % total*	*No. of foreign suppliers involved in R & D as % total*
N	40	40	40	40	40
Average	0.9	2.8	6.8	7.8	1.3
Std. Dev.	1.9	8.5	1.8	1.3	4.0

At the same time, in more than 90 per cent of the sample this ratio is less than 2 per cent. The percentage of R&D foreign expenditure on the total R&D budget is equal to 6.8 per cent in average. Such evidence seems to be consistent with the limited size of firms within the cluster.

These data provide some evidence that confirms the first proposition. The second proposition was examined by investigating the correlation between firm size and various firm activities within the cluster. A positive correlation was found between firm size (defined as both total sales and number of employees) and variables explaining commercial internationalization. However, the same positive correlation was not found between the number of employees and the percentage of foreign customers among total customers. On the contrary, an extremely significant and positive correlation was found between the number of foreign markets in which the firm is present and its size defined in terms of total turnover ($r=0.869$). Moreover, total sales are, on average, positively correlated with the commercial internationalization of the investigated start-ups. At the same time, start-ups' age is positively associated with the number of foreign markets ($r=0.738$) and the total number of foreign customers ($r=0.586$) (Table 17.5).

The size of firms seems to influence the level of supply-based internationalization, more than the sales-based. More specifically, the Pearson's correlation index result becomes more relevant. Here the number of employees is strictly and positively related to that of foreign suppliers ($r=0.904$), and the percentage of the latter of the total number of a firm's suppliers ($r=0.886$). At the same time, total turnover is positively correlated to the same variables (respectively 0.848 and 0.799). The size of firms is also strongly correlated with the percentage of foreign purchasing to total purchases and the number of suppliers' markets. In this respect, start-ups' turnover is correlated with the latter variable (0.788). Moreover, the age of firms is positively related to the level of

Table 17.5 Sales-based internationalization: correlation matrix

Variables	*1*	*2*	*3*	*4*	*5*	*6*	*7*
1 Pearson's correlation							
sig. (2-code)							
N							
2 Pearson's correlation	.751**						
sig. (2-code)	0						
N	40						
3 Pearson's correlation	.815**	.644**					
sig. (2-code)	0	0					
N	40	40					
4 Pearson's correlation	–0.114	0.004	0.131				
sig. (2-code)	0.484	0.98	0.419				
N	40	40	40				
5 Pearson's correlation	.499**	.586**	.489**	0.266			
sig. (2-code)	0.001	0	0.001	0.097			
N	40	40	40	40			
6 Pearson's correlation	.383**	0.27	0.208	0.078	0.192		
Sig. (2-code)	0.015	0.092	0.199	0.631	0.235		
N	40	40	40	40	40		
7 Pearson's correlation	.813**	.738**	.869**	0.162	.501**	.336**	
Sig. (2-code)	0	0	0	0.319	0.001	0.034	
N	40	40	40	40	40	40	

* $p < .05$
** $p < .01$

1 Employees
2 Age
3 Total sales
4 Foreign customers (per cent total customers)
5 No. of foreign customers
6 Foreign sales (per cent total sales)
7 No. of foreign markets

supply-based internationalization, more than in the case of sales-based internationalization (Table 17.6).

In order better to understand the influence of globalization and localization forces on R&D activities, attention was specifically focused on R&D partners. Here it must be noted that even if foreign customers are quite relevant in term of total turnover, joint R&D activities with such players are not very diffused (30 per cent of the total sample). On the contrary, R&D agreements are generally developed with customers within the cluster, or in the rest of Italy (70 per cent). More specifically, for more than 90 per cent of the sample, foreign customers involved in R&D partnerships are less than 2 per cent of the total foreign customers. This result might be explained by the long-lasting relationships between firms and customers belonging to the cluster.

Table 17.6 Supply-based internationalization: correlation matrix

Variables	*1*	*2*	*3*	*4*	*5*	*6*	*7*
1 Pearson's correlation							
sig. (2-code)							
N							
2 Pearson's correlation	.751**						
sig. (2-code)							
N							
3 Pearson's correlation	.815**	.644**					
sig. (2-code)	0	0					
N	40	40					
4 Pearson's correlation	.866**	.804**	.799**				
sig. (2-code)	0	0	0				
N	40	40	40				
5 Pearson's correlation	.904**	.814**	.848**	.986**			
sig. (2-code)	0	0	0	0			
N	40	40	40	40			
6 Pearson's correlation	.499**	.509**	.582**	.440**	.544**		
Sig. (2-code)	0.001	0.001	0	0.004	0		
N	40	40	40	40	40		
7 Pearson's correlation	.629**	.454**	.788**	.661**	.740**	.715**	
Sig. (2-code)	0	0.003	0	0	0	0	
N	40	40	40	40	40	40	

** $p < .01$
* $p < .05$

1 Employees
2 Age
3 Total sales
4 Foreign suppliers (per cent total suppliers)
5 No. of foreign suppliers
6 Foreign supply (per cent total supply)
7 No. of foreign markets

With respect to R&D agreements with suppliers, it must be noted that more than 90 per cent of suppliers involved in R&D partnerships are localized within the cluster, or in the rest of Italy. Only four companies of the sample (10 per cent) have declared R&D agreements with foreign suppliers, which account for around 2 per cent of the total sample.

Lastly, factors influencing R&D-based internationalization were analysed. It was found that such an internationalization process is strictly influenced by firm size, as in the case of supply-based internationalization and more than in the case of sales-based internationalization (Table 17.7). At the same time, a start-up's age positively and significantly influences the former type of internationalization. Both size and age are positively correlated also with the number of foreign suppliers involved in R&D partnerships (r=0.636 for the number

Table 17.7 R&D-based internationalization: correlation matrix

Variables	*1*	*2*	*3*	*4*	*5*	*6*	*7*	*8*
1 Pearson's correlation								
sig. (2-code)								
N								
2 Pearson's correlation	.850**							
sig. (2-code)	0							
N	40							
3 Pearson's correlation	.853**	.979**						
sig. (2-code)	0	0						
N	40	40						
4 Pearson's correlation	.695**	.895**	.858**					
sig. (2-code)	0	0	0					
N	40	40	40					
5 Pearson's correlation	.766**	.845**	.870**	.751**				
sig. (2-code)	0	0	0	0				
N	40	40	40	40				
6 Pearson's correlation	.596**	.745**	.700**	.815**	.644**			
Sig. (2-code)	0	0	0	0	0			
N	40	40	40	40	40			
7 Pearson's correlation	0.326**	.434**	0.37	0.336	0.257	.457**		
Sig. (2-code)	0.04	0.005	0.019	0.034	0.109	0.003		
N	40	40	40	40	40	40		
8 Pearson's correlation	.945**	.803**	.784**	.636**	.730**	.546**	0.311	
Sig. (2-code)	0	0	0	0	0	0	0.051	
N	40	40	40	40	40	40	40	

* $p < .01$
** $p < .05$

1	Foreign R & D partners (per cent on total	5	Age
2	No. of foreign R & D partners	6	Total sales
3	Foreign R & D investments (per cent total)	7	No. of foreign customers in R&D (per cent on total
4	Employees	8	No. of foreign suppliers in R&D (per cent on total)

of employees, $r=0.730$ for the age, and $r=0.546$ for the total turnover). Finally, firm size is also positively correlated with the percentage of foreign customers of total customers involved in R&D activities, even if at less than a significant level.

Table 17.8 shows the average correlation values between size and age of firm, and respectively sales, R&D and supply-based internationalization activities. These data also confirm that the second hypothesis has been verified in our research.

Table 17.8 Average correlation values

	Sales internazionalization	*Supply internationalization*	*R&D internationalization*
Sales	0.396	0.729**	0.608**
Employees	0.339	0.645**	0.684**
Age	0.424*	0.693**	0.754**

Notes: ** P < .01
* P < .05

Conclusions

In this chapter we have tried to investigate the interplay of localization and globalization with respect to various firm activities. In doing so, three different types of internationalization processes were analysed: purchasing, sales and R&D. The results affirm that in the Tiburtina Valley, globalization and localization are complementary forces, and that firms seem to integrate them in order to create a sustainable competitive advantage. In fact, even if globalization seems to have a relevant influence on the creation of competitive advantage, the relationships of firms with players operating inside the cluster are still critical.

Our results confirm different studies in the literature, which argue that firms tend to internationalize in areas that are centred on codified knowledge-based activities, while locating those based on implicit and unroutinized knowledge in local areas. In fact, while the firms of the sample tend to internationalize commercial activities through exporting, at the same time, the administration of supply activities where tacit and non-standardizable knowledge is critical, seem to require physical proximity, strong personal ties and reciprocal trust. Lastly, localization is relevant for the management of R&D activities; the results clearly confirm that innovation processes tends to be localized within the cluster and to be based on long-lasting relationships with local players.

The results show that for the implementation of appropriate internationalization processes it is more important to have established beneficial relations at local level for the activities based on tacit knowledge than for those based on explicit and routinized knowledge. In fact, the rate of correlation of internationalization both with the age of a firm, as a proxy of experience obtained within the cluster, and with other firm dimensions, as a proxy of resources and competencies owned by the firm inside a cluster, is bigger for the activities of R&D than for the commercial activities.

This exploratory work might be developed by expanding the analysis of the identified problem cases before generalizing the results. It would also be convenient to insert some control variables, especially at the level of financial resources of firms. It would therefore be interesting to examine the possible role that local institutions might have in favouring the opening of firms working in a cluster towards the outside, without losing the link with the local context. Such a study might lead to important indications of the ways in which the politics of local development should be implemented. Finally, improved data collection backed by improved conceptual frameworks are necessary to allow more robust statistical tests of developed hypotheses on the relationships between firm dimensions and the localization versus internationalization decisions within clusters.

References

Acs, Z.J. and Gifford, S. (1996) 'Innovation of entrepreneurial firms', *Small Business Economics* 8(3), 203–18.

Amin, A. and Wilkinson, E. (1999) 'Learning, proximity and industrial performance: an introduction', *Cambridge Journal of Economics* 23(2), 121–5.

Anderson, V., Gramah, S. and Lawrence, P. (1998) 'Learning to internationalize', *Journal of Management Development* 17(4), 492–501.

Audretsch, D. and Acs, Z.J. (1991) 'Innovation and size at the firm level', *Southern Economic Journal* 57(3), 739–44.

Boari, C. and Lipparini, A. (1999) 'Networks within industrial districts: organizing knowledge creation and transfer by means of moderate hierarchies', *Journal of Management and Governance* 3(3), 339–60.

Brown, R., (2000) *Clusters, innovation and investment: building global supply chains in the New Economy*. Canberra: Australian Project Developments Pty Ltd.

Casson, M. (1994) 'Internationalisation as a learning process: a model of corporate growth and geographical diversification', in Balasubramanyam, V.N. and Sapsford, D. (eds), *The economies of International investment*. Chelentham: Edward Edgar.

Chandler, J., Solvell, A.D. and Hagstrom, P. (1998) *The Dynamic Firm, Strategy, Organisation and Regions*. Oxford: Oxford University Press.

Cooke, P., Davies, C. and Wilson, R. (2001) *Innovation Advantages of Cities: From Knowledge to Equity in Five Basic Steps*. Cardiff: Centre for Advanced Studies, University of Cardiff Press.

Covin, J.G. and Slevin, D.P. (1990) 'New venture strategic posture, structure and performance: an industry life cycle analysis', *Journal of Business Venturing* 19(2), 190–210.

Deeds, D.L., De Carolis, D. and Coombs, J. (1999) 'Dynamic capabilities and new product development in high technology ventures: an empirical analysis of new biotechnology firms', *Journal of Business Venturing* 15(2), 211–19.

Dyer, J.H. and Singh, H. (1998) 'The relational view: cooperative strategy and sources of interorganizational competitive advantage', *Academy of Management Review* 23(4), 660–79.

Enright, M. and Roberts, B.H. (2001) 'Regional clustering in Australia', *Australian Journal of Management* 26(1), 65–85.

Forsgren, M. and Johanson, J. (1992) 'Managing internationalization in business networks', in Forsgren, M. and Johanson, J. (eds), *Managing Networks in International Business*. Philadelphia: Gordon & Breach.

Harrison, B., Kelley, M. and Gant, J. (1996) 'Innovative firm behaviour and local milieu: exploring the intersection of agglomeration firms effects, industrial organization and technology change', *Economic Geography* 72(2), 233–58.

Ibarra, H. (1992) 'Structural alignments, individual strategies, and managerial action: elements toward a network theory of getting things done', in Nohria, N. and Eccles, R.G. (eds), *Networks and Organizations: Structure, Form and Action*. Boston, Massachusetts: Harvard Business School Press.

Johansson, J. and Vahlne, J.-E. (1977) 'The internationalisation process of the firm, a model of knowledge development and increasing foreign market commitments', *Journal of International Business Studies* 8(1), 23–32.

Keating, M. (1997) 'The invention of regions: political restructuring and territorial government in Western Europe', *Environment and Planning* 15(3), 383–98.

Krugman, P. (1991) *Geography and Trade*. Cambridge, MA: MIT Press.

Lawson, C. and Lorenz, E. (1999) 'Collective learning, tacit knowledge and regional innovative capacity', *Regional Studies* 33(3), 305–17.

Marshall, A. (1920) *Principles of Economics*. London: Macmillan – Palgrave.

Nonaka, I. (1991) 'The knowledge creating company', *Harvard Business Review* 69(6), 96–104.

OECD (2001) 'World Congress on Local Clusters', Paris: Organization for Economic Cooperation and Development.

Padmore, T. and Gibson, H. (1998) 'Modelling systems of innovation: a framework for industrial cluster analysis in regions', *Research Policy* 26(4), 625–41.

Porter, M. (1990) *The Competitive Advantage of Nations*. London: Macmillan – Palgrave.

Porter, M. (1998) 'Clusters and the New Economics of Competition', *Harvard Business Review* 76(6), 77–90.

Porter, M. (2000) 'Location, competition, and economic development: local clusters in a global economy', *Economic Development Quarterly* 14(1), 15–34.

Reid, S. (1983) 'Firm internationalization, transaction costs and strategic choice', *International Marketing Review* 1(1), 44–56.

Saxenian, A.L. (1994) *Regional Advantage: Culture and Competition in Silicon Valley and Route 128*. Cambridge, MA: University of Harvard Press.

Scott, A.J. (1998) *Regions and the World Economy. The Coming Shape of Global Production, Competition and Political Order*. Oxford: University of Oxford Press.

Scott, A.J. (2001) *Global City-Regions: Trends, Theory, Policy*. Oxford: Oxford University Press.

Name Index

Note: f = figure; n = note; t = table; **bold** = extended discussion or heading emphasized in main text.

Subject Index

Note: f = figure; n = note; t = table; **bold** = extended discussion or heading emphasized in main text.